A short history of
Soviet socialism

A short history of
Soviet socialism

Mark Sandle

De Montfort University

Published in the UK in 1999 by UCL Press

UCL Press Limited
Taylor & Francis Group
1 Gunpowder Square
London EC4A 3DE

and

325 Chestnut Street
8th Floor
Philadelphia
PA 19106
USA

The name of University College London (UCL) is a registered trade
mark used by UCL Press with the consent of the owner.

ISBNs: 1-85728-354-6HB
          1-85728-355-4PB

British Cataloguing-in-Publication Data
A catalogue record for this book is available from the British Library.

Printed and bound by T. J. International Ltd, Padstow, UK

To my mother and father, with love.

Contents

List of Figures   ix

Preface   xi

Introduction   1

Part One: The genesis of Soviet socialism

Chapter 1:   The crucibles of Russian socialism   9

Part Two: The emergence of a Soviet model: from the revolution to NEP

Chapter 2:   The revolutionary settlement: state capitalism, technocracy and the transition to socialism   57

Chapter 3:   War communism and Soviet socialism: a technocratic orthodoxy?   95

Chapter 4:   NEP and Soviet socialism: departing from orthodoxy?   151

Chapter 5:   Stalin, Trotsky and Bukharin: debating a new orthodoxy   199

CONTENTS

Part Three: Orthodoxy in power: from Stalin to Brezhnev

Chapter 6: Stalinist Socialism: creating a country of
metal, 1929–39   225

Chapter 7: Khrushchev and Soviet socialism:
burying Stalin, reviving Lenin?   275

Chapter 8: Brezhnev and developed socialism:
technocratic socialism in power   333

Part Four: The demise of scientific socialism

Chapter 9: Gorbachev and Soviet socialism: the rise
and fall of Humane Democratic Socialism   371

Conclusion: history and Soviet socialism   429

Chronology of party conferences and congresses   437

Chronology of main ideological texts of Soviet socialism   439

Glossary of key terms/acronyms   441

Select bibliography   443

Index   457

List of Figures

Figure 1.1   Bolshevism in power: the institutional structure
of the Soviet State after October 1917. Formal
operation of system.   40

Figure 2.1   Bolshevism in power: the institutional
structure of the Soviet State after October
1917. The transferral of power after 1917.   75

Figure 7.1   Organizational changes to the Soviet economy
under Khrushchev 1957–63. The structure prior
to 1957 (simplified version): the centralized
"branch" system.   310

Figure 7.2   Organizational changes to the Soviet economy
under Khrushchev 1957–63. The Sovnarkhoz
reforms of 1957: decentralized regional
economic councils.   311

Figure 7.3   Organizational changes to the Soviet economy
under Khrushchev 1957–63. The further
reorganizations of Nikita Khrushchev:
recentralization creeps back.   312

Figure 7.4   Organizational changes to the Soviet economy
under Khrushchev 1957–63. Once more on the
reorganizations of Khrushchev: a new regional
structure.   313

Figure 7.5   Organizational changes to the Soviet economy
under Khrushchev 1957–63. Reorganization
mania: 1962 and all that.   314

Preface

This book has grown out of my personal attempts to understand and make sense of the Soviet period of Russian history from 1917–91, and the subsequent hours spent trying to communicate this to numerous students of mine. The contours of such a project – a broad, interpretive appraisal of the Soviet period – inevitably means that I owe a great debt to numerous scholars who have trodden this path before me, many of whom it is not possible to acknowledge in a direct way. The present book would not have been possible without the help and inspiration of many friends and colleagues. I would like to take this opportunity to note my gratitude to a whole range of teachers who helped to nurture my interest in history in general, and in Russia in particular: Gwynne Lewis, Chris Read, David Washbrook, Maureen Perrie, Bob Davies, Ron Amann. I have been particularly fortunate to work in a history department at De Montfort University with colleagues who have been constantly supportive, friendly and an inspiration to me. To David Ryan, Nick Carter, Panikos Panayi, Jason McDonald, John Martin, Chris Goldsmith, Pierre Lanfranchi, Matt Taylor, Daryl Adair, Ian Spencer, David Thoms, Wray Vamplew, and David Sadler, many thanks. A special note of thanks to David and Ed, who were so generous with their time, and whose suggestions and criticisms were invaluable in improving this work. Any flaws and errors remain the full responsibility of the present author. At UCL, Aisling Ryan has been a supportive and patient voice at critical moments. Finally, a work such as this incurs many debts with one's friends and family. I am much indebted to the support, encouragement and patience (!) of Witty without whom this work might never have been completed. I am also indebted to my children – Luke and Bethany – without whom this work would have been completed much earlier, but life would have been much less colourful and far too predictable! Finally, this book is dedicated to my parents, who have always been there for me.

Introduction

The dust has settled after the collapse of communism. The greater access to archives and the greater opportunities for dialogue and collaboration with Russian scholars are opening up new fields for research and critical inquiry into some of the long-neglected aspects of the Soviet era of Russian history. This is a most welcome development. At the same time, this new situation is also renewing some old debates and disputes. One of the enduring issues which has divided scholars is the question of how important were ideas to the course of Soviet history? Was ideology a profound determinant of events? Or was it merely a smokescreen, which rationalized a set of actions that promoted or defended the interests of particular groups or individuals? Or are these views too starkly drawn to encapsulate the complex relationship between ideas and political practice in the USSR?

It is traditional to assert that the basic historiographical divide in Soviet history lies between the totalitarian or counter-communist school on the one hand, and the "revisionist" school on the other. The totalitarian interpretation, arising out of the polemics of the cold war, looked to establish the origins of the Stalinist terror and dictatorship in the ideology of Marxism–Leninism and in the theory and practice of the Bolshevik party before and after 1917. Derived from the writings of Leonard Schapiro, Martin Malia, Robert Conquest, Richard Pipes and others, this approach identified a clear continuity between Marxism, Leninism and the Stalinist period. Transposed to the debate about the role of ideology, the totalitarian viewpoint asserted that there was a profound degree of ideological continuity between Lenin and Stalin, and that these ideas fundamentally shaped the nature of the Stalinist system.

Revisionist scholarship (defined by Sheila Fitzpatrick as "scholarship that is explicitly abandoning the totalitarian model")[1] has explored the broader socio-economic and cultural context of the early Soviet period, examining history "from below". Eschewing the totalitarian emphasis upon high politics, the state and events in Petrograd and Moscow, revisionists have explored the actions and reactions of workers, peasants, soldiers and sailors, of events in the regions. One of the outcomes of this detailed research has been that a much more diverse, complex, sprawling, chaotic picture of Soviet history emerges. As Fitzpatrick describes,

> At present, on every major issue of Soviet history, historians seem to be submerging themselves in data and periodically surfacing with a single astonished cry: "improvisation". Chaos is almost becoming the dominant principle of Soviet development as the old explanatory structures disintegrate . . . Political leaders stagger from one unexpected crisis to another, pragmatically muddling through. Their minds are empty of ideology . . . and only circumstances govern their actions.[2]

However, this totalitarian/revisionist dichotomy does not adequately characterize the nature of the disputes between historians on this issue. Counter-communist historians themselves have been unable to reach a consensus on the role of ideology. Malia asserts that the ideological imperative of "building socialism", derived from the Marxian heritage of the Bolshevik party, was the single most important feature of the Soviet system.[3] On the other hand, Pipes has argued that, "[a]s a rule, the less one knows about the actual course of the Russian Revolution the more inclined one is to attribute a dominant influence to Marxist ideas".[4]

Conversely, scholars of a more left-leaning or revisionist orientation have posited a central explanatory role. Julian Cooper, in a remarkable piece on the collapse of Soviet Marxism–Leninism, stated that,

These observations are founded on a belief that ideology has been of profound significance as a determinant of the course of Soviet development from 1917 to the present day. Throughout this period the Soviet Union has had a political regime of an essentially theocratic nature, the policies and actions of its leadership being shaped and bounded by a relatively stable body of ideas consistently presented as the highest achievement of human science.[5]

This issue appears to straddle traditional historiographical divisions, and is becoming increasingly contested as scholars reassess the Soviet era. Andrjez Walicki's recent work sought to demonstrate that ideological factors were of "decisive importance"[6] in shaping the nature and outcome of Soviet history. Orlando Figes' review of Robert Service's latest work is critical of the relatively little space devoted to ideology, and to "the ideological driving force of its [bolshevism's] murderous policies to drag backward Russia into the modern world".[7] Stephen Hanson's recent text has postulated that ideas were central in shaping the institutional architecture of the Soviet state.[8]

The central issue dividing scholars is the extent to which ideas were an active force in shaping Soviet development. A recent discussion in *The Russian Review*, devoted to Robert Daniels' view of Soviet history, outlined that "the real problem is to show how ideologies were used".[9] Many contributions have outlined that there has been an interaction between ideology and reality. But what does this mean? And how did it work in practice? It is this issue which this text seeks to address, by examining the relationship between the theory and practice of Soviet socialism. In tracing the historical development of the Soviet understanding of socialism, and how this understanding evolved in the light of the contact of Bolshevik ideals with Russian realities, this volume addresses the question of how ideology and reality interacted, and the extent to which the Bolshevik ideals about the nature of the society they were creating shaped this society. In this sense the writing of this book seems to be a worthwhile effort, complementing the more orthodox narratives and specialist monographs, and exploring a disputed issue in Soviet historiography.

This book is about ideas. More specifically, the understanding of socialism as a transitional society between capitalism and communism within the CPSU. It traces the development of a Soviet model of socialism from the pre-revolutionary heritage of Marx, Engels, Kautsky and Lenin, through the formative years of early Bolshevism, the civil war, NEP and the factional infighting of the 1920s until the consolidation under Stalin. The modifications introduced by Khrushchev and Brezhnev are followed by a detailed analysis of Gorbachev's dismantling of the traditional model and its replacement with a renewed, ethical version of socialism, vastly different to its scientific predecessor. The chapters are structured to explore the interaction between theory and practice in Soviet socialism, examining policy towards the economy, society and the political sphere, and the new theoretical synthesis that arose out of the changing practice of successive leaders. The adoption of a historical perspective allows the reader to trace both the continuities in the Soviet understanding of socialism, and the unique features of different phases of Soviet development.

In this sense it is not an orthodox narrative history of the Soviet Union from 1917–91. It is designed to be read alongside, and in conjunction with, more specialist works on social, cultural, economic and political aspects of Soviet history. It is a work that is part synthesis of secondary sources, part interpretive regarding the successive theoretical syntheses of the Soviet understanding of socialism, and part original research on the ideological innovations of each leader. Consequently, I owe a heavy debt to the work of other scholars in a variety of fields. With regret, many interesting and critical issues fell out of the remit of this work: the nationalities issue, foreign relations and the pre-revolutionary Russian heritage to name but three. In addition, it was only possible within the confines of this work to explore the dominant conceptions of socialism within the discourse of Bolshevism. The story of the other strands of Bolshevism, and the other ideas that co-existed with it is another task, for another day.

Notes

1. S. Fitzpatrick, "The legacy of the civil war", in *Party, state and society during the Russian civil war*, D. Koenker et al. (eds) (Bloomington: Indiana University Press, 1989), p. 387.

2. Ibid., p. 390.

3. M. Malia, *The Soviet tragedy: a history of socialism in Russia* (New York: Free Press, 1994).

4. R. Pipes, *Russia under the Bolshevik regime* (London: Harvill, 1994), p. 502.

5. J. Cooper, "Construction . . . reconstruction . . . deconstruction", in *Perestroika: the historical perspective*, C. Ward & C. Merridale (eds) (London: Edward Arnold, 1991), p. 166.

6. A. Walicki, *Marxism and the leap to the kingdom of freedom* (Stanford: Stanford University Press, 1995), p. 2.

7. O. Figes, Facts without feelings, in *Sunday Telegraph*, 23 November 1997, p. 15. The work under discussion is R. Service, *A history of twentieth century Russia* (London: Penguin, 1997).

8. S. Hanson, *Time and revolution: Marxism and the design of Soviet institutions* (Chapel Hill: University of North Carolina Press, 1997).

9. The Complexities of Soviet History, *The Russian Review* **54**, 1995, pp. 315–29, quotation on p. vii.

PART ONE

The genesis of Soviet socialism

CHAPTER ONE

The crucibles of Russian socialism

The history of Soviet socialism is inextricably caught up in the wider history of socialism as a political concept. The formation of a Soviet "model" of socialism after 1917 was a function of the collision of the ideas of socialism forged within Russian social democracy after 1883 with the hard reality of the Russian socio-political environment. Yet the notion of socialism which informed the post-revolutionary thinking of the Bolshevik wing of the Russian Social Democratic Labour Party (RSDLP hereafter) was itself the product of decades of Russian and European intellectual and historical development. The tensions and contradictions within socialism as both a political doctrine and a political movement, were reproduced and given specific form by their interpretation and translation into Russian conditions at the turn of the century. It is important to note that while Soviet socialism comprised a particular cluster of wider socialist values and perspectives, it was itself a complex, pluralistic phenomenon, with a good deal of internal diversity. Locating the historical and intellectual origins of Soviet socialism begins in the eighteenth century.

The origins of socialism

Socialism has always been a diverse, complex, eclectic doctrine. Socialists have been classified as "utopian", "scientific", "reformist",

9

"revolutionary". The socialist movement has divided into Social Democrats, Eurocommunists, Leninists, Maoists, Trotskyists, Marxists, Fabians, Democratic Socialists, eco-socialists and so on.[1] Universal agreement upon the core principles or features of a socialist society has been almost impossible to achieve. Scholars remain deeply divided over the reasons for this. Martin Malia argues that socialism as a term is "meaningless".[2] For Malia, it has embraced such a wide variety of meanings, and been embraced by such a bewildering spectrum of political movements, that "it corresponds to no identifiable object in the sublunary world".[3] Furthermore, there is an ineradicable tension within socialism between its economic forms and its moral principles: the former are intrinsically incapable of realizing the latter according to Malia.[4] Other scholars – Berki, Lichtheim and others – have also highlighted many of the tensions within socialism, which can be explained by a combination of philosophical and historical factors.

Although socialism emerged as a modern political phenomenon at the end of the eighteenth century in the wake of the French and Industrial Revolutions, it was the heir of a longer tradition of moral protest and indignation. From Plato, through More to Winstanley and the Diggers during the English Civil War, there has been an ethical or moral critique of the inadequacies of the present way of life, and a corresponding aspiration for a fairer, more just society.[5] The emergence of capitalism, and the demise of feudalism provided the impetus for the growth of socialism as moral critique. The extension of economic exploitation, poverty, wage labour and injustice encouraged this sense of rebellion against injustice. This was exemplified in the writings of Rousseau, Babeuf and others, who aspired to overturn the existing order, and to institute a new social order based upon egalitarianism, popular sovereignty and integral democracy. In their ideals they expressed a desire to move away from the growing individualism of modern society and to return to a society based upon harmony, fraternity and community.

An alternative strand within socialist doctrine emerged concurrently with this moralistic critique. This strand – which Berki has termed "rationalism" – was derived from the Enlightenment, and from the "Philosophes" in particular.[6] It emphasized the emancipatory power of knowledge and education, and upheld the ideals of progress, reason and efficiency. This strand was an essentially modern one, drawing upon the ideals unleashed by the French Revolution, unlike the former strand's pre-modern or classicist yearning. Socialism's rationalist strand, by enthroning human reason, argued that it was possible in a conscious way to plan and organize society rationally, so eliminating waste, inefficiency and inequality.

In its origins socialism was at the same time both a *rejection* of capitalism, and an *extension* of the principles and values of the liberal philosophy that underpinned capitalism. In Malia's words, socialism was "the maximalist wing of one broad movement of protest against the still tenacious remnants of the old regime".[7] Essentially, socialism and liberalism were at one in their desire to end the domination of feudal notions of hierarchy, privilege and inequality. They diverged over the scope and meaning of the notions of liberté, égalité and fraternité. Socialist thinkers sought to extend the values of justice, freedom and equality into every sphere of life and so effect a total reordering of society.

The presence of this philosophical divide between moralism and rationalism at the conceptual birth of modern socialism is crucial to an understanding of the subsequent development of socialism. Socialism came to incorporate a cluster of distinct, at times contradictory, values. Commentators have expressed this in a number of ways. Berki identifies the "four basic tendencies of socialism – rationalism, moralism, egalitarianism and libertarianism".[8] Bernard Crick explores the tension between liberty and equality, fraternity and individualism.[9] Zygmunt Bauman examines the antinomies at the heart of socialism: "freedom and equality, the community and the state, history as lawful process and as a creative act".[10] Common to all these (and other approaches) is the striving to communicate the ineradicable tensions running at the heart of socialism as a political doctrine, and consequently of socialism as a political movement. How can the liberty of the individual be reconciled with the wider good of society as a whole? In what sense are we to understand "equality"? The existence of these tensions helps to explain socialism's great diversity. Babeuf's primitive communism stressed a radical egalitarianism. Saint-Simon's technocratic industrial productivism emphasized the rationalism and efficiency of a socialized industrial economy. The "utopian" socialists – Charles Fourier and Robert Owen – sought to remove the underlying evils of capitalism by creating ideal communities based on mutual co-operation and harmony. English socialism stressed the Christian values of social justice, co-operation and brotherly love. The historical development of socialism expressed the philosophical tensions at the core of the idea itself.[11]

The existence of these different tendencies is crucial to an understanding of the emergence and development of Soviet socialism. In Berki's terms, Soviet socialism was marked by the domination of rationalism over moralism, and egalitarianism (the striving for a communal, collective way of life) over libertarianism (the striving to liberate humanity from all sources of oppression and exploitation).

Taylor's interpretation of the philosophical tension running at the heart of socialism is of particular pertinence for this study.[12] He identifies a distinction within socialist thinking in their conceptions of human nature. Socialists outlined both a modern and a "Romantic expressivist" conception of humanity. Socialist modernizers, in line with Enlightenment thinking, saw the individual as a conscious agent who strove to organize the world to fulfil themselves, manipulating nature to achieve this goal. Romantic thinkers emphasized co-operation and community between human beings, and between individuals and nature. Within a socialist discourse, this gave rise to two highly distinct conceptions of a socialist society. Modernizers viewed emancipation as the creation of structures to facilitate human happiness and fulfilment, enabling a greater and greater degree of manipulation and control of nature. Expressivists revolted against this utilitarian notion of humanity, seeking instead to restore the unity and creativity of person in community with person and nature. Taylor asserts that this tension runs at the heart of the dominant figure in socialist thinking in the nineteenth century: Karl Marx.[13]

The Founding Fathers: Marx and Engels on socialism and communism

The main intellectual forebear of Soviet socialism was Marx.[14] His critique of capitalism, and his views of the transition from capitalism to socialism had an enormous impact upon the form and content of Soviet socialism. Although Marx (and Engels) rarely wrote about the post-revolutionary scene, the basic contours of the transition, and of the nature of this society were apparent. It has become a commonplace to state that Marx's views on post-revolutionary society were sporadic, undeveloped and (deliberately) vague. The main texts in which he wrote about the future society were *Private Property and Communism* in the *1844 Paris Manuscripts*, *The German Ideology* (with Engels in 1845),[15] *The Communist Manifesto* (1848), *The Civil War in France* (1871), *The Critique of the Gotha Programme*[16] (1875), along with sporadic references in *Grundrisse* and *Capital*.[17] An overview of Marx's views on communism reveals a clear development in his thought that points to a possible tension in his ideas, a tension which was intensified by the interpretation of Marx put forward by Engels after his death.[18]

The future society: an overview

The term "communism" has a number of different meanings in Marx's writings. According to de George, Marx used the term "communism" in four ways:

- the stage which will succeed capitalism;
- the abolition of the private ownership of the means of production;
- the negation of the alienation, exploitation and the oppression of the worker;
- a set of positive characteristics, including the emancipation of humanity, an increase in the productive forces in society, and the all-round development of the individual.[19]

What is notable is the co-existence within Marx's view of communism of humanistic, ethical components, with impersonal, structural features of the future society. How can we account for this cluster of meanings? Some theorists argue that there was a substantial shift in Marx's writings from his early writings (emphasizing the humanistic aspect of overcoming alienation) to his later writings, which were increasingly concerned with the abolition of the social aspects of capitalism causing exploitation and oppression: division of labour and class rule.[20] Harding expresses this very starkly. He posits two models of communism within Marx's writings.[21] Model One relates to the humanistic striving to free man from the alienation of capitalist society. Man's true self-realization could only be achieved through the abolition of the two elements (state and private property) constituting the means through which the individual was dominated. Freedom would result from the emergence of a society with a voluntary division of labour and consisting of a free association of co-operative labour. For Harding (and others), this view of communism in the early writings of Marx reflected an essentially romanticist impulse, a nostalgic yearning to reconstitute a society of unity and freedom. Happiness was not found in ever increasing consumption, but in a diversity of labouring pursuits. Individuals would live in harmonious community with each other and with nature.[22] Model Two sought to remove exploitation. It had as its objective the transformation of ownership relations, in order to maximize production for the benefit of society as a whole, removing want, poverty and exploitation. The waste and inefficency of capitalist production would be overcome through the conscious control of social and economic processes (embodied in central planning). This conception sought to build upon and universalize the principles of industrial society. Fulfilment, freedom and happiness were derived from the enjoyment of material abundance in leisure time, not in creative labour. The individual would dominate nature fully for the first time.[23]

Walicki also identifies a shift in Marx's thinking. He argues that Marx was concerned to establish the conditions for the total and unconditional liberation of humanity.[24] While his conception of freedom remained virtually unchanged, Marx's understanding of the means by which this would be achieved shifted, according to Walicki. Communist society was the point in history where humanity would be fully free according to Marx. By freedom, Marx understood a mode of existence in which humans were living in harmony with themselves and with others. To achieve this required overcoming those forces and conditions that both dominated and divided humanity, and which caused individuals to be alienated from themselves. According to Walicki, Marx believed that the basis of freedom lay in "rational, conscious, collective control over economic forces",[25] and in the abolition of the divisive institutions of capitalism, namely private ownership and the division of labour.[26] In Marx's early works, he viewed human creative labour as the means for overcoming self-alienation, and the replacement of market forces with rational planning as the means to establish human freedom.[27]

14

In *Capital* and his later works, Marx retreated somewhat from this position, according to Walicki. Freedom was now to be found in the non-productive sphere (i.e. leisure time). The overwhelming priority now was to combine rational control of the economy with measures to shorten the working day. The quickest, most effective means of doing this was to develop the productive forces (technology, labour power) as rapidly as possible, thus enabling huge increases in productivity while decreasing the actual time spent by individuals on productive activity.[28]

The implications of this "duality", however it is conceived, were to become fully apparent in Russia after 1917. The earlier more "Romanticist" writings, which emphasized human emancipation, were not published until 1932. Soviet views of the future society were conditioned by the later, more sociological, empirical writings of Marx and Engels. The stress in the works which the Russian Marxists studied were derived from the modernist strand of Marx's works. Centralization, rapid development of the industrial sector and the elimination of want, exploitation and oppression were central to their understanding of the post-revolutionary society. From the later works of Marx it is possible to define communism and communist society as a set of institutional structures and features. Creating communism was, on this reading, reducible to the construction of a series of political and economic structures. The nature of these specific features is of critical importance in understanding Marx's contribution to the Soviet view of socialism.

Marx and Engels also sketched in outline the manner in which the post-capitalist society progressively unfolded. This outline was also somewhat ambiguous. The post-capitalist society contained three different stages (although the periodization was itself a little murky): the dictatorship of the proletariat, socialism (the "lower" phase of communism) and full communism (the "higher" phase). The dictatorship of the proletariat was the regime that would rule in the period after the proletarian revolution. But what did Marx (and Engels) mean by this term? How long would it last? In the *Critique of the Gotha Programme*, Marx identified the "lower" phase of communism (later termed "socialism" by Engels), as a prolonged historical period, in which capitalist society would be negated, as the foundations of capitalist exploitation were removed.[29] This however was a transitory era. The negation of the features of capitalist society would gradually evolve into the positive features of communist society, as socialism was transformed into full communism. Under this "higher" phase, the individual becomes the conscious master of nature, and of his/her destiny. History begins.[30]

Before turning to the details of these "phases" of communism, it is worth dwelling upon the implications of Marx inserting a transitional era between capitalism and communism. The idea of a transition implies two things, which were to inform Bolshevik thinking after 1917. First, there was an identifiable end to the revolutionary process which they had initiated, and the achievement of this end product was the objective of Bolshevik policy-making. The legitimacy of the Bolshevik party would rest on their ability to demonstrate that progress, the process of transition, could be achieved. This is a critical point. In the absence of a democratic mode of legitimation, the Bolsheviks would legitimate themselves through the successful construction of the features of "socialism". Their view of the future society was not just a matter of ideological correctness. It was also central to the Bolshevik party's ability to maintain itself in power. Secondly, it implied the need for conscious guidance and direction of this transition period to reach communism. The new social system could be "constructed" and built according to human design. Marx's view of the process of the transition to communism was infused with notions of constructivism and social engineering.

The future society: the "lower" phase

Although the details provided by Marx were somewhat sketchy, it is possible to outline the main features of the "transitional" phase:

> What we have to deal with here is a communist society, not as it has developed on its own foundations, but, on the contrary, just as it emerges from capitalist society; which is thus, in every respect, economically, morally and intellectually, still stamped with the birth marks of the old society from whose womb it emerges.[31]

The lower phase was marked by elements of continuity with capitalism: classes, the division of labour, wage labour and elements of inequality would still exist as remuneration would be carried out "according to work done". But the process of transformation gets underway simultaneously, as the exploitative features of capitalism – the market, private property – are negated and replaced by structures that promote the construction of the basis of communist society. These include: (a) the abolition of private property and its replacement with public ownership; (b) the means of production are brought under central direction and control; (c) measures are adopted to foment the most rapid possible development of the productive forces (which include the means of production, the labour process, technological innovations and so on).[32]

The politics of the transition period are slightly more complex. For Marx the state under all previous societies was an organ of class rule.[33] As "separate bodies of armed men" it was used by the ruling class in any epoch to oppress other classes and realize its own interests. It did this by posing its own particular interests as the embodiment of the interests of society as a whole. The division of labour, and the existence of a conflict-ridden class-based society produced the coercive state, which became a central component in the perpetuation of the alienation of the individual. This alienation, according to Kolakowski, was the separation of civil society and the state which produced a split in the essence of every individual in industrial society:

> ... the political society ... makes up the only form of (apparent) community, the only place where individuals recognise (in the abstract) the social character of their existence. This results in the almost perfect split of every individual into his real but self-centred life in civil society, on the one hand, and his communal but abstract existence as state member on the other.[34]

One of the primary tasks of the socialist revolution was to destroy the basis of this political alienation. The end to class rule would obviate the need for the coercive state. No political institutions would be needed, and the division between civil and political society would be abolished.

How did Marx envisage moving from the coercive state apparatus under capitalism to a non-class, non-state society? Marx's views on the post-revolutionary state were guarded, except in his writings on the Paris Commune in *The Civil War in France*, and ambiguous. At one point Marx talks about the need to smash the state and move immediately to a form of administration based on the Paris Commune, "the working class cannot simply lay hold of the ready-made state machinery and wield it for its own purposes".[35] At other points (and Marx is noticeably silent on the Paris Commune after 1871) it is necessary during the transition to the "higher phase" that the proletariat are able to wield power through a coercive organism: the dictatorship of the proletariat. Its function is to oppress the bourgeois classes, and appropriate the means of production for the common good. This entailed taking over and utilizing the existing state machinery.[36] This was a transitional state though. As progress towards the higher phase unfolded, the need for a coercive state would disappear.

There is some controversy over the precise shape and features of the dictatorship of the proletariat. Marx makes few references to it. In a letter to J. Wedemeyer (1852), he argued that "the class struggle necessarily leads to the dictatorship of the proletariat . . . this dictatorship only constitutes the transition to the abolition of all classes and to a classless society".[37] In the *Critique of the Gotha Programme*, Marx outlined:

> . . . between capitalist and communist society lies the period of the revolutionary transformation of the one into the other. There is a corresponding period of transition in the political sphere and in this period the state can only take the form of a revolutionary dictatorship of the proletariat.[38]

The broad contours of the proletarian dictatorship in Marx's works is highlighted in an interesting passage by Frederic Bender.[39] It was to be a state controlled by the proletariat to defend the interests of the proletariat. It was an instrument of class rule, except that for the first time this ruling class (the proletariat) was the majority in society. It was also clear that it was conceived of in democratic terms. Marx and Engels foresaw a *democratic dictatorship*. A contradiction in terms? Not according to Bertram Wolfe. He argues that Marx's conception was heavily influenced by his study of the Roman

Republic. In Republican Rome, at times of emergency a dictatorship was instituted to defend Roman democracy. It was constitutional, temporary, and self-limiting.[40] The contemporary meanings and connotations of the term "dictatorship" serve only to obscure and distort our understanding of the concept of proletarian dictatorship as outlined by Marx.

Beyond this basic conception, there is little clarity. The ambiguities in Marx's writings on the dictatorship of the proletariat centre on three issues. First, how long would the dictatorship of the proletariat last? Was it the short period between capitalism and socialism? Or was it the entire period between capitalism and the onset of full communism?[41] Expressed diagramatically, the alternative conceptions appear thus:

The second ambiguity surrounds the nature and purpose of the proletarian dictatorship. What form of democracy did Marx envisage? How would the proletariat control the state? How would the state enforce its rule over the non-proletarian classes? How would the proletariat undertake the transformation of the economy? The final ambiguity relates to the process by which the proletarian dictatorship would be transformed into the stateless society of the "higher" phase of communism. Would it be abolished by the proletariat, as envisaged by Marx? Or would it "wither away", as envisaged by Engels?[42]

Across the writings of Marx and Engels, these ambiguities remained unresolved, and indeed for some theorists, created different, incompatible models of the post-revolutionary state. Harding identified two incompatible models of the state in Marx. In the Paris Commune model there was a high degree of direct democracy and participation by the workers in the government of the city. Decentralization and the fusion of the executive, legislative and judicial functions co-existed in a body in which authority flowed from the bottom upwards. In the dictatorship model, the state was a highly centralized, coercive non-democratic organ of suppression and expropriation.[43] Bender also sees two models in Marx: a "Centralisation-Model" (derived from the *Communist Manifesto*, the *Critique of the Gotha Programme* and *Capital*), and an "Aufhebung-Model" (a process of the abolition of the state), which was derived from his early writings as well as his analysis of the Paris Commune.[44] The former was a centralized, statist conception in which political decisions and economic guidance were in the hands of an elite. The latter was a form of radical, participative proletarian democracy, with proletarian control over the functioning of the economy.

These ambiguities are further exacerbated by the subsequent interventions of Engels (of which more below). In 1892, Engels stated in his introduction to the German edition of *The Civil War in France* written in 1892 (after Marx's death) that the Commune *was* the Dictatorship of the Proletariat.[45] An understanding of the ambiguities within Marx's sketches of the post-revolutionary society is crucial in any analysis of the origins and evolution of the concept of socialism within the Russian Marxist movement.

The future society: the "higher phase"

The unfolding of the historical process would lead inexorably from the lower to the higher phase of communist society. In a vivid passage, Marx describes it thus:

> In a higher phase of communist society, after the enslaving subordination of the individual to the division of labour, and therewith also the antithesis between mental and physical labour has vanished; after labour has become not only a means of life, but life's prime want; after the productive forces have also increased with the all-round development of the individual and all the springs of cooperative wealth flow more abundantly, only then can the narrow horizon of bourgeois right be crossed in its entirety, and society inscribes on its banners, "from each according to his ability, to each according to his needs".[46]

This era is marked by the full and final self-realization of the individual: the complete humanization of mankind is finally attained as individuals are now in full control of their own destiny. The abolition of market forces promotes conscious rational control over the economy. All sources of alienation and inequality have been abolished: the social division of labour, classes, wage-labour, production for exchange-value and the coercive apparatus of the state. All the divisive dichotomies of capitalist society – mental/manual labour, town/country, male/female – would be overcome.

In economic terms, production is directed towards use-value. Ownership of the means of production is completely socialized. Developments in technology and labour productivity enable the production of a superabundance of goods. This entailed the abolition of scarcity, which was to become a central goal of the Bolsheviks after 1917. Under communism there is a totally different approach to work. Individuals contribute according to their abilities, and draw from the common supply of goods to meet their needs. The specific nature of the labour experience of communism is a little confusing though. In his earlier works, and in *Grundrisse,* Marx foresaw labour itself as part of the realm of freedom under communism. The abolition of the social division of labour would be replaced by a voluntary division of labour:

> . . . while in communist society, where nobody has one exclusive sphere of activity but each can become accomplished in any branch he wishes, society regulates the general production and thus makes it possible for me to do one thing today and another tomorrow, to hunt in the morning, fish in the afternoon, rear cattle in the evening, criticise after dinner, just as I have a mind, without ever becoming hunter, fisherman, cowherd or critic.[47]

In his later works, alienation is overcome, yet labour has a different status. Marx sets labour entirely within the realm of necessity. The "realm of necessity" (the production of requirements necessary for biological survival) still exists, but the time spent on this is greatly reduced by the growth in the productive forces, and by a voluntary division of labour arising from a process of education through labour. This creates the preconditions for the "realm of freedom", when individuals are able to develop their potential to their full ability, *in their leisure time.*[48] According to Marx in *Capital* "the sphere of material production remains a realm of necessity, and the true realm of freedom begins only in leisure time".[49]

Politics no longer exists under communism. The destruction of the division of labour and of a class-based society removes the basis for a coercive state apparatus which will disappear eventually. In its stead there would be a non-political authority, or administration of communist society which is communitarian, democratic, participative and non-coercive. Civil and political society become fused, and the dichotomy between the individual as citizen and as private individual is overcome, as:

> Only when the real individual man will absorb back the abstract citizen of the state and – as individual man, in his empirical life, in his individual work, in his individual relationships – will become the species-being, only when man will recognise and will organise his "forces propres" as social forces and, consequently, will not separate from himself the social force in form of political force any more, only then the emancipation of man will be accomplished.[50]

The individual recovers his/her true being: self-realization through self-transcendence.

Marx on socialism and communism: a summary and interpretation

The dominant themes of Marx's writings on socialism and communism were shaped by his worldview, which synthesized various intellectual currents of the nineteenth century. Attempting to distill the essence of Marx's enormous body of work is inherently reductionist and problematic. Acknowledging these limitations, five strands can be identified that were to play a significant role in shaping Soviet socialism. First, Marx was a materialist. As opposed to the idealistic philosophers, Marx considered matter to be primary in explaining the nature of the world. The world was governed by laws of nature and these laws were knowable. Secondly, Marx's view of history lies within the positivist tradition: linear, progressive and teleological. History was moving towards a preordained end, and the laws governing the historical process were also open to human understanding and explanation. Both these aspects of Marx's world-outlook place Marx firmly within the Enlightenment tradition of rationalism and the enthronement of human reason. This was scientific socialism.

Thirdly, Marx's theories were informed by a profound sense of rationalism and constructivism. Marx's faith in the ability of human reason to understand the world, and his belief in the teleology of historical materialism combined to promote an awareness that the future society could be consciously constructed. Social processes could be guided, social change directed. This is best illustrated by attitudes to the market. The market under capitalism was an anarchic mechanism, outside of human control. In the future society, there would be no market, as socalism would be a society subject to the dictates of human reason and rationality, embodied in the planning apparatus for the provision of social needs. As Julian Cooper has noted:

> At the core of Bolshevik–Marxist–Leninist ideology has been the conviction that socialism must be constructed by conscious human action according to a preconceived plan. Not only was socialism conceived as a task on a grand scale, but this very mode of development was understood to express the superiority of the new social formation . . . "But what distinguishes the worst architect from the best of bees is this, that the architect raises his structure in imagination before he erects it in reality" (Marx). Here we have one of the original sources of the constructivist discourse.[51]

This constructivist ethos found expression, in the Soviet Union after 1917, in a form of social engineering which was to have a profound influence on the form Soviet socialism was to take, and upon the nature of Soviet society.

Fourthly, Marx's view of human nature was an Enlightenment derived one. Marx had an optimistic view of humanity. Freed from the fetters and constraints of bourgeois society, individuals could live harmoniously with one another. Removing the basis for exploitation, and overcoming alienation would facilitate the emergence of a society of harmony, unity and voluntary co-operation. Human beings were essentially social beings, who discovered their true humanity in a social context. In the sixth thesis on Feuerbach, Marx wrote that, "But the human essence is no abstraction inherent in each single individual. In its reality it is the ensemble of the social relations".[52]

In this sense, Marx's view of socialism can be seen to lie on the collectivist/egalitarian/fraternalist wing of socialism as a doctrine. In the post-revolutionary discourse developed by the Bolshevik wing of Russian social-democracy, these notions of perfectability, constructivism and the absence of an unchanging core of human attributes left the way open for the Bolsheviks to consider the re-shaping of humankind in the image of the "New Socialist Person" to be both legitimate and desirable.

Lastly, Marx's writings are imbued with productivist notions. The centrality of production to human history as the motor of progress ensured that the organization of production was the key issue to be resolved by the dominant class in each epoch. Added to this is the idea encapsulated by Harding, "Humans enter society, therefore, in their capacity as labouring beings and the object of their association with others is to maximize their material satisfaction".[53] Individuals were defined as bearers of labour-power. With production as the basis of every social system, productive issues assumed primacy over all others.

From these underlying principles, it is possible to summarize the key features of the post-capitalist society envisaged by Marx, which was to exert such a profound hold on the imagination and thought of the Russian Marxists. The final outcome of history was a society free from alienation, in which individuals realize themselves fully, and become truly human for the first time. As we have seen, Marx was both vague and ambiguous beyond this very general descrip-tion. In particular, the Romanticist impulse within Marx sought to establish a society of unity, harmony and community, in which freedom was found in a society of diverse creative labour. This was a rejection of capitalism and its workings. The modernist Marx viewed freedom outside of labour, in the enjoyment of leisure and of material plenty. This conception sought to take over capitalism in order to extend and universalize its principles, especially the domina-tion of nature. Freedom would come when humanity finally con-trolled nature, and so was in control of its destiny for the first time.

It was this latter conception that came to predominate in Bol-shevik thinking. This became "orthodoxy" within the Bolshevik wing of the RSDLP because of a conjunction of factors: the non-availability of Marx's early writings before 1932, the mediation of the thought of Engels and Plekhanov and the interpretations provided by Russian Marxists. Many other outcomes or conceptions of socialism were possible from the corpus of Marx's works. The key features of the transitional or lower stage (socialism as it has become known) are summarized below.

Under socialism production would be increasingly geared towards use, not exchange. To overcome the anarchy, waste and inefficiency of the capitalist market required central control and planning of the economy. To overcome the poverty and immiserisation induced by capitalism required central equitable distribution of goods, initially based on work (and so bringing inequality) but eventually based on need. Indeed, labour in the transition era was a responsibility for all to undertake. All these measures were a negation of capitalism. At the same time, the central agencies of economic direction (whatever they may be) would introduce measures to increase the development of the productive forces in the most rapid manner possible. Only in this way could a society of material abundance and maximum leisure time be achieved. The maximization of productivity was a central aim of the transitional era.

The future society would be a collectivist, internationalist, non-political one. The transition to this was a problematic issue. Should the capitalist state be taken over and used as a repressive tool and as the central co-ordinating and directing agency for the transformation of society? Or should it be smashed and the administration of society devolved onto self-governing organs of popular control? In other words, what was meant by the Dictatorship of the Proletariat? Was it possible to combine a conception of the post-revolutionary state (the so-called "Commune model"), which tended towards the Romanticist notion of the future society, with the modernist tasks of centralization, expropriation and transformation of the productive forces? This question was to produce fierce debate within the Russian Social-Democratic Movement in the lead up to 1917.

Friedrich Engels

Engels played a significant role in the codification of a Marxist orthodoxy.[54] His interpretation of Marx's ideas had a profound influence on the understanding of socialism among Russian Marxists. Indeed, prior to 1914 Engels had a far higher reputation than Marx.[55] In what ways did Engels shape the ideas of Karl Marx?

Engels accentuated the "scientific" aspects of Marx's theories. He was interested in the links between the materialist conception of history, and the laws of nature. Engels' emphasis upon the scientific aspects of the movement of history led to a one-sided interpretation that highlighted the deterministic law-governed evolution of history. This denuded the concept of revolutionary praxis as the driving-force of history which lay at the centre of Marx's views. As Lichtheim has noted:

> In the place of the original dialectical conception, in which critical thought was validated by revolutionary action, there now appeared a cast-iron system of laws from which the inevitability of socialism could be deduced with almost mathematical certainty.[56]

Although Engels initiated this process, the evolution of Marxism into a scientistic, deterministic doctrine was an unforeseen consequence of his writings after Marx's death. The general implications of the claims for a scientific status for Marx's writings strongly accentuated the rationalist outlook of Soviet socialism. It imbued their worldview with a high degree of certitude, rendered it intolerant of alternative views and emphasized the ability of adherents to be able to plan and construct the new society. Hence, in *Socialism: Utopian and Scientific*, Engels was to write:

> These two great discoveries, the materialist conception of history and the revelation of the secret of capitalist production through surplus value, we owe to Marx. With them, socialism became a science, which had now to be elaborated in all its details and interconnections.[57]

His greatest influence can be found in *Anti-Duhring (Herr Eugen Duhring's Revolution in Science)*, published first in 1877–8.[58] This work was ostensibly aimed at countering the influence of Duhring in the German socialist movement. The nature of the text – a systematic ordering of the views of Marx and Engels across a variety of themes – soon accorded it a significant role in the codification of a particular interpretation of Marx's views. The specific emphases contained within *Anti-Duhring* "resolved" many of the tensions within the writings of Marx, contributing to the hegemony of a rationalistic, modernist, productivist interpretation of Marx. The Romanticist strand slipped quietly into obscurity as first Engels, and then Plekhanov, Kautsky, Lenin et al. began to elaborate and develop Marx's thought.

All of the central features of Marx's philosophical and doctrinal approach to the future society can be found in *Anti-Duhring*. The stress on productivism and constructivism is particularly acute:

> The materialist conception of history starts from the principle that production and, next to production, the exchange of things produced, is the basis of every social order.[59]

Engels continues to outline the central features of the future society. Social planning of production, non-commodity economy, large-scale production, viz., "the seizure of the means of production by society eliminates commodity production",[60] "the anarchy within social production is replaced by consciously planned organisation",[61] "only a society which enables its productive forces to mesh harmoniously on the basis of one single vast plan can allow industry to be dispersed over the whole country".[62] In particular, Engels uses the phrase "by generating a race of producers", encapsulating the one-sided conception of individuals as "bearers of labour-power", and the constructivist optimism that the human personality can be moulded, shaped, engineered.[63]

In *Anti-Duhring* Engels set out the classic formulae for the evolution of the post-revolutionary state. It is worth quoting at length:

> As soon as there is no social class to be held in subjection any longer, as soon as class domination and the struggle for individual existence based on the anarchy of production existing up to now are eliminated together with the collisions and excesses arising from them, there is nothing more to repress, nothing necessitating a special repressive force, a state. The first act in which the state really comes forward as the representative of the whole of society – is at the same time its last independent act as a state. . . . *The*

government of persons is replaced by the administration of
things and the direction of the processes of production. The
state is not "abolished", it withers away.[64] (my emphasis)

This conception reinforces the idea of the state as expropriator and
oppressor, which will "wither away" in the long term. In other
words, the proletariat must seize the state in order to take control
of the means of production and nullify the old classes in a political
sense. After this, it will disappear as a political entity, but will remain, in Bender's words, as an "economic planning bureau".[65] In
Engels' vision, a central public authority would remain after the
revolution, as a means of directing the economy. The abolition
of the capitalist division of labour and of scarcity (owing to the
rapid development of the productive forces) will lead inexorably
to the abolition of classes. Society will be governed by notions of
collectivism and co-operation. Interestingly, Engels also foresaw
the eventual homogeneity of communism: the town/country distinction would be abolished and the two would be "fused". Large
towns would be eliminated![66]

The nature of the "realm of freedom under communism" (freedom through creative labour, or through enjoyment of leisure time)
was resolved firmly in favour of the latter by Engels. The nature of
freedom is defined in terms of control *over* nature:

> The conditions of existence environing and hitherto domin-
> ating humanity now pass under the dominion and control
> of humanity, which now for the first time becomes the real
> conscious master of nature.[67]

In similar vein, productive work is defined as "this natural condition
of human existence", but the development of the productive forces
will "reduce the time needed for work to a point which will be
small indeed in the light of our present conceptions".[68] The stress
Engels laid upon abolishing the spontaneity of market forces, on
centralizing control of the economy, and on maximizing productivity was to shape the outlook of the Russian Marxist movement
profoundly. His influence is central to an understanding of the
emergence of a Soviet model of socialism. It is to the specific Russian context that we must now turn.

Socialism in Russia: Lenin, Bolshevism and Russian social-democracy

The ideas about socialism that became predominant in Russia prior to 1917 were produced out of the contact of Marx's ideas (mediated substantially by Engels and Kautsky) with the traditions of Russian socialism. The character of Russian social-democracy has been the subject of intense dispute, as theorists have disagreed over the extent to which the "Russianness" displaced "Marxism" from the centre of its worldview. This debate is accentuated by those who argue that the doctrinal basis of Russian social-democracy was also profoundly shaped by the socio-political and economic structure of autocratic Russia. The political activities of the Russian Marxists imposed the need to synthesize their theoretical positions with their revolutionary activities.[69]

Russian Marxism was profoundly influenced by both Russia's intellectual heritage, and also by the semi-feudal, agrarian, back-ward nature of her economic and social structure. From the time of its emergence, Russian socialism was marked by a strong tendency towards egalitarianism, maximalism and collectivism. It grew out of the general movement for change and reform that emerged from the 1840s, and which burgeoned under the impact of the reforms of the 1860s. Its maximalist tendency derived from the intransigence of the autocratic state. The prospects for liberalization or piecemeal reform were consistently frustrated. The socialist movement was the radical wing of the movement for change, expressing the desire for a total restructuring of Russian society. The so-called "parliamentary road" to socialism was not an option in nineteenth century Russia.[70]

The collectivist and egalitarian traditions of Russian socialism stem from the Populist legacy. Populists argued that the peasant commune would form the basis for the revolutionary transforma-tion of Russia into a democratic, decentralized egalitarian state. In this way, the twin evils of autocratic rule based on serfdom, and capitalist exploitation and degradation could be overcome and avoided. Populists wished, in Marxist terms, to "bypass" capital-ism.[71] Interestingly, Marx himself raised the possibility of a peculiar "Russian Road" to socialism, based on the peasant commune.[72] Although Populism suffered a serious setback in the 1870s with the catastrophic failure of the "Going to the People" movement, it influenced Russian Marxism in two ways. First, the commitment to a collectivist, egalitarian approach to post-revolutionary social and economic organization: secondly, the strategy and tactics of revolution. Populism, in varying ways, outlined a key role for the intelligentsia in the making of a revolution. The backwardness of the masses (in terms of political consciousness, and cultural and educational development), and the antipathy of the autocratic state to autonomous political and social movements created the need for an elite group of revolutionaries. Although different theorists conceptualized the role of the intellectuals in different ways – educate the masses for self-emancipation, seize control of the state through a coup, or smash the state through a revolutionary uprising – the question of revolutionary strategy was a contentious one in the history of Russian social democracy. Although Russian Marxists departed significantly from many populist ideas and approaches, the underlying influence of Populism on Russian Marxists and Russian Marxism should not be underestimated.

Russian social-democracy

Western scholarship on Russian and Soviet history has, until recently, tended to view the Russian social democratic movement and its ideology monolithically.[73] Reading history backwards, the uniform, rigid, dogmatic ideology of the Stalinist years is seen to have its origins in the Leninist interpretation of Marxism which was pre-eminent before and after 1917. This is a misleading viewpoint. Russian Marxism before the revolution was an inherently pluralistic phenomenon. It was marked by substantial disputes, debates and differences of approach.[74] The reason for this lies in the need of Russian social-democracy for doctrinal specificity.[75] Although the Russian Marxists continued to be animated in their revolutionary activities by the view(s) of the future society put forward by Marx and Engels, they also sought to fill in the details of both the revolutionary process and the aftermath of the revolution. Disputes arose as theorists attempted to apply Marx and Engels' ideas to the Russian context. It was in this crucible that a Soviet model of socialism was forged.

The acknowledged founder of the Marxist movement in Russia was Georgi Plekhanov.[76] In 1883, he along with Vera Zasulich and Pavel Axelrod, created the Emancipation of Labour Group in Geneva. In 1898, the RSDLP was formed in Minsk. At the outset, it was marked by a high degree of internal conflict over specific components of revolutionary strategy, while sharing a set of common assumptions about the future of the post-revolutionary society.

Perhaps the most consistent feature of Russian Marxism was the search for doctrinal orthodoxy. Primarily this can be explained by the sociological composition of the RSDLP, and the structure of political activity in Tsarist Russia. It was overwhelmingly a movement of intellectuals. A central feature of the Russian intelligentsia was its "search for comprehensiveness . . . and a commitment to science and rationalism".[77] Establishing the fundamental premises before identifying specifics or practicalities underpinned the outlook of much of the Russian intelligentsia, and this practice was assimilated into the Russian Marxist movement. This intellectual outlook was substantiated by the political context of Tsarist Russia. As Harding has noted, "in the absence of a strong labour movement or a mass party, the intelligentsia needed the security of proper method and undiluted theoretical orthodoxy".[78] The obsessive concern with fundamental ideological purity, with theorizing the practicalities of revolution created a climate of intellectual conflict and intolerance. The Russian Marxist movement was constantly engaged in polemical struggles, both internally and externally, and this contributed to the creation of a maximalist and extremist mindset.

The evolution of Russian Marxism into a specific body of doctrine is only understood fully in its relations with Populism. The relationship is a complex one. Many of the central figures of the RSDLP had their roots in the populist movement, and had links with the peasant socialist movement. In particular, the issues of the relationship between the revolutionary organization and the masses, and the promotion of a collectivist ethos in social and economic affairs, derived from the populist soil in which Russian Marxism grew. The precise nature of these links, and the extent of influence of populist ideals is a matter of some dispute though. Theoretically, Russian Marxism represented a fundamental break with the core ideas of Populism. The progressive role of capitalism in creating the preconditions for socialism, and the primacy afforded to the role of the proletariat in the revolutionary struggle represented a diametrical opposition to populist theorists who emphasized the need to bypass capitalism, and the central role of the peasant commune as the basis of the new socialist order. Russian Marxism both grew out of and broke with Populism at the end of the nineteenth century.

There is also another level to the relationship. Russian Marxism was formed by its polemical struggles, within and without. In the early stages (certainly up to 1914), Russian Marxists were engaged in constant polemics with the proponents of agrarian socialism, which forced them to define their attitudes across a whole spectrum of issues, including land policy, attitudes towards differentiation among the peasantry and much more besides. The position taken upon the peasant question, in particular, played a fundamental role in shaping the post-revolutionary attitudes of the Bolsheviks to the prickly agrarian question. In tandem with these disputes with the groups Lenin named "Friends of the People", Russian Marxism was also convulsed with internal disputes. Two issues stand out: the question of party organization and proletarian consciousness, and the tactics and strategy of the "first" stage of the revolution.[79]

Russian Marxism was riven with factions. In the aftermath of its formation as a political movement in 1898, different tendencies began to emerge. "Economism" (stressing the primacy of the economic struggle of the workers and the need to detach this from the wider political struggle), and Legal Marxism (stressing the potential inherent in a Bernsteinian approach combined with a movement for political reforms) being the most notable examples. The tendency for the establishment of doctrinal orthodoxy resulted in the division of the RSDLP into two wings in 1903. The issue was one of party organization.[80]

Divisions emerged over whether the party should be an elite vanguard of professional revolutionaries, or a mass movement. Lenin argued (in line with Plekhanov's earlier works) in *What is to be done?* that the workers by themselves could only attain to "trade-union consciousness", that is, a concern with their immediate material needs (wages, conditions, etc.). To attain to "Social Democrat" (that is revolutionary) consciousness required a disciplined organization of revolutionaries, armed with the "correct" ideology who would lead and guide the workers:

> Hence our task, the task of Social-Democracy, is to combat spontaneity, to divert the working class movement from this spontaneous trade-unionist striving to come under the

wing of the bourgeoisie, and to bring it under the wing of revolutionary Social-Democracy.[81]

Clearly, there was an important practical aspect to this theory. A mass movement was inappropriate in the repressive conditions of Tsarism. A tightly knit organization would be more difficult to infiltrate. The context of Lenin's writings are also vital. The pamphlet was part of the wider polemical struggle with the "Economists", and Lenin overemphasized certain points. Lenin always stressed the importance of mass action. Yet the stress on the need for a dedicated revolutionary elite separate from the mass movement caused a split at the 1903 Congress, where Lenin and Martov fell out over the definition of party membership.[82] The resulting division (Bolsheviks and Mensheviks) was a manifestation of a wider division over revolutionary strategy in the "first" phase of the revolution. Disputes arose over which class should provide the lead in the revolution against the autocracy. Classical, orthodox Marxism argued that the bourgeoisie would lead the revolution against feudal absolutist regimes and would establish untrammeled capitalism. The role of the peasantry in this revolution was also open to question. Lenin, Trotsky and Plekhanov developed distinctive and innovative analyses of the revolutionary tactics of Russian Marxism.[83]

Many issues divided Russian Marxists. Yet, Bolsheviks and Mensheviks shared a common set of values and ideas derived from their reading of Marx and Engels. Their preoccupation with organizing revolution, and with the struggle for "orthodoxy" effectively precluded a detailed treatment of the shape of the post-revolutionary society, although they did draw up a party programme in two parts in 1903 (minimum and maximum).[84] Indeed, prior to 1917, the only real dispute among Russian Marxists about post-revolutionary ideas was between Aleksander Bogdanov (one of the leading figures in Russian Marxism at the time) and Lenin over philosophical and cultural issues.[85] It was not until 1915/16 that the issue of what was to happen after the revolution began to be discussed at any length. It is to the question of how the Russian Marxists (and Lenin and Bukharin, in particular) interpreted Marx and Engels' views on the shape of socialism that we must now turn.

The central text revealing the Bolshevik wing of the RSDLP's views of the post-revolutionary society is Lenin's *State and revolution*.[86] It is at this point that the formation of a recognizable form of social-ism, peculiar to one wing of the Russian Marxist movement, began to crystallize. Lenin (and Bukharin)'s theoretical and polemical works during 1917 developed an interpretation of the view of society after the revolution that synthesized the broad framework of the Engelian view of Marxism with elements of Kautsky's thought alongside indigenous Russian notions of socialism. In analyzing Lenin's thought, an understanding of context is crucial. The writings in 1917 have to be seen against a background of a profound shift in Lenin's understanding of the nature of capitalism, and a series of polemical struggles within the international socialist movement.[87] Lenin's highly influential pamphlet, *Imperialism: the highest stage of capitalism* (published in 1917) set out, in a popular outline, the changes in the nature of capitalism that had occurred since Marx's death. Drawing heavily on the works of other theorists (in particular Bukharin, Hilferding and Hobson) Lenin argued that capitalism had reached a new stage: state monopoly capitalism.[88] Briefly, the consequences of this development were threefold.

First, the economic basis of state monopoly capitalism, in concen-trating production into fewer and fewer trusts and/or syndicates, and in creating a single banking system, had created the essential prerequisites for socialism. It would be a fairly simple procedure to socialize the production process for the benefit of the whole of society. Secondly, the capitalist state was now a degenerate, parasitical phenomenon that was accruing enormously repressive powers unto itself. The choice for Lenin was a stark one: socialism or barbarism. Thirdly, the task now was to smash the capitalist state. But what would take its place? It was this issue which animated Lenin in 1916 and 1917. Moreover, he was concerned to establish a clear Marxist doctrinal orthodoxy on the nature of the state. In *State and revolution* (and other writings, especially *Can the Bolsheviks retain State power?*[89]) Lenin clarified the tension within Marxism, and illustrated the conception of socialism that was to dominate Bolshevik thinking after the revolution. It is important to stress here that while Lenin's views were to predominate after the revolution, there were other competing visions within Bolshevism that articu-lated alternative interpretations of the Marxist future society.[90] In spite of the evident differences of interpretation over issues such as workers' control, equality, female emancipation and the structure of the forces of coercion after the revolution, most Bolsheviks shared a common set of values and worldview that informed the practice of Soviet socialism after 1917.

The meaning of Lenin's *State and revolution* has been the subject of intense dispute.[91] Does it stand squarely within the traditions of Lenin's writings, or is it a syndicalist utopia which was an anomaly within the Leninist corpus? The origins of this controversy lie in the deeper tension within Marxism about conceptions of the post-revolutionary state and, in particular, the question of the debate over whether the Paris Commune model was distinct from, or can be equated to, the dictatorship of the proletariat.[92] Lenin's pamphlet, part polemic and part practical programme, sought to establish a Marxist orthodoxy on the post-revolutionary state in the light of both the impending socialist revolution, and the opposing views of other socialist figures. In this sense, *State and revolution* was concerned with theory and practice.

On the theoretical plane, Lenin established the following points as the kernel of the Marxist view of the state. In opposition to the anarchists, Lenin argued that:

> the proletariat must destroy the existing state machine, and substitute for it a new one, consisting of an organization of armed workers, after the type of the Commune.[93]

> complete abolition of the state can only be achieved after classes have been abolished by a socialist revolution which leads to the "withering away of the state";

> the proletariat must be prepared for revolution by utilising the present state;[94]

Lenin reiterates Marxist orthodoxy. Under communism, the state will gradually wither away. In the transition period, the dictatorship of the proletariat would hold sway, in order to suppress the bourgeoisie and to organize and plan the development of the socialist economy. The critical question was, what form would the dictatorship of the proletariat take? Would it be a centralizing, repressive, expropriative body? Or would it be based on the Paris Commune model in which the state would be a decentralized version of popular self-government? An answer to this question lies in the practical ideas set out by Lenin.

Lenin sought to fuse the two ideas. He argued that it was necessary to construct an organ of suppression to crush the resistance of the old exploiting classes, and to supervise and organize industrial production. Lenin puts forward the idea that after the revolution, the dictatorship of the proletariat would not be a state in the accepted Marxist sense of being "separate bodies of armed men" organized to promote the interests of a minority. The dictatorship of the proletariat is exercised by the majority of the population:

> And since the majority of the people itself suppresses its oppressors, a "special force" for suppression is *no longer necessary*! In this sense the state begins to wither away.[95] Instead of the special institutions of a privileged minority (privileged officialdom, the chiefs of the standing army), the majority itself can directly fulfil all these functions, and the more the functions of state power devolve upon the people as a whole the less need is there for the existence of this power.[96] (my emphasis)

Lenin saw in the spontaneous growth of the Soviets of Workers' and Peasants' deputies (local representative councils) the coincidence of popular democratic organs with a force for repression. In this way the Commune model is restored to a central place in Marxist theory. However, it is not accurate to view Lenin's vision of the state as being an inherently decentralized, syndicalist conception of self-governing communes. There are strong centralizing, coercive and hierarchical elements contained within it. Lenin attempts to reconcile conflicting impulses: the need to create a state apparatus organized to administer, control and repress, and the necessity of abolishing the distinction between state and society by fostering the growth of societal self-government.

The democratic nature of the dictatorship was manifested in two ways. First, the state would be based upon proletarian representative democracy, embodied in the Soviets. The Soviets would represent the "simple organization of armed masses", and would fuse legislative and executive functions, turning them into "working bodies" not the "talking shops" of bourgeois parliamentary democracy.[97] The Soviets were to be both legislative bodies, directly elected by the people and subject to recall at any moment, and also the core of the state apparatus involved in the administration of the country. Secondly, proletarian democracy meant a high level of popular participation in the governing of the country. The workers would elect all officials, who were revocable and accountable. There would be a regular rotation of all officials, and an egalitarian wages policy. In turn all members of the proletariat would participate in the administration of the country:

> Under socialism much of the primitive democracy will inevitably be revived, since, for the first time in the history of civilised society, the mass of the population will rise to the level of taking an independent part, not only in voting and elections, but also in the everyday administration of affairs. Under socialism all will govern in turn and will soon become accustomed to no-one governing.[98]

Capitalism had created the preconditions for popular competence in the performance of administrative tasks (universal literacy, training and labour discipline, etc.), although Lenin stressed elsewhere that training would be needed for labourers, cooks, etc. before they could begin to involve themselves. The significant point for Lenin was that the proletariat had the competence and the ability to govern themselves, given the right training from the class-conscious elements of the state. This has been characterized by Sakwa as "Commune Democracy", entailing the attempt to abolish the distinction between state and society, by involving the masses themselves in the administration of the socialist system.[99] This project came into conflict in Lenin's writings with the structure and functions of the post-revolutionary state apparatus.

The state contained coercive, disciplined, centralized and hierarchical elements. Lenin argued that:

> But when the state will be a proletarian state, when it will be an instrument of violence exercised by the proletariat against the bourgeoisie, we shall be fully and unreservedly in favour of strong state power and of centralism.[100]

Strict discipline in all spheres of political, social and economic life was to be maintained. Everyone would be compelled to work. Labour conscription would operate. The measure of labour and consumption in the first phase of communism would be subject to the "strictest control by society and by the state".[101]

Lenin's vision was also thoroughly imbued with notions of centralism, primarily in the economic sphere, but also in the political. For Lenin, the issue was clear-cut: "Marx was a centralist".[102] In his writings, Lenin was equally unambiguous:

> The effort to prove the necessity for centralism to the Bolsheviks who are centralists by conviction, by their programme and by the entire tactics of the Party, is really like forcing an open door.[103]

How was this "centralism by conviction" reconciled with the self-organization and mass participation of the people? The organization of workers and peasants into self-governing communes did not signal a decentralized federation. Rather, the communes would unite voluntarily on a national scale to expropriate the bourgeoisie. Lenin talks of voluntary "amalgamation" and "fusion" of the communes. He argues that ". . . not a single Bolshevik has ever argued against centralization of the Soviets, against their amalgamation".[104] The aim was to combine the maximum possible democratization with the maximum centralization. This pattern was repeated in the economic sphere, of which more below.

Notions of hierarchy continued to underpin Lenin's thinking. It is clear that an administrative apparatus would continue to exist after the revolution, albeit with safeguards to prevent this apparatus acquiring privileges or a discrete set of interests. This administrative apparatus would in the long run be staffed by proletarians, subject to the conditions outlined above (rotation, revocation, accountability, egalitarianism). This entailed replacing the bureaucratic personnel as well as changing the structure of the control of the apparatus itself. However, there would be continuity with the capitalist phase in the use of experts. The employment of specialists would continue:

> The question of control and accounting should not be confused with the question of the scientifically trained staff

of engineers, agronomists and so on. These gentlemen are working today in obedience to the wishes of the capitalists; they will work even better tomorrow in obedience to the wishes of the armed workers.[105]

The key point was that remuneration for the specialists was to remain higher in the transition period, "in all probability we shall introduce complete wage equality only gradually and shall pay these specialists higher salaries during the transition period".[106] Furthermore, Lenin talks of paying, "the economists, statisticians and technicians good money".[107]

Lenin attempted to resolve the tension in Marxism between the Commune and dictatorship models of the state in *State and revolution*. His view of proletarian representative democracy, or commune democracy, sought to combine the need for mass popular participation/supervision on the one hand, with a transcendence of bourgeois parliamentarism, a recognition of the necessity for administration and expertise in the post-revolutionary state, and a strongly disciplined, coercive, centralist organization on the other. Many ambiguities remained. Their resolution awaited the exercise of power after October 1917.

The large question mark hanging over Lenin's view of the post-revolutionary political sphere lay in the role of the party. Lenin only refers to it openly in one section:

> By educating the workers' Party, Marxism educates the vanguard of the proletariat which is capable of assuming power and of leading the whole people to socialism, of directing and organising the new order, of being the teacher, the guide, the leader of all the toilers and exploited in the task of building up their social life without the bourgeoisie and against the bourgeoisie.[108]

In another passage Lenin describes the dictatorship of the proletariat as "the organization of the vanguard of the oppressed as the ruling class", which hints at a complex relationship between popular self-government, the centralization and hierarchy of the post-revolutionary state and the party.[109] Although the details of the relationship were hazy and ambiguous, the recurring tension in

Figure 1.1   Bolshevism in power: the institutional structure of the Soviet State after October 1917. Formal operation of system.

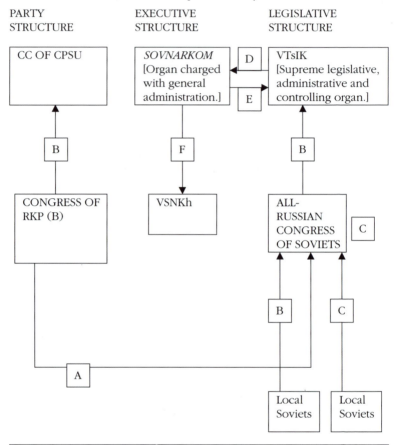

KEY:

A: Party members seek election to ARCS and agitate for Bolshevik policies.

B: Lower bodies elect delegates to higher bodies.

C: ARCS is the sovereign body: it passes legislation.

D: VTsIK (Central Executive Committee of ARCS) appoints members of *Sovnarkom* and sets tasks.

E: *Sovnarkom* passes policies for approval.

F: *Sovnarkom* passes policies to Vesenkha which draws up detailed guidelines for their implementation.

System was supposed to operate on the basis of democratic control and participation "from below", coupled with accountable direction from the elites.

Lenin's writings – between popular action and elite revolutionary consciousness and direction – is reproduced here in *State and revolution.*

Whereas the political tasks of the revolution were to smash the bourgeois state, in the economic sphere the development of state monopoly capitalism meant it was possible to take over the central economic institutions and utilize them for revolutionary goals. Indeed Lenin went further, arguing that:

> In addition to the chiefly "oppressive" apparatus – the standing army, the police and the bureaucracy – the modern state possesses an apparatus which has extremely close connections with the banks and syndicates, an apparatus which performs an enormous amount of accounting and registration work . . . This apparatus must not, and should not be smashed.[110]

Lenin reiterated his commitment to the long-term vision of the economy in the higher phase of communism. The conscious, planned control of economic processes would lead ultimately to the evolution of the classless, egalitarian society of labourers, free from exploitation, alienation and the blind tyranny of market forces, controllers of their own destiny. The disappearance of the division of labour, the abolition of the antitheses between town and country, mental and manual labour would enable society to move towards the implementation of the rule "from each according to his ability, to each according to his needs", creating the basis for actual equality. But what about his interpretation of the shape of the lower phase, or socialism? The tension between centralized direction, and popular control from below is reproduced in Lenin's writings on the economy in the first phase of communism.

The central tasks of the transitional phase were the transformation of capitalist private ownership into social ownership, and the enormous expansion of the productive forces to enable the creation of a society of material abundance and a voluntary division of labour. To achieve these aims, the defining feature of the socialist economy was the *centralized, planned* and *statist* nature of its organization and administration. There would be strict, close control of the processes of both production and distribution. Commodity production would subside and the market would be replaced by a system of centralized allocation. Production would be large-scale. Regulation of consumption would be strictly controlled by society. Indeed Lenin's writings imply a hypercentralization: a monolithic, single economic organization, centralized and hierarchical:

> All citizens are transformed here into hired employees of the state, which consists of the armed workers. All citizens become employees and workers of a single nationwide state syndicate . . . The whole of society will have become a single office and a single factory. [111]

The postal service is held up by Lenin as an example of the organizational structure of the socialist economic system: "To organise the whole national economy on the lines of the postal service . . . is our immediate aim". [112]

Lenin's analysis of state-monopoly capitalism (in particular the structure of the German war economy) demonstrated that the productive process had been consolidated, bureaucratized and simplified to such an extent that it was now possible for the people to control these economic institutions. Lenin stressed the central role played by a single state bank, "A single State Bank, the biggest of the big, with branches in every rural district, in every factory, will constitute as much as nine-tenths of the socialist apparatus". [113]

Lenin's pamphlets in the autumn of 1917 (*Can the Bolsheviks retain State power?, The impending catastrophe and how to combat it*) consistently emphasize the high degree of continuity between state capitalism and socialism. [114] At one point he argues that "socialism is merely the next step forward from the state-capitalist monopoly". [115] The critical question was how to undertake the process of "expropriating the expropriators". Interestingly, in the immediate aftermath of the revolution, Lenin did not envisage immediate confiscation of private property, although it is clear that in the socialist phase the aim was to transfer the means of production into social ownership. In *The impending catastrophe and how to combat it*, Lenin noted that:

> nationalisation of the banks . . . would not deprive any owner of a single kopek . . . Not a single one of these

certificates [shares, bonds, bills, receipts etc.] would be in-
validated or altered if the banks were nationalised.[116]

How then did Lenin envisage control of the socialist economy
being exercised by the dictatorship of the proletariat? This would
be achieved through a combination of intensified centralization of
the economy, with increased popular control. The nature of this popular control is a little unclear. Who would exercise it: the Soviets?
The workers? The vanguard?

The key tasks, identified by Lenin, were the tasks of "accounting
and control".[117] Bringing the economy directly under state control was
the crucial factor in removing the basis of exploitation. Accounting
and control was technically possible as capitalism had greatly
simplified the economic processes, and had trained the individuals
within the banks, syndicates, trusts etc. to fulfil these tasks. The
individuals are converted into state employees by a single decree,
and although they had been employees of capitalist trusts, state
control was ensured in one of two ways. Either, they would exercise control in the interests of the proletarian state as they "lead a
proletarian or semi-proletarian existence".[118] Or, as hired employees
of the state, they would carry out the instructions of state officials.

The mechanisms of control were not limited to the conversion of
the foremen, accountants, clerks, etc. into state employees. The
remaining capitalist officials would be subject to close supervision
by a variety of agencies of the state: employees unions, trade
unions, consumers' societies and the Soviets themselves. Overall,
the entire economic apparatus would be subordinated to the proletarian Soviets. Two issues are worthy of discussion in this respect.
First, the economy would be hierarchically organized. It was not
envisaged that the socialist economy would be a decentralized,
fragmented one, based around autonomous, self-governing industrial enterprises. It would be statist and centralized. It would be
a planned economy. The market would be abolished. Secondly,
workers' control was not the supervision of enterprises by the
workers themselves. Lenin is at great pains to stress that control of
the economy is subordinated to the Soviets:

> When we say "workers control", always juxtaposing this
> slogan to dictatorship of the proletariat, always putting it

immediately after the latter, we thereby explain what kind of state we mean . . . if we are speaking of a proletarian state, then workers control can become the country-wide, all-embracing, omnipresent, most precise and most conscientious accounting of the production and distribution of goods. Without the Soviets, this task would be impracticable. The Soviets indicate to the proletariat the organizational work which can solve this historically important problem.[119]

This hierarchical, centralized, regulated, statized conception of the shape of the socialist economy in the transitional phase was to exert an enormous influence on the subsequent development of the Soviet state. In particular, conflicts over the meaning of workers' control were to punctuate the early years of Soviet rule.

Land policy was another key question. The Bolsheviks were committed to the extension of socialist principles of industrial production to the agricultural sector. Farming should be undertaken on large-scale, mechanized agricultural units that were organized on either co-operative or collectivist bases. In this way Russian agriculture would benefit from the economies of scale, would be amenable to central planning and control and would promote egalitarianism, collectivism and fraternalism among the peasantry. This aspiration brought the Bolsheiks into a persistent conflict with the peasantry's own aspirations: autonomous, individual or family peasant small-holdings.

The Bolshevik adherence to Marxism profoundly shaped their vision of the structure and normative basis of society under socialism. Five features are prominent. First, the Bolsheviks were internationalists. Their long-term aim was to transform the world, not just Russia. Secondly, the Bolsheviks viewed the world in class categories, and the structure of society was conceived of in stark terms: bourgeois v. proletarian. Everything was designed to promote the interests of the proletariat, and to destroy the interests of the bourgeoisie. Thirdly, it was inherently collectivist in its orientation. Collective rights were prior to those of the individual.[120] As Carr has noted, the Bolsheviks started from the premise that "the individual could achieve self-fulfilment only through society, not against society".[121] Self-realization for the individual came through self-transcendence: personal interests were identical with the interests of the class as a whole. Fourthly, the Bolsheviks viewed a socialist society as one which would become increasingly harmonious and homogenous. The abolition of the root causes of class inequality and economic exploitation created the objective conditions for the achievement of social harmony and homogeneity under the higher phase of communism. The economic, political and cultural hegemony of the proletariat created a fundamental unity of interests among the vast majority of the population (workers and poor peasants).

Finally, the Bolsheviks were committed to an egalitarian society.[122] They sought to eradicate all forms of discrimination and injustice: gender, nationality, and class. However, the issue of egalitarianism was a complex one. The dictatorship of the proletariat sought to transcend the distinction between rulers and ruled, and to abolish the existence of a privileged and exploitative class. The policy of paying officials a workmen's wage expressed this essentially egalitarian impulse. However, actual equality would only be realized in the higher phase of communism. Inequality and injustice would still exist under socialism, for as Marx argued, workers receive articles of consumption from society according to the amount of labour performed. But, as people are unequal (in strength, talents, social circumstances, etc.) this will lead to inequalities, differentiation and injustices, although the basis for exploitation will have been removed. Lenin also argued that remuneration for specialists would be higher in the transition, emphasizing that egalitarianism was something that would evolve during socialism. Only with the abolition of scarcity, and the massive increase in labour productivity would it be possible to create a society of actual equality.[123]

Summary: Soviet socialism before the revolution

The understanding of socialism that informed Bolshevik thinking, and by extension policy-making, after 1917 comprised a cluster of different values and perspectives which were forged and tempered in the Russian Marxist movement at the beginning of the twentieth century. The particular interpretation of the ideas and outlook of Marx, mediated through Engels, Plekhanov, Kautsky, Lenin et al., was both well-defined and fluid at the same time. The understanding of the basic structures of the post-revolutionary state, and of the direction in which society was to be directed were clear. The details were almost entirely sketchy. In particular, and astonishingly, many commentators have noted that the Bolsheviks came to power in October 1917 with no detailed programme for managing the economy, just a set of precepts.

As we have seen, the understanding of socialism and communism that came to predominate in the RSDLP was heavily derived from the Engelian–Kautskian interpretation of Marxism. It rested on a rationalist, scientific, materialist premise, and was imbued with a profound sense of constructivism. It espoused a commitment to collectivism, egalitarianism and internationalism, viewed the world in stark class-based terms, and was underpinned by a view of individuals that was essentially productivist: individuals were bearers of labour-power. The transformation of the structures of the Russian economy – via the most rapid possible development of the productive forces – would not only lay the foundations for the creation of a society of material abundance, but would also overturn the values and consciousness of the population, creating the New Socialist Man/Woman. Large-scale industry was the key to social progress. Yet, some critical tensions still remained within the broad contours of the understanding of the transition between capitalism and communism.

In particular, the tension within Marx's writings between on the one hand the Romanticist understanding of communism – a society free from alienation, in which individuals lived in co-operative and creative communities expressing an essential unity between individuals, and individuals and nature – and on the other the essentially modernizing understanding of the transitional phase was manifested after the revolution within Bolshevism as a political movement. Many Bolsheviks were uncompromising modernizers. The transformation of the social, economic and political structures would facilitate the satisfaction of human desires, enabling control and manipulation of nature. The modernizing strand sought to maximize economic productivity and efficiency. Many Bolsheviks placed priority on the libertarian, radically egalitarian agenda. This "Romanticist" strand was concerned with overcoming the sources of alienation, and abolishing structures that promoted and perpetuated domination and exploitation. This tension was manifested after 1917 in the struggle between the desire to increase production, to centralize, discipline and impose hierarchies, and the impulse for decentralization, popular rule, self-government.

There were other issues to be resolved. The Bolshevik understanding of the broad contours of the transition phase did not translate into a clear, uncontested set of specific policy initiatives. The popular revolutionary movement, non-Bolshevik socialist groups, and indeed individuals and groupings within the Bolshevik party, developed alternatives, criticisms and proposals that sought to define the emphasis to be placed upon particular policies. In short, what was the specific meaning of the general features of socialism? A number of key tensions, and ill-defined terms remained within Bolshevik discourse:

- the tension between centralization and decentralization (and the precise meaning of these terms in both economic and political terms);
- the tension in the political realm between elite, technocratic direction of social processes on the one hand, and popular control and participation on the other;
- the twin imperatives of the dictatorship of the proletariat, to repress and to emancipate;
- the meaning of "central planning";
- the extent of inequality that would be tolerated under socialism as acceptable through the application of the Marxist dictum, "from each according to his ability, to each according to work done";
- the attitudes towards the "West/capitalism" were ambiguous. On one level the West was an alien civilization to be struggled against, overthrown, rejected. On another level, its technology, working practices and "modernist" nature were to be embraced, copied and borrowed;
- the relationship between the party, the state apparatus and the network of Soviets.

The emergence of a Soviet model of socialism evolved out of the contact of Bolshevik ideals with Russian society after 1917. A particular interpretation came to predominate, with a set of core features. However, this was not a wholly static conception. Subsequent adaptations in the nature of Soviet socialism can, in part, be explained by the changing interpretations of these tensions by different leaders. The chapters that follow trace the emergence of this hegemonic model, and the ways in which it was interpreted, adapted and ultimately abandoned and replaced under Gorbachev.

As Read has recently observed, "The most important factor underlying Bolshevik initiatives was utopianism, the desire to transform the world".[124] The acquisition of power in October 1917 brought them a world to transform. How was their understanding of socialism transformed by the experience of holding power? How far was the immediate nature of the post-revolutionary system shaped by the Bolshevik vision of the transition phase? The Bolsheviks were about to take their first steps in the realization of their vision.

Notes

1. The literature on socialism is too enormous and too overwhelming to document in any detail. The following are some important and/ or useful contributions: G. Lichtheim, *A short history of socialism* (London: Praeger, 1983); R. Berki, *Socialism* (London: Dent, 1975); A. Wright, *Socialisms* (Oxford: Oxford University Press, 1986); B. Crick, *Socialism* (Milton Keynes: Open University Press, 1987).
2. M. Malia, *The Soviet tragedy: a history of socialism in Russia 1917–91* (New York: Free Press, 1994), pp. 22–4.
3. Ibid., p. 23. I think this point is a good one, well made. But I also think that the problem of an absence of definitional specificity is hardly unique to "socialism". What about "ideology"? "democracy"? "liberalism"? There are many more.
4. Ibid., p. 24.
5. T. Ball & R. Dagger (eds), *Political ideologies and the democratic ideal* (New York: HarperCollins, 1991), pp. 120–1.
6. Berki, *Socialism*, p. 27.
7. M. Malia, *Alexander Herzen and the birth of Russian socialism*, (New York: Universal Library, 1961), p. 110.
8. Berki, *Socialism*, p. 25.
9. Crick, *Socialism*, ch. 1.
10. Z. Bauman, *Socialism: the active utopia* (London: Allen & Unwin, 1976), p. 60.
11. The best one volume overview of the varieties of socialism is Lichtheim, *Socialism*, chs 1–4.
12. C. Taylor, "Socialism and weltanschuuang", in *The socialist idea*, L. Kolakowski & S. Hampshire (eds) (London: Weidenfeld & Nicolson, 1974), pp. 45–58.

13. Ibid., pp. 48–58.
14. The literature on Marx is, to say the least, extensive. Useful pieces include, L. Kolakowski, *Main currents of Marxism* vol. 1 (Oxford: Oxford University Press, 1978); G. Lichtheim, *Marxism: an historical and critical study* (London: Routledge, 1961); D. McLellan, *Karl Marx: his life and thought* (London: Macmillan, 1974).
15. D. McLellan, *Karl Marx: selected writings* (Oxford: Oxford University Press, 1977), pp. 87–96, 159–91.
16. K. Marx & F. Engels, *Selected works* (London: Lawrence & Wishart, 1968).
17. The relevant extracts can be found in McLellan, *Karl Marx: selected writings*, part IV.
18. For an excellent overview of Marx's view of communism, see, B. Ollman, "Marx's vision of communism", *Critique* **8**, 1977, pp. 4–41.
19. R. de George, "Marxism and the good society", in *Marxism and the good society*, J. P. Burke, L. Crocker, L. Legters (eds) (Cambridge: Cambridge University Press, 1981), p. 13.
20. It is probably incorrect to juxtapose these two elements. Marx always focused on the overcoming of alienation as the essential feature of communism. The shift in emphasis reflects the move towards an analysis of the sociology of capitalism, rather than the philosophical bent of his earlier works. The main theorist who has argued for a break between the "young" and the "mature" Marx is L. Althusser, *For Marx* (London: Allen Lane, 1969).
21. N. Harding, "Socialism, society and the organic labour state", in *The State in socialist society*, N. Harding (ed.) (New York: Albany, 1984), p. 3.
22. Ibid., pp. 3–7.
23. Ibid., pp. 7–14.
24. A. Walicki, *Marxism and the leap to the kingdom of freedom: the rise and fall of the communist utopia* (Stanford: Stanford University Press, 1995).
25. Ibid., p. 17.
26. Ibid., p. 17.
27. The view that Marx draws a sharp distinction between "labour time" and "free time" in his later works is contested by Fetscher. He argues that the two spheres were inextricably linked. See, I. Fetscher, "Marx, Engels and the Future Society", in *The Future of Communist Society*, L. Labedz & W. Laqueur (eds) (New York: Praeger, 1962), pp. 100–10.
28. Ibid., pp. 85–6.
29. Marx & Engels, *Selected works*, p. 320.
30. For Marx, history only begins when humanity is fully in control of its own fate. Everything before communism is therefore only pre-history.

31. Marx & Engels, *Selected works*, p. 319.
32. Ibid., *The manifesto of the communist party*, pp. 52–3.
33. A slight qualification to this viewpoint has to be made. In his historical writings (e.g. The 18th Brumaire of Louis Bonaparte), Marx outlined that the state could sometimes adopt the role of neutral umpire, rising above class divisions.
34. L. Kolakowski, "The myth of human self-identity: the unity of civil and political society in socialist thought", in *The socialist idea*, L. Kolakowski & S. Hampshire (eds), p. 24.
35. Marx & Engels, *Selected works: the civil war in France*, p. 285.
36. Marx & Engels, *Selected works: letter to A. Bebel*, p. 335. Engels writes here that: "so long as the proletariat still uses the state, it does not use it in the interests of freedom, but in order to hold down its adversaries."
37. Ibid., p. 669.
38. Ibid., p. 327.
39. An excellent in depth discussion of these issues can be found in, F. Bender, "The ambiguities of Marx's concepts of 'Proletarian Dictatorship' and 'Transition to Communism'", *History of political thought* **2**(3), 1981, pp. 525–55.
40. B. Wolfe, *Marxism: one hundred years in the life of a doctrine* (New York, 1967) cited in Bender, "The ambiguities", pp. 530–1.
41. Scholars are divided over this issue. Ollman argues that it corresponds to the entire period between capitalism and communism. Walicki differs, arguing that it would last for a very short period, before the "lower" phase commenced.
42. Bender, "The ambiguities", pp. 540–1.
43. Harding, "Socialism, society and the organic labour state", pp. 4–14.
44. Bender, "The ambiguities", pp. 535–54.
45. Ibid., p. 259.
46. Marx & Engels, *Selected works: the critique of the Gotha Programme*, pp. 320–1.
47. McLellan, *Marx: selected writings*, p. 169.
48. Walicki, *Marxism*, pp. 86–7.
49. Ibid., p. 512.
50. Ibid., p. 57.
51. J. Cooper, "Construction . . . reconstruction . . . deconstruction", in *Perestroika: the historical perspective*, C. Ward & C. Merridale (eds) (London: Edward Arnold, 1991), p. 161.
52. McLellan, *Marx: selected writings*, p. 157.
53. N. Harding, "Legitimations, nationalities and the deep structure of ideology", in *The post-Soviet nations. Perspectives on the demise of the USSR*, A. Motyl (ed.) (New York: Columbia University Press, 1992), p. 83.

54. Engels has been somewhat overlooked in comparison with Marx. Good, short introductions can be found in, T. Carver, *Engels* (Oxford: Oxford University Press, 1981); D. McLellan, *Engels* (London: Collins, 1977).
55. Walicki, *Marxism*, p. 113.
56. Lichtheim, *Marxism: an historical and critical study*, p. 238.
57. Marx & Engels, *Selected works: socialism: utopian and scientific*, p. 411.
58. The edition referred to here is F. Engels, *Anti-Duhring* (Peking: Foreign Languages Press, 1976).
59. Ibid., p. 343.
60. Ibid., p. 366.
61. Ibid., p. 366.
62. Ibid., p. 385.
63. Ibid., p. 386.
64. Ibid., p. 363.
65. Bender, "The ambiguities", p. 540.
66. Ibid., p. 385.
67. Ibid., p. 366.
68. Ibid., p. 382.
69. There are a number of key works on Russian socialism and Russian Marxism: A. Walicki, *A history of Russian thought from the enlightenment to Marxism* (Oxford: Clarendon Press, 1980); M. Malia, *Alexander Herzen and the birth of Russian socialism*; J. Plamenatz, *German Marxism and Russian communism* (London: Longman, 1954); L. Kolakowski, *Main currents of Marxism* vol. 2; L. Haimson, *The Russian Marxists and the origins of Bolshevism* (Cambridge: Harvard University Press, 1955); L. Labedz (ed.), *Revisionism* (London: Allen & Unwin, 1962).
70. L. Kolakowski, *Main currents of Marxism*, pp. 305–28; A. Walicki, *A history of Russian thought*, pp. 162–182, 222–67; G. Lichtheim, *A short history of socialism*, pp. 117–68.
71. Walicki, *A history of Russian thought*, chs 12 & 18.
72. See McLellan, *Marx: selected writings*, esp. *Letter to Vera Sassoulitch*, pp. 576–80, and *Preface to the Russian edition of the Communist Manifesto*, pp. 583–4.
73. The most forceful exponent of this view is Kolakowski, *Main currents of Marxism*, vol. 2, chs 16–18.
74. N. Harding, *Lenin's political thought*, 2 vols (London: Macmillan, 1983), vol. 1, ch. 2; P. Beilharz, *Labour's utopias* (London: Routledge, 1992).
75. Harding, *Lenin's political thought*, vol. 1, p. 36.
76. S. Baron, "Between Marx and Lenin: Georgi Plekhanov", in *Revisionism*, Labedz (ed.), pp. 42–54; Kolakowski, *Main currents of Marxism*, ch. 14.

77. R. Service, *Lenin: a political life* (London: Macmillan, 1985), p. 175.
78. Harding, *Lenin's political thought*, vol. 1, p. 36.
79. A brief glance at Lenin's early writings demonstrates the enormous amount of time and attention taken up with polemical disputes up until 1914. For an analysis of these writings, see Kolakowski, *Main currents of Marxism*, vol. 2, chs 15–16; N. Harding, *Lenin's political thought*, vol. 1, ch. 2; D. McLellan, *Marxism after Marx* (London: Macmillan, 1979), chs 5 & 7.
80. The main text for Lenin's view of the party is the 1902 pamphlet, *What is to be done?* (Moscow: Progress, 1983).
81. Ibid., p. 40.
82. For details of early conflicts within the RSDLP, see L. Schapiro *The communist party of the Soviet Union* (London: Methuen, 1970), chs 1–4.
83. Details can be found in M. C. Howard & J. E. King, *A history of Marxian economics*, vol. 1 1883–1929 (Houndmills: Macmillan, 1989), chs 11 & 12.
84. The text and analysis of this programme can be found in S. White, *Soviet communism: programme and rules* (London: Routledge, 1989).
85. For a detailed analysis, see Service, *Lenin: a political life*, ch. 10.
86. The version referred to here is V. I. Lenin, *State and revolution* (Peking: Foreign Languages Press 1973).
87. Harding, *Lenin's political thought*, vol. 2, ch. 4; M. C. Howard & J. E. King, *A history of Marxian economics*, vol. 1, ch. 13; S. Cohen, "Bukharin, Lenin and the theoretical foundations of Bolshevism", *Soviet Studies* **21**(4), 1969/70, pp. 436–57.
88. Lenin's pamphlet can be found in *V. I. Lenin: Collected Works* (Moscow: Progress, 1963), vol. 22.
89. Both these pamphlets can be found in *V. I. Lenin: Selected works* (Moscow: Progress, 1970), vol. 2.
90. Early differences within Bolshevism have been documented by R. C. Williams, *The other Bolsheviks. Lenin and his critics 1904–14* (Bloomington: Indiana University Press, 1986).
91. For a fine discussion of the disputes among Western theorists about the status and content of *State and revolution*, see A. B. Evans, "Rereading Lenin's *State and revolution*", *Slavic Review* **46**(1), 1987, pp. 1–19. A recent intervention in this debate forcibly argues that this pamphlet expresses Lenin's virulent anti-statist mind set in 1916/17. See N. Harding, *Leninism* (Houndmills: Macmillan, 1996), esp. ch. 6.
92. For a good overview of the influence of Plekhanov on Lenin's conception of the dictatorship of the proletariat see, R. Mayer, "The Dictatorship of the Proletariat from Plekhanov to Lenin", in *Studies in East European Thought* **45**, 1993, pp. 255–80.

93. Lenin, *State and revolution*, p. 28.
94. Ibid., pp. 28–31;
95. Note the use of Engelian language, rather than Marxist here.
96. Ibid., pp. 50–51.
97. Ibid., pp. 53–60.
98. Ibid., pp. 51–2.
99. R. Sakwa, "Commune democracy and Gorbachev's reforms", *Political Studies* **37**(2), 1989, pp. 224–43.
100. V. I. Lenin, "Can the Bolsheviks retain state power?" in *Selected works*, vol. 2, pp. 417–18.
101. Lenin, *State and revolution*, p. 116.
102. Ibid., p. 63.
103. Lenin, "Can the Bolsheviks retain state power?", p. 417.
104. Ibid., p. 418.
105. Lenin, *State and revolution*, p. 120.
106. V. I. Lenin, "Can the Bolsheviks retain state power?", p. 412.
107. Ibid., p. 419.
108. Lenin, *State and revolution*, p. 30.
109. Ibid., p. 105.
110. Lenin, "Can the Bolsheviks retain state power?", pp. 408–9.
111. Lenin, *State and revolution*, p. 120.
112. Ibid., pp. 59–60.
113. Lenin, "Can the Bolsheviks retain state power?", p. 409.
114. Both can be found in *Selected works*, vol. 2.
115. V. I. Lenin, "The impending catastrophe and how to combat it" in *Selected works*, p. 269.
116. Ibid., p. 246.
117. Lenin, *State and revolution*, p. 120.
118. Lenin, "Can the Bolsheviks retain state power", p. 409.
119. Ibid., p. 408.
120. For an interesting discussion on the antinomy of individual/collective in Bolshevik discourse, see J. Bergman, "The idea of individual liberation in Bolshevik visions of the New Soviet Man", *European History Quarterly* **27**(1), 1997, pp. 57–92.
121. E. H. Carr, *Introduction to the ABC of communism* (Harmondsworth: Penguin, 1969), p. 43.
122. An analysis of Lenin's views can be found in S. Dobrin, "Lenin on Equality and the Webbs on Lenin", *Soviet Studies* **8**(4), 1957, pp. 337–57.
123. Lenin, *State and revolution*, pp. 109–13.
124. C. Read, *From Tsar to Soviets* (London: UCL Press, 1996), p. 222.

PART TWO

The emergence of a Soviet model: from the revolution to NEP

CHAPTER TWO

The revolutionary settlement: state capitalism, technocracy and the transition to socialism

Russian reality provided a momentous and immediate challenge for the Bolsheviks. War, economic chaos, social disruption, international hostility and political flux constituted a less than ideal milieu in which to begin the process of constructing socialism. Within this context, the Bolsheviks were confronted with the task of administering the country on a day-to-day basis, of applying their principles to a bewildering variety of problems, crises and processes.[1] Tracing the evolution of the Bolshevik understanding of the structure and content of their post-revolutionary society illustrates the way in which the conglomerate of values, principles, ideas and institutional prefigurements, which constituted the Soviet view of socialism, were modified and codified in the period after 1917.

This period can, for the purposes of this study, be divided into three chronological periods: from the October Revolution until June 1918; from June 1918 until March 1921; and from March 1921 until January 1924. Many histories of this period (both Western and Soviet) have until recently viewed these periods as distinct epochs, encompassing major shifts in policy and ideology. Indeed, many see different "models" of socialism in the respective eras of War Communism and NEP, rather than variations on a core set of values and beliefs.[2]

The realization of Bolshevik visions was always going to be a complicated affair. Unpropitious domestic circumstances and a professed dependence upon a successful international socialist revolution added an element of contingency to the Bolshevik programme. Integral to the process of overseeing the transition was the search for the optimum balance between the destruction of the old and the creation of the new.[3] Another immediate issue that confronted the party was the disparity between the aspirations of the popular movement of workers, peasants, soldiers and sailors and those of the party leadership. Throughout this nine month period between October 1917 and June 1918, a struggle between different conceptions of the social, economic and political organization of the revolutionary state can be identified, as the leadership sought to impose and substantiate their ideals in practice.[4]

The revolutionary decrees

The decrees promulgated after October represented a concession to reality on the part of the revolutionary leaders. The decrees on land and peace of 8 November and workers' control of 27 November merely legitimated the changing face of Russian life after February 1917.[5] Within these legislative acts, the long-term ideals of Bolshevism were displaced by the *de facto* reality, although occasional glimpses of future policy can be seen.

The peasant seizures of land were given official sanction. Private ownership was abolished and hired labour forbidden. Redistribution of the lands of landlords, churches and the state was placed at the disposal of rural land committees of local Soviets (peasant smallholdings were exempt from this process). Usage passed to those who were cultivating it. Absent from the text of this decree was any mention of the Bolsheviks' long-term vision of large estates of collective or co-operative farms. Indeed the Russian countryside was now a mass of small-holdings, the average size of which diminished. However, the decree noted that all mineral wealth was owned by the state, and created model farms (orchards, plantations and the like) to demonstrate the superiority of socialist techniques.[6]

The decree on workers' control similarly seemed to signal the institutionalization of control over the process of production by the workers within each factory. However, in practical terms, the decree failed to substantiate the precise role, scope and powers of factory committees, the structure of the national economy, the role of trade unions and so on. The decree represented for many, the victory of the syndicalist tendencies inherent in the factory committee movement.[7] Yet once more the decree prefigured wider Bolshevik notions: a hierarchical structure of control is implied in many clauses. For example:

> At all enterprises the owners and the representatives of the wage and salary earners elected to exercise workers control are declared answerable to the state for the maintenance of the strictest order and discipline and for the protection of property.[8]

The initial decrees posed a dilemma for the new regime: the meanings of many of the revolutionary policies and slogans adopted by the Bolsheviks during 1917 were subject to divergent and contested interpretations on the part of different social groups and their representatives. The extent of these divergences can be gauged by examining the struggle the Bolsheviks had to realize their visions.

The economics of state capitalism

The key issues for the Bolsheviks were to increase production and transform ownership relations. The transition to socialism and communism required stability in the short term, and a commitment to increasing production in the longer term. In the midst of revolution, war, social polarization and economic collapse, the Bolsheviks were faced with attempting to wed pragmatic measures to their broad ideological prescriptions. An examination of the economic policies pursued by the Bolsheviks in this period illustrates the degree to which their pragmatic responses were shaped and moulded by their underlying ideals.[9]

Ownership: the meaning of nationalization

A central part of Lenin's revolutionary strategy during 1917 was that developments in the structure of capitalism had created the basis for a fairly simple transition to socialism. All that was required was a process by which capitalist private ownership was converted into socialized ownership, via a'period in which the tasks of "accounting and control" would be exercised in the interests of the workers.[10] This would be a kind of "transition within a transition" in which there would co-exist capitalist industrialists, small-scale peasant landholdings with a Soviet state and with workers' *kontrol*.[11] The initial Bolshevik programme did not envisage wholesale immediate nationalization:

> The first step towards the emancipation of the people is the confiscation of the landed estates, the introduction of workers control and the nationalization of the banks. The next steps will be the nationalization of the factories.[12]

The first moves in the field of ownership relations appeared to substantiate Lenin's approach. The land decree abolished private ownership, but did not institute socialized ownership. The decree on workers' control established some of the tasks of the committees within each factory, yet it was clear that owners and managers were still to have a central role in the productive process. The decree on the nationalization of the banks stated that banking was from 27 December a state monopoly. Private banks were merged with the state bank. This was to be the first step in the process of establishing financial control over industrial enterprises, and formed the basis for the "expropriation of the expropriators" in due course.[13]

In the chaos after October 1917, there was very little coherence in the policy on nationalization until June 1918. This was exacerbated by a sense of conceptual imprecision on the part of the Bolshevik leadership. Beyond the shared belief in the need to expropriate financial capital, the leadership lacked any consensus on the technicalities: methods, timescale, priorities and so on. Faced with growing economic collapse, resistance and disappearance on the part of owners, the factory committees began to "nationalize" factories on their own initiative. These were designated as either "punitive" (resulting from owners' misdemeanours) or "spontaneous" (as there was no-one left to run the factories).[14] Between November 1917 and March 1918 only 5 per cent of the 836 enterprises nationalized were done so on the initiative of the centre. The centre ratified these initiatives, mainly because they did not have the resources to prevent them.[15]

A shift in the attitude towards nationalization can be discerned from the period January to February 1918. As the emphasis switched from the struggle with the owners and managers to the reconstruction of the economy, so the centre began to attempt to assert itself over the potential fragmentation inherent in seizures of individual factories "from below". The Treaty of Brest–Litovsk intensified this process.[16] Freed from the threat of foreign invasion, it offered an (albeit brief) breathing space. This resulted in attempts to nationalize entire industries or branches of industries, rather than individual factories, as the Bolsheviks sought to bring some kind of coherence to the process of reconstruction. The Bolshevik equation (more centralization = more efficiency) drove economic policy after March 1918. The nationalization of the sugar industry in May 1918 was the first such to occur.[17] The extension of this process was hampered by the absence of qualified cadres to carry it out. It was only when the leadership became aware of the implications of Brest–Litovsk – as shares in Russian industries were being bought up by German groups – that the nationalization process took on a systematic, large-scale nature, culminating in the 28 June decree.[18]

At this point in the revolutionary process the question of ownership was less important to the Bolsheviks than the question of control of the economy. Until the *Sovnarkom* decree of 28 June 1918 that nationalized all the important categories of industry, the question of the legal ownership of the factories bumbled along in a slightly haphazard fashion. The relationship between the state, private owners and factory committees/local soviets was complex and chaotic, reflecting both the circumstantial dislocation and the Bolsheviks own conceptual and theoretical imprecision over the precise meaning of "state capitalism" in practice. The attempt to develop a co-existence between private owners and state oversight was complicated by the intrusion of factory committees into this equation. The most contentious issue was the nature of the oversight that the state wished to exercise. How was this to be done, and by whom? The conflict between capitalists and proletarians receded, and in its stead state control and workers' control became the prime struggle in the economic field.

Control of the economy: centralization v. democratization

Bolshevik policy was driven by the imperative to increase production. As the emphasis shifted from expropriation to reconstruction,
stabilization and progress, so the question of the forms and structures of economic organization and control, which would most
efficiently and speedily expedite this aim, became acute.

This period – between the revolution and the onset of the civil
war in the summer of 1918 – witnessed an intense struggle between
the centralizers and the democratizers. Individuals within the Bolshevik leadership (Lenin, Larin and others) viewed centralization,
state control, hierarchy, and strong discipline as the most efficient and
speediest means to restore the economy *and* create the preconditions
for the construction of socialism. The representatives of the workers,
leftist Bolsheviks and others all viewed popular participation, decentralization and self-management as the basis of a socialist society.
Production and increasing productivity were secondary to their goals
of self-management and control over their daily existence. This
pro-worker agenda sought to restore dignity, autonomy and liberty
from exploitation to the centre of the post-revolutionary society.[19]

It is too stark and overly reductionist to describe this as a conflict
between the advocates of state control (the Bolshevik leadership)
and those of workers' control ("dissident" Bolsheviks, anarchists,
worker representatives). The conflicts occurred over the precise
meaning of workers' control. How much say, in practice, would the
representatives of the workers have in production decisions in
the factory? What would the balance between local and central representatives in the bodies of economic co-ordination and control at
all levels be? In other words, what was the balance of centralized
control "from above", and participation and control "from below"?

The broad contours of this struggle can best be illustrated by
looking at developments in three areas: organization and control
of the national economy; organization and control in the factory;
and control over labour. It is impossible, within the scope of this
work, to do justice to this period. The straight lines of the following
sections obscure the sprawling, messy and chaotic nature of the
first months of the revolution. Institution-building, disrupted communications, social conflicts, political tensions, and local and regional variations in policy implementation render generalizations

somewhat unsatisfactory, as ever. Within this framework, and given the focus of this work upon the development of Bolshevik ideas about socialism in contact with the post-revolutionary reality, the following broad parameters have been identified.

Organization and control of the national economy

It is slightly inaccurate to describe the period between October 1917 and June 1918 as marking a shift from workers' control to state control of the economy. The conception of workers' control (limited and subordinated to control by state bodies), espoused by Lenin et al., came to predominate as the factory committee movement gradually lost its political momentum. This conception was much narrower than the one outlined by the workers' representatives. It is somewhat disingenuous, though, to assert that the Bolshevik leadership cynically implemented their "real" or "hidden" agenda, having come to power advocating workers' control.

The Bolshevik conception of workers' control identified the role of the workers' organizations within the context of a centralized state.[20] The Russian word *kontrol* implies supervision, not management. Lenin's view specifically precluded control over the key decisions of production. Instead factory committees were to inspect and audit the accounts of an enterprise, uphold labour discipline and ensure that production as a whole was not disrupted. In addition, the factory committees were to be subordinated to an economic hierarchy of state bodies.[21] The representatives of the factory committees had a much broader definition, involving direct worker participation in the whole life of the factory, a form of worker self-management, in which the locus of economic decision-making rested with the proletariat itself.[22]

The decree on workers' control did not resolve this conflict over meaning. The decree was something of a compromise between a number of different platforms. The details, in institutionalizing the pre-revolutionary situation, gave substance to the agenda espoused by the factory committee movement, going beyond Lenin's narrower conception. The workers were granted the rights to supervise production, as well as inspect the books. However, the decree also imparted hierarchical and statist imperatives into the operation of the factory committees.[23]

The struggle was played out in the substantiation of the decree in practice. Divergent interpretations emerged. The Petrograd Central Council of Factory Committees put forth a radical, decentralized self-management version.[24] The Bolshevik leadership sought a restrictive conception in which management was vested in state bodies, but which reconciled the existing factory committee structure with the new state bodies of economic co-ordination. In tandem with the implementation of the decree on workers' control, the leadership introduced the Supreme Council of the National Economy (vsnkh).[25]

vsnkh was designed to provide general co-ordination for the economy. The decree stated:

> The task of the Supreme Economic Council is organization of the national economy and state finance. With this aim in view the Supreme Economic Council works out guidelines and plans for regulating the country's economy; coordinates and unifies the activity of local regulating institutions.[26]

Further on it stated that, "All institutions concerned with the regulation of the economy are subordinated to the Supreme Economic Council, which is authorised to reform them".[27] vsnkh embodied the attempt to reconcile worker supervision with centralized direction and co-ordination of the economy. This was a pivotal moment in the post-revolutionary evolution of the Soviet state.

The functions of vsnkh evolved fitfully and pragmatically, and in the chaos of the first months of 1918 many of its orders were simply ignored or were impossible to enforce. At this point there was no intention to introduce any form of central planning. vsnkh was a co-ordinating body. Control within the enterprises themselves rested with the management and the representatives of the factory committees, respectively. The structure of vsnkh reflected its composition as a form of economic cabinet, parallel to Sovnarkom (the Council of People's Commissars, the *de facto* government) to which it was attached. It was arranged hierarchically, with regional councils administering the economy at local levels guided by vsnkh. Departments quickly emerged as the complexity of co-ordinating the economy required more specialized guidance. These departments or *glavki*, quickly mushroomed to include almost every area of economic activity.[28]

At the Third All-Russia Congress of Soviets, Lenin stated that:

> From workers control we passed on to the creation of a Supreme Economic Council. Only this measure, together with the nationalization of banks and railways which will be carried out within the next few days, will make it possible for us to begin work to build up a new socialist economy.[29]

An interesting passage. Lenin appears to be arguing that the purpose of workers' control had already been fulfilled (after only 3 months!). It was an essential precondition for the transition to central control of the economy, but vsnkh was the institution that would oversee the transition to socialism.

The shift towards central control and guidance was rationalized on a number of levels by the Bolsheviks. In particular, workers' control was said to represent the priority of particular and local interests over the perceived interest of society as a whole (that is, progress towards socialism). But central control was valued in itself. The creation of vsnkh expressed the underlying constructivist and productivist outlook. Central control was the most efficient way to increase production. In the words of Kritsman, a Bolshevik chronicler, "vsnkh embodied the aspirations of the most brilliant economists to realise a new economic order as an alternative to the existing one".[30] The creation of vsnkh saw the factory committee movement relegated to a subordinate, secondary role in the economy. This trend was deepened by events in the sphere of management and labour policy.

Management of industrial enterprises

As control of macroeconomic policies gradually shifted towards the state, so the same process can be traced at the micro level. The question of who would manage the factories was a particularly acute one. The Bolsheviks suffered from a severe shortage of reliable specialists who could carry out the management of enterprises in conformity with the overall economic line. Developing a policy line was fraught with problems. A policy based on the predominance of former managers/owners carried very negative political connotations. A policy based on a pivotal role for the factory committees was deemed to be flawed in Bolshevik eyes: it was asserted that they would prioritize the immediate interests of the workers over the wider interest of society as a whole, and would prove almost impossible to guide and direct towards Bolshevik long-term aims. The overwhelming priority was to increase production. The Bolsheviks were sceptical of the ability of the factory committees to institute the necessary level of discipline within the proletariat.[31] Compromise was necessary.

In non-nationalized enterprises, owners/managers were retained, being supervised by the factory committee who were given the task of overseeing production through scrutiny of the accounts. In nationalized enterprises, a decree was passed on 3 March 1918. This decree balanced the principle of appointment with the elective principle. The central bodies (the *glavk* of the relevant industry) would appoint three figures: a technical director, an administrative director, and a commissar who was the representative of the government in the enterprise. These three figures managed the enterprise in tandem with an elected economic and administrative council.[32] How did this work in practice? The council was composed of representatives from workers, employers, technical staff, trade unionists and members of the local Soviets. This council ratified the decisions of the administrative director, and approved those of the factory committees. The technical director was subject only to the will of the commissar or the *glavk*. This arrangement represented a halfway house between a collegial, factory committee approach and the one-person management approach, and reflects the prevailing distribution of political forces within the party.[33]

The underlying trend was clear. As Kritsman identified, the move was away from "self-regulated workers control".[34] Although the road to one-person management was by no means an inexorable one in the spring of 1918, there was a strong trend in this direction. As Lenin outlined in April 1918:

> large-scale machine industry – which is precisely the material source, the productive source, the foundation of socialism – calls for absolute and strict unity of will, which directs the joint labours of hundreds, thousands and tens of thousands of people. The technical, economic and historic

necessity of this is obvious . . . But how can strict unity of will be ensured? By thousands subordinating their will to the will of one.[35]

The tendency towards centralization of decision-making in the factories was accompanied by the twin impulses of hierarchy and specialization. The heavy emphasis laid upon the need to increase productivity required the use of technical expertise and the application of strict discipline in a period of scarce resources. As Lenin said:

> Without the guidance of experts in the various fields of knowledge, technology and experience, the transition to socialism will be impossible . . . Now we have to resort to the old bourgeois method and to agree to pay a very high price for the "services" of the top bourgeois experts . . . Clearly this measure is a compromise . . . a step backward.[36]

This illustrates the central role of science and technology. The rationalist ideal was at the centre of Bolshevik ideas concerning the transition period. Expertise, disproportionately rewarded, and centralized management were essential prerequisites to the raising of productivity. Together, they represented the victory of the technocratic and centralizing strand in Bolshevik views on industrial administration over the democratic and decentralizing strand. This tendency can also be seen in the field of labour policy.

Labour Policy

Much of the labour protest in 1917 was generated by the exploitative nature of capitalist wages policy, and the strict discipline imposed within factories. Workers' control was seen by many workers as the basis for the construction of a state that rewarded work justly, and which emancipated the workers from the drudgery and servility of their day-to-day existence. But the labour movement was itself somewhat fragmented, as conflicts arose between factory committees and trade unions during the revolutionary days of 1917.

After October, the trade unions emerged as the hegemonic force in the labour movement, eclipsing the factory committees. The TU's became the agents of centralization in labour policy.[37] Their pre-dominance expressed once more the Bolshevik mistrust of spon-taneity, and their desire to guide and control social movements in order to construct socialism. Having established the hegemony of the TU hierarchy, the party sought to subject the workers to strict discipline, and to introduce a variety of measures – piece-rates, scientific management – designed to increase productivity. For the workers, it was *plus ça change*. Prior to the revolution the TU's had been Menshevik dominated.[38] Yet their roots – based on the rep-resentation of entire industries – dovetailed more closely with the ideals of the party leadership than those of the factory committees. The centrifugal tendencies perceived to be inherent in the workers' control movement could best be checked by the TU movement. Prioritizing the interests of the TU over the factory committees expressed the Bolshevik imperative of preferring the interests of the proletariat as a class, to the sectional, narrow interests of indi-vidual enterprises or industries. However, it would be misleading to see this as an alliance of equals or near equals. The TU were subordinated to the party and to VSNKh. They became the means by which labour policy was implemented and enforced. Their role in the decision-making process was rarely more than a consulta-tive one.

The institutional process was completed rather speedily. At the first All-Russian Congress of Trade Unions in December 1917, a resolution was passed which asserted that the TU were responsible for increasing production.[39] This prompted a policy to merge the factory committees with the TU, and to subordinate the former to the latter. The consequences were to subordinate the workers' move-ment as a whole to the dictates of the state. The emasculation of the social movements and groups unleashed during 1917 was well underway. The TU were now responsible for reconstruction and the increase of production. Given the nature of the shattered economy and the low educational and technical level of the Russian workforce, the TU were used to organize and discipline the labour force to achieve these objectives. Three policies stand out. Universal labour conscription was proclaimed, encompassing all those between the ages of 18–45 who were not in the Red Army.[40] The other two initiatives were put forward in the aftermath of the Treaty of Brest–Litovsk in March 1918, which brought the war with Germany to an end. There were moves to increase production through labour incentives. This entailed the introduction of piece-rates and other measures to reward labour differentially. Concurrently, the party and the TU began to emphasize the increasing importance of labour discipline within factories. If the chaos and disorganization were to be overcome, strict, imposed discipline was necessary.[41]

These initiatives reveal the centrality of the raising of productivity to Bolshevik thinking. This was not just a struggle for survival though. The specifics of these policies had a strong ideological pedigree. Marx emphasized both the necessity for universal labour service after the revolution, and that inequality would persist after the revolution. Socialism was to build upon the achievements of capitalism, which meant applying the latest developments in the organization of labour – Taylorism.[42] The ideological matrix of Bolshevik thinking on the transition period conditioned and shaped the policies adopted. As Lenin wrote in *The immediate tasks of the Soviet government,*

> The task that the Soviet Government must set the people in all its scope is – learn to work. The Taylor system, the last word of capitalism in this respect, like all capitalist progress, is a combination of the refined brutality of bourgeois exploitation and a number of the greatest scientific achievements in the field . . . The Soviet Republic must at all costs adopt all that is valuable in the achievements of science and technology . . . The possibility of building socialism depends exactly upon our success in combining the Soviet power and the Soviet organisation of administration with the up-to-date achievements of capitalism.[43]

The priorities of the Bolshevik leadership in the period of "state capitalism" were clear-cut: raise productivity, develop the productive forces. The methods adopted – centralization, concentration of industry, discipline, organization, application of science and technology – are succinctly summarized in the *Six theses on the immediate tasks of the Soviet government,* and reflect the welding of pragmatic imperatives with the broad ideological framework the Bolsheviks brought to government.[44]

The agricultural sector under state capitalism

The agricultural question proved a constant thorn in Bolshevik flesh. The momentum of the revolution and the revolutionary settlement had fulfilled the expectations of the peasantry: the land was "theirs" to farm. For the Bolsheviks this was only the start. Their vision was of a large-scale, mechanized highly efficient socialized agricultural sector, far removed from the reality of the Russian countryside. More immediately, they faced the problem of restoring grain production in order to feed the population. Once again, it is startling to note the desperate unpreparedness of Bolshevik thinking on the details of agricultural policy, and the extent to which their pragmatic measures were conditioned by their preconceptions.

The question of landholdings was "resolved" by the peasants themselves. In spite of the expressed Bolshevik desire to retain the large estates, to create and extend model co-operative farms, and their hostility to private landholdings in particular (and smallholdings in general) the party leadership were unable to enforce their preferred solution. The peasantry reverted to traditional forms of farming, which were notoriously inefficient and unproductive. This led inexorably, given the chaos and disorganization of the times, to a shortage of food. It is in this area in particular, grain supplies to the state, that the influence of Bolshevik preconceptions can be clearly seen.

The Bolshevik mindset was heavily influenced by the motif of class struggle. Their rather reductionist Marxist sociology led the Bolsheviks to apply simplistic class formulae to a bewilderingly complex social, economic and cultural milieu. Bolshevik analysis of the Russian peasantry was based on the perceived coalition of interests between the proletariat and the "poor" peasantry.[45] The latter's class interests lay in supporting the proletariat against the "rich" (or *kulaks*) and "middle" peasantry (such clear-cut categories existing solely in the mind of the urban intellectual, not in the Russian countryside).

Translated into policy, this created highly schematic and dogmatic initiatives.[46] Food shortages? Expropriate the surpluses from the rich peasantry who were hoarding grain. This led to the institution of the so-called "food dictatorship" in May 1918, whereby armed detachments of workers, and units from the CHEKA (Extraordinary

Commission for the Suppression of Counter-revolutionary Sabotage and Speculation) went into the villages to requisition this grain for the state.[47] The fact was that this grain did not exist in anything like the quantities the Bolsheviks believed. Patenaude argues that this was not just about food policy. It marked the beginning of the attempts to establish political control over the countryside.[48] The demonization of the *kulaks* and the existence of a grain surplus were ideological fictions that were to reoccur periodically over the next 15–20 years.

The apogee of the class-based approach to agriculture came on 11 June 1918 with the institution of the *kombedy*, the committees of poor peasants.[49] The Bolsheviks attempted to fan class war in the countryside by setting the rural proletariat (poor peasants) against the rural bourgeoisie (*kulaks*). Its purpose was to encourage the poor peasants to "confiscate" the grain, livestock, tools, etc. of the *kulaks* and deliver them to the state. It failed. Leaving aside the practical problems it both created and exacerbated, its failure can be adduced to the flawed nature of Bolshevik assumptions. The poor peasants did not identify with the proletariat, less still the Bolshevik party. Rural solidarity (in its many guises) was a much stronger determinant of peasant behaviour than class allegiance.

By the onset of the civil war in the summer of 1918, the Bolsheviks had made little headway in rural areas in shifting towards their maximum programme: centralization, socialization and concentration of resources. Moreover, the fundamental issue of supplying enough food was still unresolved.

The politics of state capitalism: the dictatorship of the proletariat?

Developments in the political sphere were equally complex. Twin processes – the destruction of the institutions of the capitalist state and the setting up of the dictatorship of the proletariat – were at work. Prior to October, Lenin had adhered to Marxist orthodoxy *pace* Engels on the state: under communism the state would "wither away". In the transition period the dictatorship of the proletariat would hold sway, suppressing the bourgeoisie and other counter-revolutionary forces. The specific shape of the dictatorship was a little less clear. Lenin sought to reconcile seemingly conflicting impulses: the need for a centralized, coercive repressive apparatus, and the need to foster the growth of societal self-government, drawing all people into the governing of the country.

This tension within Lenin's specific theorization of the orthodox Marxist model – between centralization and self-organization/mass participation – was reproduced in the period after October. As in the sphere of economics, the interests and aspirations of the popular movement for self-government, democratization and popular participation came into conflict with the Bolsheviks' own assumptions and preconceptions. The Bolshevik desire to transform the world in conformity with their ideals saw the state begin its evolution into a highly centralized, statified, bureaucratized, repressive organ. The democratizing, pluralist and participatory elements in Bolshevik discourse were gradually displaced as the process of state-building in a time of political, social and economic chaos and flux became increasingly acute during 1918.

Destroying the institutions of the Provisional Government's administrative machinery proved easier than constructing a viable new order. The nature of central and local government, the structure of the army, the role of the secret police, the content of a new constitution and the relationships between the Bolshevik party and other parties, and the party and the new state structures, were all the focus of a great deal of dispute.

All power to the Soviets?

"All power to the Soviets" was a central part of the Bolshevik revolutionary strategy during 1917. But what did they mean by it? And what did the workers, soldiers, sailors and peasants think they meant by it? Soviet power expressed the aspiration of the people to govern themselves, an aspiration that seemed to be buttressed by Lenin's writings which stressed mass participation in the administration of society. In order to establish a political system based on Soviet power it was necessary for the Bolsheviks to deal with the question of the Constituent Assembly.[50]

During 1917 the Bolsheviks had given wholehearted support to the calls for the election of a national representative assembly to resolve many of the issues central to the shape of the post-Tsarist system. On taking power in October on the basis of the slogan "All power to the Soviets", this confronted the Bolsheviks with something of a dilemma. Should they hold the elections to the Constituent Assembly? They went ahead, believing (mistakenly) that they would win a majority of the popular vote. When the results were published, the Bolsheviks won only 175 seats out of 707. The Socialist Revolutionaries (SRS) had 410. On 18 January 1918, the date of its convocation, the Constituent Assembly was dissolved by the Bolsheviks.[51]

The Bolsheviks had many explanations for this act of dissolution. At times they emphasized detailed practical issues: the split in the SRS meant the peasantry were not voting for the party that best represented their views; or the proximity of the elections to the October revolution meant the policies of the Bolsheviks were not yet widely known, which stressed that this particular election was not representative of the opinions of the Russian people. On other occasions they outlined a deeper philosophical hostility. The Bolsheviks did not believe in representative democracy. For them it was a fraud and a sham, concealing and perpetuating the class rule of a privileged minority. Soviet proletarian democracy, emphasizing the participation of the people themselves in government was a superior form of democracy. While this latter point had been a constant part of Bolshevik doctrine, it sounded rather hollow after an election defeat.[52] Undoubtedly the Constituent Assembly would have survived had the Bolsheviks won (though its precise role would have been problematic). Yet its indecently hasty demise, while demonstrating that the relationship between Bolshevism and democracy was a complex, ambiguous one, should have created the preconditions for the triumph of Soviet power. It did not.

Soviet democracy was said to be superior to bourgeois democracy. Soviet power envisioned the Soviets not as purely representative assemblies, but as bodies that fused legislative and executive powers. The right of recall enshrined accountability to the voters. Proportional representation ensured that it would be a genuinely representative assembly. Regular rotation would provide high levels of participation by the people in the administration of the locality. In terms of its structure, it was envisaged that local Soviets, which would oversee the administration of the affairs of the locality, would elect delegates to regional conferences. These regional conferences would in turn elect delegates for the All-

Russian Congress of Soviets (ARCS), which would be the national legislative assembly. The ARCS was the official, sovereign organ of power. This would elect an executive committee (VTSIK). VTSIK would legislate when the ARCS was not in session (it was supposed to sit four times a year), and would in turn elect the government (*Sovnarkom* or Council of People's Commissars).[53] The institutional structure was reasonably clear-cut (see Figure 1.1, p. 40). But what did it mean in practice?

It meant different things to different people. The divergence over the meaning of Soviet power was twofold. First, the Bolsheviks envisaged a hierarchical structure where power flowed down from the top, but which was organized democratically. The popular movement saw the power flow as being a bottom-up one. Secondly, many of the functions of the Soviets (expropriation, coercion, repression, administration) were impossible for the workers to fulfil because of the educational and cultural level of the population, and the general chaos and shortages of this period. These factors, alongside the powerful pressures towards centralization in the economic sphere, saw a gradual retreat from the principles of Soviet power during 1918. Twin processes were at work: a concentration of power at the centre at the expense of local organizations; and the domination of *Sovnarkom* over VTSIK and the ARCS.

This latter process is of particular interest. The marginalization of VTSIK was accomplished gradually throughout 1917 and 1918 in favour of *Sovnarkom*. Initially, VTSIK was created to be the key legislative and executive organ, expressing the hegemony of Soviet power. This position was eroded by a number of factors. First, the composition of VTSIK was increased when it was merged with the executive of the peasant Soviet in mid-November 1917. This, plus other additions, made the total number of members 366. As Figes has argued, this made it far too unwieldy to act as an efficient executive body.[54] This unwieldiness was exacerbated by the increasing need for quick, efficient decision-making in the aftermath of October. *Sovnarkom* stepped into this void, decreeing on 4 November that it had the right to act in areas requiring urgent action, without reference to VTSIK. *Sovnarkom* increasingly acted unilaterally, subverting the whole idea of "All power to the Soviets". The dominance of *Sovnarkom* was not purely a circumstantial matter, however. The Bolshevik leadership were increasingly intolerant of

Figure 2.1   Bolshevism in power: the institutional structure of the Soviet state after October 1917. The transferral of power after 1917.

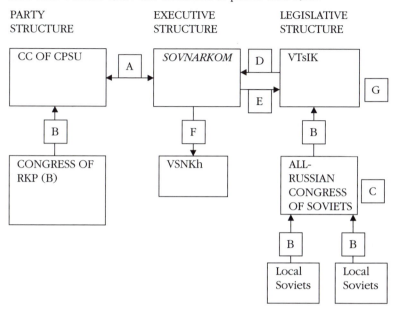

PARTY STRUCTURE   EXECUTIVE STRUCTURE   LEGISLATIVE STRUCTURE

KEY:

A: Overlapping membership between the two bodies ensured Bolshevik predominance.

B: Lower bodies elect delegates to higher bodies. Lower bodies begin to meet less frequently. More decisions taken at higher levels.

C: ARCS is still the sovereign body. However, it is reduced to being little more than a rubber stamp for the decisions of *Sovnarkom*.

D: VTsIK (Central Executive Committee of ARCS) increasingly defers to *Sovnarkom* in day-to-day running of system. Under the Constitution of 1918, *Sovnarkom* was permitted "measures requiring immediate execution". As a result, *Sovnarkom* acquires both legislative and executive functions.

E: *Sovnarkom* passes policies to VTsIK for ratification.

F: *Sovnarkom* passes policies to Vesenkha which draws up detailed guidelines for their implementation.

G: Bolshevik domination of VTsIK was ensured after October 1917 through overlapping membership. Sverdlov, the secretary of the Bolshevik party was also Chairman of VTsIK after November 1917.

The general trend in this period was towards the concentration of power and decision-making at the top of the hierarchy, and towards the party and *Sovnarkom*, and away from the Soviet/legislative structure. Although this was only beginning in the period before June 1918, the trends were already underway.

institutions and groups who could obstruct or hinder their freedom of action. Sverdlov, a loyal colleague of Lenin's, became the Chairman of VTSIK. By the end of 1917, VTSIK was meeting once or twice a week, *Sovnarkom* once or twice *a day*.[55] The interesting corollary to this is the extent of overlapping membership between *Sovnarkom* and the Central Committee of the party. The emergence of a shadow government structure within the party itself prefigured subsequent political developments. By the summer of 1918, these processes – of centralization and the domination of the party and state hierarchy over the Soviet structure – were well underway, although the full implications were not apparent until a little later.[56]

The repressive organs: the army and the CHEKA

During 1917, Lenin had envisaged that the processes of repression and expropriation would be carried out under the guidance of democratic militias, by armed units of the people themselves. This vision soon foundered in the aftermath of October. The destruction of the old army continued after October. Its replacement by a democratic decentralized militia foundered on the threat of military intervention from abroad, and of counter-revolution at home. The institutions and practices that had blossomed during 1917 (soldiers committees, democratic election of officers, abolition of death penalty) were gradually eroded during 1918 as the threat intensified.[57] The restoration of hierarchy, of appointments (instead of elections) culminated in the return of Tsarist officers as military specialists. Overseeing this latter group were the so-called political commissars: a politically reliable appointee, ensuring compliance with party orders. The reasons behind this move were twofold, and reflect developments elsewhere in this period: absence of technical skills, and susceptibility to central control.[58]

The party did not have "experts" who were "Red". The lack of suitably qualified personnel (in factories, the army, etc.) meant a reliance upon representatives of the old classes: officers, managers, scientists, until Bolshevik experts could be trained. The political commissars would provide the "Red" orientation. This dichotomy, expressed in the uneasy co-existence of political commissar with Tsarist officer, would be abolished when the educational programme combined the two roles in one person. The development of the Red

Army is also an illustration of the manner in which the tension between centralization and popular rule in the dictatorship of the proletariat was resolved in favour of the former across a range of institutions.

In December 1917, a *Sovnarkom* decree created the All-Russian Extraordinary Commission for Suppression of Counter-Revolutionary Sabotage and Speculation (VECHEKA or more usually CHEKA).[59] At local levels, the branches were ostensibly under the auspices of the local Soviets. It became a political and economic police force, and during the civil war it exercised great powers and constructed a substantial economic "empire". In its initial stages, it grew by a process of accretion, as more and more powers accrued to it, and became the kernel of many new institutions. The notable element in the growth of the CHEKA in the first few months was not its numerical size, but the expansion in the scope of its functions. The repression of the old classes quickly evolved into measures that defined counter-revolution in terms of "if you are not for us, you are against us". Economic crimes were invested with counter-revolutionary significance: speculators were shot. The central issue, unresolved by the summer of 1918, concerned the relationship between Bolshevism and repression.[60]

The need for repression was inevitable in the post-revolutionary context if the new system was to survive. Yet it was, according to dictates of ideology, due to die out. Bolshevism, as a political movement had no aversion to the use of terror. Its class-based view of morality, its maximalist and extremist mindset were powerful forces pushing for the adoption of uncompromising measures. Moreover, Figes argues that terror and repression sprang up from below after October, as the masses unleashed a war against privileged groups. The Bolsheviks merely institutionalized and channelled this spontaneous force for its own particular ends.[61] What remained unresolved in the early years of the revolutionary state were the criteria with which to decide whether to use repression, and what type, and the measures to control the institutions of repression, having established them in the body politic.

Rights and freedoms under the dictatorship of the proletariat

The rights and freedoms enjoyed by individuals were set forth in two documents: The Declaration of the Rights of the Working and

Exploited People (adopted on 25 January 1918), and the RSFSR Constitution (adopted on 10 July 1918).[62] The provisions and principles within these documents gave clear expression to the class-based, discriminatory, inegalitarian ideals of the dictatorship of the proletariat. The constitution also sets out the underlying structure of the dictatorship of the proletariat as it had evolved in practice by the summer of 1918. This reveals the nature of state power, and the relationship between the state and the individual.

The purpose of the constitution was not to set out the limits on the powers of the state. The constitution was to substantiate the intentions of the dictatorship of the proletariat: suppression of the bourgeoisie and the former classes, and the empowerment of the majority: workers and peasants. Thus while labour was a compulsory duty for all, the rights set out in the constitution privileged the workers and poor peasants over the other classes. While the freedoms of conscience, expression, assembly, association were declared for all the working people, the proletariat and poor peasantry were privileged by being granted unequal access to the resources to substantiate these rights in practice.

The starkest example of the discrimination on class grounds within the constitution came in the sphere of the franchise. The constitution cocked a snook at One Person One Vote. Article 65 stated that:

> The right to elect and to be elected is denied to the following persons:
>
> - persons who employ hired labour for profit;
> - persons living on unearned income;
> - private traders and commercial middle-men;
> - monks and ministers of religion;
> - employees and agents of the former police, as well as members of the former imperial family;
> - persons declared insane by illegal proceeding;
> - persons condemned for pecuniary and infamous crimes.[63]

Article 23 "the RSFSR deprives individuals and groups of rights which they utilize to the detriment of the socialist revolution" acted as a catch-all with which to suppress opposition to the state.[64]

Within the ranks of the toiling masses, the constitution also discriminated. Expressing the privileged position of the proletariat and of urban society, the workers enjoyed greater proportional representation than the peasantry. Article 25 stated that:

> The ARCS is composed of representatives of urban Soviets on the basis of one deputy for every 25,000 electors, and representatives of gubernia [provincial] congresses of Soviets on the basis of one deputy for every 125,000 of the population.[65]

In other words, the vote of an urban elector (which included intellectuals, specialists, professionals, etc.) was worth five times that of a peasant.

In general terms, the constitution enshrined the gradual centralization which had been occurring since October, although it failed to set out clearly the respective roles of the ARCS, VTSIK and *Sovnarkom*. It also reflected the conception of rights and freedoms of the individual. The Bolsheviks, in line with Marxism, saw rights residing with the state which, acting in the interests of the proletariat as a whole, would intervene to guarantee various freedoms. The state was thus a kind of benefactor. No rights of the individual against state encroachment were recognized. No internal checks – separation of powers for instance – upon the state were set out. The different arms of the state were all designed to achieve the same goal: the realization of the class interests of the working class as a whole. In this sense, the 1918 constitution embodied a view of state/society and state/individual relationships in which statist, centralist, collectivist, and proletarian class values were predominant.

Building a one-party state?

One of the critical issues after October concerned the role, structure and functioning of the party after October. Did they intend to institute a one-party system? What was the relationship between the party and the soviets? Why was there a growing tendency to concentrate power at the top? Why did bureaucratization defeat democratization in the internal functioning of the party? Although many of these tendencies did not come to full fruition until the 1920s and after, this period between October 1917 and June 1918 saw the first moves in these directions.

The role of the party after the revolution was thoroughly un-theorized prior to 1917. The critical questions were, who was the vanguard? How, as the party underwent the transition from revolutionary organism to ruling group, would the vanguard role work in practice? The rationalization of the vanguard role was that the party was the repository of the "true" interests of the proletariat, and the embodiment of scientific Marxism, enabling it to perceive the correct policy line at any given moment, and to raise the consciousness of all the people to the level of the vanguard. On this basis, the party would exercise an educational, supervisory role in society, and would form the "guiding nucleus" of state organizations.[66] The composition of the vanguard would combine the full-time professional revolutionaries, the revolutionary activists, with the members of the working class who had attained to a revolutionary consciousness. The reality was that the party membership had expanded enormously during 1917, and so bore little resemblance to the theory.[67] The party leadership was faced with a dual problem: first, with the mass expansion in membership, close control by the central leadership was critical if the party was to retain its higher consciousness. Secondly, in the face of the low levels of class consciousness of the mass of the working people, the party gradually began to substitute itself for the workers' organizations, and to play a more dominant role in state institutions in order to ensure that the correct decisions and policies were taken.

This issue of the composition and consciousness of party and society respectively lies at the heart of the reasons for the changes in the role and structure of the party. It would be unwise though to downplay the role of other factors. The legacies of being an underground party, the shift towards becoming a governing party, and the commitment to democratic centralism as an internal organizational method all contributed to the processes of centralization, bureaucratization and substitutionism. Let us examine a few examples.

The period between October and the summer of 1918 began the process by which the Soviet state became a one-party one. The Bolshevik attitude towards other parties – socialist and non-socialist – was laid bare in the first few days after the revolution.[68] A number of different newspapers (including socialist, liberal and conservative organs) were closed down, and vtsik issued a decree on the press, granting emergency powers to (the Bolshevik dominated)

Sovnarkom.[69] The question of a coalition was a vexed one. Debates raged in the Central Committee in early November. It was resolved in December 1917 when the Left srs joined the Bolsheviks, in a coalition that was to last until March 1918. The general intolerance towards other parties (of whatever hue) can be seen throughout this time. The Kadets were outlawed in December 1917. The cheka moved against the anarchists in April 1918. vtsik excluded both the Right srs and the Mensheviks from it in June 1918. By the summer of 1918, the Bolsheviks and the Left srs were the only really effective political movements in Russia.[70]

In terms of its internal organization, the party experienced a growing degree of centralization. The party leadership sought to place a greater emphasis upon the need for unity. Dissent continued, but tolerance of it was beginning to wane. The party congress (the supreme body within the party) was becoming increasingly displaced as the main decision-making forum by the central committee, the main executive organ. The congress was supposed to meet annually, the cc every two months. The same process in the Soviet network – the gradual concentration of power in the hands of the executive committee (vtsik) and the peripheralization of the representative organ (arcs) – was replicated in the party.[71] The larger, representative assemblies were deemed to be too unwieldy and slow to be decision-making forums. The party was still wracked with conflicts, debates and disputes. But the locus of decision-making was drifting towards smaller, appointed organs, and away from the elective democratic bodies. It is important to contextualize these developments in the party. As Schapiro argues, in the first 15–20 months of Bolshevik rule, the party structure was secondary to the soviet network in the day-to-day administration of the country. The appointment of Bolshevik figures – Lenin, Sverdlov et al. – to the key administrative positions enabled the party to exercise control through the Soviets at first. The civil war and the death of Sverdlov were to change this.

Society and culture under state capitalism

Within this brief period, the broad contours of the social and cultural policy of the Bolsheviks can be discerned. Social and cultural developments expressed the fundamentals of the Bolshevik *weltanschuuang* (worldview). The class-based approach to the world, a commitment to collectivism, egalitarianism and internationalism all shaped policies towards Soviet society, social policy, education and so on.

Social policy – aspects of egalitarianism

The question of egalitarianism was, as we saw, a complex and ambiguous one in Bolshevik theory, an ambiguity that was accentuated by the issue of Russia's economic and cultural backwardness. It is here, in this most ideologically sensitive area, that the conflict between technocracy and democracy, productivism and libertarianism was manifest. Attitudes to privilege and remuneration attempted to synthesize the political imperatives of destroying the gap between rulers and ruled, with the productivist stress on rewarding "specialists". In Lenin's mind the two could be reconciled without any contradiction, because the Bolsheviks had no belief in absolute equality as an end in itself. Egalitarianism and inegalitarianism were means for the achievement of their vision of socialism. Destroying the differentials between workers and the administrators was essential to prevent the emergence of a new ruling elite. Instituting inequality in the economic sphere was necessary for productivity to be increased: the guiding-light of all Bolshevik policies. What did this mean in practice?

In November 1917 the decree "On the extent of rewards for People's Commissars, his employees and officials" was issued.[72] It set a limit of 500 roubles a month (100 roubles more per dependent), with living space restricted to one room per person maximum. A further decree in early 1918 sought to restrict wage differentials between skilled and unskilled workers.[73] With regard to specialists, a decree of 27 June 1918 substantiated the regime's softened attitude to bourgeois expertise. Salaries of 1,200 roubles per month (cf. people's commissar 800, clerks 350) were introduced.[74] This pattern was to be maintained and extended in the months and years to come. The questions of access to scarce goods (housing, perks, travel, education) were to become acute during the civil war.

Social equality is best illustrated by the issue of female emancipation.[75] All subscribed to the ideal of full equality for women under socialism. How to achieve this was more contentious. This tension expressed (again) the conflict within Bolshevism between the libertarians and technocrats. Elements on the left viewed female emancipation as an end-in-itself, as part of socialism's mission to destroy the bases of exploitation and oppression.[76] Other strands emphasized that female emancipation was a crucial contributor to the wider goal of the establishment of socialism, in particular the creation of its economic and social basis.[77] This latter group had, in Lapidus' words, an "instrumental" approach to the *zhenskii vopros*'.[78] The emancipation of women was part of the overall strategy to increase economic efficiency and so raise productivity. This technocratic impulse ran at the heart of much of Bolshevik thinking on the need for social reconstruction and modernization, and increasingly displaced the libertarian and emancipatory elements from Bolshevik discourse.

In the early years, the Bolsheviks undertook emancipatory measures via legislation. A number of decrees sought to remove the obstacles to women becoming full citizens: at work, in the home, within marriage. Wives were no longer forced to reside with their spouses. Either surname could be adopted. Women were given freedom of movement. Restrictions on divorce were removed. Legislation was designed to create the preconditions for the economic autonomy of women.[79] The modernization of Russia's social structure would accompany the economic transformation inherent in the construction of socialism. Subsequent measures – in the period after 1918 – to extend emancipation were the subject of significant disputes.

The norms and values of Bolshevism

The Bolsheviks saw the world through class-tinted spectacles. As we saw with regard to the peasantry, this approach profoundly influenced the shape and thrust of their policy initiatives: food requisitioning was premised on the basis of fomenting class war in the countryside. The franchise excluded members of the old classes. The privileging of the toiling masses in general, and the proletariat in particular, has to be understood though within the context of the Bolshevik promotion of collectivism, and its theory of revolutionary consciousness. The interests of the class as a whole were prior to and higher than those of individuals, or groups, within that class. This collectivist orientation, so different from the liberal-democratic notions of the priority of individual rights, explains some of the apparent disparities between Bolshevik theory and practice (although the explanation is not always convincing or defensible). The shift away from workers' control, the subordination of workers to managers, the subsidiary role played by the trade unions seem problematical in a system designed to put the proletariat into power. Bolshevik discourse placed the interests of the proletariat as a whole (as perceived by the party via scientific Marxism), defined in terms of the construction of socialism and communism, above the localistic, craft or sectional interests of the workers themselves.[80]

The Bolsheviks were also modernizers, Europeanizers and internationalists. This is exemplified by the decree on the introduction of a new calendar. Russia and western Europe had been on different calendars (a 13 day difference). The Bolsheviks decided that changing the calendar would reflect the aspiration to become both Modern (part of the socialist project within Russia) and European (part of the international socialist project). In the preamble to the decree, it was stated that:

> In order to establish the system of time reckoning used by almost all cultured nations, the Council of People's Commissars resolves to introduce into civil life, after the expiry of the month of January of this year, a new calendar.[81]

Further evidence of the modernizing bent of Bolshevik policies is reflected in the increasing importance placed upon science and technology. The application of new technology and of scientific methods expressed the Bolshevik faith in the ability of the new regime to plan and order society rationally, and symbolized the priority of the productivist ideal – raising productivity – over the libertarian ideal – emancipation from the multiform exploitation associated with capitalism.

Bolshevik visions sought the transformation of the world, not just Russia. This internationalist dimension imparted into Bolshevik thinking the imperative to take the revolution beyond Russia's borders. Realizing this vision caused great controversy within the party. The October Revolution could only succeed, according to Lenin, if it was accompanied by revolution in western Europe. But what was the best way to achieve this, and what should happen about the First World War? Many on the radical wing of the party wished to turn the First World War into a revolutionary war, to foment revolution, initially in Germany, but eventually spreading throughout Europe. Lenin wished to use a peace treaty with Germany to give Russia a breathing-space in order to build up her productive and military power to equip her for the inevitable imperialist onslaught.

The Treaty of Brest–Litovsk, signed on 3 March 1918, was incredibly unpopular in the party. In part this was due to the great concessions made to Germany. Primarily its unpopularity was because it represented a victory for a national perspective (defend the revolution in Russia) over the international perspective (promote revolution in Europe).[82] This was the issue over which the first signs of a serious split within the post-revolutionary Bolshevik party emerged. A group of Left Communists – Bukharin, Bubnov, Uritsky and Lomov – opposed the peace treaty and resigned from office in protest. In their view the whole *raison d'être* of the October Revolution was to promote an international revolution. Any other approach was an unacceptable compromise.[83] Yet Lenin's approach was entirely consistent within the wider context of Bolshevik ideas: the interests of the international proletariat equated to the construction of socialism and communism. Only the survival of Soviet power would guarantee the creation of the first socialist state, and provide the foundation for future revolutions. The equation, Defend Soviet State = Defend Socialism, was born. This ambiguity between international and national perspectives was a constant element in the subsequent history of the USSR.

Education was a critical area for the Bolsheviks. Inculcation of the correct consciousness required the conscious propagation of the Bolshevik worldview: materialist, atheist, internationalist, proletarian, collectivist, egalitarian. There was also an instrumentalist rationale. Progress towards socialism was rooted in overcoming economic backwardness. Practical, technical education would equip the people to function in an industrial economy. The combination of the two – political and technical education – was the key to overcoming the Red/Expert dichotomy, and emphasized how notions of constructivism and social engineering were central to Bolshevik thinking.

Two future chickens: state capitalism and Soviet power in Bolshevik ideology

In May 1918 Lenin wrote that:

> And history . . . has taken such a peculiar course that it has given birth in 1918 to two unconnected halves of socialism existing side by side like two future chickens in the single shell of international imperialism. In 1918 Germany and Russia have become the most striking embodiment of the material realization of the economic, the productive and the socio-economic conditions for socialism on the one hand, and the political conditions on the other.[84]

Germany continued to cast its shadow over Bolshevik thinking. Much of Lenin's political writings grew out of the polemical disputes with Kautsky. Likewise, Bolshevik views on the economy were profoundly shaped by the experience of the German war economy. The German experience runs at the heart of Lenin's analysis of the first eight months of Soviet rule.

Lenin was provoked into a defence of the policies of the Soviet state by the criticisms of the Left Communists after the Brest–Litovsk Treaty. Bukharin, along with Kollontai, Ryazanov, Uritsky and Radek published a series of attacks on the economic policies of "state capitalism", having been defeated over the question of peace with Germany. They were highly critical of the return of former managers, the use of, and unequal rewards for, bourgeois specialists, the imposition of strict discipline in the factories. They wished to move towards the socialization of the means of production and to restore workers' control of industry. For the Left the ideals of the revolution were being sacrificed to the consolidation of state power.[85] It was a theme that was to recur during the initial years of the Soviet state, and it provoked a series of challenges to the party leadership as divergences over the form of socialism which was being constructed became acute.[86]

Lenin's response was typically forthright, mixing invective, polemic and shrewd analysis. He took them to task over their international and domestic policies. Lenin defends state capitalism not as a necessary evil, but as a "step forward" towards socialism.[87]

State capitalism – defined as a monopolistic economy centred around large trusts nominally owned by private capitalists but in reality supervised very closely by the state – was progressive for Lenin in two senses. First, through the processes of concentration and centralization, it created the preconditions for socialism. Secondly, as Carr puts it, state capitalism was an ally of socialism because it "was an enemy of socialism's enemies" (i.e. *petit bourgeois* capitalism).[88]

In his analysis, Lenin makes a number of telling points that illustrate the development in Bolshevik ideology. The experience of holding power, developing policies and solving problems sharpened their thinking on the nature of the transition period, and began the resolution of many of the tensions in pre-revolutionary Bolshevik discourse on socialism. Lenin identified two phases: the era of expropriation under workers' control (until around February 1918) and the era of organization and raising productivity (under state supervision). The task now was to:

> study the state capitalism of the Germans, to spare no effort in copying it and not shrink from adopting dictatorial methods to hasten the copying of it.[89]

This analysis and the debate that sparked it illustrate two important factors. First, the nature of Bolshevism as a pluralist movement in which a number of competing visions co-existed, as had been the case prior to 1917. The centralized, monolithic party did not exist. Secondly, the predominant motifs in Lenin's understanding of socialism were those of productivism, technocracy and centralization:

> Socialism is inconceivable without large-scale capitalist engineering based on the latest discoveries of modern science. It is inconceivable without planned state organisation, which keeps tens of millions of people to the strictest observance of a unified standard in production and distribution.[90]

This represents a resolution of the tension in Bolshevik thinking between the emancipatory, participatory, self-managing, democratic strand on the one hand, and the technocratic, centralizing, statist, productivist strand on the other. It is not accurate to see this as a major shift from a wholly libertarian, quasi-anarchistic approach during 1917 to a wholly technocratic one after the revolution. Lenin attempted to hold the two elements together, but the circumstances, his own mindset, and the values of key figures in the new hierarchy (particularly Larin and Milyutin) all pushed Bolshevism to resolve this tension in favour of the technocratic strand. Subsequent events witnessed a deepening of this process. A distinctive Soviet model of socialism was being forged.

Notes

1. There are a number of good general texts which narrate the details of this period. See, E. H. Carr, *The Bolshevik revolution 1917–23* vols. 1–3 (London: Pelican, 1966); A. Nove, *An economic history of the USSR* (Harmondsworth: Pelican, 1992); G. Hosking, *A history of the Soviet Union* (London: Fontana, 1992); C. Read, From Tsar to Soviets (London: UCL Press, 1996); O. Figes, *A people's tragedy. The Russian revolution 1891–1924* (London: Pimlico, 1996).
2. M. Lewin, Political undercurrents in Soviet economic debates (London: Pluto Press, 1975); L. Szamuely, *First models of socialist economic systems* (Budapest: Akademiai Kiado, 1974).
3. Figes, *A people's tragedy*, p. 502.
4. Read, *From Tsar to Soviets*, chs 7–9.
5. The text of these decrees can be found in Y. Akhapkin (ed.) *First decrees of Soviet power* (London: Lawrence & Wishart, 1970), pp. 18–23, 36–8.
6. Ibid., pp. 23–7.
7. Details of the decree can be found in ibid., pp. 36–8. For an analysis, see Carr, *The Bolshevik revolution*, pp. 64–80; S. Malle, *The economic organization of War Communism* (Cambridge: Cambridge University Press, 1985), pp. 89–98.
8. Akhapkin, *First decrees of Soviet power*, p. 37.
9. The keynote articles and pamphlets by Lenin in this period are, *How to organize competition?* on 6–9 January 1918, pp. 517–24; *Report on the activities of the Council of People's Commissars at the Third All-Russia Congress of Soviets*, 10–18 January 1918, pp. 541–65; *The immediate tasks of the Soviet government*, April 1918, pp. 643–77; *Draft plan of scientific and technical work*, April 1918, p. 681; *Speech at the First Congress of Economic Councils*, 26 May 1918, pp. 723–8. All are in *V. I. Lenin: selected works*, vol. 2 (Moscow: Progress, 1970).
10. Malle, *The economic organization of War Communism*, pp. 35–57.

11. *Kontrol'* in Russian implies supervision or oversight, rather than "control".
12. "How to organize competition", in *V. I. Lenin: selected works*, vol. 2, pp. 517–18.
13. Akhapkin, *First decrees of Soviet power*, pp. 62–3.
14. Carr, *The Bolshevik revolution*, vol. 2, pp. 87–9.
15. Read, *From Tsar to Soviets*, p. 246.
16. The details of this treaty can be found in Carr, *The Bolshevik revolution*, vol. 3, pp. 48–55.
17. Carr, *The Bolshevik revolution*, vol. 2, p. 101.
18. The details of the text can be found in Akhapkin, *First decrees of Soviet power*, pp. 147–53. For analysis, see Carr, *The Bolshevik revolution*, vol. 2, pp. 103–5; Nove, *An economic history of the USSR*, pp. 52–9.
19. A number of works detail the different perspectives within both Russian society and the Bolshevik party. See, Malle, *The economic organization of War Communism*, chs 2–3, 5–6; Carr, *The Bolshevik revolution*, vols. 1–2; R. Service, *Lenin: a political life, vol. 3 The iron ring*, ch. 3; L. Schapiro, *Origins of the communist autocracy: political opposition in the Soviet state* (London: Macmillan, 1977); R. V. Daniels, *The conscience of the revolution: communist opposition in Soviet Russia* (Cambridge: Harvard University Press, 1960).
20. For details on workers' control and the labour movement, see M. Brinton, *The Bolsheviks and workers' control, 1917–21* (London, 1970); C. Sirianni, *Workers' control and socialist democracy* (London: New Left Books, 1982); W. Rosenberg, "Russian labour and Bolshevik power: social dimensions of protest in Petrograd after October", in *The workers revolution in Russia in 1917: the view from below*, D. Kaiser (ed.) (Cambridge: Cambridge University Press, 1987).
21. Malle, *The economic organization of War Communism*, pp. 89–96; T. Remington, *Building socialism in Bolshevik Russia* (Pittsburgh: University of Pittsburgh Press, 1984), pp. 23–47.
22. Malle, *The economic organization of War Communism*, pp. 96–107.
23. The key points in the decree are articles 5–8 which established the rights of the factory committees within the factory. Article 10, which enshrined that the factory committees were answerable to the state. See Akhapkin, *First decrees of Soviet power*, p. 37.
24. S. Farber, *Before Stalinism* (Cambridge: Polity, 1990), pp. 65–6; Remington, *Building socialism in Bolshevik Russia*, pp. 43–4.
25. The text of the decree can be found in Akhapkin, *First decrees of Soviet power*, pp. 50–1.
26. Ibid., p. 50.
27. Ibid., p. 50.
28. Malle, *The economic organization of War Communism*, pp. 202–26.

29. Lenin, "Report on the activities of the Council of People's Commissars", in *Selected works*, vol. 2, p. 551.
30. Cited in Malle, *The economic organization of War Communism*, p. 209.
31. Read has set out the broad contours of the Bolshevik attitude towards workers control in, *From Tsar to Soviets*, pp. 244–54.
32. Carr, *The Bolshevik revolution*, vol. 2, p. 92.
33. Malle, *The economic organization of War Communism*, p. 112.
34. Ibid., p. 107.
35. Lenin, "The immediate tasks of the Soviet government", in *Selected works*, vol. 2, p. 671.
36. Ibid., pp. 654–5.
37. Carr, *The Bolshevik revolution*, vol. 2, pp. 105–20; Remington, *Building socialism in Bolshevik Russia*, pp. 78–82; Malle, *The economic organization of War Communism*, pp. 98–104.
38. Carr, *The Bolshevik revolution*, vol. 2, pp. 107–8.
39. Malle, *The economic organization of War Communism*, pp. 108–10.
40. Remington, *Building socialism in Bolshevik Russia*, pp. 82–92.
41. Lenin, "The immediate tasks of the Soviet government", in *Selected works*, vol. 2, pp. 651–3; Carr, *The Bolshevik revolution*, vol. 2, pp. 113–20.
42. The example of the Bolshevik attitude towards Taylorism is an excellent example of Bolshevik ambivalence towards capitalist practices. Before the revolution Lenin was highly critical of the exploitative tendencies inherent within Taylorism. See, "The Taylor system: man's enslavement by the machine", in *V. I. Lenin: Collected works*, vol. 20 (Moscow: Progress, 1963), pp. 152–4. At the same time, it was viewed as having the potential for a rational organization of labour that could achieve massive increases in productivity, which would underlay the development of socialism and finally communism. What was crucial was the political and economic context in which Taylorism was applied. Under capitalism it was exploitative. Under socialism, it was the rational reordering of production for the good of society. For analyses, see K. Bailes, "Alexei Gastev and the Soviet controversy over Taylorism", *Soviet Studies* **29**(3), 1977, pp. 373–94; Z. Sochor, "Soviet Taylorism revisited", *Soviet Studies* **33**(2), 1981, pp. 246–64; S. Smith, "Taylorism rules OK?", in *Radical Science Journal* **13**, 1983, pp. 5–27.
43. Lenin, *The immediate tasks of the Soviet government*, in *Selected works*, p. 663.
44. Ibid., pp. 678–80.
45. For analyses of early Bolshevik policies towards the peasantry see, R. Pipes, *The Russian Revolution 1899–1919* (London: Harvill, 1990) ch. 16; Read, *From Tsar to Soviets*, pp. 225–38; Carr, *The Bolshevik*

revolution, vol. 2, pp. 35–61; D. Atkinson, *The end of the Russian land commune 1905–30* (Stanford: Stanford University Press, 1983), pp. 165–205; Nove, *An economic history of the USSR*, pp. 59–63; J. Channon, "The Bolsheviks and the peasantry: the land question during the first eight months of Soviet rule", *Slavonic and East European Review* **66**, 1988, pp. 593–624.

46. An excellent analysis of Bolshevik grain policy between 1917 and 1921 can be found in B. Patenaude, "Peasants into Russians: the utopian essence of war communism", *The Russian Review* **54**, October 1995, pp. 552–70.

47. Atkinson, *The end of the Russian land commune*, p. 191.

48. Patenaude, "Peasants into Russians", p. 554.

49. Ibid., pp. 554–5. Atkinson, *The end of the Russian land commune*, pp. 191–6.

50. The best works on the early politics of Bolshevik rule include, Read, *From Tsar to Soviets*, chs 8, 10; Service, *Lenin: a political life*, chs 1–3; S. Farber, *Before Stalinism* (Cambridge: Polity, 1990) part 1; M. Liebman, *Leninism under Lenin* (London: Merlin, 1975) part 3; Pipes, *The Russian revolution*, ch. 18; Carr, *The Bolshevik revolution*, part 1; L. Siegelbaum, *Soviet state and society between revolutions 1918–29* (Cambridge: Cambridge University Press, 1992); R. Service, *The Bolshevik party in revolution 1917–23*, 3 vols (London: Macmillan, 1979).

51. Lenin's analysis of the Constituent Assembly can be found in "Theses on the Constituent Assembly" in *Selected works*, vol. 2, pp. 506–9. For analyses, see Pipes, *The Russian revolution*, pp. 537–55; Read, *From Tsar to Soviets*, pp. 179–90.

52. Details of the Bolshevik analysis of proletarian and bourgeois democracy can be found in, Lenin, *State and Revolution*, pp. 102–9; "Theses on the Constituent Assembly", in *Selected works*, vol. 2, pp. 506–9; "Theses on the present political situation", in ibid., pp. 706–9.

53. Details of the institution-building in the post-revolutionary political system are treated a little sketchily in most texts. Perhaps the best piece is still Carr, *The Bolshevik revolution*, vol. 1, pp. 191–219. See also Farber, *Before Stalinism*, pp. 19–61.

54. Figes, *A People's Tragedy*, p. 506.

55. Ibid., p. 506.

56. Carr, *The Bolshevik revolution*, vol. 1, pp. 192–9; Farber, *Before Stalinism*, pp. 19–43; Pipes, *The Russian revolution*, pp. 506–65.

57. Details of the political aspirations of the soldiers and sailors can be found in A. Wildman, *The end of the Russian imperial army* (Princeton: Princeton University Press, vol. 1, 1980, vol. 2, 1987); Read, *From Tsar to Soviets*, pp. 121–42, 209–11; F. Benvenuti, *The Bolsheviks and the Red Army 1918–22* (Cambridge: Cambridge University Press, 1988).

58. Read, *From Tsar to Soviets*, pp. 209–10.

59. The decree was first published in *Pravda*, 18 December 1917.
60. For details of this relationship, see Carr, *The Bolshevik revolution 1917–23*, vol. 1, pp. 166–78. See also G. Leggett, *The Cheka: Lenin's political police* (Oxford: Oxford University Press, 1981); Farber, *Before Stalinism*, pp. 113–43; Read, *From Tsar to Soviets*, pp. 209–210.
61. Figes, *A People's Tragedy*, pp. 522–36.
62. Akhapkin, *First decrees of Soviet power*, pp. 76–8, 154–68. Carr analyzes this in depth in, *The Bolshevik revolution 1917–23*, ch. 6.
63. Akhapkin, *First decrees of Soviet power*, p. 165.
64. Ibid., pp. 156–7.
65. Ibid., p. 157.
66. Read, *From Tsar to Soviets*, pp. 211–18.
67. Carr, *The Bolshevik revolution 1917–23*, vol. 1, p. 211.
68. Ibid., pp. 169–78; O. Radkey, *The sickle under the hammer: the Russian socialist revolutionaries in the early months of Soviet rule* (Columbia: Columbia University Press, 1963); V. Brovkin, *The Mensheviks after October: socialist opposition and the rise of the Bolshevik dictatorship* (London: Cornell University Press, 1987); Schapiro, *Origins of communist autocracy*.
69. Farber, *Before Stalinism*, pp. 90–112. The decree on the press can be found in Akhapkin, *First decrees of Soviet power*, pp. 29–30.
70. Pipes, *The Russian revolution*, pp. 506–65; Liebman, *Leninism under Lenin*, pp. 232–70.
71. Carr, *The Bolshevik revolution 1917–23*, vol. 1, pp. 197–200; Liebman, *Leninism under Lenin*, pp. 278–97.
72. The details are found in M. Matthews, *Privilege in the Soviet Union* (London: Allen & Unwin, 1978), p. 62.
73. Ibid., p. 62.
74. Ibid., p. 63.
75. There are a number of excellent texts covering this topic. For good general introductions, see G. Lapidus, *Women in Soviet society* (Berkeley: University of California Press, 1978); M. Buckley, *Women and ideology in the Soviet Union* (London: Harvester Wheatsheaf, 1989).
76. See Buckley, *Women and ideology in the Soviet Union*, pp. 44–56.
77. Lapidus, *Women in Soviet society*, pp. 73–82.
78. Ibid., p. 73.
79. The details of the early legislation can be found in ibid., pp. 57–63.
80. Carr, *The Bolshevik revolution 1917–23*, vol. 1, pp. 150–59.
81. Akhapkin, *First decrees of Soviet power*, p. 93.
82. The debates over Brest–Litovsk are succinctly summarized in Carr, *The Bolshevik revolution 1917–23*, vol. 3, pp. 16–68; Service, *Lenin: a political life*, pp. 43–9. Lenin set out his own position at the Extraordinary Seventh Congress of the RCP (B) in March 1918, in *Selected*

works, vol. 2, pp. 577–617. See also the Report on the Ratification of the Peace Treaty, in ibid., pp. 626–40.

83. R. V. Daniels, *The conscience of the revolution: communist opposition in Soviet Russia* (Cambridge, Mass.: Harvard University Press, 1960), pp. 70–80.

84. Lenin, "'Left-wing' childishness and the petty-bourgeois mentality", in *Selected works*, vol. 2, p. 694.

85. A good analysis of the Left Communist position in 1918 can be found in S. Cohen, *Bukharin and the Bolshevik revolution* (Oxford: Oxford University Press, 1980), pp. 62–78.

86. Daniels, *Conscience of the revolution*, pp. 81–91.

87. Lenin, "'Left-wing' childishness and the petty-bourgeois mentality", p. 690.

88. Carr, *The Bolshevik revolution 1917–23*, vol. 2, p. 98.

89. Lenin, "'Left-wing' childishness and the petty-bourgeois mentality", p. 694.

90. Ibid., p. 694.

CHAPTER THREE

War communism and Soviet Socialism: a technocratic orthodoxy?

The civil war casts a long and distressing shadow over the period between June 1918 and the winter of 1920/21. Enormous devastation, terrible human losses and suffering, famine, deprivation and trauma engulfed Russia and beyond. That story has been related admirably well elsewhere, and is beyond the scope of this work.[1] The organization of the system during the civil war has been the subject of intense dispute. The series of measures adopted – economic, political, socio-cultural – have attracted the epithet of "war communism". But the meaning of this term has been heavily contested.

Lih and Siegelbaum argue that "war communism",

> is a contradiction in terms, a conceptual trap that has hindered more than it has helped to make sense of Bolshevik attitudes and behaviour before 1921. The only reality assumed by War Communism was retrospective, as a foil against which could be highlighted more "realistic" or even "human" policies . . . it should be dropped from our vocabulary.[2]

Others accept its existence, yet differ greatly over its meaning.[3] Was it, as first set out by Maurice Dobb, a pragmatic set of measures designed to run a wartime economy?[4] Was it an attempt "to march

95

straight into communism"? Was it a complex interplay of the two? Malia highlights the impeccable ideological origins and credentials of war communism. All the actions and policies of the Bolsheviks in this period were derived from, and shaped by their ideology.[5] Figes argues that both poles of the argument – the ideology perspective, and the pragmatic approach – are seriously flawed.[6] Furthermore, the argument set out by Lih has been challenged recently by Bertrand Patenaude, who has identified a utopian essence running at the heart of "war communism".[7] Major interpretative differences remain.

Finally, a wider question. Does war communism lie firmly within the Bolshevik understanding of the nature of the transition period, or does it mark a significant departure? Is it a conceptually distinct model of the transition from capitalism to communism, or does it represent one particular interpretation of the broad understanding of socialism in Bolshevik discourse? The significance of this period lies not just in the measures adopted during the civil war. During 1919 onwards, the Bolshevik Party began to debate and theorize the transition period and its specifics in the light of the practice of governing the country. Out of these debates, a more definite view of socialism began to emerge.

The economics of "war communism"

The breathing-space after Brest–Litovsk was short-lived. As the civil war began in May/June 1918, the Bolsheviks adopted a series of measures which extended the trends towards centralization, nationalization, concentration, hierarchy and technocracy. The Bolshevik experiences in running the economy during the civil war fed into the theoretical debates about the nature of Soviet socialism.[8]

Industry and economic organization: patterns of ownership and control

On 28 June a decree "On Nationalisation" was issued.[9] This was in part prompted by the Brest–Litovsk Treaty. German investors were rapidly purchasing shares in Russian heavy industry. To prevent control passing into the hands of foreign nationals meant rushing through a decree nationalizing a whole variety of industries: mining, metallurgy, textiles, engineering, railways, public utilities and many others. However, the decree really was nothing more than a paper recognition of the transfer of ownership. Section 3 of the decree stated that:

> Pending a special decision of the Supreme Economic Council regarding each particular enterprise, the enterprises declared under this Decree to be the property of the RSFSR are regarded as leased to their former owners gratis; their boards and former owners continue to finance them and receive profits in the usual manner.[10]

Actual control by *Vesenkha* (VSNKh) awaited direct intervention from above. Underlying the immediacy imposed by the actions of German investors was the long-term project of accelerating the process of "trustification": the creation of huge state monopolies administered by the centre. Nationalization created the essential preconditions for this. The process was not an orderly one though. Local appropriations still continued, emphasizing the continued gap between declaration of intent and implementation. In early 1919, the Bolsheviks attempted to bring small rural industries under state ownership. Full-scale nationalization was not completed until November 1920, when small-scale industrial enterprises were brought under central control.[11] In the conditions of growing armed foreign intervention on Russian soil, the question of the control of industry was of much greater import than the question of legal ownership.

Maintaining production and supply during the civil war rapidly posed the question of how best to organize the economy. Three issues in particular stood out. What role should *Vesenkha* play? What would the relationship between *Vesenkha* and the local organs of economic power be? How would the central organs of power configure themselves?

The Bolsheviks viewed trustification as a marriage of convenience and ideology. The creation of huge state industrial trusts, based on the German wartime economy, was seen as the economic basis of socialism. Yet they were also seen as simplifying the processes of administering the industrial sector. The exigencies of a civil war simplified industrial administration through territorial shrinkage (facilitating central control) and by providing a clear set of priorities for production. By the end of 1919 around 90 of these trusts had been created. They were answerable to their local *glavk*, under the overall guidance of *Vesenkha*.[12] *Vesenkha*'s role gradually shifted from a more supervisory, regulatory role (as initially envisaged), to a more managerial and administrative one. This was grounded in a decree of August 1918 which outlined that *Vesenkha* was to "administer all the enterprises of the republics".[13] This closer, more detailed administrative function brought about a change in the internal workings of *Vesenkha*. This decree detailed its composition and its structure. Most significantly, a praesidium of nine members was created (the president and deputy being appointed by *Sovnarkom*). Given the new role and the civil war, the praesidium quickly became the main policy-making body, supplanting the larger council. Indeed, the full council failed to meet again after the autumn of 1918.[14]

As *Vesenkha* increasingly attempted to administer the economy, through distributing materials, supplying orders, setting priorities, so conflicts began to grow at the centre between the different central agencies and committees. In particular, the Council of Labour and Defence (STO), the Commissariat of Food Procurement (*Narkomprod*) and *Sovnarkom* created a proliferation of committees and agencies, bureaucratizing economic processes.[15] This was evidence of how the impulse for centralization began to run counter to the desire for economic efficiency. Conflicts at the centre were overlain with disputes over the precise nature of the division of powers between centre and locality, an issue that punctuated the whole Soviet period. That strand of Bolshevism which had an instinct for centralization, concentration and statification of socio-economic processes began during the civil war to confront the issue of what this meant in practice. The continuous debates and policy revisions demonstrate the struggles within the party between centralizers and decentralizers, and also between those with differing conceptions of centralization.

The conflicts arose over the administration of industry at local and regional levels. Two approaches began to come into conflict. One based around a vertically organized system, divided into branches of industry: *glavkism*. The other was a horizontal division centred on a geographical basis: *sovnarkhozy*. The *glavki* were initially designed to stand between the specific sections of *Vesenkha* and the enterprises themselves. Their function was to regulate all enterprises within a particular branch of production. They quickly became management organs, as they began to assimilate the functions of *Vesenkha*'s productive sections. In the conditions of civil war, some Bolsheviks began to see in the *glavki* the basis for a system of central co-ordination of the economy, in contrast to the regionalization inherent in the *sovnarkhozy*.[16]

The *sovnarkhozy*, or regional economic councils, had been created in the immediate aftermath of the revolution. Arising out of the desires of local Soviets to co-ordinate the chaotic post-revolutionary circumstances, the *sovnarkhozy* embodied the democratizing, participatory strand of industrial administration (although it was often rationalized as a more efficient method, through being nearer to the actual point of production and having more accurate information).[17] The *sovnarkhozy* evolved its own hierarchy, but conflicts with *glavki* emerged as the leadership attempted to demarcate the division of responsibilities of the different levels of the *sovnarkhozy*. The pre-eminence of centralization saw the *glavki* gradually accrue more powers at the expense of the *sovnarkhozy*. However, the *sovnarkhozy* retained their status within the economic structure, and indeed enjoyed something of a revival at the end of 1919 when an attempt to draw up a precise division of responsibilities was made. The resultant proposal – dividing enterprises into three groups – represented something of a compromise between centralization and provincial administration of the economy.[18] Within the context of the civil war, the trends towards centralization were extremely powerful. Yet it is important to remember that these trends antedated the civil war, and that this conflict became inherent in the Soviet economic system. The growing predominance of *glavkism* cannot be explained solely by the struggle for survival.

Patterns of distribution: trade, finance and allocations

Socialists viewed the capitalist market as a source of waste, inefficiency, irrationality and injustice. Precisely what to replace this with was the subject of some dispute. During the civil war, the idea of central planning (and a particular conception thereof) gradually evolved, as the Bolsheviks' faith in their ability to reorder and manage society scientifically and consciously merged with their experiences of managing the problems of supply and distribution under war communism. Lenin's vision of the socialist economy – akin to the postal service on a national, and ultimately international scale – was imbued with notions of a centralized distribution of raw materials, finished goods and so on. In the conditions of the civil war, scarcity, rationing and the priority of military supply gave a great impetus to the growth of administrative allocation of goods, culminating in the attempt to eliminate private trade and establish a state trading monopoly.[19]

It would be misleading to view the growing role of the state in the distribution of resources as the outcome of a conscious, planned process to replace market relations. The civil war witnessed a desperate, chaotic and bitter struggle to maintain production and feed the population. The whole process was built on improvization, resulting in administrative confusion and bureaucratization. The role of the state in requisitioning agricultural produce, one of the central aspects of war communism, will be dealt with in more detail below. In terms of the industrial sector, the complete collapse of the rouble created a "moneyless" economy. Wages were often paid in kind. Services in municipal areas were free. Money transactions were replaced by paper transactions by enterprises within the state controlled sector: firms delivered supplies without cash payment, and received goods in the same manner.[20]

In an attempt to control this process, private trade was declared illegal, and a state trading monopoly instituted. Rationing, fixed prices, and bartering became part of everyday Russian economic life. Administering this monopoly was intensely difficult. *Vesenkha* attempted to distribute resources, but was gradually displaced as other administrative organs – sTo and the Commission of Utilisation – began to exercise more authority. At local levels, the disputes between *glavki* and *sovnarkhozy* were reproduced by the use of co-operatives and local Soviets as central parts of the distributive network. Inexorably, a black market emerged.[21] It was out of this milieu of centralization, administrative allocation, moneyless economic transactions, bureaucratic chaos, rationing and the militaristic mentality fostered by the civil war that the notion of central planning emerged.

Management and labour under war communism: triumph of technocracy?

Perhaps the greatest source of conflict under war communism was the distribution of power within the factory, and the attitude of the regime to the proletariat. Prolonged debates over one-man management, specialists, labour policy and the role of the trade unions took place within the party. War communism saw a decisive victory for the technocratic, statist strand of Bolshevism culminating in the development of Taylorism and the scientific management of labour in the early 1920s.

One-man management, expertise and hierarchy

The tendency throughout this period was for an increased dependence upon the use of specialists, and for a turning away from collegial, participatory forms of management towards one-man management in enterprises. Yet again this was not a uniform pattern, with significant variations at different times. Neither were these developments uncontested. Debates between individuals and factions within the party-state hierarchy punctuated this period, in the party, the economic bureaucracy, the trade unions and elsewhere.[22]

The trend for employing specialists, prefigured in *State and revolution*, gathered apace after March 1918. Carr noted an increase from 300 in March 1918 to over 6,000 within 2 years.[23] The rationale behind their use lay in the priority accorded to the raising of productivity, especially acute during the civil war, and the continued absence of reliable Bolshevik experts. The employment and unequal rewards for these "bourgeois" specialists was dictated by the economic and cultural backwardness of the Russian proletariat. The issue of management was even more profoundly contested. The parameters of the discussion – collegial boards or one-man management – show how far the debate had shifted from the Bolshevik pre-revolutionary slogan of workers' control. The issue of whether to continue with collegial boards (and what the composition of these boards should be) divided the party, and widened the gap between the technocratic and democratic strands of Soviet socialism.[24] The defenders of collegiality – the trade unions, Tomskii, Osinskii, and interestingly some specialists and members of *Vesenkha* – argued their case from a number of positions. For the trade unions and Left-communists it expressed the survival of elements of economic democracy, of participation by workers and other representatives, of the continued autonomy of localist interests against centralization. For technical staff and members of *Vesenkha*, it represented the best means of administering centralization at local levels. It would prevent the emergence of tensions between management and labour, and best ensure local compliance with central directives.[25]

Lenin and Trotsky demurred. For Lenin, one-man management was the best (i.e. most efficient and effective) method of raising productivity, of instilling strict discipline in the workforce, of taking quick decisions. Collegiality was once again rationalized as part of the development of Soviet industrial administration. The time had come now to move on, towards one-man management.[26] Bukharin theorized it thus. The dictatorship of the proletariat expressed the interests of the workers and was embodied in the authority of the factory manager. A collegial system embodied the attempt to reconcile a plurality of interests that no longer existed.[27] The forum for the resolution of this dispute was the 9th Party Congress of March 1920, in which Lenin's view prevailed, in the face of stern opposition.[28] One-man management came to predominate (particularly in military industries) but not exclusively. Collegial forms continued to exist at the end of the civil war in 1920/21. Indeed, as Carr, Nove and others have noted, four forms co-existed, mixing specialists, commissars, managers and collegial forms.[29] One principle that became established during this time was the inclusion of political guidance at the level of the day-to-day operation of the system. This paved the way for the future selection of specialists from within the party, as the Bolsheviks sought to synthesize the "Red" and "Expert" functions from within their own ranks, rather than from the proletariat as such. The question of one-man versus collegial management had profound ramifications for the further refining of the role of the trade unions, and the wider issue of the labour policy under a socialist system.

Labour policy: mobilization, militarization and the statification of the trade unions

Labour policy proved to be a highly charged issue. Contained within this debate lay the wider questions of the relationship between the state and the workers, and the state and workers' organizations. Soviet labour policy encompassed a variety of forms – universal mobilization, militarization, voluntary labour service and punitive labour camps – which involved a massive extension of state power in its dealings with the workers (and other classes). At the same time, the state began to institute measures to create a scientific organization of labour, as the compulsion to raise productivity and the worship of scientistic and rationalistic methods began to reach new heights.

Scholars disagree over the extent to which the circumstances of the civil war were responsible for the mobilization of labour under war communism. Marx had asserted that labour was a universal duty, and this principle had been enshrined in the Constitution of July 1918. The details were elaborated in October 1918 with the promulgation of a Labour Code, which set out the terms of the obligation to labour.[30] What was absent at this point were the sanctions for transgressors: the principle was not enforced. Workers were returning to the countryside in droves without intervention from the state. The moves to enshrine a universal obligation to labour, directed by the state, coincided with the onset of the severest period of the civil war. At the 8th Party Congress in March 1919, the trade unions were seen as the main vehicle for the instilling of the labour discipline necessary for "the individual mobilisation of the whole population".[31] Legislation soon followed. A decree of 10 April 1919 called for a general mobilization for military service.[32] The distinction between military service and labour service was soon blurred, and the one evolved inexorably into the other over the course of 1919, as the migration from town to country gathered pace. It was not until January 1920, however, that a *Sovnarkom* decree established the principle of universal labour conscription.[33] Alongside universal labour service, the state also adopted other measures, attempting to marry the revolutionary ardour of the committed elements of the proletariat with the use of labour as a punitive tool against the old classes and enemies of the regime. In 1918 forced labour camps and concentration camps were set up.[34] In May 1919, the Bolsheviks set up the "Communist Saturdays", by which workers voluntarily donated their labour to the state for a day.[35]

The issue that was to cause most controversy was the one surrounding the way in which labour was mobilized, disciplined and organized: the Militarization of Labour. The first moves came in January 1920, during a brief breathing-space in the civil war. On 15 January 1920 a decree established a "labour army" out of an existing military unit of peasant soldiers.[36] This practice was gradually extended throughout the first half of 1920. They were engaged in heavy manual labour, and were organized using militaristic discipline. Differences of opinion emerged among the leadership over the rationale behind militarization. Trotsky was the foremost advocate of militarization of labour as a principle of economic reconstruction. The industrial workforce should be organized along the same lines as the labour armies in order to achieve the most rapid and most efficient increases in productivity. It was, as Figes argues, a potential "short-cut" to communism.[37] According to Trotsky, in his pamphlet *Terrorism and communism*:

> We . . . oppose capitalist slavery by socially regulated labour on the basis of an economic plan, obligatory for the whole people and consequently compulsory for each worker in the country . . . But obligation and . . . compulsion are essential conditions in order to bind down the bourgeois anarchy, to secure socialisation of the means of production and labour, and to reconstruct economic life on the basis of a single plan.[38]

For Lenin, the militarization of labour was a useful expedient during the civil war, not a principle for reconstruction in the post-war era.[39] Yet militarization of industrial labour, and the labour armies, played a central role in the economics of "war communism". The labour armies are highly illustrative of the hegemony of modernizing, productivist attitudes towards labour. The workers were little more than a resource to be exploited in the construction of socialism.[40] The moves towards mobilization and militarization threw into sharp relief the question of the role of the trade unions. This debate engulfed the party until its resolution in 1921.[41]

The same battle-lines were drawn. Trotsky emerged as the main proponent of the statification of the trade unions: in a workers' state, the trade unions' prime function was as agents of production. There was no need for them to assume their traditional role as defenders of workers' interests: that had been secured by the establishment of the dictatorship of the proletariat. Trotsky's views were firmly in line with his views on centralized control of the economy and the militarization of labour, and were primarily a response to the virtual disappearance of the industrial proletariat during 1920 (through unemployment, migration, conscription, hunger and so on).[42] The defence of the unions was taken up by Tomsky (the head of the trade unions) and the Workers Opposition faction within the party. They wished to see independent trade unions representing the interests of the workers, and agitating for an increase in industrial democracy.[43]

The debate was sparked by a practical issue of great importance: the running of the railways. The chaos on the railways during 1919 and 1920 led to calls for the imposition of "iron discipline" on the rail unions. After the 9th Party Congress in March 1920, it was decreed that a new central committee of the rail union – *Tsektran* – would take over. The dispute rumbled on until the winter of 1920, and gripped the party until the 10th Congress in March 1921. The most notable development was the emergence of several intermediary platforms between Trostsky's statification and Shlyapnikov's independence positions. Both Lenin, and a group around Bukharin (known as the "buffer group") put forward proposals for discussion.[44] The trade union debate was finalized at the 10th Party Congress. The intensity of the disputes demonstrates the extent to which – even in the midst of the civil war – the Bolshevik party was able to theorize and discuss issues central to the running of the country, and to the nature of the transition phase. The growing role of the state in the running of the economy and the management of labour was not without opposition. Yet it is evident that the party was also intent on the acceleration of the use of science and technology in all fields. Labour policy was no exception.

The triumph of technocracy: Taylorism, scientific management and GOELRO

The Bolshevik party held a deep-seated conviction that the best and most efficient method of transforming Soviet society and economy was through the consistent application of science and technology. Allied to the growing commitment to planning and managing social and economic processes, the Bolshevik vision of the transition phase was gradually evolving in a technocratic direction, emphasizing the rationalist strand over the democratic libertarian one, combining science and Soviet power. This is best illustrated by examining the plans for electrification, and the moves to bring in Taylorist labour practices.

Taylorism was a movement, created by the American F. W. Taylor, for the scientific organization of labour under capitalism. Taylor studied the labour process in order to discover the most efficient working practices and impose these upon the workers. It was designed to maximize efficiency and productivity. For many socialists it represented the further exploitation of the workers under capitalism. Yet it also expressed the potential inherent in the application of scientific methods to raise productivity, and bring about progress towards so-called "higher" social forms. In this sense, the Bolshevik attitude towards Taylorism exemplified the wider issue of socialism as both negating and evolving out of capitalism.[45]

In 1914, Lenin wrote that:

> What does this scientific system consist of? In wringing from the worker three times more work in the same working day . . . It ruthlessly drains all the strength, sucks every last drop of nervous and muscular energy from the wage slave at three times the normal speed.[46]

Yet Lenin also noted the enormous increases in productivity. In the post-revolutionary situation, this same ambiguity towards Taylorism persisted, yet was tempered by one crucial difference: proletarian state power. Taylorist methods could now be applied and extended across the whole industrial sector (not just in individual factories) because the proletariat were exercising political control. As Sochor has argued, the "proposition which emerges from Lenin's discussion of Taylorism is that capitalist methods could be employed to build socialism".[47] This brought Lenin into confrontation once more with Alexander Bogdanov, who disagreed over whether bourgeois science, practices and culture could be adopted and used to build socialism. For Bogdanov, a wholly new proletarian culture and science had to be created.[48]

The first moves towards the implementation of Taylorism came from within the trade union movement in 1918, in particular from the metalworkers union. In 1920, a Central Institute of Labour was created to study the Scientific Organization of Labour (NOT). It was headed by Alexei Gastev who was to become the main proponent of Taylorism in the Soviet state. Gastev was a technocratic visionary, poet and enthusiast for the co-ordination, symmetry and unity of an industrial society. He espoused a form of machine collectivism, a utopia built upon a culture of labour in which both the individual and society would be transformed. Gastev's views were extreme.[49] Yet Taylorism promised the resolution of the Bolsheviks' short-term problem – scarce resources and a culturally and educationally backward workforce – by raising productivity, as well as contributing towards the longer-term transformation of Soviet society by inculcating a set of cultural values and norms based around collectivism, technocracy and the application of scientific rationalism. The discussions surrounding the implementation of Taylorism, set within the context of the mobilization and militarization of labour and the statification of the unions, demonstrate the extent to which the Bolshevik commitments to workers' control, industrial democracy and the emancipation of the worker from capitalist exploitation and alienation had been displaced by the commitment to productivism and the mobilization of science and technology for the construction of socialism.[50]

In February 1920, VTSIK created a State Electrification Commission (GOELRO), comprised of 200 specialists and engineers, which united and co-ordinated the disparate and disjointed efforts at electrification that had grown since 1918.[51] The commission presented its plan to the 8th Congress of Soviets in December 1920. Under the leadership of Krzhizhanovskii, the electrification programme became a core part of the economic development of the country, of the modernization of backward rural Russia, and of the provision of cultural enlightenment through the electric light bulb.[52] Lenin's report at the 8th Congress makes fascinating reading, expressing so clearly the modernizing, constructivist, productivist ethos underpinning Bolshevism during the civil war. Lenin was fascinated by this project. He called it the "second programme of the party". He went on to state:

> Communism is Soviet power plus the elctrification of
> the. whole country. Otherwise the country will remain a

small-peasant country, and we must realize that . . . Only when the country has been electrified and industry, agriculture and transport have been placed on the technical basis of modern large-scale industry, only then shall we be fully victorious . . . We must see to it that every factory and every electric power station becomes a centre of enlightenment; if Russia is covered with a dense network of electric power stations and powerful technical installations, our communist economic development will become a model for a future socialist Europe and Asia.[53]

The generation of this project to bring electrical power across the country was more than just another expression of the industrializing, modernizing impulse of Bolshevism. The practical aspects of organizing this proposal gave a clear stimulus to the emergence of a formal planning mechanism. By the end of the civil war, the electrification programme had brought the question of the production of a single economic plan for the whole country to a central place in party discussions.

The emergence of Soviet planning

The creation of the State Planning Commission (GOSPLAN) in April 1921 was the culmination of a number of interrelated developments. The experiences of war communism generated a sharp debate about what exactly was meant by "planning". The works of Marx and Engels provided few clues. Lenin talked generally about the need for the central organization and control of the economy, akin to a single factory.[54] Guroff also argues that Lenin was profoundly influenced by the heritage of Russian economic thought, which emphasized the "necessity of viewing the economy in its totality, and investigating the interrelationships of all the sectors of the economy".[55] Experience was also a great teacher. The German War Economy – centralized, concentrated and state-directed – exercised a great hold on the imagination and theorizing of Larin, Bukharin, Lenin and many other leading figures in the Bolshevik party. Yet the meaning of planning remained elusive. Some (Larin and Trotsky in particular) spoke of the need to generate a single economic plan. Another strand argued for the planning of different sectors or branches which would then be amalgamated. Others argued for a regional focus. Initial moves were made in early 1918 by *Vesenkha* to draw up a programme of public works. The civil war interrupted this process, and it was not until the lull in the spring of 1920 that the debate was rejoined.[56]

The divide was between a general single state plan, in which the broad contours of state economic policy would be drawn up by a single economic authority, and a more specific approach which highlighted a number of key projects to be carried out. The turning-point came in December 1920 with the approval of the specific plans for electrification and transport, but which also established the STO as the body that would draw up a single economic plan for Soviet Russia. In February 1921, *sovnarkom* decreed the establishment of GOSPLAN, against Lenin's judgement who favoured the GOELRO approach.[57] The first steps towards Soviet planning had been made. Yet the debates about the optimal means and method of planning were unresolved, and were to punctuate the period between 1921 and 1928.

Agriculture under war communism

Food supply dominated the economics of the civil war.[58] The thrust of Bolshevik policy towards the peasantry under war communism contained two main impulses: the centralization of state control over food supply and the socialization of land tenure. In both areas the Bolsheviks were forced to temper their ideological leanings in the face of the exigencies of the civil war, and the overwhelming resistance of the peasantry to the extension of party/urban control of the countryside.

The issue of food supply is often viewed as the central defining feature of war communism. In the spring of May 1918, Bolshevik policy took a radical turn. A decision was taken to set up Committees of Poor Peasants (*kombedy*) and a food supply dictatorship. The impulse underlying these moves, according to Patenaude, was the wholly pragmatic one of increasing the supply of grain. The chosen method, however, was conditioned by the Bolshevik class-based, urban, conflictual view of the world. The food supply dictatorship was based upon the existing practices of a state grain monopoly, and centrally fixed prices. The peasants were required to supply any grain surplus to the state. The state had recourse to coercion, if necessary, and in the conditions of civil war the central authorities created armed food supply detachments to collect the grain.[59] The *kombedy* were designed to extract grain for the state by fomenting class war in the countryside. This had a twofold purpose. In food collection terms it would increase the amount of grain as the *kombedy* took grain from the rich to give to the state. In political terms it was hoped that this would divide the peasantry along class lines and increase support for Soviet power in the rural areas.[60]

The *kombedy* were a total failure. The party began to shift its stance in late 1918, adopting a less hostile posture towards the "middle" peasantry. In early 1919 the party declared that it was moving towards a "firm alliance" with the middle peasantry, ending its prioritization of the interests of the poor peasantry through the *kombedy*. Reconciling this new conciliatory approach with the harsh realities of civil war food supply proved impossible. From late 1918, local authorities adopted the practice of requisitioning the total amount of grain they required. This practice became known as *razverstka*, the policy of "requisitioning" grain from the peasantry by strict quotas.[61] Lih argues that the policy of *razverstka* marks a retreat from the confrontation of the food supply detachments. He defines *razverstka* as a policy of quota assessment, which was introduced because of the signal failure of the food supply dictatorship and the *kombedy* to deliver grain to the towns. Food supply officials recognized both the desirability of a state grain monopoly and its impracticability in the conditions of the civil war. Rather than trying to fan the flames of civil war in the countryside, the *razverstka* meant dealing with the peasant village as a whole, and levying a quota from it.[62] The party were still committed to the imposition of state control and the elimination of market relations. The civil war merely imposed a sense of realism in their dealings with the peasantry.[63]

A similar process was at work in the area of land tenure. The party was committed to the socialization of the land. Large-scale, mechanized collective farms would be the centrepiece of a socialist agricultural sector. They would promote socialist ideals among the peasantry, increase the productivity of the land and extend state control. The party recognized, however, that a policy of forced or coerced collectivization was foolhardy. The party pursued a policy based around persuasion through the creation of model state and collective farms. A decree of 2 November 1918 established, alongside the already existing state farms or *sovkhoz*, three types of collective farm: *kommuna*, *artel'* and *TOZ*.[64] Whereas the state farms gave the peasantry no claims to the land itself, merely providing remuneration for the peasants who worked them, the different types of collective farms exhibited a variety of approaches to land tenure and remuneration. The *kommuna* were socialistic in their entire internal organization. All belongings, land and produce were equally divided. The *artel'* were something of a midway point between the *kommuna* and the traditional peasant farming methods. The *artel'* was run by a general assembly. This assembly decided how much time the members of the *artel'* would devote to the collective labouring projects. The rest of the time could be spent on their own plots. Private property was recognized by the assembly, although it was to be made available for the use of all. The *TOZ* was a fairly loosely organized organ, in which members farmed their landholdings together and received back produce in proportion to the land they provided.[65]

The process of socializing the land was given impetus by a decree of February 1919, which outlined that the land previously belonging to the nobility that was not being farmed would pass to these new state and collective farms. This was deeply unpopular with the existing peasant farmers, who had aspirations on all noble land.[66] These model farms proved to be anything but shining examples of the superiority of socialist, collectivized agriculture. Generally run by either urbanites or non-agricultural specialists, and composed of the indolent, inebriated and/or incompetent, most failed to generate any genuine economic dynamism.[67] To contextualize the moves towards collectivization during the civil war, by 1921, and after significant promptings from the state, less than 1 per cent of the rural population were in the collective sector. The peasant question, alongside the issues of international revolution and cultural backwardness, remained unresolved at the end of the civil war.

The politics of war communism

Political developments between 1918 and 1920 were marked by a growth in centralization, bureaucratization and militarization, and a concomitant decline in democracy, popular participation and local autonomy. The use of coercion was established within the fabric of the Soviet state, and the organs of decision-making emerged that were to survive for almost the whole of the Soviet period. The debate in western literature has focused on the respective roles played by ideology, political choices and circumstances in conditioning these developments.[68]

Coercion, authoritarianism and the militarization of the Soviet state

Repression and violence were embedded deeply into Bolshevik rule during the civil war. The emergence of the "Red Terror" during the summer of 1918 (after the attempted assassination of Lenin and the execution of the Imperial family in July 1918) was formalized by a decree of 5 September 1918.[69] It lasted until the end of the civil war, and along with the terror perpetrated by the "Whites", led to a number of appalling atrocities being committed against individuals and groups and to the creation of a series of labour and concentration camps (under the control of either the CHEKA or the NKVD).

The rationale was clear: to defend the revolution. As Dzerzhinsky asserted:

> The Cheka is not a court of law. The Cheka, like the Red Army, is the defence of the Revolution, and just as the Red Army in the Civil War cannot take account of the fact that it might harm particular individuals but must concern itself solely with the victory of the Revolution over the bourgeoisie.[70]

As Latsis argued in a famous passage, the Red Terror was the extension of the class struggle in wartime conditions:

> We are not waging war against individuals. We are exterminating the bourgeoisie as a class. During investigation, do not look for evidence that the accused acted in word or deed against Soviet power. The first questions that you ought to put are: to what class does he belong? What is his origin? What is his education or profession? And it is these

questions that ought to determine the fate of the accused. In this lies the significance and essence of the Red Terror.[71]

Yet it proved impossible to reconcile a broad definition ("Defend the revolution"!) with a restrictive one ("Exterminate the bourgeoisie"!). The Red Terror became violent and indiscriminate. Not only were "counter-revolutionaries" executed, but it soon engulfed speculators, prostitutes and informers. Statistical evaluations differ on the precise extent.[72] Yet the general pattern of an escalation in violence was clear. Although this provoked dissensions within the leadership, much of this disagreement stemmed from institutional and personal rivalries, as the Ministry of Justice sought to have its powers restored, or as individuals tried to curb the position of Dzerzhinsky. Kamenev was one of the few who spoke out against the arrest of "innocent" people. Yet almost all Bolsheviks shared a belief in the efficacy of state violence in the pursuit of revolutionary goals. Differences were a matter of extent and method.[73]

The CHEKA is significant for reasons other than the extension of violence and coercion. The CHEKA became one of the central executive organs of the state during the civil war, along with the Red Army. Its disciplined and efficient operations made it a reliable tool in times of emergency and scarce resources. It began to supplant existing institutions, forming the core of a new administrative structure, further displacing the elements of popular control and participation from the dictatorship of the proletariat. The CHEKA became involved in combating crime and banditry, controlling firearms, combating epidemics, conscripting and militarizing labour and, somewhat bizarrely, the care of orphans![74] Along with the NKVD, it began to occupy a central role in the solution of economic problems.

The Red Army became the central administrative organ during the civil war. Its priority claim on resources, its personnel and its hierarchical and centralized organization enabled it to fill the gap left by the erosion of the civilian administration. But the Red Army was also a moving force in this very process of eroding local autonomy. The lines of cause and effect are neither clear nor easily explicable. Although the party continued to profess its belief in a democratic popular militia, Trotsky maintained the pace of constructing a Red Army organized along traditional lines. The symbol and bearer of revolutionary values and consciousness in the army was the political commissar, who had extensive civilian and military powers. It was through this agency, that the local autonomy of Soviets and other organs were gradually eroded as the Red Army became the nucleus of the Soviet state.[75]

The impact of an increased role for the CHEKA and the Red Army was not just an institutional one, which powerfully catalysed the growth of centralization and bureaucratization in the system. The systematic use of violence, of political methods to solve economic problems, the attempts to identify internal "enemies" and the general militarization of Bolshevik attitudes towards decision-making and governing were to shape the nature of Soviet-style socialism for decades to come. The outlook of both the central leadership and the middle-ranking strata of the administration were profoundly influenced by these developments.[76] The dictatorship of the proletariat was stamped with a pervasive and creeping authoritarian, militaristic operating culture.

Bureaucratization, centralization and the demise of local autonomy

The process of resurrecting the Russian state occurred amid "a disintegrating economy and a decomposing social fabric".[77] In these conditions, and within the framework of the central role of the military and the CHEKA, it was the organs of local autonomy, and the democratic practices inherent in the Soviet system that were the main casualties. By 1920/21, the Soviet state was highly centralized and bureaucratized at all levels.

Sovnarkom and VTSIK became the central decision-making organs, as the All-Russia Congress of Soviets met less and less frequently, being too large and unwieldy for rapid decision-making in the context of a desperate struggle for survival. This same process was mirrored throughout the system. The Soviets' position as organs of local autonomy and popular representation was systematically eroded. The processes of centralization during the civil war reinforced the moves towards a vertical branch system of administration, as opposed to a horizontal, territorially-based approach. The Red Army represented the extension of central directives and control over local areas, as the priority of military objectives took precedence over local autonomy. Increasingly the Soviets became little more than "transmission belts" for central directives.

This process of centralization was exacerbated by the increasing bureaucratization of the system. The number of officials within the system increased, according to Liebman, from approximately 14,000 in 1918 to approximately 5,880,000 in 1920.[78] A suffocating plethora of committees, agencies and departments sprang up to adminster the war. It would be wrong to see this central intervention as being wholly intrusive to the practices of local democracy. Many local bodies were appealing for greater central intervention to assist them in their administration of local areas. Indeed, the Soviets themselves underwent the same process, whereby the executive committees of local Soviets supplanted the representative assembly as the decision-making organ in local areas.[79] This poses an interesting paradox, whereby the vast numbers of personnel within the system increased levels of popular participation in the administration (derived from a variety of motives – idealism, careerism, heroism, self-interest), while simultaneously witnessing a decline in the democratic functioning of the system. Appointmentism, bureaucratism and vertical centralism replaced elections and democratic centralism, vastly increasing the scope and character of central power.

The communist party: building a one-party state?

Developments within the party occurred along four main axes. The internal structure and functioning of the party saw a growing degree of centralization and a concentration of authority at the top of the hierarchy. The role of the party shifted from a body of revolutionaries to a mass movement forming the core of the new state administration. The status of the party was altered, as the system became less pluralistic and the party increasingly adopted a monopolistic position. Finally, the social composition of the party was changed irrevocably.[80]

The tension between democracy and centralism within the party was laid bare during the civil war. The same processes that affected the state organs flowed through the party as well. In the party statutes, the Party Congress (the apex of the pyramidical structure of party organs) and the Central Committee (cc) (elected by the Party Congress) were the sovereign decision-making and executive organs. The concentration of authority at the top of the party took the form of the creation of new organs of power. At the 8th Party Congress in March 1919, the Politburo was reconstituted and the Orgburo was created. In 1920, the Secretariat also emerged. The functions of the three bodies were as follows:

- the Politburo: a small body of (initially) five people. Its remit was to deal only with urgent issues, and to report to the full cc;
- the Orgburo: subordinate to the cc and the Politburo, the Orgburo carried out organizational and administrative tasks, particularly the appointment and selection of personnel;
- the Secretariat: subordinate to the Orgburo, the secretariat was a board of cc secretaries that dealt with specific issues that did not require the intervention of the Orgburo.[81]

The cc met less and less frequently, as the locus of decision-making shifted to the Politburo and elsewhere (the sto in particular). The overlapping membership on these new organs meant, in effect, a vast concentration of power in the hands of a few key individuals. The only person enjoying membership of all four bodies by 1922 was Stalin.

This process spawned a proliferation of bureaux and committees as the party began to create a working apparatus to enable it to undertake the tasks of governing the country. The cc developed nine different departments (including the *Orgotdel*, the *Uchraspred* and the *Informotdel*). Bureaux were created for working among non-Russian groups. The cc extended its control, by tying the work of local party committees more directly to itself, by appointing officials rather than having them elected from below, and by devolving greater powers to the secretaries of party committees at all levels of the hierarchy.[82] In sum, these developments represented an intense bureaucratization of the activity of the party. Problems were resolved by administrative means. Appointmentism supplanted the elective principle. Centralism dominated democracy.

The change in the role of the party was brought about at the 8th Party Congress after the death of Sverdlov who had headed up both the party and Soviet hierarchies. A Resolution "On the Organisational Question" was passed, which sought to delineate the respective roles of party and soviet organs. The resolution solved very little in practice:

> It is absolutely necessary that a party fraction be set up in all soviet organisations, and that such fractions be strictly subordinated to party discipline . . . In no case would it do to confuse the functions of party collectives with the functions of state bodies such as the soviets . . . The party must implement its decisions through the soviet bodies, within the framework of the Soviet constitution. The party strives to direct the work of the soviets, not to replace them.[83]

The difficulty was political practice. How could direction be exercised without emasculating the independence of the soviets? The precedent had been created at the elite level, whereby the locus of decision-making moved inexorably from VTSIK and the ARCS to *sovnarkom* and in particular to the CC. At lower levels, the party (through individual members) attempted to form the core of all public organizations. Key figures were appointed by the secretariat to ensure politically reliable individuals occupied the important positions. Party fractions were to organize themselves in all non-party bodies in order to agitate for the adoption of the party line. Maintaining this division of functions proved impossible. The local party secretary soon replaced the chairman of the soviet executive committee as the main official in local areas.[84] Within the system as a whole, authority flowed from the state to the party. Within the party, authority flowed to the top and to the full-time apparatus, away from the localities and the rank and file. The party had rapidly become the "directing nucleus" of the administration.

The consolidation of the Bolshevik monopolization of power extended the trends that had been apparent prior to the civil war. The other socialist parties were marginalized and harassed during the civil war, but both the Mensheviks and the SRS survived at grass-roots level. Indeed the Mensheviks were the most popular movement within the trade unions, and had made headway in elections to urban Soviets. The SRS retained considerable support in the countryside.[85] At the elite level however, the Bolsheviks were hegemonic. Opposition at the elite level was on the whole confined to the emergence of factions within the party. Between 1918 and

1920/21, a series of opposition movements sprung up, opposing the leadership across a whole spectrum of issues. The Left Communists, the Workers' Opposition, the Military Opposition, the Democratic Centralists and others all became restless and discontented with the thrust of Bolshevik policy. The significant issue is the persistence of public debate, dispute and dissension in the midst of the civil war. At this point, the predominance of the party at the elite level did not yet equate to the suppression of all dissent, within and without of the party.

Finally, the social composition of the party was radically altered, irrevocably. During the civil war, it became a mass party, growing to reach approximately 600,000 by March 1920 (having been only *c.*24,000 at the start of 1917). It was the social background, experiences and outlook of the new entrants that is worthy of note. As Siegelbaum has noted, the proportion of manual workers gradually fell, and those of peasants and white-collar workers grew. By January 1921, the party comprised: 240,000 workers (41 per cent); 165,300 peasants (28.2 per cent); 138,800 employees (23.7 per cent); 41,500 origins unknown (7.1 per cent).[86]

The vast majority had joined after the revolution, often for careerist notions, or to acquire scarce rations or privileges, and were imbued with notions of militaristic methods of rule. Figes skilfully narrates how the outlook of party members influenced the nature of Bolshevik rule and shaped the practices of the post-revolutionary state.[87] The party membership was overwhelmingly short on education and long on pragmatism. Whereas the majority remained ideologically submissive to the diktats of the cc, the system became increasingly riven with corruption and patronage at local levels. The party had changed in profound ways.

The (Less) politics of war communism

At the 8th Congress of Soviets in December 1920, Lenin said:

> We have no doubt learnt politics; here we stand as firm as a rock. But things are bad as far as economic matters are concerned. Henceforth less politics will be the best politics. Bring more engineers and agronomists to the fore, learn from them, keep an eye on their work, and turn our

congresses and conferences, not into propaganda meetings but into bodies that will verify our economic achievements, bodies in which we can really learn the business of economic development.[88]

Lenin advocated "less politics" within the context of his plans for electrification. Earlier in his speech he said that:

This marks the beginning of that very happy time when politics will recede into the background, when politics will be discussed less often and at shorter length, and engineers and agronomists will do most of the talking.[89]

Lenin's remarks were in part generated by his growing impatience with the factional struggles within the party. At a deeper level though, it expresses the deep-seated hostility to "politics", and the preference for a technocratic, scientific approach to the management of society, and to subordinating everything to the need to increase productivity. This underlying attitude, almost Saint-Simonian in outlook, conditioned the choices and policies made in this period.

The processes at work – bureaucratization, coercion, centralization, hierarchicalization – were all symptoms of the statization of Soviet political life. The democratic elements established during 1917 – workers' control, local Soviets, trade unions – were destroyed or severely weakened.[90] The causes of this statization are manifold. The desperate shortage of resources and personnel entailed a massive process of institution-building and bureaucratization, often encouraged from below by local officials struggling to cope. The wartime circumstances brought a corrosive coercion and authoritarianism into politics, along with the introduction of an enemy motif. Failure to support the revolution actively could lead to the charge of counter-revolution. Soon, failure to support the leadership line would bring the same charge.

Social historians have produced a great deal of excellent research on the decimation and outmigration of the industrial proletariat during the civil war. Figes notes that in "1921 there were twice as many bureaucrats as workers in Russia".[91] Two consequences flowed from this. First, the Bolsheviks became increasingly isolated as its basis of support narrowed. Secondly, the party increasingly came to see that the requisite socialist consciousness that would enable the people to participate in the governing of the system was "missing". The party, its activists, its commissars and its officials were forced to substitute for the people in the administration of the country, as the only ones with the "correct" socialist consciousness.[92] These factors gave a great impetus to the growth of coercion, bureaucratization and to the prioritization of the use of specialists and experts in the administration of the system. More agronomists, less politics.

It would be wrong to see these developments as being accepted uncritically, either within the party as a whole, or within the leadership. A variety of opposition movements – Workers' Opposition, Democratic Centralists, Military Opposition, a group of Ukrainian communists agitating for greater autonomy – sought to restore the democratic impulse, to revive the local, representative organs of Soviet society (albeit within the framework of exclusive Bolshevik rule). Criticism intruded spasmodically as the military threat ebbed and flowed. The unifying theme in all this criticism was a desire to place the democratic, emancipatory, libertarian strand of Soviet socialism in the centre of the post-revolutionary state. The surge of Left-libertarian criticism probably peaked at the 8th Party Congress of March 1919. Here the party retained its commitment to a popular militia, to industrial democracy through trade union participation.[93]

The leadership itself was acutely aware of the problems within the system. A number of solutions were devised. Lenin instituted a series of purges of the party membership to remove those considered to be "unsuitable". Greater rotation of officials (both occupational and geographical) was also encouraged to prevent corrupt networks consolidating their position. Perhaps the most interesting developments, which illustrate the emerging hegemony on the nature of politics under Bolshevik rule, occurred in the area of popular control of the state and party apparatuses. In May 1918, the Bolsheviks created the People's Commissariat of State Control (NKGK) to weed out "red tape". After further reorganizations in 1919, in February 1920 the Commissariat of Workers' and Peasants' Inspection (RABKRIN) was created. Its function was to promote greater popular control and involvement, thereby reducing the bureaucratic nature of the state. Through a variety of means – usually assistance cells and mass investigations – RABKRIN sought to involve the masses in the oversight of officialdom. It had something of a chequered existence.[94] Simultaneously, new organs were created to oversee the work of the party. These party control commissions – both at elite and local levels – had a minimal impact upon the drift towards centralism, appointmentism and bureaucratization within the party.

The tension within the dictatorship of the proletariat between popular control and elite revolutionary consciousness remained. The circumstances of the civil war pushed the Bolshevik conception of the dictatorship of the proletariat further in the direction of centralization, elitism and technocracy, adding bureacratization and coercion. But this conception *redefined* the tension between popular participation and centralized direction, it did not eradicate the former. Lenin attempted (unsuccessfully) to synthesize the two, by turning the organs of Soviet society into "transmission belts" of party policy, in so far as the conditions of the civil war allowed, and by creating popular organs to oversee the work of party and state officials. This amounted to the hegemony of a technocratic approach to societal management, supported by state directed popular participation, which would perform an educative function.

Society and culture under war communism

One of the most surprising things about the study of the civil war is the time and attention that was devoted to debating and developing the cultural, educational and social policies of the state. On one level, it appears to be a distraction from the overriding concern to establish control and secure military victory. Yet within the Bolshevik worldview, concern with society and culture was an intrinsic part of the attempt both to secure control and to construct socialism, by embedding the values of the regime into the population. In transforming the workers and peasants, the system itself would be transformed. The key issue was not how to create a socialist culture, or how could a society be created that was dominated by socialist norms and values. No, the issue was how could culture and social policy be used to construct socialism?

Equality and inequality under war communism

Economically speaking, war communism produced a greater degree of inegalitarianism and stratification in Soviet Russia. This was partly a function of the context. War produced scarcity produced rationing. In turn the Bolsheviks inevitably privileged certain groups within the system upon whom they were particularly reliant for survival. The following privileges emerged during the civil war period, as the party gradually abandoned its commitment to the "maxima" (a ceiling on earnings, although given the collapse of the rouble, the benefits-in-kind were the most tangible and useful ones).[95]

The main beneficiaries of high wages were the specialist and technical personnel in state enterprises. Increased income differentiation was formalized in March/April 1920, when the practice of minimizing differentials was renounced by the trade unions.[96] The main beneficiaries of the system of rationing of goods and food were the manual workers and the party/state officials. Manual workers, white-collar workers and persons who did not work received rations in the ratio of 4:2:1.[97] The most privileged group were those in the Red Army, who qualified for special rations. This practice of allocating special rations gradually spread to include CHEKA personnel, selected workers, political agitators and others. Other benefits – accommodation, travel, educational opportunities – also became subject to discretionary allocations.[98]

These practices were deeply unpopular with Left-libertarians and workers alike. Indeed, Lenin and other party leaders recognized the undesirability of this growing inequality. Yet the twin imperatives – physical survival and expansion of the productive forces – compelled the leadership to promote inequality, and to prioritize productivism over egalitarianism. It is interesting to juxtapose this progressive growth in inegalitarianism with the supposed radicalism of the economic policies of war communism. Can the two be reconciled? There is certainly nothing anomalous in terms of Lenin's pre-revolutionary writings, in which he predicted the need for unequal rewards, nor with the general thrust of transition economics (increase productivity). The answer may well lie in the interpretations and theorizing of war communism, of which more below.

The main initiative *vis-à-vis* attitudes towards the emancipation of women during the civil war concerned the creation of *Zhenotdel*

(The Women's Department of the CC Secretariat).[99] In November 1918 the first All-Russian Congress of Working Women was established. Out of this Congress, *Zhenotdel* was created. Its activities were designed to raise the educational and cultural level of women in order to draw them into the public arena. The idea was to create a large cadre of female workers who would undertake work for the party and for the state at all levels of the hierarchy, establishing a link between liberating women from the traditional roles they still occupied and the construction of socialism.[100] Radical differences between *Zhenotdel* activists and the Bolshevik leadership emerged. As Clements has noted,

> The *zhenotdelovski* called for a world of new women building a communalised society neighbourhood by neighbourhood. Leading Bolshevik theoreticians (Lenin, Trotsky and Bukharin) however, believed that huge centralised organisations would construct communism by rearranging economic structures, producing as a result the social transformation of which women's emancipation was a part.[101]

As the initial emancipatory and liberational elements in Bolshevik discourse died down, the technocratic, instrumentalist attitude of the leadership became dominant. *Zhenotdel* became one of the party's transmission belts, mobilizing women for the fulfilment of particular tasks in constructing socialism. This is not to say that there were not significant changes that liberated women or which challenged traditional social mores. These developments occurred within a context of a shift in state policy towards a more instrumentalist approach to the *zhenskii vopros*.[102]

Instilling a new worldview: education, propaganda and the debate over proletarian culture

The sphere of culture acquired increasing importance for the Bolsheviks as the likelihood of imminent European revolution receded. The construction of socialism in Soviet Russia was hindered not just by the material backwardness of the Russian economy, but also by the technical and cultural backwardness of the Russian workers and peasants. Rapid large-scale industrial development, and the application of science and technology to the productive process was only possible with a skilled workforce. Popular participation in the processes of administering socialism required a literate and educated populace. Bolshevik rule was also increasingly threatened by the low levels of the socialist consciousness of the population. Embedding the rule of the communist party would be problematical in a country perceived to be dominated by a *petit bourgeois* peasantry. The developments in the cultural sphere saw an attempt to remake the worldview of the people. Conflicts arose over the content of this culture, a conflict expressing some of the deeper tensions running throughout the Bolshevik movement.

The theoretical dispute about the nature of culture after the revolution re-emerged with the growth of the *Prolet'kult* movement.[103] Basing themselves on the views of Bogdanov, Lunacharskii and others (including, interestingly, Bukharin and Kollontai), the *Prolet'kult* movement worked for the creation, development and propagation of a distinctly proletarian culture. For the *prolet'kult*ists (a very broad and amorphous grouping) culture was autonomous from politics and economics, and so a cultural transformation would have to occur simultaneous with economic and political developments (or perhaps even prior to them). Indeed many radical *prolet'kult*ists wished, while creating a new proletarian culture, to reject all bourgeois cultural and scientific developments entirely. At the first conference of *Prolet'kult* in Moscow in September 1918, Bogdanov called for the "socialization of science" as the basis for creating a genuinely proletarian culture.[104]

Although staffed mainly by intellectuals, the purpose of *Prolet'kult* was not merely the creation of a proletarian culture, but also the promotion of workers themselves to manage the development of this culture. This was to be accomplished in two ways: Workers' Universities and the Workers' Encyclopaedia.[105] The *Prolet'kult* movement espoused a faith in the creative potential of both the workers themselves, and in the autonomy and centrality of cultural transformation in the establishment of socialism in Russia.[106] The Bolshevik who most vehemently opposed it was Trotsky. He prioritized the transformations in the economic sphere, and along with Lenin strongly criticized those who wished to reject all bourgeois culture and values. For Lenin and Trotsky, the raising of productivity was the primary task: all spheres had to contribute to this. In asserting this, Trotsky in particular denied the autonomy of the cultural sphere, and assigned it a secondary role in the construction of socialism.[107]

Lenin occupied something of an intermediary position (as in so many other instances). Lenin accepted the need for a "cultural revolution", but with two important qualifications. First, his concern was with material culture: literacy, scientific knowledge and so on. He had little time for artistic experimentation or avant-garde movements in developing a new proletarian culture. Secondly, Lenin vehemently rejected the ideas of those who sought to reject the developments of capitalism in the fields of culture and science. The cultural and educational backwardness of the Russian worker and peasant could only be overcome through the widest possible dissemination of the latest advances in human culture.[108] This is the application to the cultural sphere of Lenin's view of socialism as growing out of capitalism, as its heir. The imperatives of modernization and productivism imparted a strong utilitarian bent into Lenin's attitude towards culture.

During the civil war period (and after) the sphere of culture saw struggles and conflicts over the management and content of cultural policy, as the ambiguities and tensions within Bolshevism over culture were played out. As in so many other areas, the civil war period saw a massive growth in institution building to oversee cultural policy. A Commissariat of Enlightenment (*Narkompros*) was created under Lunacharsky, which became responsible for all aspects of cultural policy: arts, literature, education, the press, the cinema, theatre.[109] Ideas, values and policies were popularized and transmitted to the population through a number of different organizations (*zhenotdel*, *Komsomol*, trade unions) as the party gradually extended the scope of its activities. Concurrently, they shut down organizations that cut across class cleavages (most notably the Boy Scouts!). This tension between societal autonomy and state control ran throughout this period. There was no definitive resolution though. While *Prolet'kult* dwindled in influence after 1920, the universities, the Academy of Sciences, scientists and some famous cultural figures retained considerable autonomy from the state.[110]

The content of cultural policy combined a number of different strands designed to inculcate a new worldview, and also to impart more narrow educational and technical values, as part of the modernization of society. The process of forming a new worldview entailed the destruction of alternative explanations of the world (religious and secular) and the propagating of a communist viewpoint through an extensive propaganda network. The party adopted a policy of militant atheism, and started to uproot organized religion in Russia, expecting personal faith to dwindle automatically as a consequence of modernization and education. Priests were impoverished by the ending of state subsidies and the confiscation of church property. Religious buildings were converted for a variety of different uses (including museums of atheism). Religious education was outlawed, being replaced with atheistic propaganda. Religious festivals were replaced by secular and communist alternatives. A vast propaganda network – incorporating cinema, theatre, the press, posters – was created to spread the atheistic gospel.[111] Censorship was applied increasingly extensively during the civil war, as alternative viewpoints were suppressed. One of the main obstacles to the success of this attempt to create a socialist person was the extensive illiteracy in Russia. The Bolsheviks commenced a campaign to abolish illiteracy. A network of literacy schools were created, notably in the Red Army, but also in factories and elsewhere.[112]

Underlying these social and cultural initiatives was the Bolshevik desire to transform the world, and their faith in the ability of the human mind to order this process. The constructivist tendencies of Bolshevism expressed itself in this aspiration to undertake a profound degree of social engineering. This aspiration was continually frustrated and confounded by the material conditions of the civil war, in which the Bolsheviks lacked the resources to undertake this transformation. The civil war period is notable for the gradual predominance of the Leninist utilitarian line on cultural policy, emphasizing the struggle to overcome backwardness and construct socialism, reinforcing the technocratic, productivist line, over the democratic, libertarian approach which sought a proletarian culture developed by the workers themselves.

War communism – details and debates

War communism has generated a great deal of interpretive controversy, among both Western and Soviet scholars. The specific features of the Soviet state in this period are very well-documented in many texts. Summarizing these, and the above analysis, the following features can be identified:

- a growing statization and central control of all aspects of life;
- extensive nationalization of industry;
- the administrative allocation of goods, services, raw materials, and labour;
- the attempt to suppress private trade by eliminating market relations and by abolishing money;
- the extensive use of coercion, terror and authoritarian practices;
- a bureaucratization of political and social processes;
- a massive growth in institution building.[113]

The debates over the origins of these policies is more difficult to delineate. The basic divide surrounds the ideology versus circumstances or ideology and circumstances debate. Early Soviet writings, such as Kritsman, emphasized the ideological element, writing of how "war communism" was "an experiment in the first steps of the transition to socialism".[114] He went on to label it as the "Heroic Period". Later Soviet writings focused instead upon circumstances and necessity causing the introduction of a range of extreme policies designed to deal with an extreme situation. The end of the war brought an end to the policies.[115]

Non-Soviet literature has also tended to emphasize one explanation or the other. Nove views it as an interaction of the two:

> Was War Communism a response to the war emergency and collapse, or did it represent an all-out attempt to leap into socialism? I have already suggested that it could be both these things at once. Perhaps it should also be said that it meant different things to different Bolsheviks, and this is an important element in our understanding their view of the about-turn in 1921.[116]

Szamuely argues that the ideological legacy of Marxism did provide some broad parameters within which the Bolsheviks made their policy decisions.[117] Boettke went further, arguing that,

This task of eradicating market relations and "taking over the whole process of social production from beginning to end" constitutes the economic policy followed by the Bolsheviks from 1918 to 1921. War communism represents the conscious and deliberate attempt to realize Marx's utopia.[118]

However, many of the radical messianic interpretations stemmed from the coincidence of aspects of the Bolshevik war economy with Kautsky's identification of the essential features of a socialist economic system. This encouraged theorists to view them as permanent features of the transition period.

Recent writings have argued that war communism was nothing more than a *post hoc* construct composed by Lenin in order to justify the turn towards moderation under NEP. Siegelbaum, *pace* Lars Lih, has argued that Lenin created "war communism" in order to defend NEP and attack his critics. On some occasions, Lenin referred to it as a desperate response to emergency circumstances. On others as a premature attempt to march straight into communism. Siegelbaum and Lih maintain that Lenin imposed an interpretative framework upon post-revolutionary developments that cannot be sustained:

October 1917–May/June 1918 = State Capitalism [MODERATION]
May/June 1918–March 1921   = War Communism [RADICALISM]
March 1921–   = NEP [MODERATION][119]

First, they argue that there is no *a priori* reason for equating state capitalism with moderation. Secondly, there were many instances of *retreats* from pre-civil war ambitiousness: the turn to the middle peasants in 1919, the policy of foreign concessions. The processes of statization were generated as much by the experiences of wartime Imperial Germany and Russia as the doctrines of Marx and Engels. On this reading there was nothing conceptually distinct about this period.[120]

From the above analysis, it is apparent that the policies adopted during the civil war were generated by a complex array of motives, and that each policy initiative needs to be examined in detail. It is too simplistic and one-sided to explain developments in the civil war as either an attempt to march straight into communism, or as a system conditioned purely by emergency and desperation. What is remarkable on one level are the elements of continuity over the period after October. Within the framework of a desire to raise productivity as the overwhelming factor guiding Bolshevik policy, and given the tendency to favour large-scale, statist and centralist solutions, then one can see a basic consistency in the actions of the party. The inconsistencies between Bolshevik doctrine and practice occur not at the level of their ideas about the transition phase and the reality, but in the gap between their political pronouncements during 1917 (for example workers' control of factories) and their actions afterwards. Let us examine a few policies in order to high-light the complex factors at play.

Many policies – the return to one-man management, the use of specialists, inegalitarian wages policy, foreign concessions, strict labour discipline – reflected the priority of increasing production. The specific shape of these policies were defined by the circum-stances of civil war. But the original impulse lay in Bolshevik ideas about the nature and purpose of the transition phase. Some policies reflected the national–specific conditions of the transition, causing an extension and deepening of a particular idea. This is best illustrated with regard to the post-revolutionary franchise. Marxist–Engelian theory on the nature of the dictatorship of the proletariat spoke of the need to institute a revolutionary democracy in which legislative and executive functions were fused, and where the proletariat ruled. Nothing specific was said about the franchise. The particular conditions of the Bolshevik struggle for survival imposed the need to interpret the dictatorship function of the post-revolutionary state in terms of restricting the franchise. But Lenin was at pains to stress that this was a national–specific extension of a general principle, not a universal feature of the post-revolutionary state.

Other policies were an extension and deepening of a particular idea because of international conditions. The extension of the pro-cess of nationalization in June 1918 was the result of the con-sequences of Brest–Litovsk, accelerating a process that had been developing fitfully and gradually. The question of the elimination of money and the creation of an economy of direct exchange was the result of the civil war conditions, and was only rationalized after the event by Preobrazhensky and others as being a conscious decision taken on ideological grounds. Both the 1919 Party Programme and *The ABC of Communism* expressed the long-term goal of a moneyless economy, and an intermediate phase in which money would be essential:

> In the first period of transition from capitalism to communism, while communist production and distribution of products is not yet organised, it is impossible to abolish money . . . the All-Russian Communist Party strives towards the adoption of a series of measures which will render it possible to extend the field of operations without the aid of money, and which will lead to the abolition of money.[121]

The conditions of the civil war encouraged an identification of certain elements of crisis management with elements of full blown communism, and the monetary issue was one of these.

Other policies represented a readjustment, although within the general productivist framework. This is most obvious with regard to the turn towards the middle peasants in 1919. This "retreat" from the policy of class war (committees of poor peasants) was due to the recognition of the past failures of food procurement, but also an adjustment in light of the fact that many poor peasants had become middling peasants as a result of the revolutionary land settlement. The poor peasants retained a central role in Bolshevik strategy, particularly in creating collective and co-operative farms.

In short, it is impossible to generalize. Each policy initiative needs to be examined, paying close attention to the ideological and circumstantial matrix out of which it arose. The term "war communism" does appear to be a *post hoc*, artificial construct, concealing more than it reveals. However, the inherent ambiguity within the term itself, highlighting ideological and circumstantial features, may mean that the concept can be saved, although not in the form envisaged by Lenin et al. Of greater significance perhaps are the debates within the party generated by the experiences of governing during the civil war. Out of these, there emerged a new theoretical synthesis about the nature of socialism as a transitional society. It is to an analysis of this understanding of socialism that we must now turn.

War communism and Soviet socialism: a model of Soviet socialism?

By the end of the civil war the Bolshevik party had begun to refine its view of socialism, as the contact of their ideals with the reality of Russian society brought forth a new theoretical synthesis. But how did this interaction between theory and practice work. It can best be described as a dialectical process:

1) The general ideas and principles about the transition period, which were developed prior to the revolution, represented a loose framework within which there were many unresolved tensions and undeveloped ideas;

2) This framework acted as something of an ideological filter, which led the party leadership to favour some approaches at the expense of others, conditioning the choice of specific policies;

3) The application of these policies to the circumstances of the civil war helped to define the nature of the transitional society in two ways. First, it resolved many of the tensions within the Bolshevik understanding of socialism. Secondly, it provided a specific content/meaning for many of the rather vague principles in Bolshevik ideology.

From this process emerged the first definitive post-revolutionary theorization of the transition phase. The contested issue here concerns the extent to which this theoretical synthesis outlined below represents an historically and conceptually distinct view of socialism, or whether it forms the basis of the Soviet model of socialism which was to remain virtually unmodified until *perestroika*.

The theoretical basis of Soviet socialism: statism, technocracy, productivism and collectivism

Lenin, Bukharin and Trotsky all made significant contributions to theorizing the transition process, although there were differences between them. Additionally, these views were also subject to significant criticisms generated by factions within the Bolshevik party. The most significant theoretical writings from this period were: the

Party Programme of March 1919; *The ABC of Communism* (drafted by Bukharin and Preobrazhensky);[122] Lenin's "The Proletarian Revolution and the renegade Kautsky";[123] Bukharin's "The economics of the transition period";[124] Trotsky's *Terrorism and communism*.

The 1919 Party Programme was an update of the 1903 Programme, and occupied a central role in Bolshevik discourse, setting out the long-term perspectives of the party alongside its specific short-term policy commitments. *The ABC of Communism* was written as a means of popularizing and explaining the Programme in more depth. The other three pieces were partly derived from the ongoing polemic within the international socialist movement. Lenin, Trotsky and Bukharin continued their polemical struggle with their old adversary Karl Kautsky. Taken together, these works are highly significant. Amid a devastating, destructive civil war, the key Bolshevik theorists thought it essential to begin to theorize their experiences, to assert the ideological correctness of their stance in the light of stringent criticism from within and without, and also to reorient themselves on their journey from capitalism to communism.

Interpreting these texts is by no means straightforward though. Lih has convincingly demonstrated the problems with the existing views of *The ABC* currently in circulation.[125] Given the diverse ends to which these works were directed, and the shifting context within the civil war itself as the military struggle waxed and waned, it is possible to extract the essential features of the emerging orthodoxy concerning the shape of the transition period. The orthodoxy that emerged from this period was forged in the heat of the party's multiple struggles: ideological, polemical, military, political, cultural, survival.

The economics of Soviet socialism

It is clear that by 1921 the conception of socialism which held the upper hand in Bolshevik discourse lay on the modernizing, productivist, technocratic, rationalist wing of Marxism. Soviet socialism was conceptualized as a phase in which economic, social and political structures would be transformed, and in which maximum effort was devoted to a massive increase in the productive forces. Only in this way, through modernization, rapid large-scale industrialization and technological change, could domination over nature be brought about and the satisfaction of mankind's basic needs be met. Socialism, and by extension communism, was thus about transforming structures to enable mankind to dominate nature and finally be free. It was not about the creation of a society of relationships in which humanity would find unity and live in harmony with each other and with nature. Consequently, the transition phase had to adopt those policies that most quickly, effectively and efficiently expedited this transformation of the economic, social and political structures of Soviet society. As Bukharin wrote in *The ABC of Communism*:

> The communist method of production will signify an enormous development of productive forces. As a result, no worker in communist society will have to do as much work as of old. The working day will continually grow shorter, and people will be to an increasing extent freed from the chains imposed on them by nature. As soon as man is enabled to spend less time upon feeding and clothing himself, we will be able to devote more time to the work of mental development. Human culture will climb to heights never attained before. It will no longer be a class culture, but will become a genuinely human culture. Concurrently with the disappearance of man's tyranny over man, the tyranny of nature over man will vanish.[126]

This was freedom outside of labour, not through creative labour. Soviet socialism viewed leisure time as the "realm of freedom".

In this way, two critical notions became central to Soviet socialism:

1) The central objective of socialism was the maximization of productivity through the expansion of the productive forces;
2) The individual under socialism was defined as a bearer of labour-power, and the status of the individual under socialism was determined by their productive contribution.

Flowing from this productivist definition of socialism, the Bolsheviks posited a central role for the state, and for science and technology in this process. Enormous power was concentrated in the hands of the state to bring about this transformation. Enormous faith was vested in the ability of science and technology, of scientists and experts to achieve it. The technocratic dimension to Soviet social-ism arose from the contact of the Bolsheviks' own emphasis upon modernization and their rationalist tendencies with the realities of the cultural and technical backwardness of Russia. The statist aspect of Soviet socialism arose from a similar process. The devastation of civil war Russia – scarce resources, low levels of consciousness, wartime emergencies, the decimation of the proletariat – left the state as the main agent of social transformation. The Bolshevik conception of the dictatorship of the proletariat was underpinned with notions of centralism, coercion and hierarchy.

The theoretical rationale of this statist approach was provided by Bukharin in "Economics of the transition period". Bukharin, and Trotsky, adopted the view that the dictatorship of the proletariat required the growth of the most powerful state possible in order to effect the social transformation towards communism, so that a state-less society could emerge. This theme runs throughout Bukharin's "Economics", but has been most vividly put by Trotsky:

> . . . the road to socialism lies through a period of the highest possible intensification of the principle of the state . . . Just as a lamp before going out shoots up in a brilliant flame, so the state, before disappearing, assumes the form of the dictatorship of the proletariat, i.e. the most ruthless form of the state, *which embraces the life of the citizens authorita-tively in every direction.*[127] (my emphasis)

Bukharin set out the theoretical justification for viewing the state as the agent of social and economic transformation under socialism: "it is an active force, a functioning organisation that uses every means to strengthen the productive base upon which it arises".[128] He argued that, "The collective reason of the working class, in turn, is materially embodied in its highest and most universal organisation – in its state apparatus".[129] The proletarian state came to represent the "organised consciousness of society".[130] Bukharin went on to state what this would mean in practice:

> It is obviously necessary in a formal sense for the working class to adopt exactly the same method that the bourgeoisie

used during the epoch of state capitalism. In organisational terms that method consists of subordinating all proletarian organisations to the most universal organisation . . . to the Soviet state of the proletariat. The "statification" of the trade unions and the genuine statification of all proletarian mass organisations results from the innermost logic of the transformation process. Even the smallest cells of the workers' apparatus must be integrated into the general organisational process.[131]

The rationale for the universalization of state power in the transition period arose from the dual challenge posed by this phase: destroying the old and creating the new. Violence and coercion are required to destroy the forces of counter-revolution. The creation of the new requires an agent of "unity, organisation and construction".[132] The chaos of the revolutionary period, and the disparate nature of post-revolutionary proletarian consciousness requires the use of compulsion in the transitional period for all classes. Yet as the state is the organized consciousness of society, Bukharin argues that compulsion under the dictatorship of the proletariat is very different from that under a bourgeois dictatorship. It represents self-organization and self-discipline, not something imposed from outside,

> . . . discipline is not established by some outside force, but represents the collective will of all and is obligatory for each . . . In the transition period the working class experiences both self-regulation and coercion . . . all forms of proletarian compulsion, beginning with executions and ending with obligatory labour service, are methods of forging communist mankind out of the human material left by the capitalist epoch.[133]

This theoretical rationale of a universalized state power exerting compulsion over all social groups, and constructing a new society out of human bricks and mortar is best illustrated with reference to the question of the organization of labour.

The labour question – along with the increased use of technology in the productive process – was central to the raising of productivity. As Trotsky asserted:

> The whole of human history is the history of the organisation and education of collective man for labour, with the object of attaining a higher level of productivity.[134]

During the civil war, labour was brought under the direct control of the state. The autonomous agencies for defending workers' interests were subordinated to the state. Universal compulsory labour service was introduced, and labour was organized along militaristic lines. Strict labour discipline, one-man management, piece-rates were all imposed. All these developments were justified on the basis of the following. First, people were intrinsically lazy and needed discipline to work. Secondly, the task of construction was taking place in conditions of misery, poverty and chaos. Thirdly, there was an identification of the individual interests of the workers and the group interests of the unions with the overall collective interests of the class as a whole, represented by the state which was the embodiment of the collective reason of the working class. Trotsky related that:

> Naturally it is quite clear that the state must, by means of the bonus system, give the better workers better conditions of existence. But this not only does not include, but on the contrary presupposes, that the state and trade unions – without which the Soviet state will not build up industry – acquire new rights of some kind over the worker. The worker does not merely bargain with the Soviet state: no he is subordinated to the Soviet state, under its orders in every direction – for it is his state.[135]

Compulsion, militarization and other methods were,

> essential conditions in order to bind down the bourgeois anarchy, to secure socialisation of the means of production and labour and to reconstruct economic life on the basis of a single plan.[136]

By 1920/21 the foundations of the Soviet concept of socialism – productivist, collectivist, technocratic, constructivist, statist, class-based – had crystallized. On these foundations, there was beginning to be erected an edifice of features, the institutional architecture of the transition phase. The following features of socialism Soviet-style can be identified:

- state ownership and control of the economy;
- centralized allocation and direction of all resources;
- the abolition of market relations;
- the abolition of money and the replacement of trade with direct product exchange;
- the development of a single economic plan;
- the maximum use and application of science and technology in the productive process;
- one man, appointed, management in the factories.

What was unresolved in this concept of Soviet socialism at this point is the precise meaning of these terms. What form would centralization take? What forms would state control of the economy take? What role would the trade unions have? What type of planning? Who would undertake the planning? How would the agricultural sector be organized? Specifying the meaning of socialism in practice had yet to be established fully. Debates, conflicts and disputes still continued within the party, although very few groups or individuals challenged the dominant understanding of the transition phase. The differences were essentially concerned with the best means to achieve this.

The politics of Soviet socialism

The tensions in pre-revolutionary Bolshevik discourse on the nature of the dictatorship of the proletariat had begun to be resolved by 1920/21. The democratic impulse within *State and revolution* – popular participation and control in the processes of governing – had been displaced and redefined as the universalization of state power accentuated the impulse towards centralization, hierarchy, coercion and bureaucratization. The imperatives of raising productivity and winning the civil war meant a resolution of this tension *in practice* in favour of state power. Social organizations and popular participation became an adjunct of the latter, expediting the functions of the state. All social organizations and political institutions

– trade unions, local Soviets, Communist Youth League – were to become "transmission belts" for party policy. Democratic practices within state bodies – for example the Red Army – were ended and replaced with a return to discipline and hierarchy. Although there were nuanced differences between Lenin and other leaders (most notably Trotsky) over the scope and extent of popular participation, there was substantial consensus on the overall pattern of the distribution of power and authority between state and society.

The politics of the transition phase were dominated by the growth of centralization, bureaucratization, coercion, hierarchy and monism over local autonomy, accountability, popular participation and political pluralism. These developments were fed by the immediate context of war and chaos, but also by the low cultural and educational levels of the population, which presented a barrier to Lenin's vision of extensive popular participation in the administration of the country. The realities of the civil war intruded into this equation, pushing towards a resolution in favour of elitism, centralization and coercion. How was this theorized?

In terms of theoretical advances, the arena of politics remained rather undeveloped. The assumption of power by the proletariat, exercised by the party, did not produce any detailed theoretical pronouncements on the distribution of power under socialism. Indeed, Lenin argued in "The proletarian revolution and the renegade Kautsky" that it was necessary to draw a distinction between the form of state and the form of government. Once the rule of a class has been established, the form of government was an irrelevance. The role of the law, the division of powers between centre and locality, executive and legislative bodies received no detailed treatment.[137]

The general features of the politics of the dictatorship of the proletariat can be deduced from an examination of four main questions: the relationship between the state and the individual; the relationship between the state and society; the relationship between the state and the party, and the role of the party.

The identification of the state as the embodiment of the collective reason of the working class, combined with the underlying premise that individual self-realization came through self-transcendence created a system in which the individual could have no rights outside of or against the state. What emerged from the key texts of this period was a top-down approach, in which rights and freedoms were vested in the state, and delegated to individuals. The universalization of state power, the priority of the collective over the individual, overturned the notions of individual freedom within liberal discourse. Individuals could have no rights against the state. There was no autonomous sphere within which the state must not encroach. The law was not a means for defending the individual against state power:

> The revolutionary dictatorship of the proletariat is rule won and maintained by the use of violence by the proletariat against the bourgeoisie, rule that is unrestricted by any laws.[138]

Bolshevik ideology was concerned with the economic basis of the rights of the workers, not the "fictitious" freedoms arising from the legal and political rights that liberal democracy proclaimed. Freedoms under socialism concerned the freedoms of the proletariat as a class, not as individuals.

The relationship between state and society, and social organizations in particular, was more complex. The theoretical works attempted to maintain the balance between centralized elite direction and guidance on the one hand, and popular participation and control on the other. In Lenin's words,

> The Soviets are the direct organisation of the working and exploited people themselves, which helps them to organise and administer their own state in every possible way.[139]

In the 1919 Party Programme, there was a continued commitment to upgrade the role of the trade unions in the production process, in the midst of a wider debate within the party over their precise position within the system:

> Trade unions . . . must actually concentrate in their hands the management of the whole system of public economy as an economic unit . . . The participation of trade unions in the management of production and the attraction by them of the broad masses are the principal means to carry

on a struggle against bureaucracy in the economic apparatus of the Soviet state, and afford the opportunity of establishing real democratic control over the results of production.[140]

Yet these ideas of popular participation in the making and control of the system came into conflict with the universalization of state power, through which the state would use all resources, institutions and organizations to raise productivity, relegating social organizations to a subordinate role. The implications of this (although it had not been realized in practice at the end of the civil war) were that all organizations would be agencies of the state. No independent organizations outside of the state could exist. The unresolved issue concerned the degree of autonomy that different organizations might acquire and exercise within this statized system. The precise role, functions, structure and composition of these social and political organizations – trade unions, Soviets, *Komsomol* – remained to be resolved.

Finally, the role of the party. Trotsky expresses the reasons for the development of political monism and the gradual transformation of the Soviets into transmission belts rather than organs of local and national power:

> The exclusive role of the Communist Party under the conditions of a victorious proletarian revolution is quite comprehensible. The question is of the dictatorship of a class. In the composition of that class there enter various elements, heterogenous moods, different levels of development. Yet the dictatorship presupposes unity of will, unity of direction, unity of action . . . The revolutionary supremacy of the proletariat presupposes within the proletariat itself the political supremacy of a party, with a clear programme of action and a faultless internal discipline . . . We have more than once been accused of having substituted for the dictatorship of the Soviets the dictatorship of our party. Yet it can be said with complete justice that the dictatorship of the soviets became possible only by means of the dictatorship of the party. It is thanks to the clarity of its theoretical vision and its strong revolutionary organisation that the party has afforded to the soviets the possibility of becoming

transformed from the shapeless parliaments of labour into the apparatus of the supremacy of labour. In this substitution of the power of the party for the power of the working class there is nothing accidental, and in reality there is no substitution at all. *The communists express the fundamental interests of the working class.*[141] (my emphasis)

The role of the party in the post-revolutionary system was becoming clearer. The party was to exercise leadership and general control over the path of development. It would develop the programme to be followed and would guide the activities of all state bodies through the work of communist members within them. The monopoly position of the communist party was justified on the basis of the following propositions:

- political parties express the interests of a class;
- the proletariat has a homogenous, fundamental set of interests;
- these interests are expressed by the communist party, as it alone expresses the course of historical development;
- there is no justification for other socialist parties;
- guaranteeing the dominance of the communist party will guarantee the predominance of the proletariat and the realization of the fundamental interests of the working masses;
- the form of this government does not alter the fact of the rule of the proletariat, albeit through the communist party;

It was emphasized that the party was not to administer, but to guide and provide leadership. Administration would be the task of the different state organizations.

From this analysis, the theoretical basis for the dictatorship of the party was becoming evident. The socio-economic and cultural reasons for this are well known. In theoretical terms, it could be summarized thus:

1) Communist party expresses the fundamental interests of the workers.
2) The Soviet state embodies the collective reason of the working class.

3) The dictatorship of the proletariat = the supremacy of the Soviet state = the dictatorship of the communist party. QED!

The general contours of the politics of Soviet socialism, of the dictatorship of the proletariat, represented the predominance of state power, centralization, coercion and terror, monism and a tendency to favour technocratic approaches. The tendency towards popular participation, democracy, local autonomy had been eroded during the entire post-1917 period, although it retained a significant place in the party programme, emphasizing the persistence of the democratic impulse in Bolshevik discourse and the attempts of Lenin in particular to synthesize communist direction and leadership with the participation of a society with a low cultural and educational level.

What remained unresolved in this sphere concerned the relationship between the party and the state organizations (Soviets, trade unions, etc.). How could the party lead and guide, without interfering in the day-to-day work of these institutions? How could the problem of bureaucratization be countered? How could the balance between democracy and centralism within the party be maintained?

Socio-cultural aspects of Soviet socialism

The socio-cultural sphere was viewed in instrumental terms by the Bolshevik leadership. The struggle between the desire to emancipate and liberate, to realize justice and equality, and the urge to subordinate everything to the wider goal of constructing the material and technical basis of socialism was resolved firmly in favour of the latter. Wage inequality was fostered to reward the experts and those engaged in essential work during the civil war. Gender equality was promoted in order to liberate women to contribute to the process of increasing production, rather than removing the bases of exploitation *per se*. Cultural policy was designed to equip the workers for the demands of a technologically advanced economy.

Not only was it instrumentalist, it was also constructivist. The party sought to create a socialist society by moulding the consciousness, worldview, morality and outlook of the Soviet people. This had the benefit of destroying the basis of non-socialist thinking. Atheism was propagated. The education system was imbued with socialist ideas. Morality was based on class notions. The press was dominated by the norms of Soviet-style socialism. The Bolsheviks sought to remake individuals, and in so doing to remake the world.

Conclusion

The emerging model of Soviet socialism represented the victory of rationalism, collectivism, productivism and technocracy over the tendency towards democracy, libertarianism, moralism and egalitarianism.[142] Yet it would be wrong to overstate this point at this stage. Two points in particular need to be added.

First, Lenin himself was acutely aware of the problems of bureaucratization and centralization, and of the importance of mass participation in the administration of the system. The problems of cultural and economic backwardness accentuated the elitist and hierarchical nature of the Soviet state. But the importance of mass participation was a central concern of Lenin's. Secondly, there continued to exist within the party a number of groups or factions, whose specific concerns about the development of the system after 1917 were at a deeper level articulating alternative conceptions of socialism. The Democratic Centralists (greater democracy within the party), the Workers' Opposition (revival of the Soviets as functioning democratic organizations and genuine workers' control in industry), the Military Opposition (democratization in the army), all expressed the yearning for greater democracy and egalitarianism within the system. In subsequent Soviet history, these ideas were to become the basis for movements to reform the system. At the end of the civil war though, the technocratic tendency held the upper hand.

It is often argued that the system underwent something of a sea-change in the period after March 1921 with the adoption of the New Economic Policy (NEP hereafter). The extent to which NEP represents an alternative model of Soviet socialism, or merely a shift in emphasis within the parameters of the model of Soviet socialism is a matter of some dispute. It is to this question that we must now turn.

Notes

1. See B. Lincoln, *Red victory* (New York: Simon & Schuster, 1990); G. Swain, *The origins of the Russian civil war* (London: Longman, 1996); O. Figes, *Peasant Russia, civil war* (Oxford: Oxford University Press, 1990).

2. L. Siegelbaum, *Soviet state and society between revolutions 1918–29* (Cambridge: Cambridge University Press, 1992), p. 66.

3. The best survey of views, with a perceptive analysis, is S. Malle, *The economic organisation of War Communism* (Cambridge: Cambridge University Press, 1985), pp. 1–28. See also P. J. Boettke, *The political economy of socalism: the formative years, 1918–28* (Boston: Kluwer, 1990). By the same author, "The Soviet experiment with pure communism", in *Critical Review* **2**(4), 1988, pp. 149–82.

4. M. Dobb, *Soviet economic development since 1917* (New York: International Publishers, 1948).

5. M. Malia, *The Soviet tragedy: a history of socialism in Russia* (New York: Free Press, 1994), pp. 127–32.

6. O. Figes, *A people's tragedy. The Russian revolution 1891–1924* (London: Pimlico, 1997), pp. 612–15.

7. B. Patenaude, "Peasants into Russians: the utopian essence of war communism", in *The Russian Review*, vol. 54, October 1995, pp. 552–70. See also the subsequent exchange in ibid., vol. 55, July 1996, pp. 494–7.

8. On economics, see A. Nove, *An economic history of the USSR* (Harmondsworth: Penguin, 1992), pp. 46–82; E. H. Carr, *The Bolshevik revolution 1917–23*, vol. 2 (London: Pelican, 1966), pp. 151–279; Malle, *The economic organisation of war communism*; T. Remington, *Building socialism in Bolshevik Russia* (Pittsburgh: University of Pittsburgh Press, 1984); Siegelbaum, *Soviet state and society between revolutions*; M. Lewin, *Political undercurrents in Soviet economic debates* (London: Pluto Press, 1975), pp. 73–84; M. Dobb, *Soviet economic development* (London: Routledge, 1966).

9. Y. Akhapkin, *First decrees of Soviet power* (London: Lawrence & Wishart, 1970), pp. 147–53.

10. Ibid., p. 151.

11. Malle, *The economic organization of war communism*, pp. 63–7.

12. Carr, *The Bolshevik revolution*, vol. 2, pp. 179–82.

13. Ibid., p. 180.

14. Ibid., p. 181.

15. Nove, *An economic history of the USSR*, p. 70.

16. Carr, *The Bolshevik revolution*, vol. 2, pp. 181–5.

17. Malle, *The economic organisation of war communism*, pp. 255–67.

18. The details on the divisions of enterprises, and the conflicts between *glavkism* and *sovnarkhozy* can be found in Remington, *Building socialism in Bolshevik Russia*, pp. 72–4.

19. For distribution, see Nove, *An economic history of the USSR*, pp. 59–71; Carr, *The Bolshevik revolution*, vol. 2, pp. 229–46.

20. Nove, *An economic history of the USSR*, pp. 63–7.

21. Carr, *The Bolshevik revolution*, vol. 2, pp. 229–36.

22. Malle, *The economic organisation of war communism*, pp. 128–42; Remington, *Building socialism in Bolshevik Russia*, pp. 92–101.

23. Carr, *The Bolshevik revolution*, vol. 2, p. 186.

24. Ibid., pp. 190–94; Remington, *Building socialism in Bolshevik Russia*, pp. 116–17; Malle, *The economic organisation of war communism*, p. 142.

25. Carr, *The Bolshevik revolution*, vol. 2, pp. 190–4.

26. Lenin made this point forcefully in his speech to the third All-Russian Congress of Councils of the National Economy, cited in ibid., p. 192.

27. Remington, *Building socialism in Bolshevik Russia*, p. 87.

28. A brief survey of the discussion can be found in R. Service, *Lenin: a political life*, vol. 3, pp. 162–6.

29. Carr, *The Bolshevik revolution*, vol. 2, p. 194; Nove, *An economic history of the USSR*, p. 72.

30. Carr, *The Bolshevik revolution*, vol. 2, pp. 200–1.

31. This quotation is from the new Party Programme of the RCP, adopted at the 8th Party Congress from 18–23 March 1919, pp. 144–5. The full text can be found in *Soviet communism: programs and rules* (San Diego: Chandler, 1962); J. F. Triska (ed.), pp. 130–53.

32. Carr, *The Bolshevik revolution*, vol. 2, p. 208.

33. Ibid., p. 211.

34. R. Pipes, *The Russian revolution 1899–1919* (London: Harvill Collins, 1990), pp. 832–7.

35. W. Chase, Voluntarism, Mobilisation and Coercion: *Subbotniki* 1919–21, *Soviet Studies* **41**, 1989, pp. 111–28.

36. Service, *Lenin: A political life*, p. 106.

37. Figes, *A people's tragedy*, pp. 720–2.

38. L. Trotsky, *Terrorism and communism* (London: New Park Publications, 1975), p. 151.

39. Service, *Lenin: A political life*, p. 107.

40. Figes, *A people's tragedy*, p. 723.

41. Ibid., pp. 152–6, 161–6.

42. See the entire chapter, "Problems of the organisation of labour", pp. 140–82, in Trotsky, *Terrorism and Communism*.

43. A good, brief discussion of the Workers' Opposition can be found in Siegelbaum, *Soviet state and society between revolutions*, pp. 79–83. This summarizes a number of different positions taken by western

scholars. See also R. V. Daniels, *The conscience of the revolution* (Cambridge, Mass.: Harvard University Press, 1960).

44. A good summary can be found in Service, *Lenin: A political life*, pp. 154–6.

45. Details on Taylorism and Bolshevism can be found in Remington, *Building socialism in Bolshevik Russia*, pp. 136–45; K. Bailes, "Alexei Gastev and the Soviet controversy over Taylorism, 1918–24", *Soviet Studies* **29**(3), 1977, pp. 373–94; Z. Sochor, "Soviet Taylorism revisited", *Soviet Studies* **33**(2), 1981, pp. 246–64; S. Smith, "Taylorism rules OK? Bolshevism, Taylorism and the technical intelligentsia in the Soviet Union, 1917–41", *Radical Science Journal* **13**, 1983, pp. 5–27.

46. Cited in Smith, *Taylorism rules OK?* p. 13.

47. Sochor, *Soviet Taylorism revisited*, p. 248.

48. A good overview of the conflicts between Lenin and Bogdanov can be found in P. Scheibert, "Lenin, Bogdanov and the concept of proletarian culture", in B. Eissenstat (ed.), *Lenin and Leninism* (Lexington: Lexington Books, 1971), pp. 43–57.

49. Bailes, *Alexei Gastev*, pp. 374–81.

50. Remington, *Building socialism in Bolshevik Russia*, pp. 136–45.

51. Remington, *Building socialism in Bolshevik Russia*, pp. 131–6; Carr, *The Bolshevik revolution*, vol. 2, pp. 369–73.

52. Lenin, "Report of the All-Russia Central Executive Committee to the Eighth Congress of Soviets, 22 December 1920", in *Selected works*, vol. 3, pp. 495–521.

53. Ibid., p. 519.

54. Lenin spoke of this in *State and revolution* prior to 1917. See ch. 1.

55. G. Guroff, "Lenin and Russian economic thought: the problem of central planning", in B. Eissenstat (ed.), *Lenin and Leninism* (Lexington: Lexington Books, 1971), p. 202.

56. Carr, *The Bolshevik revolution*, vol. 2, pp. 358–73 is excellent on the debates in the party.

57. Ibid., pp. 373–4.

58. Agricultural policy is analyzed in Pipes, *The Russian revolution 1899–1919*, pp. 714–44; D. Atkinson, *The end of the Russian land commune 1905–1930* (Stanford: Stanford University Press, 1983), pp. 189–230; Nove, *An economic history of the USSR*, pp. 59–63; Siegelbaum, *Soviet state and society between revolutions*, pp. 38–50; L. Lih, "Bolshevik razverstka and war communism", *Slavic Review* **45**, 1986, pp. 673–88.

59. Patenaude, "Peasants into Russians", p. 554.

60. Ibid., p. 554.

61. Ibid., p. 555–6.

62. Lih, *Bolshevik razverstka*, pp. 674–8.

63. Ibid., pp. 676–80.
64. Details can be found in Atkinson, *The end of the Russian land commune*, pp. 206–23.
65. Ibid., pp. 218–23.
66. Figes, *A People's Tragedy*, pp. 729–30.
67. Ibid., p. 730.
68. For a good discussion on the civil war in western historiography, see S. Fitzpatrick, "New perspectives on the civil war", in *Party, state and society in the Russian civil war*, D. Koenker et al. (eds) (Bloomington: Indiana University Press, 1989), pp. 3–23.
69. Details of the decree and other measures can be found in Pipes, *The Russian revolution*, pp. 816–22.
70. Cited in Carr, *The Bolshevik revolution*, vol. 1, p. 175.
71. Cited in G. Hosking, *A History of the Soviet Union* (London: Fontana, 1992), p. 70.
72. Ibid., p. 71.
73. Service, *Lenin: A political life*, p. 291; Trotsky, *Terrorism and Communism*, is probably the most forthright exposition of this viewpoint.
74. See G. Leggett, *The Cheka: Lenin's political police* (Oxford: Oxford University Press, 1981); Figes, *A People's Tragedy*, pp. 627–49.
75. M. Von Hagen, "Civil-military relations and the evolution of the Soviet socialist state", *Slavic Review* **50**(2), 1991, pp. 268–76.
76. See S. Fitzpatrick, The legacy of the civil war, pp. 385–99, and D. Orlovsky, "State-building in the civil war era: the lower middle strata", in *Party, state and society*, Koenker et al. (eds), pp. 180–209.
77. M. Lewin, "The civil war: dynamics and legacy", in ibid., p. 403.
78. M. Liebman, *Leninism under Lenin* (London: Jonathan Cape, 1975), p. 285.
79. M. McAuley, *Politics and the Soviet Union* (Harmondsworth: Penguin, 1979), pp. 58–79.
80. Carr, *The Bolshevik revolution*, vol. 1, pp. 191–219; L. Schapiro, *The communist party of the Soviet Union* (London: Methuen, 1970), pp. 180–200.
81. An excellent overview of the changes in the party's internal structures is Schapiro, *The communist party of the Soviet Union*, pp. 235–55.
82. Ibid., pp. 248–50.
83. R. Gregor (ed.), *Resolutions and Decisions of the CPSU, vol. 2, 1917–29* (Toronto: University of Toronto Press, 1974), p. 88.
84. Schapiro, *The communist party of the Soviet Union*, pp. 248–9.
85. Ibid., pp. 195–6. More details on the fate of the Mensheviks, srs and other parties can be found in L. Schapiro, *The origins of the communist autocracy* (London: Macmillan, 1977).
86. Siegelbaum, *Soviet state and society between revolutions*, pp. 22–3.
87. Figes, *A people's tragedy*, pp. 682–96.

88. V. I. Lenin, Report of the All-Russia Central Executive Committee to eighth Congress of Soviets, in *Selected works*, vol. 2 (Moscow: Progress, 1971), p. 517.

89. Ibid., p. 517.

90. Fitzpatrick, "The legacy of the civil war", in Koenker et al. (ed.), *Party, state and society*, p. 416.

91. Figes, *A people's tragedy*, p. 688.

92. Read, *From Tsar to Soviets*, pp. 211–18, 238–44.

93. The continued existence and tenacity of the democratic, emancipatory impulse can be seen from the 1919 party programme which was ratified at the eighth party Congress. See, Gregor, *Resolutions and decisions of the CPSU*, vol. 2, pp. 54–72. For a commentary, see Daniels, *Conscience of the revolution*, ch. 4.

94. E. A. Rees, *State control in Soviet Russia: the rise and fall of the Workers' and Peasants' Inspectorate, 1920–34* (London: Macmillan, 1987); J. Adams, *Citizen inspectors in the Soviet Union. The People's Control Committee* (New York: Praeger, 1977), pp. 21–8.

95. M. Matthews, *Privilege in the Soviet Union* (London: Allen & Unwin, 1978), pp. 60–70.

96. Ibid., p. 65.

97. Ibid., p. 73.

98. Ibid., pp. 68–78.

99. B. Clements, "The utopianism of the zhenotdel", *Slavic Review* **51**(2), 1992, pp. 483–96; G. Lapidus, "Sexual equality in Soviet policy: a developmental perspective", in *Women in Russia*, D. Atkinson et al. (eds) (Hassocks: Harvester Press, 1978), pp. 115–38; M. Buckley, *Women and ideology in the Soviet Union* (Hemel Hempstead: Harvester Wheatsheaf, 1989).

100. M. Buckley, *Women and ideology in the Soviet Union*, pp. 65–9.

101. B. Clements, "The utopianism of the zhenotdel", p. 488.

102. Ibid., pp. 483–90.

103. There are a number of good works on Bogdanov, and also cultural policy in general. See C. Read, *Culture and power in revolutionary Russia* (London: Macmillan, 1990); S. Fitzpatrick, "The 'soft' line on culture and its enemies: Soviet cultural policy, 1922–27", *Slavic Review* **33**, 1974, pp. 267–87; S. Fitzpatrick, "The Bolsheviks' dilemma: class, culture and politics in early Soviet years", *Slavic Review* **47**, 1988, pp. 599–613; A. Gleason et al. (ed.), *Bolshevik culture* (Bloomington: Indiana University Press, 1985); J. McClelland, "Utopianism versus revolutionary heroism in Bolshevik policy: the proletarian culture debate", in *Slavic Review* **40**, 1980, pp. 403–25; P. Scheibert, "Lenin, Bogdanov and the concept of proletarian culture", in *Lenin and Leninism*, B. Eissenstat (ed.) (Lexington: Lexington Books, 1971).

104. J. McClelland, "Utopianism versus revolutionary heroism", pp. 410–11.

105. Ibid., pp. 410–11.
106. P. Scheibert, "Lenin, Bogdanov and the concept of proletarian culture", pp. 51–3.
107. J. McClelland, "Utopianism versus revolutionary heroism", pp. 421–5.
108. Service, *Lenin: a political life*, pp. 149–50.
109. S. Fitzpatrick, *The Commissariat of Enlightenment: Soviet organisation of education and the arts under Lunacharsky* (Cambridge: Cambridge University Press, 1970); Pipes, *Russia under the Bolshevik regime 1919–24*, pp. 284–7.
110. J. McLelland, "Utopianism versus revolutionary heroism", p. 425; S. Fitzpatrick, "The 'soft' line on culture", pp. 267–78.
111. Pipes, *Russia under the Bolshevik regime 1919–24*, pp. 340–6.
112. Ibid., pp. 325–8.
113. Nove, *An economic history of the USSR*, pp. 74–82; M. Lewin, *Political undercurrents in Soviet economic debates*, pp. 83–4; Malle, *The economic organization of war communism*, pp. 495–515; Szamuely, *First models of socialist economic systems*, pp. 10–22.
114. Cited in Malle, *The economic organisation of war communism*, p. 9.
115. Ibid., pp. 9–11.
116. Nove, *An economic history of the USSR*, p. 78.
117. Szamuely, *First models of socialist economic systems*, pp. 23–8.
118. Boettke, "The Soviet experiment with pure communism", p. 159.
119. Siegelbaum, *Soviet state and society between revolutions*, pp. 63–6.
120. Ibid., p. 66.
121. *1919 programme of communist party*, p. 149.
122. N. Bukharin & E. Preobrazhensky, *The ABC of communism* (Harmondsworth: Penguin, 1969). For a stimulating treatment of this text, see Lars T. Lih, "The mystery of the ABC", *Slavic Review* **56**(1), 1997, pp. 50–72.
123. V. I. Lenin, "The proletarian revolution and the renegade Kautsky", in *Selected works*, vol. 3, pp. 65–149.
124. N. Bukarin, *Selected writings on the state and the transition to socialism*, R. B. Day (ed.) (New York: M. E. Sharpe, 1982).
125. Lih, "The mystery", pp. 50–1.
126. Bukharin & Preobrazhensky, *ABC of communism*, p. 121.
127. Trotsky, *Terrorism and communism*, p. 77.
128. Bukharin, "Economics of the transition period", in Day, *Selected writings on the state*, p. 46.
129. Ibid., p. 57.
130. R. B. Day, "Introduction", in ibid., p. 4.
131. Ibid., pp. 56–7.
132. Ibid., p. 76.
133. Ibid., p. 78.

134. Trotsky, *Terrorism and communism*, p. 155.
135. Ibid., p. 176.
136. Ibid., p. 151.
137. Lenin, "Proletarian revolution and the renegade Kautsky", pp. 71–86.
138. Ibid., p. 75.
139. Ibid., p. 84.
140. *1919 programme of communist party*, p. 144.
141. Trotsky, *Terrorism and communism*, pp. 122–3.
142. A good overview of these developments can be found in N. Harding, "Socialism, society and the organic labour state", in *The state in socialist society*, N. Harding (ed.) (New York: Albany, 1984), pp. 15–38.

CHAPTER FOUR

NEP and Soviet socialism: departing from orthodoxy?

The end of the civil war brought the first respite for the Bolshevik leadership from armed conflict. Yet social peace remained elusive, and the prospects for constructing a socialist society looked bleak. The economy was devastated, the urban population hungry and restless, the countryside rebellious and resentful, the infrastructure collapsing and international revolution receding over the horizon. In the midst of these events, the leadership were confronted with a profoundly disturbing rebellion at the Kronstadt naval base.[1] This rebellion, carried out by a group which had been a core part of the revolutionary vanguard of 1917, presented a deep-rooted political and ideological challenge to the legitimacy of Bolshevik rule. It was against this background that the party met at its 10th Congress and introduced the NEP (New Economic Policy) and the resolution "On Party Unity".

A great deal has been written about NEP.[2] At the time it provoked controversy because of the apparent turn away from socialism and the restoration of capitalism implied by its policies. It has provoked controversy subsequently because historians have debated the inevitability or otherwise of Stalinism, and have seen in NEP an alternative model for the construction of socialism. Yet the meaning and significance of NEP remain deeply contested. Was it a departure from the Bolshevik understanding of the transitional phase, or was it merely a shift of emphasis, which affirmed the basic principles but

151

differed in its interpretation or implementation? This has not been a purely academic debate. The early years of *perestroika* saw a conscious attempt by Gorbachev to redefine Soviet socialism. The example of NEP – defined *pace* Lenin as "a radical modification in our whole outlook on socialism" – was used to legitimize Gorbachev's project by disassociating it from the Stalinist–Brezhnevite model.[3]

The genesis of NEP

Although the 10th Party Congress is traditionally viewed as the inaugural point of NEP, this is a little misleading. NEP evolved fitfully during 1921 and 1922. It was not a ready-made package of measures implemented all at once. It was at the 10th Party Congress, however, that the initial moves – the introduction of the *prodnalog* or tax-in-kind to replace the requisitioning of grain from the peasantry – were brought in. This move had been mooted before. In February 1920, Trotsky had suggested that the problem of bread shortages could best be solved by ending forced requisitioning of grain in favour of a return to private trade (albeit in selected areas of the country: Ukraine, the Don, Siberia).[4] He was defeated in the CC by eleven votes to four, and was severely criticized by Lenin for wanting to restore private trade.[5]

Exactly a year later, the proposal re-emerged. The catalyst for this was the end of the civil war, which brought in its wake both a review of the state of the country and social unrest. The conclusion to the armed conflict abruptly destroyed the fragile support for the Bolsheviks among the Russian population. No longer benefiting from being the lesser of two evils, social strife erupted. Urban and rural Russia were in turmoil. The Kronstadt sailors were threatening to join with restless workers in Petrograd. The resolution of the food issue became a matter of political survival, and it was this that placed it in the forefront of party policy. A *rapprochement* between the state and the peasantry was crucial to the survival of Bolshevism. Would the Bolsheviks be willing to abandon requisitioning in favour of a restoration of (limited) market relations, and by extension of capitalism? A clandestine and contentious debate ensued within the party in February and March 1921. The first full discussion took place in the Politburo meeting of 8 February.[6]

The premise was a simple one. In order to increase production it was necessary to give the peasants an incentive to work harder. By replacing the forcible requisitioning with a tax, levied in kind, and set below the level of the state procurement quota, it left the peasants with a surplus to dispose of as they wished. The higher their production, the greater their surplus. The leadership proceeded cautiously, aware of the ideological dilemmas raised by the *prodnalog*. The discussion turned on the disposal of the surplus. Lenin initially envisaged the emergence of "local economic exchange" (i.e. a local, limited market where peasants could receive industrial goods in exchange for their produce). There was no intention to restore market relations to the economy as a whole. A Politburo commission, set up on 19 February, deliberated on technical aspects of the food tax. The commission, composed of some individuals unsympathetic to the new turn,

> proceeded to excise "local economic exchange" from Kamenev's earlier draft. Their aim was to restrict the peasants to bartering with the People's Commissariat of Food Supplies, which had access to the warehouses of the state-owned factories . . . An entire economy run from Moscow remained the objective.[7]

The return of "local economic exchange" to the final draft was guaranteed when Lenin became personally involved in its drafting, as popular rebellions increased during early March.[8] These deliberations demonstrate the tenacity of Bolshevik principles on the shape of a socialist economy – statist, centralist, non-market – as well as the continued disputes and debates within the party. In spite of the clear determination of the leadership to hedge this in with limitations, the *prodnalog* quickly snowballed, transforming the socio-economic landscape of Russia.

The economics of NEP

Prodnalog, *food policy and the agricultural sector*

On 15 March 1921 at the 10th Party Congress the resolution "On the replacement of requisitions with a tax-in-kind" was passed. The central parts of the decree outlined the following:

- in order to ensure a correct and tranquil working of the land on the basis of greater freedom on the part of the farmer to dispose of his economic resources, to strengthen his peasant holdings and raise their productivity . . . the requisitions, as a means of state procurements of food, raw materials and forage are replaced by a tax-in-kind.
- the tax is to be lower than the amount levied by the requisitions.
- the tax is to be a progressive one. Hardworking peasant proprietors who increase the sown area of their holdings, or who increase the productivity of their holdings as a whole, are granted advantages in the payment of the tax-in-kind.
- all stocks of food, raw materials and forage that remain in the possession of the farmers after they have paid their taxes are completely at their disposal and can be used by them to improve and strengthen their holdings, to increase personal consumption and to obtain, in exchange, products of factory and cottage industry and agricultural produce. Exchanges are permitted within the bounds of the local economic turnover.[9]

The resolution was passed, although not without some disquiet. The full extent of this disquiet only became apparent two months later at the 10th Party Conference in May 1921, when the party had a full and frank debate. How did Lenin theorize this policy shift?

From Lenin's two speeches (10th Congress and 10th Conference), and his pamphlet – "On the tax-in-kind" sandwiched in between – it is clear that he was attempting to defend it on both political and economic grounds.[10] For Lenin, it was necessary to defend the revolution, to get the economy working, and to effect the transition to socialism. The emphasis in Lenin's writings and speeches shifted subtly according to the context and the audience. In the initial report to the 10th Party Congress, Lenin emphasized the political benefits of NEP, of its political expediency, "we know that as long as there is no revolution in other countries, only agreement with the peasantry can save the revolution in Russia".[11] The need to establish an economic alliance (*smychka*) between the mass of the peasantry and the proletariat dictated a shift in the nature of the economy, "we must adapt our state economy to the economy of the middle peasant".[12] The emphasis lay upon satisfying the disgruntled peasantry, and creating an economic breathing-space for the restoration of the country.

By the time Lenin came to write his pamphlet, and even more so by the 10th Party Conference, Lenin had begun to theorize this move in order to defend it from the growing criticism within the party. Less was made of "adapting" to the demands of the peasantry, than to the immediacy and pragmatism of a "breathing-space". In "On the tax-in-kind", Lenin attempted to demonstrate that NEP stood full square within the Bolshevik post-revolutionary economic approach to the construction of socialism. Lenin talked of a return to the construction of "state capitalism" (à la May 1918), which would advance Russia towards socialism. State capitalism would help to eradicate petty capitalism, and lay the basis for large-scale production. By creating a food policy that restored economic exchange between town and country, this would assist industrial growth and thus restore large-scale industry.[13] At the 10th Conference, faced with vehement criticism, Lenin reiterated the ideological rectitude of NEP. Here Lenin described NEP as a "stepping-stone to further measures".[14] What were these measures? To restore large-scale industry, which would create the material basis for socialism, and for the development of proletarian class-consciousness. This could only be achieved by accumulating stocks of food. Increasing food production required incentives for the peasant to produce more, and goods for the peasant to buy. The long-term goal had not changed one iota. In the interim, the peasant (and light industry) were to be placed in the forefront of party policy.[15] This shift in Lenin's public utterances illustrates the dilemma facing the Bolsheviks: how could a successfully functioning economy be restored while demonstrating progress towards the construction of socialism?

Lenin's line prevailed. But unease lingered in the party. The wider theoretical issues relating to Lenin's writings about the food tax will be explored below. Suffice to note at this point that Lenin argued that capitalist relations could be combined with proletarian state power. The key point, he noted, was the extent. Could the state limit exchange, and prevent the wholesale restoration of the market? The initial intention was that centralized statist control of the economy could be maintained by bartering manufactured goods for the peasant surplus. The progress of NEP after its introduction testify to the difficulty the party had in controlling the "genie" of petty capitalism. Not only did it transform the agricultural sector, but it also had far-reaching consequences for the industrial sector.

The immediate benefits were political rather than economic. The countryside retreated from open rebellion, and began to return to their farms. However, the accumulation of grain by the Bolsheviks was undermined by a severe drought in the spring of 1921. The aim had been to acquire 240 million *puds* of grain via the *prodnalog*, with a further 160 million acquired through barter exchange. Only 128 million *puds* were brought in through the tax; none via barter.[16] After 1921, the economic ramifications were enormous, bringing ideological conundrums in their wake.

Economic exchange stubbornly refused to remain "local". Unable to provide sufficient manufactured goods, private trade in agricultural produce mushroomed. By 1924, the *prodnalog* had been replaced by a monetary tax. Market relations sprung up. Private traders (the so-called NEPmen) emerged. Money returned. The whole atmosphere of rural Russia was overturned as buying, selling, bartering and exchange were revived. A notable feature of this period was the growth of co-operative trading, which was greatly encouraged by the party as a means of implanting collectivist practices into the countryside.[17]

The growth of private trade, and the incentives this gave to peasant productivity had further ramifications. First, it threw traditional Bolshevik class analysis into further disarray. The poor peasants had been viewed as the allies of the proletariat; the rich *kulaks* their enemies. The middle peasants were to be tolerated. But given the encouragement within NEP for peasants to increase their output, this would increase the numbers and wealth of the middle peasants and *kulaks*. Restricting their economic activities would undermine the whole thrust of NEP. This dilemma vexed the party throughout the 1920s.

Secondly, the land tenure situation was formalized with the adoption of the Land Code which became operational on 1 December 1922.[18] This reinforced the abolition of private ownership of land, as all land was the property of the state. However, the form of land tenure exercised by the peasantry was left open to the discretion of the peasantry. While the state framed the code so as to encourage the peasant household (the basic unit) to transfer to collective forms of tenure, it was still possible for individuals to consolidate their landholdings. This latter practice (along with leasing of land and hiring of labour) became increasingly prevalent, running counter to the Bolshevik ideals of a collectivized, large-scale, modernized and mechanized agricultural sector. Indeed, NEP seemed to be creating a fragmented, archaic, quasi-medieval system.

The industrial sector: trustification and commercialization

The ripples caused by NEP extended beyond the waters of rural Russia. Placing the peasant at the centre of economic policy effected changes in the structure, organization and operating principles of Soviet industry. The most notable changes encompassed a higher priority for small and light industry, a shift towards commercial principles (production for the market, profit and loss indicators), and a greater degree of autonomy for enterprises in managing their affairs, acquiring supplies, dealing with employees and so on.[19]

The priority of supplying goods in exchange for peasant produce led to the restoration of market relations and a shift in emphasis from large-scale state heavy industry, towards small and medium-sized firms producing for the market. In the period after March 1921, a greater degree of diversity returned to the industrial sector. Nationalization remained the overwhelming form of ownership. Yet there was a realization that the attempts to nationalize all manufacturing enterprises were erroneous. Following a decree of 17 May 1921, the industrial sector comprised:

- the "Commanding Heights" of the economy (banking, transport, foreign trade, large-scale strategic industry) still in state hands.
- many state enterprises, especially those under the jurisdiction of local economic councils that were in some difficulty, were leased, at times to private entrepreneurs, but more often to co-operatives and other forms.
- some small firms, which had not been nationalized prior to 17 May 1921, were returned to private ownership.[20]

These changes aimed to restore flexibility to the sector, fostering a more consumer-oriented approach, but also to restore *expertise*.

Lenin was typically blunt on this point. Communists had to "learn to trade".[21] Without this the restoration of the economy was impossible.

The growth of the market and the return of money as the unit of exchange slowly dissolved the operating principles of civil war economics. During the summer of 1921, the bureaucratic edifice of wartime supply was dismantled. The centralized supply of raw materials, fuel, the practice of producing to order, and the payment of wages in kind, rationing and so on were all deemed to be incompatible with the new commercialism of NEP. In August 1921, there were the first moves towards this with the adoption of the policy of *khozraschet* (profit and loss accounting). This decentralized economic decision-making to the enterprises themselves. They were given the scope to acquire raw materials themselves, and to sell their products on the market. Internally, enterprises were to operate on the basis of profitability, paying workers wages, shedding excess labour and forcing them to become financially autonomous. Hard budget constraints had arrived.[22]

Financial autonomy in turn affected the organizational structure of the economy. A conscious retreat from the mindset that treated the industrial sector like the post office, or a single large firm was apparent. The major initiative in this area saw the creation of "trusts". "Trusts" were a group of enterprises (be they factories, mines, etc.) engaged in a similar field of production, which became fused into one entity. Part of the rationale for this process of trustification, according to Carr, was to cushion the switch to *khozraschet*, by allowing for rationalization within larger units that could better absorb downturns in production, redundancies and so on.[23] From the end of 1921 to March 1923, 478 trusts were formed, employing 75 per cent of all workers in the industrial sector.[24] The independence of the trusts was confirmed by a *sovnarkom* decree of 10 April 1923, which set out their position as legal entities with the right to enter into contracts, buy and sell and so on. However the trusts were not joint-stock or private companies, merely "trustees of the state".[25] In this sense, NEP meant both a decentralization in the economy, and a concentration of economic activity in fewer hands.

One of the most interesting and contentious developments in this period came with the inauguration of foreign concessions. Lenin hoped to utilize the expertise and resources of foreign businessmen to help in the reconstruction of the Russian economy.

Although this policy was subject to severe criticisms by other Bol-sheviks, who saw this as capitalism making further inroads into socialist Russia, Lenin defended it as he defended so many other initiatives: this was the quickest way to restore the productive forces of the country. In the end the heat generated by the debate was out of all proportion to the importance of the concessions movement: only 42 agreements were concluded.[26]

Labour, management and trade unions

NEP came to be known as the "New Exploitation of the Proletariat". As the peasants took centre stage, managers and former owners returned, the market was restored and factories were run according to the principles of *khozraschet*, it was the workers who had to bear the brunt of the change in policy. The ending of free services and priority rations, the return of wages and piece-rates, inflation, a free market in labour, and unemployment all contributed to the growing discontent and insecurity of the Russian proletariat. The coercive discipline of the state (the militarization of labour, com-pulsory labour service) during the civil war was replaced by the economic discipline of the market. Labour relations deteriorated, and strikes became commonplace.[27]

The restoration of a labour market, wages linked to productivity and the decline of labour service compelled the state to redefine the relationship between workers, unions, the state and manage-ment. The framework for this relationship was defined by the 1922 Labour Code. The main points of this code were: a minimum wage was set (in practice wage rates were determined by local bargain-ing between employers and unions); the workers were entitled to an eight-hour day, two weeks holiday and welfare benefits; the rights of employers were also protected; unions were recognized as the sole body for the defence of workers' interests, but were also given responsibility for helping to increase production.[28]

This allowed for the defence of workers' rights, as well as estab-lishing minimum conditions for all workers. But the gap between the reality of NEP labour conditions and the heady days of "workers' control" seemed to be wider than ever, and growing.

The position of the trade unions under NEP was a difficult one. The debate within the party on the trade union issue was resolved at the 10th Party Congress with the adoption of the resolution "On the role and tasks of trade unions".[29] They were described as "schools of communism", and were to occupy an intermediary position between full independence and full statization: educating the workers, dealing with housing and welfare issues, aiding in the restoration of the economy.[30] The thrust of this resolution was undermined by the logic of NEP. Wage rates, unemployment, local collective bargaining and the return of former managers and owners shifted the unions into the position of being the defenders of workers' interests, and away from their intermediary role. Yet the unions were still expected to expedite the development of the productive forces, reflecting the ambiguities of defending workers' immediate interests (wages, conditions, etc.) and promoting their longer-term interests (as defined by the party) of effecting the most rapid transition to socialism.

This paradox was expressed in many ways. Strikes were permitted, but it was emphasized that they retarded economic recovery. The unions could participate in the administration of a factory, but could not interfere in the day-to-day production decisions. As NEP unfolded and the unions became the defenders of the interests of the workers, the party moved to prevent the trade unions developing any institutional autonomy within the system by asserting a greater degree of political control over the trade union hierarchy.[31]

The precise arrangements for the management of the state enterprises and trusts were quite convoluted. The triumvirate approach was revived. vsnkh proposed an "audit committee" of three individuals (manager, party secretary and trade union secretary) who would supervise transactions, inspect the accounts and so on. This became a method of dual oversight of the work of the trust directors: the committee would provide information for higher bodies (vsnkh in particular), as well as providing oversight from representatives of the workers. The trusts were run by a board of directors (appointed by vsnkh), each member of which had responsibility for a section of work of the trust. Managers of individual factories within the trust were appointed by the directors, and they had the responsibility for the internal functioning of the factory. Commercial dealings rested with the directors. Management–labour deliberations were settled through production commissions.[32]

The economic developments under NEP appeared to represent something of a liberalization: the ending of compulsory labour service, the granting of incentives to the peasantry, and greater autonomy in economic decision-making for enterprises. Was this process replicated in the political sphere?

The politics of NEP

On 27 March 1922, at the 11th Congress of the RCP, Lenin stated that:

> During a retreat, however, discipline must be more conscious and is a hundred times more necessary, because, when the entire army is in retreat, it does not know or see where it should halt ... the slightest breach of discipline must be punished severely, sternly, ruthlessly; and this applies not only to certain of our internal party affairs, but also, and to a greater extent, to such gentry as the Mensheviks ... And the Mensheviks and Socialist-Revolutionaries, all of whom preach this sort of thing, are astonished when we declare that we shall shoot people for such things. They are amazed; but surely it is clear. When an army is in retreat a hundred times more discipline is required than when it is advancing.[33]

On one reading, the politics of NEP were an ominous precursor of the practices of the 1930s: the suppression of debate, show trials, bureaucratization, purges and the consolidation of the monopoly of power of the party. Yet NEP has traditionally been viewed as the calm before the Stalinist storm, as an era of cultural pluralism, relative liberalism and genuine debate.[34] Lenin's speech at the 11th Congress summarizes the political developments of this period, covering three areas: the move to political monism, the growing preponderance of bureaucracy over democracy, and the extension of repression, coercion and terror.

The one-party state: pluralism and dissent, within and without

While the adoption of the *prodnalog* at the 10th Party Congress represents something of a liberalization in economic terms, the other resolutions concerning political developments were moving in the opposite direction. The 10th Party Congress was crucial in this respect. Not only were there further initiatives consolidating the one-party domination of the RCP, but there were parallel moves to suppress alternative groupings or "factions" within the party itself. Three factors fostered these resolutions. The first factor relates to the internal politics of the Bolshevik party during 1920/21. Lenin was clearly becoming increasingly exasperated by the growth of organized opposition within the party. Valuable time and effort was being expended on inner-party debates and bickering. Increasingly, Lenin himself was the subject of criticism from rank and file party members and other key party figures. In the midst of the trade union debate, the party appeared to be unravelling as a unified political organism, as platforms – Workers' Opposition, Democratic Centralists – became well-organized groupings.[35]

Secondly, the mounting social crisis at the end of the civil war concentrated the minds of the leaders on the meaning of "opposition". The revolts at Kronstadt and in the countryside as a whole provide the essential backdrop to the events at the 10th Party Congress. Opposition to the party was mounting. International revolution was looking an increasingly remote possibility. This crisis scenario focused the attention of the leadership (and Lenin in particular) on political dangers to Bolshevik party rule, both within and without of the party.

Thirdly, there was a theoretical rationale for the suppression of factions. If concessions were being made to capitalism, to the petty bourgeois peasantry as part of the transitional phase, then every measure had to be taken to prevent the economic power which the bourgeoisie might accrue being converted into political power. The consolidation of proletarian state power was the guarantee that NEP would lead to the building of socialism, not the restoration of capitalism. On this basis, any opposition to the party line could be interpreted as being "counter-revolutionary". For instance, in the resolution "On the anarchist and syndicalist deviation in our party", it states that:

> the views of the Workers' Opposition and similar elements are not only theoretically false, but serve in practice as the expression of petty bourgeois and anarchist vacillations;

in practice they weaken the steadfast guiding line of the
cp and in fact aid the class enemies of the proletarian
revolution.[36]

In response to these issues, Lenin resolved to deal with the particular factions within the party, but also with the practice of factionalism
itself. During the 10th Party Congress, Lenin held secret meetings
with his supporters (the Platform of the Ten) to devise a means of
destroying factions and factionalism.[37] Two resolutions were passed.
The resolution entitled "On party unity" referred to the practice of
factionalism. It contained seven clauses (although the last one was
kept secret and not published until after the 13th Conference in
1924) and was described as being "temporary". The resolution talked
of the need to restore "unity and cohesion" to party ranks. The key
points can be summarized thus:

- unity of will of the proletarian vanguard was a basic condition of the success of the dictatorship of the proletariat;
- deviations from the party line weaken the party and aid the
  struggle of the international bourgeoisie;
- criticisms, proposals, analyses should be put forward for discussion by all party members, not by groups derived from a
  particular platform;
- all factions were to be immediately dissolved.[38]

Clause 7 outlined that if factionalism continued, party members
would be disciplined, up to and including expulsion, which included members of the cc.[39] The cc itself was vested with these
powers. Henceforth, in theory, criticism of the leadership had to
remain at an individual level, and great powers were to accrue
to the party elite. Although the practice of Bolshevism in this period
was to remain marked by conflicts and debates, a marked shift in
the nature of politics under the dictatorship of the proletariat had
been initiated. Politics were to become an inner-party preserve.

Concomitant with the representation of inner-party factions as
unwitting agents of Whiteguardism and counter-revolution, was a
similar development with regard to the Mensheviks and srs. Within
the ideological paradigm of nep Bolshevism, all non-Bolshevik
groupings were labelled as "counter-revolutionary" *irrespective of*

their pronouncements or actions. On this point, Lenin was, as usual, uncompromisingly brutal,

> And when a Menshevik says, "You are now retreating; I
> have been advocating retreat all the time, I agree with you,
> I am your man, let us retreat together," we say in reply,
> "For the public manifestations of Menshevism our revolu-
> tionary courts must pass the death sentence . . . Permit us
> to put you before a firing squad for saying that. Either you
> refrain from expressing your views, or if you insist on ex-
> pressing your political views publicly . . . then you will only
> have yourselves to blame if we treat you as the worst and
> most pernicious whiteguard elements.[40]

Although many Mensheviks were arrested during the spring and summer of 1921, they were to suffer less than the srs. The latter were viewed as more of a threat because of their following among the peasantry. In this sense NEP represented a stepping up in the nature and extent of repression compared with the civil war. At that time the Mensheviks and srs had been tolerated (as long as they were loyal), and indeed were able to organize and disseminate ideas publicly. In the aftermath of the 10th Party Congress, the Bolsheviks became advocates of "zero tolerance". Lenin targeted the srs who, during 1922 were subjected to the first "Show Trial". Thirty-four were put on trial, and found guilty of spurious charges and sentenced to death (commmuted to 5 years in jail in 1924).[41] Alongside a similar public trial for the leadership of the Orthodox church, and the deportation of thousands of non-Bolshevik activists in 1922–3,[42] these developments represent the emasculation of political pluralism, and the formalization of the dictatorship of the Bolshevik party.

From democratic centralism to bureaucratic centralism

By the end of the civil war, a vast administrative machine had been spawned. The civil war rationale – the need for speedy responses and quick decisions, the greater efficiency of the Red Army struc-ture over the network of local Soviets – no longer applied. Rumblings in the party over the evils of "bureaucratism" were increasingly being heard. Yet the tension within Bolshevism as a wider move-ment (and in Lenin's thinking also) between its predilection for expertise, for technocratic solutions to problems of societal man-agement on the one hand, and its desire to draw the people into the administration of the system on the other, posed something of a dilemma for the leaders. How could the system be administered in a way that fostered expertise, popular participation and the correct socialist consciousness? Could they construct a bureaucracy without bureaucratism, an administrative structure that combined expertise and ideological rectitude, political zeal and training in administrative techniques? This search for a "Third Way" between "bureaucratic centralism" and "direct democracy" hinged on the role of the party within the system, and the nature of the party itself.

The relations between the party and state bodies under NEP ex-tended and deepened the processes inaugurated during the civil war: party domination over the Soviet network and the state admin-istrative organs (the commissariats). At the centre, the Politburo became the locus of policy-making. Domination over the state insti-tutions was exercised through overlapping membership: all the Polit-buro members headed up key state institutions.[43] At lower levels, the local party committees increasingly substituted for the *excoms* of the corresponding Soviet. All non-party social organizations (trade unions, co-operatives) contained a party grouping agitating for align-ment with party policy.[44] This fusion between party and state left two key issues unresolved. How could the wider population be trained and educated to participate in the administration within the system? How would the party's administrative apparatus be organ-ized and supervised to ensure that it fulfilled its functions, especially given the vast influx of officials into the party during the civil war?

Oversight of the state institutions (the commissariats), which were overwhelmingly staffed by ex-Tsarist officials, was devolved to RABKRIN (Commissariat of Workers' and Peasants' Inspection). The representatives were elected by the same electors who chose the delegates for Soviets, and were to serve for a short time only. High turnover would promote the greatest possible opportunity for maxi-mum participation by workers and peasants. The career of RABKRIN was dogged with controversy, and in 1923 it was fused with a party control commission. The party was now exercising oversight of the Soviet network through the (supposed) organ of popular oversight.[45]

The central role of the party in the administration of the system threw the spotlight on to its internal functioning. The NEP period continued the process whereby the democratic practices within the party were eroded (without disappearing) whereas the central party apparatus vastly increased its power and authority. In order to address the question of how to make the administrative structure more responsive to the diktats of the party leadership, a number of different initiatives were implemented. First, commissions were created to oversee the activities of the party. At the 10th Party Congress, a resolution was passed creating Control Commissions. Its tasks were defined as: (a) combating bureaucratism and careerism; (b) combating misuse of party and Soviet positions by party members; (c) violations of comradely relations within the party (and many more besides).[46]

Secondly, the process by which decision-making was concentrated at the top of the party during the civil war was extended as the centre succumbed to appointmentism: selection of personnel equipped with the requisite levels of expertise and communist consciousness. This was another blow to inner-party democracy. The organs of the party apparatus – the CC Secretariat, Orgburo – began to consolidate their control over the party as a whole (and Comrade Stalin over these organs) and the issue of assigning personnel was the catalyst for this. From the middle of 1922 onwards, the party undertook to assign individuals to key roles in the hierarchy through *Uchraspred* (the Account and Distribution Section). As Carr noted:

> Uchraspred thus became an inconspicuous but powerful focus of the control exercised by the party over the organs of state, political and economic. It also proved, under the management of the general secretary, a serviceable instrument for building up Stalin's authority in the state as well as in the party machine.[47]

One key point to note. The practice of appointmentism as a means of consolidating the personal authority of the leader, and in removing and undermining opposition to the party line, was inaugurated by Lenin in his struggles with the Workers' Opposition at the 10th Party Congress.

Finally, the party sought to sift "undesirable" elements from its ranks in order to ensure its vanguard status. The 10th Party Congress wrought a change in the recruitment policy to the party. Purity of communist consciousness was essential in a period of restoring capitalist economic relations. This required a "purge" or cleansing (*chistka*) of its ranks of those who had flooded into the party during the civil war for careerist or other reasons. On 30 June 1921 *Pravda* announced a purge to begin on 1 August that year.[48] The purge was to be directed at purifying the party on the basis of the ideological outlook of party members, as well as their behaviour. The ostensible targets were ex-Tsarist officials and ex-members of other parties. However, in the midst of growing rank and file criticism of NEP, it also became a means by which the leadership could remove opponents to the new line. Approximately 24 per cent were expelled in this first wave.[49] Interestingly, this was not a one-off. At the 11th Party Conference in December 1921 a resolution "On the question of strengthening the party in connection with a study of experience of the verification of its personnel" was passed, outlining measures for recruitment.[50] At the 11th Party Congress in March/April 1922 a further resolution "On the strengthening of the party and its new tasks" set out the details for admission to the party.[51] The purge had now become a continuous part of party life.

In sum, the party continued to be an organism in which centralism, appointmentism and bureaucratism dominated over local autonomy, elections and democracy. Crucially, Lenin's analysis of this situation merely compounded the problem. Rather than searching for solutions in the system itself, Lenin instead focused upon the quality of the personnel within it:

> The key feature is that we have not got the right men in the right places; that responsible communists who acquitted themselves magnificently during the revolution have been given commercial and industrial functions about which they know nothing . . . Choose the proper men and introduce practical control.[52]

An administrative solution to an administrative problem.

Terror, coercion and the law

NEP brought an end to the Red Terror. But terror itself continued. The more relaxed atmosphere in the country with the end of foreign intervention led to calls for the abolition of the CHEKA. However, the need for vigilance and discipline in the "retreat" meant the leadership would maintain a security organ. The functions of the CHEKA were transferred to the Commissariat of Internal Affairs (NKVD). Within this latter organ there was created the GPU (state political administration), which was to exercise the functions of the old CHEKA, only this time political crimes were now out of the purview of the courts completely. The GPU, in fact, had far greater discretionary and arbitrary powers than the CHEKA had had.[53] Far from limiting the use of arbitrary coercion in the system, NEP created a set of extra-judicial organs through which the party could repress any opposition.

In the legal sphere, the same instrumental approach (law as a means of building socialism) that emerged after the revolution was continued.[54] Although the legal system was put on a more regularized and stable basis, by which individuals on the whole were aware what behaviour would be liable for arrest, this was still a long way short of a state based on the rule of law. The introduction of market relations under NEP brought forth the need to provide a legal framework for economic activities, which in turn compelled the regime to formalize relations between the state and the individual. Lenin sent Bolshevik jurists to study legal codes of western Europe (Germany, Switzerland and France).[55] Between 1922 and 1926 they produced, a Judiciary Act; Civil Code; Code of Civil Procedure; Criminal Code; Code of Criminal Procedure; Land Code; Labour Code; Family Code.[56]

As with the economic system, which mixed socialist and capitalist elements, so the legal system reflected the duality of NEP. Many elements reflected the practices of mainstream European law (for example protection of private property). Yet NEP law also constrained the concessions given to petty bourgeois capitalism. Article One of the Civil Code (1922) stated that, "Civil rights shall be protected by law except in instances when they are exercised in contradiction with their social-economic purpose".[57] In defending Bolshevik ideals, the law became an instrument of the state in building socialism. Not only did the party prescribe the content of the law, but party control over the courts was maintained through the system of state procurators, who supervised their activities.[58] Bolshevism, as a movement, was – in legal terms – nihilistic.

The politics of NEP saw the consolidation of the forces of centralization, hierarchy, bureaucratization and repression. One of the underlying causes of these processes was the lack of "communist consciousness" within both the party rank and file, and within the wider Russian society, and a comcomitant absence of technical expertise among the population. Having adopted a series of essentially capitalist measures to reconstruct the economy and develop the productive forces in order to construct the material basis of socialism, the leadership became increasingly aware of the importance of consciously engineering a society compatible with these tasks.

Society and culture under NEP

The growing recognition of the importance of socio-cultural affairs in the construction of socialism forced the leadership to resolve the tensions within Bolshevism surrounding its approach to societal management. During the civil war, the social and cultural policy of the party was subordinated to the tasks of constructing socialism and winning the war. However, there continued to exist an emancipatory, libertarian, egalitarian, utopian impulse among party rank and file, activists in the *zhenotdel* and elsewhere, who worked to implement a more radical socio-cultural approach. How would this tension be realized after the end of the armed conflict?

The consolidation of power within the party, and the party's expanding control over all autonomous social institutions inexorably suffocated the emancipatory impulse. Yet, Bolshevik attempts to transform the society and culture of Russia to promote the wider processes of modernization and industrialization ran up against the reality of Russian society during the 1920s. The persistence of traditional pre-revolutionary attitudes and patterns of behaviour was a severe obstacle to the realization of the wider Bolshevik goals. As the economics of NEP expressed a more gradualist approach to the development of the productive forces, so socio-cultural policy under NEP represented an accommodation of party ideals with Russian realities.[59]

Egalitarianism and inegalitarianism: social and economic aspects

The issue of female emancipation illustrates the manner in which the emancipatory impulse was snuffed out in favour of party directed objectives. The aim of the party was to mobilize all constituencies behind the work of constructing socialism. This would increase the resources available to the party in its work, but also accorded with the productivist, instrumentalist strand of Bolshevism, which saw female emancipation as flowing from the changed socio-economic status of women. In contrast, the activists within *zhenotdel* sought to liberate women as an end in itself. By the end of the decade, the party's productivist strand had triumphed over the libertarian strand across the whole range of issues: family life, sexual relations, child-rearing and so on.[60]

The programme of the *zhenotdel* activists laid its emphasis upon self-emancipation. Women would organize themselves in order to confront the daily obstacles to full equality, and to defend their interests as women. This meant prioritizing the issues of domestic life: child-rearing, sexuality, domestic labour. Moreover, as Clements has argued, the *zhenotdel* focus was not just self-organization. It was *local* self-organization,

> women themselves would build the communal institutions that would revolutionise the family and make new women possible . . . Crucial to the process of mobilising women to these revolutionary tasks was developing their independence and initiative . . . the *zhenotdel*'s utopians did not wax lyrical, as Bukharin and Trotsky did over the transforming activities of the centralised institutions of the dictatorship of the proletariat.[61]

To some extent, this agenda was undermined by the socio-economic consequences of NEP. The growth of unemployment meant that activists spent a great deal of time trying to defend the gains of 1917: a women's right to work. Economic uncertainty also tended to reinforce the traditional role divisions of the family, at the time when *zhenotdel* activists were seeking to transform and modernize it. *Zhenotdel* also suffered from funding cuts, hindering its ability to act.

The Bolshevik leadership, and in particular Lenin and Stalin, were diametrically opposed to the fundamentals of the agenda of the *zhenotdel* activists in the period after 1921. The Bolsheviks favoured centralization and large-scale solutions, which prioritized economic issues, not domestic issues. There was a profound suspicion in the party over special sections for women and ethnic minorities. It was felt that they would dilute the wider struggle to establish socialism, by dividing the attention and energies of the masses. The adoption of NEP required measures to integrate and stabilize Russian society if the partial restoration of capitalism was to be managed successfully. The *zhenotdel* agenda, involving a frontal challenge to social mores and practices, seemed to many Bolsheviks to be portending further social disruption, confrontation and chaos.[62]

From 1923 onwards, *zhenotdel* increasingly became transformed into a party transmission belt, rather than a vehicle of self-emancipation. On one level the hegemony of the productivist conception of social roles appeared to signify continued subordination for women. Women still bore the brunt of child-rearing and domestic labour. Men maintained their authority roles at work. Yet the party was also forced to recognize the precarious position of women in unregistered marriages created by the economic uncertainties of NEP. The 1926 Marriage Code granted registered and unregistered marriages equal rights in law. In this way, the husband was forced to provide financial support.[63] Although one of the motivations for this was concern for vulnerable women with children, the state also had an economic interest in shifting the burden of financial support onto the male partner. As Lapidus states,

> conflicts over family policy and sexual liberation brought into sharp focus the growing tension between libertarian and instrumental concerns within Bolshevism. The growing predominance of views hostile to any further strain in family and communal relations accompanied an increasing willingness to subordinate a broader definition of liberation to the need for social stability, control and productivity

– to the need in sum for harnessing the energies of men and women alike to the common cause of socialist construction.[64]

NEP resolved the tension within Bolshevism firmly in favour of the productivist and instrumentalist wing, dashing the hopes of the libertarians and egalitarians, as the party accommodated itself to the attitudes and norms of Russian society. A similar accommodation and retreat occurred in the field of privilege.

NEP witnessed an extension of the growth of privilege within the system. The restoration of capitalist practices fostered a sharp increase in differentials across a spectrum of goods – material and non-material. However, the type of privilege, and the manner of its distribution varied greatly. In terms of social groups and material rewards, the most favoured groups were as follows. Specialists in state enterprises generally enjoyed higher salaries. In 1922, the upper limit for their salaries was raised from 3,000 roubles to 60,000 roubles. At the beginning of the following year, there emerged a system of personal salaries and special awards that qualified them for wages above the state-set rates.[65] Party-state officials, although operating within a narrower band than the specialists, still enjoyed steadily increasing salaries during the 1920s, alongside a number of other privileges (of which more below).[66] Red Army officers in particular, but also members of the creative intelligentsia, were also privileged in various ways.[67]

The distribution of housing stock is a good example of the priorities of the party under NEP, and provides an insight into the principles underlying Bolshevik attitudes towards privilege and inequality in the transition period. In August 1921, engineers became eligible for better quality flats.[68] In January 1922, scientific workers were allowed the use of an extra room. In 1924, this latter privilege was extended to five categories of person: (a) officials of state institutions, enterprises, co-operatives, trade unions and party organizations; (b) military and naval administrators; (c) scientific research workers; (d) doctors and dentists in private practice; (e) members of Society of Former Political Prisoners.[69]

In terms of rents, the levels were set very low (1 per cent of the minimum wage of a worker in a state enterprise). Excluded from low rents were workers in private enterprises, and persons who were living on "unearned income". This penalized those in the private sector, and heavily favoured the higher earners from the state sector, reinforcing the material privileges outlined above.[70]

From this it is clear that the Bolsheviks privileged its closest supporters, the skilled and technical staff it required and those engaged in its defence. Hardly surprising. The notable thing is that NEP society saw an extension of privilege and a deepening inegalitarian strand to social policy. The party was accommodating itself to the tasks of economic reconstruction and the political isolation of a proletarian party in a peasant country through a varied set of rewards, privileges and benefits. Once more the radical, egalitarian strand within Bolshevism was eclipsed and marginalized by the socio-economic processes of NEP Russia.

The structure and consciousness of Russian society also modified the Bolshevik commitment to the prioritization of the interests of the proletariat. Attempts were made to widen access to higher education for the masses and to increase the provision of vocational education. Unified labour schools were created during the 1920s, which combined vocational training with elementary secondary education.[71] Privileging access to higher education for workers was attempted through Workers' Faculties (*Rabfaki*), which were attached to HE institutions, in order to prepare workers for enrolment on degree programmes. Purges of students from "elitist" backgrounds served to consolidate the position of students from worker backgrounds.[72] The aims of these initiatives were to overcome the lack of expertise among the general population, and to create a communist worker elite. As Fitzpatrick has demonstrated though, the policy was unsuccessful, "academic standards dropped sharply. The universities were overcrowded, and their graduates of such poor quality that employers complained".[73]

A retreat from this policy of class prioritization occurred in 1925. Measures were adopted to raise academic standards, which produced revised quotas and included the children of specialists. A year later, enrolment was entirely open, whereby children of specialists were declared to be equal to the children of workers. Academic criteria were re-established in the selection process. The need for expertise, and to conciliate the intelligentsia, defeated the attempt to engineer the social composition of the student body.[74]

Culture and education under NEP

Cultural and educational policy was riddled with the tensions, ambiguities and accommodations of NEP as a transitional society. The Bolshevik party developed institutional and other measures to control the processes of cultural production and dissemination, and also to shape the educational system. Yet, it also became clear that the party had to accommodate itself to the expertise provided by the old intelligentsia, setting clear limits to the pace of the transformation, if not its overall direction.

In educational terms, the Bolsheviks undertook a massive literacy campaign. This was a wildly enthusiastic but chaotic attempt to abolish illiteracy in both rural and urban Russia. Many thousand individuals, who had a formal education, were drafted into the campaign. Crash courses, lasting 2–3 weeks, were created in thousands of towns and villages across Russia. In numerical terms it appeared to be quite successful: 5 million people are estimated to have been schooled between 1920 and 1926.[75] However, the notion of literacy was set at a very low level. People were designated as literate if, (a) they could recognize written words on signs or posters; (b) they could sign their names.[76] It appears that this crash programme created a semi-literate society, with little follow-up for the vast majority of citizens.

Control over the HE curriculum was seen as critical in embedding Bolshevik norms among the new elite. In 1921 the Institute of Red Professors was created, to train up professors who would teach from a Marxist perspective.[77] From 1921 onwards, the Bolsheviks attempted to slant the curriculum, imposing the compulsory study of historical materialism, history of the Bolshevik party, and replacing old history and philosophy faculties with faculties of social sciences.[78] Shaping the content was combined with political control over appointments and governing of universities. The right to appoint rectors and professors was vested in *Narkompros*, although the appointments were made from lists drawn up by professors, students, trade unionists and soviet officials. The autonomy of the universities was gradually undermined, in spite of strikes by university professors.[79] However, this should not be overemphasized. As Fitzpatrick noted:

The policy of the Soviet government at this time was to avoid open conflict at all costs except that of loss of political control. The old professors kept their jobs, a fair part of their freedom of teaching, and a share in university administration; the appointed rectors were mild.[80]

The situation in the cultural field was similarly complex, reflecting the contradictory currents and tensions that ran throughout NEP. The conflicts over cultural policy emerged along two axes: form and content. The party leaders and leading revolutionary cultural figures concurred over the instrumental role of culture in constructing socialism. But what form should this take? Should it too be expressed in a revolutionary idiom, reinforcing the message? Or should it be couched in such a way as to appeal to the cultural tastes of the people? In addition, the conflicts over content revolved around the clash between popular "commercial" culture of NEP society, and a culture designed with more "enlightening" and "noble" themes.

In general, the forms of cultural policy reflected those of the party leadership, fusing elements of the old with elements of the new in order to communicate their message. According to Stites,

Its cultural code proscribed eroticism, mysticism, religion or upper-class fluff ... As a counterweight it promoted a new proletarian morality based upon mutual respect and equality of the sexes, atheism rooted in science, a spirit of collective comradeship; and a veritable cult of technology and the machine.[81]

The Bolsheviks developed an elaborate propaganda network that was designed to disseminate their worldview to the widest possible audience. The Bolsheviks foresaw the vast potential inherent in theatre and cinema as a means of propagation. Agit-trains and boats toured the country. Street theatre, carnivals and a panoply of new rituals, parades and assemblies were created that combined regime-directed ideological content with cultural forms which were familiar to the people.[82] The greatest cultural threat to the Bolsheviks came in the popularity of "bourgeois" culture under NEP. The partial restoration of capitalism led to a partial revival of pre-revolutionary cultural practices, and western forms remained popular throughout this period.[83]

In this sense, cultural policy in this period reflected the uncertainty, ambivalence and contradictory nature of NEP. It was a transitional society which was itself in transition.[84] Conflicts within the party itself, and between the party and society, expressed the fundamental socio-cultural dilemma of the Bolsheviks in the 1920s: how could a society be transformed both consciously and consensually, without causing instability? Changing the institutions of Russian society had proved relatively easy. Changing the outlook, consciousness and behaviour of the people was proving far more problematical.

Understanding NEP: a new model of Soviet socialism?

NEP raises many interesting issues. Within the confines of this work, only one will be explored here. Namely, to what extent did NEP represent a departure from the broad understanding of socialism in Bolshevik discourse? Resolving this issue is a complex affair. Three issues stand out. First, the degree of filiation between "state capitalism", "war communism" and NEP. Secondly, the meaning of Lenin's last works "On co-operation", in which he outlined that "we have to admit that there has been a radical modification in our whole outlook on socialism". Thirdly, the place of NEP within Soviet socialism.

NEP and "peculiar war communism": of retreats, mistakes and advances

Many commentators point to the inconsistencies in Lenin's analyses and descriptions of NEP.[85] Much of this can be explained by examining the particular context within which Lenin was speaking or writing. Lenin, the consummate politician, shifted the emphasis of the message depending upon the audience being addressed and the wider economic and political context. Within this framework, terms such as NEP and "war communism" can appear to have a variety of meanings. The question is whether there is any consistent line visible across this period. Lenin's analysis can be divided (broadly) into two periods – March 1921–October 1921; October 1921–January 1923.

NEP and the politics of the worker–peasant smychka:
March–October 1921

In the spring of 1921, Lenin set forth his views on NEP in three forums: (a) speech to the 10th Party Congress (March 1921); (b) the pamphlet "The tax-in-kind" (The significance of the new policy and its conditions) (April 1921); (c) speech to the 10th All-Russia Party Conference (May 1921).

The dominant themes from this period stressed the pragmatic, political aspects of the *prodnalog*. The severity of the internal unrest confronted the party with the necessity of adopting measures to ensure the survival of the revolution. In lieu of an international revolution, it was imperative to establish an economic basis for the alliance with the peasantry. The alliance with the peasantry, which had been forged during the civil war, was based upon the military necessity of defeating the Whiteguard forces,

> As soon as we had done away with the external enemy –
> and this became a fact only in 1921 – another task confronted us, the task of establishing an economic alliance between the working class and the peasantry.[86]

An economic alliance could only be forged on the basis of a policy that reconciled the interests of the peasantry (an incentive to produce) with the needs of the state (food for the industrial and urban sectors). Lenin's initial analysis of the reasons for the adoption of NEP stressed politics and pragmatism.

How was "war communism" described? The food policy of surplus appropriation under war communism was described variously as "crude", "imperfect", "inconvenient and onerous" and a "makeshift".[87] They had been forced into adopting it because of the severity of the conditions in the civil war, and although it had been the only possible option then, it had now to be abandoned. To reassure the party faithful, Lenin stressed that if NEP marked a break with war communism at this point, it was still in line with economic policy prior to the civil war, and so was not a major departure from Bolshevik theory on the transition phase.

Lenin argued, in particular in "The tax-in-kind", that there was substantial continuity between NEP and the state capitalism of May 1918.[88] The *prodnalog* was described as a key part of the transition to a "regular socialist exchange of products" (i.e. the non-monetary exchange of goods between state industry and the peasant) and away from the state monopoly on trade during the civil war. The key to promoting the transition to "proper" socialist exchange, was to direct the economics of NEP down the path of state capitalism, as this would represent a step towards socialism, as Lenin had argued in May 1918. This could not be an immediate return to proper socialist exchange though, as Lenin realized the Soviet industrial sector was in no state to supply all the goods the peasantry required.

It is clear that Lenin downplayed the "change" aspect of NEP and stressed the "continuity" aspects, in the spring of 1921, as part of the politics of gaining acceptance for NEP, and persuading the party of its correctness (politically, economically and ideologically). As Szamuely has argued,

> As a good politician, he [Lenin] must have known that sharp, too radical, turns frequently cause incomprehension ...We believe this also explains why Lenin so strongly emphasized in the first few months that the introduction of the tax-in-kind did not mean a radical turn in policy, and that this was why he stressed legal continuity with previous economic policy, and why he characterized War Communism then as a unique detour.[89]

NEP: *from frontal assault to slow siege:*
October 1921–January 1923

In autumn 1921, Lenin began to theorize NEP. Inexorably, he was drawn into an analysis of prior economic policies, reappraising the short history of Bolshevik economic policy after 1917. He outlined his views in four pieces:

1) Fourth Anniversary of the October Revolution (14 October 1921).[90]
2) "The new economic policy and the tasks of the political education departments" (17 October 1921).[91]
3) "Report on the new economic policy at 7th Moscow Gubernia Conference of RCP" (29 October 1921).[92]
4) "The importance of gold now and after the complete victory of socialism" (5 November 1921).[93]

The reason for this theorizing arose partly out of the inability to restrict NEP to local product exchange. The return of free trade, monetary exchange and market relations brought ideological questions in their wake, requiring a theoretical response. The time lapse (over six months) also created a degree of distance from the original decision which, given the nature of the audience (political education workers, and local party figures), allowed Lenin to reflect upon the wider meaning and significance of NEP, "war communism" and "state capitalism".

From this analysis, NEP was described as a correction to the mistakes and excesses of the attempt to go over directly to communist production and distribution. At first Lenin reiterated the continuity between NEP and the pre-civil war period, defining NEP as a return to the gradualist transitional economics of state capitalism. The pragmatic, political aspects of NEP began to disappear from Lenin's analysis as the emphasis shifted from NEP as primarily a set of political measures taken to save the revolution towards NEP as an alternative, more gradual, more prolonged transition to socialism. In theoretical terms the civil war period represented an attempt to "leap" stages of historical development. NEP was a recognition of "defeat", and the need to retreat.

At the 7th Moscow Party Conference, Lenin evaluated the sense in which the civil war policies represented a "mistake". In an interesting passage, Lenin drew a military parallel, which is worth quoting at length,

> I would like to take, for the purpose of analogy, an episode from the Russo–Japanese War, which, I think, will enable us to obtain a clearer picture of the relationship between the various systems and political methods adopted in a revolution of the kind that is taking place in our country. The episode I have in mind is the capture of Port Arthur by the Japanese General Nogi. The main thing that interests me in this episode is that the capture of Port Arthur was accomplished in two entirely different stages. The first stage was that of furious assaults, which ended in failure and cost the celebrated Japanese commander heavy losses. The second stage was the extremely arduous, extremely difficult and slow method of siege, according to all the

rules of the art. Eventually, it was by this method that the problem of capturing the fortress was solved.[94]

In developing this analogy, Lenin sharpened his thinking upon the nature of NEP, and also upon the periodization of economic policy before 1921, without always maintaining consistency with earlier pronouncements.

The first revision from the spring 1921 pronouncements saw Lenin reduce Bolshevik post-revolutionary economic policy from three periods down to two,

> I think this analogy [above] can serve to illustrate the position in which our revolution finds itself in solving its socialist problems of economic development. Two periods stand out very distinctly . . . The first the period from approximately the beginning of 1918 to the spring of 1921; and the other, the period from the spring of 1921 to the present.[95]

Here Lenin destroyed an earlier distinction between the pre-civil war gradualist policy of "state capitalism", and the civil war radicalism of "war communism". Lenin implied that the period from March 1918 onwards was similarly infused with notions of proceeding immediately with transition to the construction of socialism. Lenin does still argue for a continuity between NEP and the earlier period, but this is a continuity with the *initial intentions* of the Bolsheviks, that the transition would be a gradual, complex and tortuous affair. The practice of the first months had run ahead of Bolshevik notions of caution. Why? Well, the logic of the struggle of the Russian proletariat with the bourgeoisie was such that the latter would not participate in a gradual transition to a new order. The opposition of the old classes compelled the state to take measures that were more extreme, more desperate. At the same time the Bolsheviks did not establish the relationship between the system of state production and distribution on the one hand, and the questions of the market, trade, incentives on the other. The key point for Lenin was that the practice of state capitalism was radicalized by the opposition of the bourgeoisie, and pushed it beyond the cautious, gradualist framework that Lenin hoped to maintain.[96] The problem at this point was that Lenin was using the term "state capitalism" rather promiscuously. He did not define it clearly or consistently, leading to a good deal of ambiguity and confusion.[97]

The civil war policies (the term "war communism" was no longer mentioned, as it was no longer deemed to be specific to the civil war period) were also reinterpreted, albeit inconsistently. The whole policy of state monopoly on trade, and in particular the policy of surplus-appropriation or grain requisitioning was described somewhat paradoxically by Lenin. On many occasions, Lenin described the civil war policy as a "mistake":

> What had been done before had to be resolutely, definitely and clearly regarded as a mistake in order to remove all obstacles to the development of new strategy and tactics.[98]

But Lenin qualifies this "mistakenness" in two ways. First, given the intensity of the struggle in which they were engaged, he argued that "they were the only possible tactics that could have been adopted under the conditions then prevailing".[99] Secondly, they were "necessary" and "useful" mistakes.[100] In the same way that the Japanese had learnt from their mistakes in capturing Port Arthur, so the Bolsheviks would learn from their mistakes, and so adapt their strategy accordingly. It was in this latter sense, of necessary mistakes, that Lenin viewed the pre-NEP policy in a positive light.

Lenin saw the civil war policy also as both response to desperate necessity and a long-term attempt to construct socialism. For instance, at one point he says,

> Partly owing to the war problems that overwhelmed us and partly owing to the desperate position in which the Republic found itself when the imperialist war ended . . . we made the mistake of deciding to go over directly to communist production and distribution.[101]

Elsewhere, Lenin maintained that,

> By the spring of 1921 it became evident that we had suffered defeat in our attempt to introduce the socialist principles of production and distribution by "direct assault", i.e. in the shortest, quickest and most direct way.[102]

Lenin's rather inconsistent analysis of the civil war period stemmed partly from the need to provide an ideological rationale for Bolshevik economic policy in the light of the many critics – domestic and international – who were beginning to voice their opinions, but also partly from a genuine theoretical dilemma that the leadership found themselves in, following the failure of international revolution. The desperate measures were adopted because of the intense struggle with the forces of international capitalism, and were justified as the only feasible means by which the civil war could be won. The mistakes were committed in seeking to construct socialism rapidly, immediately and directly. (Quite how measures of desperate necessity can also be part of a long-term strategy to construct socialism was unelaborated.) NEP had the same aim. What was required was a change of strategy: more gradual, cautious. Extending his military parallel, Lenin thus viewed NEP as a retreat, in order to resume the advance towards socialism by siege tactics, not direct assault. But retreat to where? And for how long? In answering these questions, Lenin began to spell out the wider meaning and significance of NEP.

The reasons for this rather obscure and ambiguous (and one could say inaccurate) re-evaluation of the economic development of Bolshevism were to provide an ideological and historical rationale of NEP. Lenin justified NEP as a retreat. But this was a retreat not only beyond the policies of "direct socialist construction", but also, in October 1921, beyond state capitalism. In this sense, the analysis of autumn 1921 went further than had been envisaged in the spring of 1921. Then Lenin argued that,

> The whole problem – in theoretical and practical terms – is to find the correct methods of directing the development of capitalism . . . into the channels of state capitalism.[103]

In the spring of 1921, the aim had been to use the *prodnalog* as the basis for a policy of direct product exchange, and on this basis to restore large-scale industry. However, economic developments had speeded up so greatly in the intervening period, with the restoration of money, market relations and free trade, that it became necessary to retreat to a pre-state capitalist position. However, to prevent accusations that this position amounted to nothing more than the full-scale restoration of capitalism (the stance of non-Bolshevik socialists in Russia and elsewhere who viewed the events of October 1917 as "premature"), it was also a return to the initial Bolshevik ideas about economic policy, about a gradual transition. Lenin outlined that,

> We must admit that we have not retreated far enough, that we must make a further retreat . . . from state capitalism to the creation of state-regulated buying and selling, to the money system . . . Only in this way, a longer way than we expected, can we restore economic life.[104]

Looking back over the four years of the revolution in October 1921, Lenin succinctly summarized the lessons that economic experience had taught him,

> Experience has proved that we were wrong. It appears that a number of transitional stages were necessary . . . in order to prepare . . . for the transition to communism. Not directly relying on enthusiasm, but aided by the enthusiasm engendered by the great revolution, and on the basis of personal interest, personal incentive and business principles, we must first set to work in this small-peasant country to build solid gangways to socialism by way of state capitalism.[105]

Lenin constantly affirmed that this retreat had not changed the objective. This remained the restoration of large-scale industry, the speediest and most effective development of the productive forces. The party activists, according to Lenin, must never lose sight of the reasons for the retreat of NEP. By way of a "siege", a socialist society would be built.

How long would the retreat last? Although this appears to be a fairly straightforward issue, it does in fact touch upon one of the most contentious debates in Soviet history: what was NEP? A method of building socialism? Or a period of economic reconstruction, before going over to direct socialist construction? On the surface, the pronouncements of Lenin appear a little confusing. For instance:

> May 1921: "the Party regards this policy as being established for a long period of years", and "seriously and for a long time".[106]

November 1921: "there are visible signs that the retreat is coming to an end; there are signs that we shall be able to stop this retreat in the not-too-distant future".[107]

March 1922: "For a year we have been retreating. On behalf of the Party we must now call a halt. The purpose pursued by the retreat has been achieved. This period is drawing, or has drawn, to a close."[108]

The retreat was over. But NEP was not. A close reading of Lenin's writings reveals no fundamental inconsistency here. First, in what sense was the retreat over? The policy line was now clear – the state had to learn to trade, to create an economic link with the peasant producer in order to strengthen the economy. What was required now was to implement this policy. No further concessions to capitalism were required.

But was NEP the basis for the subsequent advance, as the retreat was now over? Many scholars argue (accurately in the present author's opinion) that NEP would be the means of the advance towards socialism. NEP was both retreat and advance. As Lars Lih has so persuasively argued,

The retreat was to free trade from a state trade monopoly . . . the decriminalisation of free trade was a concession to the small individual owner-peasant and cleared the way for forms of advance understandable and accessible to peasants. As soon as economic recovery made it possible, the advance would start again – private trade would be "crowded out" by the combined forces of state trade and the cooperative apparatus, using peaceful economic measures . . . While including an undeniable element of retreat, NEP also included subsequent advance towards a planned economy. The overcoming of NEP would be NEP's own doing.[109]

NEP represents, on this view, an alternative method of building socialism, utilizing the capitalist tools of personal interests and incentives, profit and loss commercial principles and the use of monetary relations. It would "overcome itself" and construct socialism in two ways. First, the retention of state power in the hands of the representatives of the proletariat. Secondly, through competition between the forces of capitalism and communism. In lieu of a successful international revolution, the class struggle took on a national-specific form within Russia. If socialist enterprises could be made more efficient and business-like, if communists could learn to trade, then the forces of capitalism inside Russia would recede and disappear.

Lenin was adamant on this point. Competition with the forces of private capitalism was described as the "pivot" and "quintessence" of NEP.

> If we beat capitalism and create a link with peasant farming we shall become an absolutely invincible power. Then the building of socialism will not be the task of that drop in the ocean, called the Communist Party, but the task of the entire mass of working people. Then the rank and file peasants will see that we are helping them and they will follow our lead. Consequently, even if the pace is a hundred times slower, it will be a million times more certain and more sure.[110]

The road to socialism was now paved with market relations and monetary incentives.

NEP and "On co-operation": a note

Much attention has been focused recently upon an article (in two parts) written by Lenin in January 1923, entitled 'On co-operation".[111] In particular, Soviet theorists after 1985 saw in this article a Leninist rationale for shifting the meaning and content of Soviet-style socialism. Lenin outlined that, "the system of civilised cooperators is the system of socialism",[112] and that it was necessary "to admit that there has been a radical modification in our whole outlook on socialism".[113] Does this equate to a significant revision of the Bolshevik understanding of socialism?

No. Lenin was turning his attention to the two critical questions facing the party under NEP: the relationship of the peasantry and the peasant economy to the state economic sector, and the problem of the cultural backwardness of the masses. Lenin saw these two elements as critical to the establishment of socialism in Russia. The long-term task of establishing large-scale industry required prioritizing the interests of the peasantry. A socialist country required a cultural revolution. Lenin's emphasis on co-operatives must be viewed in this context. Having legalized private trade, co-operation acquired great significance under NEP,

> We went too far when we introduced NEP, but not because we attached too much importance to the principle of free enterprise and trade – we went too far because we lost sight of the co-operatives, because we now underrate the co-operatives.[114]

Lenin envisaged retail (NB, not producer) co-operatives drawing the peasant population into a co-operative trade sector, and in this way the growth of private trade would be restricted. The nature of these co-operatives was fundamentally different from those under capitalism, because of the social ownership of the means of production, and because the state was a proletarian one. It is in this sense that Lenin was to argue that there was a "radical modification" in their outlook on socialism. The emphasis had now shifted to work of an educational or cultural character, and away from the issues of winning political power. We will leave the last words to Lenin,

> This cultural revolution would now suffice to make our country a completely socialist country; but it presents immense difficulties of a purely cultural (for we are illiterate) and material character (for to be cultured we must achieve a certain development of the material means of production, must have a certain material base).[115]

NEP and Soviet socialism: an alternative model?

Opinions over the precise status of NEP in Bolshevik ideological discourse are deeply divided. For Lewin, NEP represented a distinct model, the fact remains that the realities and policies of the NEP inspired Lenin to promulgate a doctrine that allowed a concept of "socialism" which could be disassociated from the exclusive statism that prevailed both earlier and later.[116]

The central issue concerns the extent to which the policies introduced under NEP constituted a shift in the Bolshevik understanding of socialism or was nothing more than a shift of emphasis in certain areas. While it is possible in certain areas to identify clear constants and variables, it is also clear that a number of the tensions extant in Bolshevik thinking remained unresolved, and that NEP added another layer of unresolved tensions.

NEP *and the economics of Soviet socialism*

The core features of the socialist economy remained unaltered. NEP reaffirmed the constancy of the Bolshevik commitment to a large-scale industrial sector, which was socialized, technologically advanced, consciously planned. A mechanized, collectivized large-scale agricultural sector remained their vision of the "good" rural society. The Bolshevik vision was still infused with notions of productivism, rationalism and technocracy. On numerous occasions, Lenin asserted that the central task was to increase the productive forces, increase output, restore large-scale industry. This was the essential condition for the emancipation of the workers.

The commitment to rationalism and technocracy continued to be expressed in a number of ways. The Bolsheviks remained committed to the use of planning, expressing faith in their ability purposively and consciously to order economic life. Their belief in the transformatory potential inherent in science and technology remained undimmed. The electrification of Russia was still a priority for Lenin,

> A large-scale machine industry capable of reorganising agriculture is the only material basis that is possible for socialism . . . Large-scale industry based on the latest achievements of technology and capable of reorganising agriculture implies the electrification of the whole country.[117]

Technology was the motor for economic progress. This also applied in the case of labour, where the principles of Taylorism and the scientific management of labour continued to dominate. Although there was a clear division in the NOT movement (Scientific Organization of Labour) after 1921, this' was resolved at the March 1924 NOT Conference.[118] In its final resolution, this conference set forth the principles for the implementation of scientific management in industry. According to Smith, the conference outlined:

- the improvement of the means of production through mechanisation and electrification.
- rationalization of the workshop via a reorganisation of labour and labour processes and the standardization of materials and products.
- increased productivity of labour via an improvement in the quality and qualifications of labour and via labour intensification.[119]

Alongside the application of science to the labour process, NEP reaffirmed a deference to specialists, and to managerial authority within the factory:

> Unless our leading bodies, i.e. the RCP, the Soviet government and the trade unions, guard as the apple of their eye every specialist who does his work conscientiously and knows and loves it – even though the ideas of communism are totally alien to him – it will be useless to expect any serious progress in socialist construction.[120]

Yet, the situation is far less clear with regard to the more detailed aspects. In particular, the questions of the proper scope of state control, and the issue of the relationship between the use of planning and the use of market incentives as economic mechanisms.[121] The civil war period had seen the abolition of market relations, and a system of centralized administrative allocation of resources through an all-embracing plan. Under NEP, Lenin emerged as an ardent defender of competition, enterprise, initiative and the discipline of the market. Communists had to learn to trade. As Lenin remarked in a letter to Krzhizhanovsky in December 1921, the use of market relations could become a means by which the economy moved towards planning: "the NEP does not change the integrated state economic plan, nor does it exceed its framework, it merely changes the ways of its implementation".[122]

Resolving this particular issue is made more difficult by Bolshevik imprecision on the nature of "planning". There is, as Nove, Davies and others have shown, no real evidence to suggest that Lenin envisaged the type of all-embracing centralized planning that was adopted by Stalin after 1929. Indeed, as Davies maintains, "until 1928 everyone assumed that plans must be made compatible with market equilibrium, and with a non-coercive relationship with the peasantry".[123] NEP – with its greater scope for market elements, for decentralization, for a private sector, for free trade, monetary mechanisms, personal incentives (albeit within a one-party dictatorship and with fairly strict ideological conformity) – seems to represent a significant revision of the civil war model, although a constant core ran at the heart of both. The crux of the issue lies in the timetable of the transition envisaged. Were the policies of NEP for the whole transitional period between the revolution and communism? Or were they merely a transition until the transition, i.e. a preparation for the lower stage of communism (socialism) which would then see a reversion to the former model in order to usher in full-blown communism? No definitive answer exists. Lenin was convinced of the correctness of a gradualist, market-based evolutionary path in 1922–3. But Lenin was also firmly committed to planning, central direction and heavy industry. A strong case can be made, as Lewin and Szamuely have done, for viewing Lenin at this point as being a proponent of a socialist planned economy using market methods. Equally though, Brus has argued that the existence of the market was due to the survival of non-state sectors of the economy.[124] Once these were removed the basis for the use of commodity–money relations would disappear.

It is probably accurate to argue that both NEP and the civil war "models" represent modifications of the pre-revolutionary model of Soviet socialism. As the Bolsheviks sought to apply their ideas, in different contexts, so their emphases and policies shifted in response to the differing priorities of winning an armed struggle, and effecting a transition to socialism in an economically devastated country and a hostile capitalist world. The model displayed a strong core of constants. The variables within this model – the scope of state activity, the relationship between centralized planning and market relations, the relationship between the state and the non-state sectors, the nature of economic incentives – were forged from the application of these constants to Russian realities. In this sense, both NEP and the civil war model have a clear filiation with the pre-revolutionary understanding of socialism in Bolshevik discourse, and represent the outcome of the process of the interaction of theory and reality, culminating in a refining and specifying of the original theories. After the civil war, the theory was refined in the direction of universalizing state power. With NEP, the use of money, market relations and personal incentives became part of the transition to socialism. But the essential understanding of Soviet socialism remained unchanged.

NEP *and the socio-cultural aspects of Soviet socialism*

It is in this sphere that the most "clear water" exists between NEP and the civil war model. In particular, NEP represents a reassessment of the Bolshevik commitment to proletarian internationalism and to the prioritization of the interests of the proletariat at home. The two issues are inextricably linked.

The proletarian internationalist perspective was mitigated in favour of an approach that promoted class collaboration within Russia, as the prospects of an international revolution receded. International revolution was still the firm goal of the Bolsheviks. The realities of Russia, however, meant a shift in emphasis towards a national, class collaborative approach. Beilharz asserts that NEP represents a populist multi-class utopia, which differs from the westernizing, modernizing, proletarian utopia of *State and revolution*.[125] The creation of a more inclusive socio-cultural base incorporated concessions to personal interests and material incentives in the construction of socialism. This strengthened the tendencies towards inegalitarianism, stratification and hierarchy. Bourgeois specialists were retained in post as the Bolsheviks were forced to recognize that they would have to build socialism with non-socialist hands.

But it would be wrong to overemphasize the extent of this socio-cultural "retreat". The Bolshevik approach continued to be underpinned by notions of proletarianism, internationalism, collectivism, constructivism and instrumentalism: culture in the service of the construction of socialism. The Bolsheviks still believed that human nature could be altered by changing the external environment. Human beings were still viewed as a malleable resource who could be moulded and shaped to create a New Socialist Man.[126] The interesting issue here is the extent to which the Bolshevik understanding of the socio-cultural sphere had become accommodated to the realities of Russian society, rather than the discourse reflecting an accommodation between competing ideas within the party itself. The party line was dominated by the leadership's rationalist, constructivist approach, as opposed to the libertarian, emancipatory line (although the latter still existed at this point).

NEP *and the politics of Soviet socialism*

In 1917, the conquest of political power dominated Bolshevik thinking. In 1924, questions of culture and economics predominated. Somewhat paradoxically, while in the latter two fields the Bolsheviks were "accommodating" themselves to the stubborn reality of Russian socio-economic structures, in the political sphere, there was greater pressure towards centralization, monism and dictatorship, extending the patterns of control and rule established during the civil war. The two issues were linked of course. In the course of a retreat, strict discipline was required. In the NEP period, the control of state over society was deepened and extended, while the party itself became increasingly centralized and bureaucratized.

The predominance of centralism, appointmentism, bureaucratism, the continuation of the use of terror, the suppression of other socialist parties, the repression of the clergy all reflected the need for "discipline" during the retreat. In particular, this meant preventing the emergence or expression of dissident or discrepant voices and organizations. This entailed strict ideological controls and more importantly political controls. What was central to the politics of NEP was that this was now applied to the party itself, not just to organizations outside of the party. The ban on factions and the prevalence of appointmentism reflected the continued predominance of elitism, hierarchy, centralization. Even measures designed to combat bureaucratism and careerism, and maintain the purity of the consciousness of the vanguard – purges and control commissions – tended to reinforce the powers of the centre. The key issue here is that of "consciousness". The retreat required close supervision and leadership by politically and ideologically orthodox figures.

This emphasis upon the necessity and desirability of centralized elite direction and control was still framed alongside the need for mass participation. The enduring tension within Bolshevism between technocratic, depoliticized, expertise based approaches to the management of society, and those favouring mass participation, democracy, accountability and local autonomy still existed under NEP. What was becoming clearer by the time of Lenin's death was the nature of the latter. Mass participation was to be directed and supervised by the party, and was to be channelled into tasks defined by party. The question which thus came to dominate the politics of NEP were the composition of the party, the quality of its personnel, and the means by which supervision from below could be combined with specialist guidance from above. Essentially, the hegemony of the technocratic tendency within Soviet socialism was deepened under NEP.

Conclusion: the Soviet model of socialism

By 1924, the contours of the understanding of socialism in Bolshevik discourse were becoming slightly clearer. While the first seven years of Bolshevik rule had resolved many of the tensions extant within the pre-revolutionary writings of Marx, Engels, Lenin and Kautsky, many tensions, ambiguities and imprecisions remained. The core features of this model included:

- a worldview that was productivist, technocratic, constructivist, collectivist;
- the leading role of the communist party in guiding and managing social and economic processes, excluding other political organizations;
- an economy that was planned, centralized, nationalized, industrialized, technologically advanced, and which prioritized large-scale heavy industry.
- a central role for the state as an agent of social and economic transformation.

The post-1917 practice, however, left many issues unresolved. These included:

- what was meant by "planning"?
- what was the locus of decision-making within the economy? What was the balance between centralization and decentralization?
- what would the extent of inegalitarianism be under socialism? Which group would be privileged?
- what was the relationship between the interests of the international proletariat and the domestic interests of the Soviet state?
- what was the relationship between state control and popular participation in the administration of the system?
- should the process of transition be viewed as something to be accomplished rapidly and coercively, or gradually and consensually?
- how could the rural/urban divide be overcome? By what means should the countryside be socialized/collectivized?
- how could the peasantry be transformed into a rural proletariat?

Neither NEP, nor the practices established during the civil war, supplied a definitive resolution to these questions. The death of Lenin in 1924 witnessed a fierce struggle between different individuals for control of the party. Within this power struggle, there emerged competing interpretations of the correct manner to construct socialism. Bukharin, Trotsky, Preobrazhensky, Stalin and others engaged in a wide-ranging debate that was finally resolved in 1929 with Stalin's victory in the factional struggles.

Notes

1. A good description of the contours of the crisis facing the party is L. Siegelbaum, *Soviet state and society between revolutions* (Cambridge: Cambridge University Press, 1992), pp. 67–84.
2. Among the best pieces, see ibid., pp. 85–187; M. Lewin, *Political undercurrents in Soviet economic debates* (London: Pluto Press, 1975), pp. 84–96; R. Pipes, *Russia under the Bolshevik regime* (London: Harvill, 1994), pp. 369–435; A. Nove, *An economic history of the*

USSR (Harmondsworth: Penguin, 1992), pp. 83–118; G. Hosking, *A history of the Soviet Union* (London: Fontana, 1992), pp. 119–48; E. H. Carr, *The Bolshevik revolution 1917–23*, vol. 2, pp. 269–357; S. Fittzpatrick et al. (eds), *Russia in the era of NEP* (Bloomington: Indiana University Press, 1991); S. Cohen, *Rethinking the Soviet experience* (Oxford: Oxford University Press, 1985), pp. 71–92; O. Figes, *A People's Tragedy* (London: Pimlico, 1997), pp. 721–72. For excellent technical analyses of economic developments, see R. W. Davies, M. Harrison, S. G. Wheatcroft (eds), *The economic transformation of the Soviet Union 1913–45* (Cambridge: Cambridge University Press, 1994); R. W. Davies (ed.), *From Tsarism to the New Economic Policy* (Houndmills: Macmillan, 1990).

3.   M. von Hagen, "The NEP, perestroika and the problem of alternatives", in *Socialism, perestroika and the dilemmas of Soviet economic reform*, J. Tedstrom (ed.) (Boulder: Westview Press, 1990).

4.   R. Service, *Lenin: a political life*, vol. 3 (London: Macmillan, 1995), p. 107.

5.   Ibid., p. 107.

6.   Ibid., pp. 169–70.

7.   Ibid., p. 170.

8.   Ibid., pp. 171–2.

9.   R. Gregor (ed.), *Resolutions and decisions of the CPSU, vol. 2, 1917–29* (Toronto: University of Toronto Press, 1974), pp. 129–30.

10.   V. I. Lenin, "Report on the substitution of a tax-in-kind for the surplus-grain appropriation system", in *Selected Works*, vol. 3, pp. 568–80; Lenin, "Tax-in-kind", in ibid., pp. 589–619; Lenin, "Report on the tax-in-kind", in *Collected Works*, vol. 32 (London: Lawrence & Wishart, 1965–70), pp. 402–32. For a Western assessment see A. Ball, "Lenin and the question of private trade in Russia", in *Slavic Review* **43**, 1984, pp. 399–412.

11.   Lenin, "Report on the substitution of a tax-in-kind", p. 569.

12.   Ibid., p. 578.

13.   Lenin, "the tax-in-kind", pp. 601–7.

14.   Lenin, "Report on the tax-in-kind", p. 406.

15.   Ibid., pp. 407–8.

16.   Pipes, *Russia under the Bolshevik regime*, pp. 391–2. Carr dissents from these figures slightly, *The Bolshevik revolution*, vol. 2, pp. 283–4.

17.   Nove, *An economic history of the USSR*, pp. 83–118 is probably the best brief description of the impact of NEP.

18.   D. Atkinson, *The end of the Russian land commune 1905–30* (Stanford: Stanford University Press, 1983), pp. 234–9.

19.   M. Dobb, *Soviet economic development since 1917* (London: Routledge, 1966), pp. 132–4.

20. Carr, *The Bolshevik revolution*, vol. 2, pp. 296–302.
21. Lenin, "The NEP and the tasks of the political education departments", in *Collected Works*, vol. 33 (London: Lawrence & Wishart, 1965–70), p. 72.
22. Dobb, *Soviet economic development*, pp. 130–2.
23. Carr, *The Bolshevik revolution*, vol. 2, pp. 302–9.
24. Dobb, *Soviet economic development*, p. 135.
25. Ibid., p. 136.
26. Nove, *An economic history of the USSR*, p. 89.
27. Siegelbaum, *Soviet state and society between revolutions*, pp. 100–113.
28. Carr, *The Bolshevik revolution*, vol. 2, pp. 328–9.
29. Gregor, *Resolutions and Decisions*, pp. 126–9.
30. See article 4 in ibid., p. 126–7.
31. Carr, *The Bolshevik revolution*, vol. 2, p. 327.
32. Dobb, *Soviet economic development*, pp. 136–8.
33. Lenin, "Political report of the CC of the RCP", in *Selected Works*, vol. 3, p. 690.
34. For a good overview of the place of NEP in Soviet historiography, see Cohen, *Rethinking the Soviet experience*, pp. 38–92.
35. Service, *Lenin: a political life*, pp. 176–82.
36. Gregor, *Resolutions and decisions*, vol. 2, p. 124.
37. Service, *Lenin: a political life*, pp. 172–6.
38. Gregor, *Resolutions and decisions*, vol. 2, pp. 119–21.
39. Ibid., p. 121.
40. Lenin, Political report of the CC of the RCP to the 11th party Congress, 27 March 1922, in *Selected Works*, vol. 3, p. 691.
41. Pipes, *Russia under the Bolshevik regime*, pp. 403–9.
42. Ibid., pp. 347–56.
43. Schapiro, *Communist party of the Soviet Union*, pp. 242–8.
44. Ibid., pp. 249–50.
45. Carr, *The Bolshevik revolution*, vol. 1, pp. 231–5.
46. Gregor, *Resolutions and decisions*, vol. 2, p. 124.
47. Carr, *The Bolshevik revolution*, vol. 1, p. 235.
48. Schapiro, *Communist party of the Soviet Union*, pp. 236–7.
49. Ibid., p. 246.
50. Gregor, *Resolutions and decisions*, vol. 2, pp. 151–2.
51. Ibid., pp. 157–62.
52. Lenin, Political report of the CC of the RCP to 11th Congress, 27 March 1922, in *Selected Works*, vol. 3, p. 708.
53. Carr, *The Bolshevik revolution*, vol. 1, pp. 188–9.
54. Good introductions to this field include, J. Burbank, "Lenin and the law in revolutionary Russia", *Slavic Review* **54**(1), 1995, pp. 23–44; E. L. Johnson, *An introduction to the Soviet legal system* (London:

Methuen, 1969); H. J. Berman, *Justice in the USSR* (Cambridge, Mass.: Harvard University Press, 1966).

55. Berman, *Justice in the USSR*, p. 33. Lenin demanded a new code in three weeks according to Berman! He got it in four months.

56. Ibid., p. 34.

57. Cited in ibid., p. 36.

58. Burbank, "Lenin and the law", pp. 41–2.

59. See W. G. Rosenberg, "Conclusion: understanding NEP society and culture in the light of the new research", in *Russia in the era of NEP*, Fitzpatrick et al. (eds), pp. 310–20.

60. B. Clements, "The utopianism of the zhenotdel", *Slavic Review* **51**(2), 1992, pp. 483–96.

61. Ibid., pp. 492–3.

62. G. Lapidus, "Sexual equality in Soviet policy", in *Women in Russia*, D. Atkinson et al. (eds) (Hassocks: Harvester Press, 1978), pp. 119–24.

63. M. Buckley, *Women and ideology in the Soviet Union* (London: Harvester Wheatsheaf, 1989), pp. 40–3.

64. G. Lapidus, *Women in Soviet society: Equality, development and social change* (Berkeley: University of California Press, 1978), p. 94.

65. M. Matthews, *Privilege in the Soviet Union* (London: Allen & Unwin, 1978), pp. 64–5.

66. Ibid., pp. 67–8.

67. Ibid., pp. 68–70.

68. Ibid., pp. 75–6.

69. Ibid., p. 76.

70. Ibid., pp. 76–7.

71. S. Rosen, *Education and modernisation in the USSR* (Reading, Mass.: Addison-Wesley, 1971), p. 38.

72. S. Fitzpatrick, "The 'soft' line on culture and its enemies: Soviet cultural policy, 1922–27", *Slavic Review* **33**, 1974, pp. 270–5; Pipes, *Russia under the Bolshevik regime*, pp. 322–5.

73. Fitzpatrick, "The 'soft' line on culture", p. 272. This complaint seems vaguely familiar.

74. Ibid., p. 274.

75. Pipes, *Russia under the Bolshevik regime*, pp. 325–8.

76. Ibid., p. 326.

77. Ibid., p. 323. S. Fitzpatrick, *The cultural front: power and culture in revolutionary Russia* (Ithaca: Cornell University Press, 1992).

78. Pipes, *Russia under the Bolshevik regime*, p. 323.

79. Fitzpatrick, "The 'soft' line on culture", pp. 270–1.

80. Ibid., p. 271.

81. R. Stites, *Russian popular culture: entertainment and society since 1900* (Cambridge: Cambridge University Press, 1992), p. 40.

82. Pipes, *Russia under the Bolshevik regime*, pp. 303–9.
83. Stites, *Russian popular culture*, pp. 37–63.
84. The nature of this "transition" is explored in W. G. Rosenberg, "Introduction", in Fitzpatrick et al. (eds), *Russia in the era of NEP*, pp. 1–11.
85. See for example, A. Nove, "Lenin and the New Economic Policy", in B. Eissenstat (ed.), *Lenin and Leninism* (Lexington: Lexington Books, 1971), pp. 155–71; M. Lewin, *Political undercurrents in Soviet economic debates* (London: Pluto Press, 1975), pp. 84–96; L. Szamuely, *First models of socialist economic systems* (Budapest: Akademia Kiado, 1974), pp. 45–79; A. Walicki, *Marxism and the leap to the Kingdom of Freedom* (Stanford: Stanford University Press, 1995), pp. 366–97.
86. Lenin, "Report on the tax-in-kind to the tenth party conference", in *Collected works* vol. 32, p. 405.
87. See Lenin, "The tax-in-kind", p. 600; Lenin, "Theses for a report on the tactics of the RCP", in *Selected works*, vol. 3, p. 626.
88. Lenin, "The tax-in-kind", pp. 600–2.
89. Szamuely, *First models of the socialist economic system*, pp. 74–5.
90. *Selected works*, vol. 3, pp. 641–8.
91. *Collected works*, vol. 33, pp. 60–79.
92. Ibid., pp. 83–108.
93. *Selected works*, vol. 3, pp. 649–55.
94. Lenin, "Report on the New Economic Policy", pp. 84–5.
95. Ibid., pp. 86–7.
96. Ibid., pp. 87–93.
97. Lewin, *Political undercurrents in Soviet economic debates*, pp. 85–6, fn. 14; Walicki, *Marxism and the leap to the Kingdom of Freedom*, pp. 366–7. Walicki argues that the two forms of state capitalism were different. Pre civil war state capitalism was marketless capitalism. NEP state capitalism was market-centred. On this reading he argues that NEP was a "conscious retreat from the programme of a direct transition to the marketless economy" (p. 367). The analysis here differs somewhat, as Lenin's later analysis clearly demonstrates that NEP had to retreat to a pre-state capitalist position. The next step would be an advance towards marketless state capitalism, and then socialism.
98. Lenin, "Report on the New Economic Policy", p. 86.
99. Ibid., p. 86.
100. Ibid., p. 86.
101. Lenin, "The New Economic Policy and the tasks of the political education departments", p. 62.
102. Lenin, "Report on the New Economic Policy", p. 93.
103. Lenin, "The tax-in-kind", p. 602.
104. Lenin, "Report on the New Economic Policy", p. 96.

105. Lenin, "Fourth anniversary of the October revolution", p. 647.
106. Draft resolutions on questions of the New Economic Policy, in *Selected works*, vol. 3, p. 433; Lenin, "Speech in closing the conference", in *Selected works*, vol. 3, p. 436.
107. Lenin, "The importance of gold now and after the complete victory of socialism", p. 655.
108. Lenin, "Political report of the CC of the RCP to the 11th Congress", pp. 688–9.
109. L. Lih, "Political testament of Lenin and Bukharin and the meaning of NEP", *Slavic Review* **50**(2), 1991, p. 248.
110. Lenin, "Political report of the CC of the RCP to the 11th party Congress", p. 693.
111. V. I. Lenin, "On Co-operation", in *Selected works*, vol. 3, pp. 760–6.
112. Ibid., p. 763.
113. Ibid., p. 765.
114. Ibid., p. 761.
115. Ibid., p. 766.
116. Lewin, *Political undercurrents in Soviet economic debates*, p. 95.
117. Lenin, "Theses for a report on the tactics of the RCP at Third Congress of Communist International", in *Selected works*, vol. 3, p. 627.
118. For details on this conference, see Z. Sochor, "Soviet Taylorism revisited", pp. 249–54.
119. Smith, "Taylorism rules OK?", p. 20.
120. Lenin, "The role and functions of the trade unions under the New Economic Policy", in *Selected works*, vol. 3, pp. 664–5.
121. Lewin, *Political undercurrents in Soviet economic debates*, pp. 88–96.
122. Cited in Szamuely, *First models of socialist economic systems*, p. 79, fn. 88.
123. R. W. Davies, "Gorbachev's socialism in historical perspective", *New Left Review* **179**, 1990, p. 9.
124. W. Brus, "Utopianism and realism in the evolution of the Soviet economic system", *Soviet Studies* **40**(3), 1988, pp. 435–8. See also Lewin, *Political undercurrents in Soviet economic debates*, pp. 73–96; Szamuely, *First models of socialist economic systems*, pp. 70–9.
125. P. Beilharz, *Labour's utopias* (London: Routledge, 1992), p. 21.
126. O. Figes, *A People's Tragedy*, pp. 732–51.

CHAPTER FIVE

Stalin, Trotsky and Bukharin: debating a new orthodoxy

Introduction

The victory of Stalin in the factional struggles in the 1920s brought a resolution of the tensions extant in the Soviet conception of socialism between 1917 and 1924. This conception was to dominate the thinking and practice of the CPSU until the accession of Gorbachev in 1985. The central themes and features of the Stalinist model of socialism are often said to have been a reanimated version of the civil war policies, representing a radical "break" with the policies of NEP, as coercion, terror and the overwhelming application of state power over society and the economic sector replaced the relative calm and pluralism of NEP. Yet it becomes clearer that the successive phases of the post-revolutionary era represent syntheses of the clash of Bolshevik ideals with Russian realities. The Stalinist model was forged out of a similar process, emphasizing particular aspects of Bolshevik theory (distilled from the conflicts with Trotsky, Bukharin, Preobrazhensky et al.), and substantiating the meaning of many of their ideals in practice (for example, "planning"). Before turning to explore the Stalinist model, the nature of the alternatives put forward by Bukharin and Trotsky need to be elaborated.

Bolshevism after Lenin: unitarian or trinitarian?

How distinct were the alternative views of the transition period developed by the leading Bolshevik figures after Lenin's death? The highly politicized nature of the historical writings on this period – both East and West – has tended to obscure and obfuscate the central issues in the debates on economic policy, party democracy and relations between the peasants and the workers. The vogue to rehabilitate Bukharin after 1985, the contested place of Trotsky in Marxist discourse (both East and West), and the relative lack of attention paid to the ideas of Preobrazhensky, all reflect the way the history of this period has been subject to the shifting sands of highly politicized historiography.

In the following analysis, the views of Trotsky, Bukharin, Preobrazhensky and Stalin are set out. It is crucial to bear two things in mind. First, the economic perspectives outlined below were developed against a backdrop of intense political in-fighting. Secondly, the views of the major protagonists changed and developed during 1924–9. Stalin is the figure who is most often quoted as having shifted his position, but he was by no means alone. From the debates and oscillations of the factionalism of the 1920s, it is possible to identify the essential features of the platforms of Bukharin, Trotsky and Stalin.

Bukharinism and Soviet socialism

Bukharin is viewed as the defender of NEP, of gradualism, of the peasantry, of a "national" or "separate" road to socialism.[1] His vision of the transition period is said to stand in stark contrast with that of Trotsky and the other "super-industrializers", with their emphasis upon rapid industrialization, the workers and the international revolution. Bukharin is said to be an advocate of the socialist market, of an all-embracing non-class populist vision of a worker–peasant socialism. Can this view be sustained?

Only the broad contours of Bukharin's thought can be outlined here. Extrapolating from his works written during the period 1921–9, Bukharin was consistent in subscribing to the general ideas of Bolshevism concerning the transition period.[2] Hence, Bukharin was a consistent advocate of a centralized, unified economy. He believed in the inherent superiority of planning. Industrialization was indispensable to the construction of socialism, and the growth of the capital goods sector was a prerequisite for the emergence of an industrial society. The dictatorship of the Bolshevik party had to be maintained. Disagreements and disputes emerged over how to reach this goal. In particular, differences emerged over the methods, limits and tempos of constructing socialism. In terms of specifics, Bukharin constructed an original and distinct synthesis of the tensions within Bolshevik discourse: the balance of plan/market, urban/rural, industry/agriculture, worker/peasant, production/consumption, international/national, democracy/bureaucracy in this transitional phase.

The balance of market and plan stands at the centre of Bukharinism. In Bukharin's thought, the market was to be a central feature of the construction of socialism. But it was part of the transition *to* socialism, not an integral part *of* the transition phase (i.e. the lower phase of communism). Bukharin saw an expanding consumer market as the key to industrial growth.[3] Within the NEP framework of a mixed economy (state industrial sector and private agricultural and industrial sector), the emergence of a prosperous peasantry would stimulate demand for consumer goods. This would benefit the state industrial sector (because of its greater efficiency and competitiveness, economies of scale, etc.), which would gradually displace the private part of the industrial sector, strengthening the socialist forces at the expense of the capitalist ones. In the agricultural sector, the poor and middle peasants would be encouraged to create rural consumer co-operatives to purchase goods. This would give them a comparative advantage over the individual farms of the *kulaks*. In the long-term, these co-operative societies would prove to be more efficient, displacing individual private farming and inculcating in the peasantry collectivist economic norms, as co-operation expanded into production as well as consumption.[4]

Three points to note. First, as Lih, Cohen and others have noted, Bukharin outlined overcoming the market "through the market".[5] There was no sense of a future "assault" on market relations and the private sector through the rapid, forced expansion of the state sector. In other words, Bukharin was advocating an evolutionary, gradualist approach to the construction of socialism. This would be a prolonged process. Secondly, this economic competition between the private and state sectors, mediated through the market, was the form in which the class struggle would now take place. Bukharin was advocating a peaceful construction of socialism. This stood in marked contrast to those who saw the construction of socialism as being accompanied by increased class conflict within the rural sector.[6] Thirdly, Bukharin stressed the sphere of circulation over the sphere of production, overturning the traditional Bolshevik emphasis upon production as the key process in the construction of socialism.[7]

The centrality of market relations inexorably shaped Bukharin's views on planning. Bukharin believed in planning, but stressed that the plan had to be realistic, scientific, flexible and designed to maintain the proportionality and equilibrium in the economy. Planning would enable a more rational, controlled approach to economic management, and through a flexible framework, would interact with the spontaneous forces of the market. Although Bukharin became increasingly convinced of the benefits of a more comprehensive form of planning by the late 1920s, he was still critical of approaches to planning that were overly centralist or bureaucratic.[8] For Bukharin, planning would grow and extend its scope of operation organically along with the growth of the socialist sector and the displacement of the market. It should not be seen as a process that embraced the entire economic life of the state immediately.

Bukharin's approach to the question of the relationship between peasants and workers, town and country, also turned many Bolshevik assumptions on their head. Bukharin viewed the peasantry more as allies than enemies, professed faith in their revolutionary potential, and sought to build socialism through civil peace between peasants and workers, not conflict.[9] The essence of his position was the maintenance of the *smychka*. Without this support from the peasantry, socialism could not be constructed in Russia. Bukharin acknowledged that the peasantry had two "souls": a labouring soul, and a proprietorial soul. The task of the party was to create the economic and cultural conditions in which the former would gradually displace the latter.[10] The key peasant group for Bukharin were the middle peasants. If they could be won over to collectivist ideals, then the agricultural sector would evolve in a socialist direction. If not, then the likely outcome would be capitalism. This accounts for Bukharin's support for co-operation rather than collectivization in the medium term, as co-operation would demonstrate the superiority of collectivism over individualism, without undermining the peasants proprietorial instincts. Collective farming – large scale, mechanized and efficient – would eventually displace individual farming, but only by proving to be more productive and prosperous. Bukharin supported moves to limit the *kulaks*, but these were to be economic and non-coercive. Although Bukharin remained within the general framework of Bolshevism – priority of the proletariat – his view of the peasantry was far more positive, optimistic. Soviet society, in Bukharin's eyes, was a more inclusive, complex and differentiated organism than traditional Bolshevik class categories usually set out, and was to be based on civic peace and consensus rather than strife and conflict.[11]

Bukharin also shifted the basis of Bolshevik thought on the international arena. Bukharin (along with Stalin) is credited with shifting Bolshevism from an internationalist perspective to a nationalist one, with the development of the idea of "socialism in one country". Stalin first adopted the slogan in December 1924, but it was Bukharin who elaborated its theoretical significance. This concept, has been subject to a certain degree of misrepresentation, much of it deriving from the polemical disputes between "Left" and "Right" in the 1920s. It is necessary to correct many of these one-sided and distorted views. First, Bukharin never disavowed the long-term possibility of a proletarian revolution in western Europe. However, he did argue that with the failure of insurrection in Germany, and the apparent stabilization of the western economy, a rethink about the approach to the construction of socialism in peasant, isolated Russia was necessary. In the light of this new situation, Bukharin reconceptualized the internationalist outlook of the party. He argued that it was possible to build socialism in Russia, or more specifically, it was possible for Russia to modernize and industrialize on her own. Through the economic processes described above, Russia would grow into socialism through the *smychka*.[12]

Bukharin responded to the charge that he was promoting a nationalist form of socialism in a number of ways. First, he argued that the ultimate victory of socialism in Russia could not be guaranteed without revolutions elsewhere. Secondly, the nature of socialism in Russia would reflect the backward peasant socio-economic structure. On a global basis socialism would display a high degree of heterogeneity, because of the differences in cultural levels, ethnic composition, levels of economic development, social structure, etc. It was possible to construct socialism in Russia, but it would not conform precisely and immediately to the vision espoused by Marx and Engels.[13] Thirdly, Bukharin theorized the *smychka* on a global scale. As the peasants could legitimately be viewed as revolutionary allies within Russia, then might they not prove to be international revolutionary allies? Bukharin began to preach the potency of the peasantry as a force for revolution in the non-capitalist colonies, and by extension of the possibility of a peasant-based, non-capitalist path to socialism. Bukharin maintained a revolutionary, internationalist stance, but shifted the focus from Europe to Asia, from proletariat to peasantry.[14]

Bukharin's position within Bolshevism's ideological matrix is an interesting one. While subscribing faithfully to the broad features of the transition period, Bukharin provided an original resolution of many of the unresolved tensions in Bolshevik thought on the shape of the entire transition period. His inclusive socio-class analysis, the emphasis on balanced growth, and realistic flexible planning, the growth of socialism through the market, and the possibility of building socialism in one country, distinguish Bukharin from his contemporaries. Yet, it would be wrong to overestimate the distinctiveness of Bukharin's platform. He remained an advocate of a centralized, large-scale, concentrated, planned industrial economy. Bukharin cannot be held up as the defender of market relations under socialism, or of a form of market socialism. He abhorred the anarchy and spontaneity of market forces. But he also opposed the overbureaucratization and overcentralization of the economy. He wished to establish the political hegemony of the proletariat, and continued to advocate unequal franchise arrangements that favoured the worker over the peasant. Yet this was not a platform of socialist political pluralism: Bukharin fully supported the one-party monopoly. The role of the state should be that of educator. Politics should be carried out on the basis of consensus, of revolutionary legality, of persuasion. The key for Bukharin was to draw the masses more fully into the work of local Soviets, to create space for voluntary organizations and associations as a way of combating bureaucratism without undermining the role of the party.[15] As with Lenin, Bukharin sought to steer a course between pluralist (socialist) democracy and a bureaucratized state standing above the masses, unaccountable and undemocratic.

Trotsky and Preobrazhensky

The views of Trotsky are no less controversial and disputed than those of Bukharin. Trotsky is often characterized as a "super-industrializer": as a consistent proponent of rapid industrialization, central planning, class war in the countryside and international revolution. In other words Trotsky is often portrayed as the inheritor of the "socialist offensive", "heroic" tradition of "war communism". Yet a close reading of Trotsky's views reveals a far greater degree of correspondence between the views of Trotsky and Bukharin than the labels "Leftist" and "Rightist" would indicate.[16]

On markets and planning, Trotsky followed a similar approach to Bukharin. Trotsky remained committed to the market during the transition to socialism. The framework of NEP – market, material incentives and the *smychka* with the peasantry – was to be maintained. Although Trotsky emphasized the importance of strengthening and building up the socialist industrial sector and of moving towards a planned economy, this was to be accomplished via the market.[17] Trotsky argued that:

> We must adapt the Soviet state to the needs and strength of the peasantry, while preserving its character as a workers state; we must adapt Soviet industry to the peasant market.[18]

In similar vein to Bukharin, Trotsky saw planning developing in tandem with the market: that is, it would have to be a rational, realistic, flexible approach. By restricting the operation of the plan to the socialist industrial sector, this would enable the practice of planning to be perfected and to be adapted to the peasant market economy. Although Trotsky continued to assert the necessity and priority of industrialization, in 1923–4 this was to be achieved through the market. Trotsky and Bukharin only really began to differ after 1926–7, when Trotsky became increasingly critical of the gradualist, pro-peasant orientation.[19] Industrialization, pro-workerism and central planning were an increasing necessity as the international situation worsened and the peasants began to withdraw from the market.

It is here that the differential emphasis of the two theorists becomes evident. Trotsky was far less tolerant of the market, far less content with the growth of capitalism in the countryside, and placed a greater emphasis upon the need to industrialize as quickly as was economically possible. Trotsky wished to industrialize within the framework of NEP, but this was to be accomplished through the exploitation of the agricultural sector. Priority was to be accorded to the industrial sector.[20]

The differences between Trotsky and Bukharin became more evident in their respective attitudes towards the international arena. In the course of the factional struggles in the 1920s, Trotsky was labelled as the advocate of "permanent revolution" in opposition to the views of Stalin and Bukharin who espoused the idea of "social-ism in one country" (of which more below). Trotsky's doctrine had two separate but related components. First, that in Russia the anti-feudal revolution would grow into the proletarian revolution (which had essentially been Lenin's position in 1917). Secondly, that the revolutionary impulse would shift out from Russia to the rest of the world, and the victory of socialism in Russia required the victory of the international revolution.[21] Trotsky opposed the implications of "socialism in one country" on a number of grounds. First, he denied that the Soviet economy could develop using its own resources. Economic autarky was an error, for Russia required imports from the West to make good shortfalls in consumer goods, and to provide capital goods for industrialization. On its own, the Russian economy could not withstand the economic pressures and greater efficiency of the western economies. Secondly, the technical and cultural backwardness of Russia meant that autarky would doom Russia to permanent underdevelopment. Thirdly, "socialism in one country" rendered foreign policy defensive – preventing capitalist intervention to allow Russia to develop on her own basis – rather than foment-ing and promoting revolution in the West. In this way it would contribute to the long-term defeat of the international revolution.[22] Trotsky never denied that it was possible to set in motion the pro-cess of socialist construction in Russia. Neither did he believe that the international revolution was imminent. Trotsky, like Bukharin agreed that world revolution remained an essential objective. The differences with Stalin will be highlighted below; however, there appears to be agreement on underlying principles, but differences of emphasis: Trotsky's essentially internationalist emphasis versus Stalin and Bukharin's essentially nationalist emphasis.

Clearly, Trotsky shared many basic assumptions with Bukharin, although his vision of the future was more industrialist, modernist, centralizing and technocratic, and this influenced the manner in which he conceptualized the transitional phase. The differences were ones of emphasis, nuance, tempo, degree. In fact there appear to be greater differences between Trotsky and Preobrazhensky, erstwhile "Leftist" allies, than between Trotsky and Bukharin. In particular, Preobrazhensky stressed the need to prioritize the growth of state industry.[23] In this way the forces of socialism were consolidated, the basis for a collectivized, mechanized agriculture was lain, and the organizational advantages of planning (the central factor in socialist economic superiority) could be exploited. For Preobrazhensky, the development of state industry required the privileging of heavy industry over light industry. The resources would be provided through "primitive socialist accumulation": acquisition of the resources for industrialization from the peasant sector and from integration into the global socialist economy. In other words, owing to the need to exploit the peasantry and to benefit from the advances in the world economy, Preobrazhensky was deeply convinced of the need for support from the western proletariat: he was opposed to the idea of "socialism in one country". The construction of socialism would not be possible without assistance from outside.[24] In sum, Preobrazhensky's emphasis on the need for comprehensive planning to be developed immediately, the priority of heavy industry and the absolute imperative of international revolution places him at the other end of the spectrum from Bukharin, with Trotsky occupying something of a middling position.

Within this debate there was a high degree of consensus on the central aspects of economic policy and the construction of socialism. The application of labels ("super-industrializer" and "permanent revolutionary", or "communist populist") was a consequence of the factional struggles within the party. They obscure the shared set of assumptions held by the main protagonists. Yet the differences – over priorities, emphases, assessments of danger – were real ones also. The defeat of Trotsky and Bukharin in the factional struggles between 1927 and 1929 opened the way for the application of the platform espoused by Stalin.[25]

The emergence of a Stalinist model

Stalin's contribution to the forging of a distinctive model of Soviet socialism in practice is uncontested. Stalin's policies infused Bolshevik concepts – planning, centralization, industrialization – with a specific content. On this basis Stalin occupies a key role in establishing an orthodox interpretation of Soviet socialism. His contribution to the theoretical development of Soviet socialism is more contentious. Scholars have tended to question the originality, depth and meaning of Stalin's infrequent incursions into the field of theory. Can this view be sustained?

"Like a cat avoiding hot porridge": Stalin, Trotsky and "socialism in one country"

Stalin's contributions to the theoretical debates in the 1920s are inextricably linked with the factional struggles. Only with this context in mind is it possible to understand the emergence of Stalin's idea of "socialism in one country".[26] Only within this context is it possible to understand how a minor technical difference over the meaning of terms such as "building" or "completion" or "victory", became the basis for a major doctrinal dispute between Stalin and Trotsky.

Although Stalin is credited with the first use of the phrase in December 1924 (in an article entitled "October revolution and the tactics of Russian communists")[27] the notion that it would be possible to construct socialism in Russia was implicit in Bukharin's idea of "growing into socialism". The phrase emerged somewhat haphazardly. In April 1924, in a series of lectures at Sverdlov University entitled "Foundations of Leninism", Stalin outlined that,

> . . . does it mean that with the forces of only one country it can finally consolidate socialism and fully guarantee that country against intervention, and, consequently also against restoration? No it does not. For this the victory of the revolution in at least several countries is needed. Therefore the development and support of revolution in other countries is an essential task of the victorious revolution.[28]

This was a restatement of orthodoxy concerning the relationship of the *construction of socialism* and its dependence upon help from the European proletariat. However, Stalin also asserted that a socialist *revolution* could be successful within one country. This was the onset of Stalin's concerted attack on the idea of permanent revolution, arguing that it was anti-Leninist and attempting to disassociate Trotsky from Lenin and set himself up as Lenin's rightful heir. It is in this context – the struggle to discredit Trotsky – that "socialism in one country" emerged.

In December 1924, Stalin began to revise the ideas of "Foundations of Leninism", shifting the emphasis towards the possibility of constructing "socialism in one country". Quoting Lenin from 1915 ("the victory of socialism is possible first in several or even in one capitalist country, taken singly"),[29] Stalin outlined that the basis existed within Russia for the construction of socialism, rather than the Russian proletariat having to depend upon developments elsewhere. The idea remained undeveloped for several months, as Stalin continued to assert the necessity of the world revolution. With the publication of two works – *The results of the work of the Fourteenth Party Conference* (May 1925) and *On the problems of Leninism* (January 1926) – Stalin began to elaborate his ideas more fully, as he became aware of the political potential and the popularity of the slogan. The essence of Stalin's views were that there were two sets of contradictions in the contemporary world that had to be overcome. The first was between the proletariat and the peasantry within Russia. The second was between the USSR and the capitalist countries.[30]

Stalin's argument was that socialism can and must be completed in Russia, but that the final victory of socialism in Russia could not be guaranteed. Socialism could be built in Russia because she had sufficient resources, expertise and revolutionary ardour to complete the task. Socialism had to be built because with the stabilization of the capitalist countries of the West, the alternative was either to press forward with socialist construction or to degenerate. Final victory could not be guaranteed, though, because of the continual possibility of capitalist intervention. International revolution was still a necessity. The essential distinction drawn by Stalin related to the reasons for the inability to ensure the complete victory of socialism. Stalin asserted that both Trotsky and Zinoviev supported the process of constructing socialism in Russia, but believed that economic and technical backwardness would prevent the completion of this task.

In other words, the Russian workers could not finish what they had started. By way of contrast, Stalin asserted that the inability to complete the victory of socialism was solely due to the hostile international environment.[31]

The conceptual differences between the protagonists were minimal. What distinguished them was faith. Faith in the ability of the Russian people to construct socialism,

> Without such a possibility, the building of socialism is building without prospects, building without being sure that socialism will be built. It is no use building socialism without being sure that we can build it, without being sure that the technical backwardness of our country is not an insuperable obstacle to the building of a complete socialist society. To deny such a possibility is to display lack of faith in the cause of building socialism, to abandon Leninism.[32]

Trotsky's views appeared to be defeatist and negative, Stalin's optimistic and positive. Stalin was appealing to a pride in the achievements of the revolution, asserting that Russia was no longer dependent upon the West. Indeed Russia would now take the lead in the revolutionary movement worldwide. Russia was now the centre of the world socialist revolution. The weakest link in the imperialist chain had become the fulcrum of the revolution.

How significant was this concept? In terms of inner-party developments, it pushed Stalin into the forefront of the ideological struggle. Stalin, in Deutscher's words, "became an ideologue in his own right".[33] It was also a central part in Stalin's attempts to discredit Trotsky: he was labelled a defeatist, a pessimist, an adventurist, a Menshevik and an anti-Leninist. This was because Stalin argued that the doctrine of "permanent revolution" required risky adventures abroad, while demonstrating little faith in Russian workers. Similarly, "permanent revolution" was a deviation from Leninism, and could best be described as a form of Menshevism. The message contained within "socialism in one country" was particularly potent for the party: it promised stability, continuity and also progress towards socialism. Its significance went far beyond the original intent to discredit Trotsky.[34]

This concept synthesized Marxist and Leninist orthodoxy with nationalist ideals, linking Russian specifics with Marxian universals. The emphasis on the self-sufficiency and self-reliance of Russia promoted the idea that Russia was now the centre of world revolution, and would be the centre of the new future post-capitalist civilization. This appears to be Russian exceptionalism with a Marxist face.[35] Yet Stalin went to great lengths to assert the Leninist credentials of "socialism in one country": it was the continuation of the process of constructing socialism initiated under NEP by Lenin. Yet, as Carr has maintained, it also meant the end of NEP.[36] The move away from a professed dependency on the West to industrialize was now combined with a faith in Russia's internal capacity to industrialize. In this way, the dependence on the peasantry (a central pillar of NEP) was also overcome. "Socialism in one country" expresses a new resolution of the tensions within Soviet socialism, incorporating the orthodox faith in industrialization and a privileged place for the proletariat, alongside a new emphasis upon nationalistic–patriotic motifs.

Soviet socialism and Stalin: theorizing self-sufficiency

On one level, Stalin appears to subscribe to orthodox Bolshevik thinking on the nature of the transition phase. He was committed to creating a society that was industrialized, collectivized, centrally planned and technologically advanced. Industrialization would create the material and technical basis for the abundance of communism, and would turn peasants into proletarians. The creation of a numerically and politically dominant proletariat would solve the problem of the party ruling in a peasant country. He was opposed to the market and private ownership. He openly advocated policies that fomented class war in the countryside. He supported the continuation of the communist party's monopoly of power, and the ban on factions within the party. Yet a closer look at Stalin's writings and speeches during the period 1925–9 show that Stalin shifted the thinking of the party in subtle yet profound ways. In particular, the elaboration of the doctrine of "socialism in one country", while linked to the factional struggles, also had significant theoretical consequences. The notions of autarky and self-sufficiency inherent in this doctrine caused a reassessment of the Bolshevik commitment to the development of the productive forces in the USSR, and shaped the priorities of industrial development, which in turn shaped the nature of the economic basis of Soviet socialism.

The turn "inwards" inherent in "socialism in one country" had a number of significant repercussions. All the extant issues to be resolved in the transition to socialism and communism – technical backwardness, industrialization, collectivization of agriculture, elimination of the market – now had to be accomplished internally. This imposed a new set of priorities and policies *in order to achieve self-sufficiency.* This shifted the nature of the transition itself. The construction of a socialist society now had to be achieved via the route of national self-sufficiency. Self-sufficiency entailed a particular form of modernization, a particular form of industrialization. As we have seen before, whereas ends can justify means, the means shape the ends. Stalin's programme, by fusing Marxism and nationalism, imparted a particular content to the key processes of the transition period: technical advance, modernization, raising productivity. Stalin invoked that, "It is not just any kind of increase in the productivity of labour of the people that we need."[37] These processes were not to be driven purely by the need to construct the basis of socialism: the imperative to defend the country also now came into the equation. The emphasis upon self-sufficiency shaped the nature of the transition in a number of ways.

In economic terms, Stalin opted to prioritize industrial development, and in particular large-scale capital goods industries. In 1928, Stalin said,

> Our theses proceed from the premise that a fast rate of development of industry in general, and of the production of the means of production in particular, is the underlying principle of, and the key to, the industrialization of the country, the underlying principle of and key to, the transformation of our entire national economy along the lines of socialist development.[38]

Stalin advocated shifting priority not just away from the agricultural sector, but also away from the production of the means of consumption. If the USSR was to industrialize on its own basis, the priority was to manufacture the key producer goods to create the basis for the further industrialization of the country, for the defence of the country and, significantly, for the collectivization of agriculture. Stalin realized the Bolshevik preference for heavy industry.

Collectivization of agriculture was crucial to the industrialization process. Industrialization required reliable, increased supplies of grain. The scattered and small-scale nature of the pattern of landholding in Russia was deemed to be incapable of delivering an increase in the volume of grain. A collectivized, large-scale mechanized agricultural sector was the Bolsheviks' preferred solution. A socialist society required peasants with a collectivist outlook and collectivist values. The long-term political viability of the Soviet state required the transformation of the peasants into proletarians. Yet industrialization was integral to collectivization. Without agricultural machinery, the collective farms would not be viable. This symbiosis between collectivization and industrialization ensured a priority for the production of the means of production. This priority was reinforced by the requirements of defence,

> This applies not only to the building of socialism. It applies also to the independence of our country in the circumstances of the capitalist encirclement. The independence of our country cannot be upheld unless we have an adequate industrial basis for defence. And such an industrial basis cannot be created if our industry is not more highly developed technically.[39]

The perception that the international atmosphere was one of hostile capitalist encirclement – fuelled by the 1927 war scare – also imparted notions of haste or speed into the Stalinist programme.[40] A crash programme of modernization and industrialization entailed prioritizing key sectors of the economy – fuel, metallurgy, machine-tools, chemicals – rather than advancing a balanced approach to industrial development.

In socio-cultural terms, the drive for self-sufficiency reanimated Bolshevik notions of class war and class conflict, superceding the NEP emphasis upon social peace and class consensus. Eschewing the Bukharinite approach, which advocated the elimination of capitalism via the market, Stalin sought to resume the "offensive" against capitalist elements. Throughout 1929, Stalin set out his views on the necessity of mobilizing the proletarian elements for a struggle against capitalist elements (i.e. the *kulaks*),

> The policy should be to arouse the working class and the exploited masses of the countryside, to increase their fighting capacity and develop their mobilised preparedness for the fight against the capitalist elements in town and country, for the fight against the resisting class enemies.[41]

Indeed, Stalin asserted that the class struggle would intensify with the onset of the construction of "socialism in one country",

> The dying classes are resisting, not because they have become stronger than we are, but because socialism is growing faster than they are, and they are becoming weaker than we are. And precisely because they are becoming weaker, they feel that their last days are approaching and are compelled to resist with all the forces and all the means in their power.[42]

The intensification of the class struggle has been greatly vilified by opponents of Stalin, owing to its later use in the justification of the terror of the 1930s. Yet at the end of the 1920s it was really a restatement of the Trotskyist/Leftist position. The assertion by Trotsky that state power is at its peak just before it disappears reflects the position inherent within the doctrine of permanent revolution: the problem for the proletariat within Russia would be to consolidate power, not the seizure of power itself. The preponderance of the peasantry would make necessary a further form of conflict. The capitalist elements in the country – *kulaks*, bourgeois specialists, entrepreneurs – would have to be defeated as part of the process of constructing socialism. Industrialization required class war.

Stalin's assertion of the need for self-sufficiency also shifted the Soviet approach to international revolution. This was not abandoned. Stalin revised the definition of internationalism, prioritizing the national interests of the USSR,

> A revolutionary is one who is ready to protect, to defend the USSR without reservation, without qualification, openly

and honestly . . . for the USSR is the first proletarian revolutionary state in the world, a state which is building socialism. An internationalist is one who is ready to defend
the USSR . . . unconditionally; for the USSR is the base of the
world revolutionary movement, and this revolutionary
movement cannot be defended and promoted unless the
USSR is defended. For whoever thinks of defending the world
revolutionary movement apart from, or against, the USSR,
goes against the revolution and must inevitably slide into
the camp of the enemies of the revolution.[43]

The cause of world socialism was best served by constructing
socialism in the USSR, by defending the revolutionary gains of
1917. There was now a complete coincidence of the interests of the
international working class and those of the Soviet state. Now,
though, the former were subordinated to the promotion of the latter,
rather than vice versa. The fusion of nationalism and Marxism
was complete.

Finally, in political terms, the drive for self-sufficiency
strengthened the tendencies towards political and ideological
monism, discipline and party unity. The intensification of the class
struggle highlighted the political dangers thrown up by the twin
processes of modernization and industrialization. Stalin highlighted
three issues. First, the combination of capitalist encirclement and
economic and technical backwardness constantly generated "deviations" within the party of different political hues,

And since our proletariat does not live in a vacuum, but in
the midst of the most actual and real life with all its variety
of forms, the bourgeois elements arising on the basis of
small production "encircle" the proletariat on every side
with petit-bourgeois elemental forces, by means of which
they permeate and corrupt the proletariat . . . thereby introducing into the ranks of the proletariat and of its Party a
certain amount of vacillation, a certain amount of waver-
ing . . . There you have the root and basis of all sorts of
vacillations and deviations from the Leninist line in the
ranks of our party.[44]

215

Stalin emphasized that while the dangers of the "Right" and "Left" were different (the former underestimated the strength of capitalism, the latter overestimated it), the outcome of either in power would be the same: the restoration of capitalism. Stalin argued that in a situation of isolation, there could only be one correct line. A deviation from that line would give rise to factionalism, weaken the party and undermine the dictatorship of the proletariat. Unity and monolithism were imperative.

Secondly, Stalin warned against the dangers of bureaucratic inertia and routine among officials. Stalin's prescription for this particular ailment was a revival of the Leninist ideal of popular participation in the workings of the state, albeit channelled, mobilized and controlled by the party. Stalin asserted the importance of "self-criticism" and criticism from below. In the conditions of isolation, the safeguards of the revolutionary purity of the dictatorship lay in preserving the revolutionary consciousness of its personnel. This could only be achieved from within the party itself, given that it represented the most advanced, conscious element of the proletariat,

> Since our country is a country with a dictatorship of the proletariat, and since the dictatorship is directed by one party, the Communist Party, which does not, and cannot, share power with other parties, is it not clear that, if we want to make headway, we ourselves must disclose and correct our errors – is it not clear that there is no-one else to disclose and correct them for us? Is it not clear, comrades, that self-criticism must be one of the most important motive forces of our development.[45]

Self-criticism was to be allied with criticism from below. Criticism of the party leaders by the masses was designed to prevent them from becoming detached from the masses, from developing an interest of their own outside those of the Soviet state. It was also designed to upgrade the political consciousness of the workers themselves, rendering them more aware of problems, more willing to criticize, more engaged in the operation of the system. Stalin set clear limits to criticism though. It was not to be confused with "promotion" from below, of which Stalin had more to say elsewhere. As Stalin argued,

It is not a question of bringing new leaders to the fore, although this deserves the party's most serious attention. It is a question of preserving the leaders who have already come to the fore and possess the greatest prestige by organising permanent and indissoluble contact between them and the masses.[46]

The second limit was the type of criticism. Only criticism that aimed at,

improving the organs of Soviet rule, of improving our industry, of improving our party and trade-union work. We need criticism in order to strengthen the Soviet regime.[47]

An interesting omission from the criteria to be applied to criticism was proximity to truth. What was important was the class content of the criticism and the class origins of the critics. The following quote is archetypal Bolshevism with its class-tinted spectacles displacing norms of truth and falsehood,

How can you expect an ordinary worker or an ordinary peasant, with his own painful experience of shortcomings in our work and in our planning, to frame his criticism according to all the rules of the art? If you demand that criticism should be 100% correct, you will be killing all possibility of criticism from below, all possibility of self-criticism. That is why I think that even if criticism is only even 5 or 10% true, such criticism should be welcomed, should be listened to attentively, and the sound core in it taken into account. Otherwise, I repeat, you would be gagging all those hundreds and thousands of people who are devoted to the cause of the Soviets, who are not yet skilled enough in the art of criticism, but *through whose lips truth speaks itself.*[48] (my emphasis)

The implications from this are clear. Criticism from below that the leadership deemed acceptable would be unleashed in order to "correct" shortcomings, irrespective of its accuracy or correctness. The full disturbing ramifications of this policy were not felt until the

1930s. Arguably, this was a policy with a clear Leninist pedigree: establishing a symbiosis between rule by the vanguard and participation by the people as set out in *State and revolution*. Although this was a much more restrictive and limited notion of participation than that originally envisaged by Lenin, this does accord with a political framework that seeks to combine a one-party monopoly of power with popular participation. The criticism campaign highlights that the relationship between Bolshevism and "truth" was always a problematical one. The class-based view of the world, which conditioned Bolshevik attitudes across a whole range of issues, was woven deep into the fabric of Bolshevism.

Lastly, the party once more stressed the essential requirement of creating Red Specialists: to combat bourgeois specialists as part of the intensification of the class struggle meant finding replacements who were both Red and Expert. The pursuit of self-sufficiency imparted a new urgency to the creation of politically reliable, politically conscious, technical cadres. The combination of these varied political measures was to focus attention upon personnel within the system: factions and deviations within the leadership, bureaucratic inertia, errors and shortcomings in the work of officials, and the class/national background of key personnel. The roots of the terror and the purges of the following decade go far back into Bolshevism.

But the central defining feature of the Stalinist synthesis was the co-existence in Bolshevik discourse of nationalist and Marxist themes. The implications of this fusion have been underestimated and untheorized in the main. The legitimation of Stalin's project fused modernization to create the material basis for the abundance of communism, with modernization to solve the age-old question of Russian backwardness. The clearest expression of this came in Stalin's speech of 4 February 1931, delivered at the First All-Union Conference of Managers of Socialist Industry. It is worth quoting at length,

> It is sometimes asked whether it is not possible to slow down the tempo a bit . . . No comrades, it is not possible! To slacken the tempo would mean falling behind. And those who fall behind get beaten. But we do not want to be beaten. One feature of the history of old Russia was the

continual beatings she suffered for falling behind, for her backwardness. She was beaten by the Mongol khans. She was beaten by the Turkish beys. She was beaten by the Swedish feudal lords. She was beaten by the Polish and Lithuanian gentry. She was beaten by the British and French capitalists. She was beaten by the Japanese barons. All beat her – due to her backwardness: military backwardness, cultural backwardness, political backwardness, industrial backwardness, agricultural backwardness . . . But now that we have overthrown capitalism, and power is in the hands of the working class, we have a fatherland and we will defend its independence. Do you want our socialist fatherland to be beaten and to lose its independence? If you do not want this you must put an end to its backwardness in the shortest possible time and develop genuine Bolshevik tempo in building up its socialist economic system. There is no other way . . . We are fifty or a hundred years behind the advanced countries. We must make good this distance in ten years. Either we do it, or they crush us . . . There are no fortresses which Bolsheviks cannot capture.[49]

Reflecting upon this co-existence of nationalism and Marxism in the Stalinist synthesis of Soviet socialism, it is interesting to note that the pursuit of self-sufficiency inaugurated a change in the philosophical basis of Bolshevism. The stress laid on vulnerability, isolation and the overcoming of backwardness inserted an alternative priority into the transition period. The immediate task was to achieve self-sufficiency, and to achieve it quickly. This was the essential precondition to the building of socialism. Yet the latter aim was constantly invoked, and remained the ostensible destination point of the transition. "Self-sufficiency" did not *displace* the "construction of socialism" in the Bolshevik understanding of the transition phase, but came to co-exist with it. This co-existence of objectives created a number of new tensions and contradictions as the demands for rapid national modernization came into conflict with, and in extreme cases subverted, the ideals and principles of the dominant understanding of socialism. This policy of overcoming backwardness became in Lewin's words the "official ethos" of the Stalinist programme for the transformation of Russia.[50]

This focus on immediate tasks, and the selection of policies appropriate to this end, profoundly shifted the way in which the communist party sought to legitimize itself. The legitimacy of the party was based upon establishing the scientific correctness of Marxism's vision of the future. Having seized power proclaiming the advent of a new chapter in world history, their claims to be the legitimate rulers rested on a practical demonstration of the validity of this doctrine. This mode of legitimization remained. However, the insertion of the task of achieving self-sufficiency – outstripping the capitalist countries, solving the problem of Russian backward-ness – added new ways in which the party would seek to legitimate itself. The party could now portray itself as a nationalist, patriotic organization, upholding the independence of Russia. More sig-nificantly, the Marxist stance that socialism was superior to, and the historical successor of, capitalism, was reduced to the level of a competition or race – primarily but not exclusively of an economic nature – between the two systems. On this basis the system could be legitimized relative to the performance of capitalism, rather than with reference to their underlying ideological framework (or as well as with reference to Marxism–Leninism). This co-existence of tasks – self-sufficiency and construction of socialism – funda-mentally shaped the form and content of Soviet socialism as it developed from the late 1920s onwards.

Notes

1. Probably the best piece on Bukharin remains S. Cohen, *Bukharin and the Bolshevik revolution* (Oxford: Oxford University Press, 1980). See also A. Erlich, *The Soviet industrialisation debate* (Cambridge, Mass.: Harvard University Press, 1960); M. Lewin, *Political undercurrents in Soviet economic debates* (London: Pluto Press, 1975), pp. 3–72; R. Bideleux, *Communism and development* (London: Methuen, 1985).
2. The keynote articles written by Bukharin were, "Concerning the New Economic Policy and our tasks" (1925); "The road to socialism and the worker–peasant alliance" (1925); "Notes of an economist" (1928). All can be found in R. Day (ed.), *N. Bukharin: selected writings on the state and the transition to socialism* (New York: M. E. Sharpe, 1982).
3. Cohen, *Bukharin and the Bolshevik revolution*, pp. 173–4.
4. Bukharin, "The road to socialism", pp. 245–56.

5. L. Lih, "Political testament of Lenin and Bukharin and the meaning of NEP", *Slavic Review* **50**(2), 1991, pp. 241–52. Cohen, *Bukharin and the Bolshevik revolution*, pp. 180–1.

6. Cohen, *Bukharin and the Bolshevik revolution*, pp. 198–200.

7. Lih, "Political testament", p. 251.

8. Lewin, *Political undercurrents*, pp. 56–68.

9. Cohen, *Bukharin and the Bolshevik revolution*, pp. 200–8.

10. Bukharin, "The road to socialism", p. 288.

11. M. Matthews, *Soviet social structure* (London: Penguin, 1972), pp. 36–9.

12. Cohen, *Bukharin and the Bolshevik revolution*, pp. 147–8, 186–8.

13. Bukharin, "The road to socialism", pp. 289–94.

14. Cohen, *Bukharin and the Bolshevik revolution*, pp. 252–4.

15. Bukharin, "The road to socialism", pp. 268–74, 285–9.

16. A. Nove, "New light on Trotsky's economic views", *Slavic Review* **41**, 1981, pp. 84–97; I. Deutscher, *Trotsky: the prophet unarmed* (Oxford: Oxford University Press, 1959); R. Day, *Leon Trotsky and the politics of economic isolation* (Cambridge: Cambridge University Press 1973).

17. A. Nove, "Trotsky, markets and East European reforms", in *Studies in economics and Russia* (Houndmills: Macmillan, 1990), pp. 71–9.

18. Cited in Nove, "New light on Trotsky's economic views", p. 90.

19. Ibid., p. 92.

20. Ibid., pp. 92–7; R. V. Daniels, "The 'Left Opposition' as an alternative to Stalinism", *Slavic Review* **50**(2), 1991, pp. 277–85; Day, *Leon Trotsky*, pp. 126–52.

21. Deutscher, *The prophet unarmed*, pp. 422–5.

22. I. Deutscher, *Stalin* (London: Penguin, 1966), pp. 283–95.

23. D. Filtzer, "Preobrazhensky and the problem of the Soviet transition", in *Critique* **9**, spring–summer 1978, pp. 63–84; Bideleux, *Communism and development*, pp. 111–15; L. Kolakowski, *Main currents of Marxism*, vol. 3, (Oxford: Oxford University Press, 1978), pp. 30–1.

24. Filtzer, "Preobrazhensky and the problem of the Soviet transition", pp. 67–75.

25. On the factional struggles, see the excellent summary of perspectives in C. Ward, *Stalin's Russia* (London: Edward Arnold, 1993), pp. 7–38. For the details see, L. Schapiro, *Communist party of the Soviet Union* (London: Methuen, 1970), pp. 271–312, 365–81.

26. For the theory of "socialism in one country", see Deutscher, *Stalin*, pp. 283–95; Kolakowski, *Main currents of Marxism*, pp. 21–5; E. H. Carr, *Socialism in one country 1924–26*, vol. 2 (London: Macmillan, 1965) pp. 36–51; A. Evans, *Soviet Marxism–Leninism* (Westport: Praeger, 1993), pp. 29–43.

27. In J. Stalin, *Problems of Leninism* (Moscow: Foreign Languages Publishing House, 1947), pp. 96–109.

28. Ibid., p. 38.
29. Ibid., "The October revolution and tactics of Russian communists", p. 103. This phrase was quoted *ad nauseam* by Stalin in his struggles with Trotsky.
30. Evans, *Soviet Marxism–Leninism*, pp. 29–32.
31. Stalin, "On the problems of Leninism", in *Problems of Leninism*, pp. 156–77.
32. Ibid., p. 160.
33. Deutscher, *Stalin*, p. 291.
34. Ibid., pp. 290–5.
35. Carr, *Socialism in one country*, p. 50.
36. Ibid., p. 49.
37. J. Stalin, "The Right deviation in the CPSU", in *Collected works*, vol. 12 (Moscow: Foreign Languages Publishing House, 1955), pp. 84–5.
38. Stalin, "Industrialisation of the country and the Right Deviation in the CPSU", in ibid., vol. 11, p. 256.
39. Stalin, "Industrialisation and the Right Deviation", in ibid., vol. 11, p. 258.
40. A. Meyer, "The war scare of 1927", *Soviet Union/Union Sovietique*, **1**, 1978, pp. 1–25.
41. Stalin, "The Right deviation in the CPSU", in *Collected works*, vol. 12, p. 41.
42. Stalin, "The Right Deviation in the CPSU", in ibid., pp. 40–41.
43. Stalin, "Joint plenum of the CC and CCC of the CPSU", in ibid., vol. 10, pp. 53–4.
44. Ibid., vol. 11 p. 239.
45. Stalin, "Work of the April joint plenum of CC and CCC", in ibid., vol. 11, p. 32.
46. Ibid., p. 35.
47. Ibid., p. 37.
48. Ibid., p. 36.
49. Stalin, "The tasks of business executives", in ibid., vol. 13, pp. 40–1.
50. Lewin, *Political undercurrents in Soviet economic debates*, pp. 97–101.

PART THREE

Orthodoxy in power: from Stalin to Brezhnev

CHAPTER SIX

Stalinist socialism: creating a country of metal, 1929–39

The great change: a country of metal, tractors and automobiles

In November 1929, on the eve of the massive transformation of the socio-economic landscape of the USSR, Stalin wrote that

> We are advancing full steam ahead along the path of industrialisation – to socialism, leaving behind the age-old "Russian" backwardness. We are becoming a country of metal, a country of automobiles, a country of tractors. And when we have put the USSR on an automobile, and the muzhik on a tractor, let the worthy capitalists, who boast so much of their "civilisation", try to overtake us. We shall yet see which countries may then be classified as backward and which as advanced.[1]

Industrialization and collectivization changed the USSR irrevocably. This chapter takes the narrative up until 1939, with the convocation of the 18th Congress of the party, and relates the processes by which the Soviet state would proclaim in 1936 that the first socialist society had been built. The war and the latter years of Stalinism are discussed in the next chapter. The following analysis highlights how the implementation of the Stalinist programme gave substance and content to many of the core concepts of Soviet socialism, and profoundly shaped the nature of the Soviet system in the process.

Content and context

The particular features of the Stalinist economic model emerged out of a complex and shifting socio-political atmosphere. The factional struggles within the party saw Stalin adopt a stance that combined rapid industrialization, collectivization and class war. The precise reasons for Stalin's shift away from the gradualist programme espoused by his erstwhile ally Bukharin are the subject of no little dispute. Scholars remain divided as to the relative importance of the political struggle for supremacy, as opposed to the changing internal and international situation after 1927.[2] This stance partly arose out of and partly fostered an atmosphere that was hostile to moderation, implacably anti-capitalist and was mediated through a language and imagery highly reminiscent of the civil war: militaristic, ruthless, uncompromising. Social historians have recently demonstrated the coincidence of central policies and initiatives on the one hand, and the aspirations of the masses, in particular the urban factory workers, on the other.[3] This generated an atmosphere of revolutionary Leftism, utopian prognoses, ideological ambitiousness and militant radicalism: "there are no fortresses the Bolsheviks cannot conquer".[4] Money would soon wither away, and the market would be completely abolished. Industrialization became an ideological offensive against capitalism.[5] The deteriorating international environment added to this atmosphere an emphasis upon vulnerability and hostile capitalist encirclement. The sense of isolation imparted a need for haste. "Bolshevik tempos" became a defining slogan. In this atmosphere, it became impolitic to counsel moderation, gradualism, evolution, reformism. Approaches to industrialization that promoted progress as rapidly and effectively as possible were favoured.

The conjunction of these two distinct themes accounts for oscillations and shifts in the industrialization process. Between 1928 and 1941, it is often argued that the system moved from "radicalism" to "conservatism". It is more accurate to suggest that the emphasis on seeking the most effective means to overcome backwardness supplanted the revolutionary Leftist aspects of the programme. A key year in this respect was 1931, as the leadership openly proclaimed a move away from ideological ambitiousness. The chronology of industrialization reflects the fluctuating perspectives of the leadership, and their struggle to maintain a vestige of control over a process that became, in Lewin's words "a massive improvisation", resting upon a "quicksand society".[6] There were three 5 Year Plans (5YP) between 1929 and 1941:

1) 1st 5YP 1928–32 (although it was completed in 4 years): this plan was an agglomeration of ambitious proposals to increase the heavy industrial sector. In essence it comprised building as many factories and projects as big and as quickly as possible.

2) the year 1932–3 was something of a crisis year in which shortages and problems mushroomed. During this period, the leadership asserted that the priority was the "mastery of technology". As a result the targets for the 2nd 5YP were revised downwards as the leadership adopted a more realistic approach during 1933–7.

3) the 3rd 5YP (1938–41, interrupted by the German invasion), revived a more ambitious heavy industrial bias, although the approach of war caused a drastic reorientation towards higher investment in military spending.[7]

A centrally planned economy?

The whole concept of planning was supposed to embody the conscious and rational control of economic processes, to provide a long-term, precise scientific framework for economic decision-making, in which all the irrationality, spontaneity and waste of the market would be overcome. The reality of Soviet planning was far removed from this ideal. Scholars have identified that the economy was not "planned" in the meaning outlined above, but was rather administered on an *ad hoc* basis, using commands and instructions sent down from the centre, having the status of a law. This administrative system produced its own distinct brand of irrationality.[8] Additionally, market forces still remained in a few areas.

The specific form of planning that emerged in the 1930s arose out of a bureaucratic struggle between the two main agencies engaged in planning: GOSPLAN and *Vesenkha*. In an atmosphere encouraging ambitiousness and maximalism, the more moderate perspectives of GOSPLAN (the geneticist school) were displaced in favour of the optimum outlook of *Vesenkha* (the teleological school). Right from its very inception, the Soviet planning process was shaped by the need for speed, and for massive progress in a few key areas. This politicized context brushed aside questions of balance, equilibrium, rational calculations and precise information flows.[9] How did it evolve in practice?

The party CC and the Council of People's Commissars set down the general policy guidelines and identified the priority targets to be achieved. The co-ordinating role was played by GOSPLAN, which attempted to reconcile the general policy guidelines with the information it received from agencies at lower levels of the hierarchy. GOSPLAN would draw up a balance sheet in quantitative terms: a general 5YP and a more specific annual plan. The Commissariats for each branch of industry then drew up a plan for each enterprise, broken down into annual and monthly targets. The central feature of the plan was that the target was expressed in physical terms: gross output was the overriding indicator. The factory director received a quota to be fulfilled. This was an obligatory directive. Within the political atmosphere of intensified class war and suspicion of moderation, fulfilling the quota became an incantation for factory managers.[10]

The hierarchy of priorities for the "plan" was clear. Heavy industry (metallurgy, capital goods, energy supplies) had primacy. The most rapid development possible of the productive forces possessed a number of powerful arguments in its favour. First, it would rid Russia of her lingering backwardness, and drag her towards the modernist utopia embodied in American industrial efficiency. Secondly, it would create a large urban proletariat, breaking the political power of the peasantry and legitmizing the political rule of the communist party. Thirdly, it would lay the basis for the creation of the future material abundance of communism. Rapid industrial and technological advance was required to bring the future society within sight. Lastly, it laid the basis for national defence. The ability to defend "socialism in one country" was increasingly urgent, as the international situation deteriorated during the 1930s.[11]

As Lewin has so vividly described, "in this planned economy, the very idea of planning was sacrificed".[12] The process became an all-out effort to meet a series of short-term targets. Any means were warranted. As Davies has shown, the system also failed to eradicate market forces from the system: in the *kolkhozy*, in limited retail choice for consumers and in a market of sorts for labour, which was not centrally allocated (except in the forced labour sector).[13] By the mid to late 1930s the system was an overwhelmingly administrative one, with quasi-market elements. Accompanying the growth of planlessness, the economy became highly centralized, as decision-making was concentrated at the centre, and state power and control grew exponentially after 1929.

The organization of the economy

The story of the organizational evolution of the Soviet economy during the 1930s is impenetrably complex.[14] The key question centred around the relationship between centralization and decentralization, and how, if at all, it would be possible to combine decentralized control of factories with centralized planning. As the process of rapid industrialization got underway, so industry became heavily centralized, the economic bureaucracy multiplied and the administrative tentacles of the state spread throughout the system.

One of the enduring paradoxes of this period was the contrast between the legal structure of authority, and the practice of the system. The organizational changes introduced after 1928 destroyed the NEP structure: the administration of factories on a regional basis through the umbrella trust system. Management was now to be organized along entire industrial branches, irrespective of their geographical location. Factories engaged in the production of similar products were grouped together under the authority of an agency known as an industrial production association. Many of the powers of the trusts and the old *glavki* were embodied in the associations, giving them a central role in the administration of the system. In many respects, this move was a rationalization of what had been a very confused bureaucratic tangle in the 1920s. However, in formal legal terms authority was vested in the individual factory. Under the *khozraschet* system (profit and loss accounting), the factory had financial autonomy.[15]

In practice, as the industrial sector grew, more and more authority accrued to both "associations", and the Commissariats with responsibility for each branch. The associations interfered increasingly in the day-to-day running of the factories. The number of Commissariats grew. The party also involved itself in the running of factories. The officials of the NKVD also became integrated into the running of the state industrial sector, alongside the huge economic empire of the forced labour camps. These multiple proliferations – bureaucracies, agencies, interventions – were a function of the command-administer/Bolshevik tempo synthesis. Targets had to be met at any cost. Officials responsible for meeting targets intervened to ensure they were met. The secret police interfered to ensure that correct procedures were adhered to. This all added up to an "ever-growing concentration of state power".[16] A centralized, planned economy based around large-scale, heavy industry had become a bureaucratic, overcentralized, coercive administrative system, albeit with quasi-market elements. This in turn profoundly affected the relationship between management and labour.[17]

Management, labour and specialists

By the end of the 1930s, the extension of state power not only eradicated the last vestiges of workers' control from the factories, but also fully subordinated the trade unions to the party and to the factory director. The changes in the nature of the labour process during 1928–41 evolved fitfully across this period.[18] The initial surge of popular enthusiasm among many of the urban population for the tasks of industrialization was gradually tempered by the experiences of the workers themselves. The established workers in the factories resented both the accumulation of power by managers, and the massive influx of workers from the countryside, with all the attendant social problems this created.[19] These tensions within the factory were overlain by a profound shift in the nature of the labour process. The combination of the impact of collectivization (increasing the scarcity of food supplies), falling urban living standards, the rapid pace of industrialization (which abolished unemployment) created a situation of high labour turnover. Workers migrated constantly in search of better conditions, better jobs. The pressure on managers to increase production meant increased pressure on the workers to fulfil their output.[20] Increased labour productivity was seen as the key to the success of the industrialization drive.

In response to this, the state developed a plethora of initiatives to maintain the required tempo. A strict regime of labour discipline was inaugurated founded on the 1929 and 1932 Soviet labour laws. Truancy and absenteeism (defined as absent from work for one full day without just cause) were to be punished by dismissal, loss of ration card and removal from housing. This legislation was only partially effective. Managers and workers often colluded to subvert this legislation, as managers needed both to keep skilled workers, and to hoard labour, in order to fulfil the plan targets sent down from above.[21] In 1938 and 1940, the regime introduced further, more coercive legislation, including a new definition of absenteeism (20 minutes late for work), as well as lengthening both the working day and the working week.[22] Alongside the "free" labour sector, the NKVD oversaw the growth of a vast economic empire of labour camps, whose primary aim was to earn foreign currency and undertake labour-intensive construction projects: canals, dams and so on. Labour was mobilized on a vast scale for the achievement of an autarkic industrial economy.

There was carrot as well as stick. Mobilization and coercion was combined with enthusiasm and incentives. A number of initiatives were developed – material and non-material – to intensify the labour process. Pay scales were to reflect the premium upon skilled work. Stratification returned to the working class. Privileges and perks (paid and unpaid) were developed for industrial managers.[23] Material incentives were combined with non-material initiatives. Campaigns – shock brigades, socialist emulation, Stakhanovism – which mobilized the enthusiasm of sections of the working class, were combined with a series of awards and honours to reward hard-working, dedicated workers. During the course of the 1930s labour productivity rose substantially, and the Stakhanovite movement – based upon the raising of the amount of work each worker was expected to do in a given period of time – made a substantial contribution to this.[24] The position of the worker in the Stalinist industrial system seemed to represent the final defeat for the workerist, emancipatory impulse within Bolshevism. The total subordination of the trade union to the needs of the state encapsulates the relationship between state and society under Stalinism. Workers, according to Filtzer, were forced to pursue their grievances individually. The basis for collective action from below had been eroded.[25]

The authority of the factory managers was increased substantially. Yet the position and actions of this social group was profoundly affected by the ambiguities and paradoxes of Stalinist industrialization. In particular, the acute personal and political pressure to fulfil quotas forced the managers to adopt "flexible" approaches to managerial practice. In other words, they adopted many practices that subverted the policies of the centre. For instance, in order to retain labour to meet targets, managers would often collude with workers to evade the harsh labour decrees. Information was falsified. Capacity was underestimated. At other times the managers would step up the pressure on the workers, ignore safety regulations, increase overtime and so on. The whole stratum of management was caught between the political pressures of the process of taut planning and frantic industrialization on the one hand, and the attempt to impose a regime of economic rationality and technological efficiency within the factory.[26]

The attitude of the regime towards the technical specialists in industry is also illustrative of the shifting and complex relationship between pursuing an efficient, rational balanced industrialization process, and the pursuit of a politically directed campaign to industrialize as quickly as possible, to achieve self-sufficiency via the creation of a stratum of politically reliable technical experts.[27] In the period between 1928 and 1931, the regime developed a twin-track policy. First, bourgeois experts came under suspicion of "sabotage" and "wrecking" after the the Shakhty Trial of 1928. This generated an urgent need to develop technical specialists drawn from proletarian, not bourgeois backgrounds. Priority in recruiting specialists to higher education at engineering colleges was accorded to applicants who were either workers or communists. During the period 1928–33, thousands of communists and workers entered fulltime study. At the same time, the shortage of reliable administrators and technical specialists required the direct promotion of workers into these positions.[28]

June 1931 and Stalin's "Six conditions" speech marked a shift in the attitudes of the regime.[29] The policy of promotions from below was halted, and the old experts were rehabilitated under pressure from the industrial managers. In order to achieve the goals set out in the 1st 5YP it became necessary to improve the living and working conditions of specialists by providing them with increased material incentives, and to increase their authority in the workplace. These moves were partly a recognition that the radicalism of 1928–31 was inimical to the wider economic goals, but also partly a function of the assurance that a new cohort of communist technical specialists were waiting in the wings. In this sense, the technical specialists played a key role in the economic achievements of the 1930s, helping to legitimize the Stalinist system, and also providing levels of technical knowledge essential to industrialization.[30] The promotion and privileging of the technical specialists, at the expense of the position, status and rights of the workers, affirms the hegemony of the technocratic strand of Soviet socialism. Yet, the constant emphasis upon tempos, taut planning and the like also brought the state into conflict with technical specialists and managers who were trying to adopt a more rational, balanced approach to planning. The party and the NKVD constantly intervened in industry to assert the primacy of the political agencies, and of politically-directed priorities.

In sum, the Stalinist economic programme created an industrial system that was orthodoxically Bolshevik in content (centralized, planned, large-scale, heavy industry, technocratic), yet its particular content was defined primarily by the drive for self-sufficiency and autarky. The core features of the Stalinist model were:

- an economy resting on administrative approaches;
- a centrally organized, state directed economy;
- a preference for large-scale projects;
- prioritization of heavy industry;
- removal of the last residues of workers' control and imposition of one-man management;
- orientation towards quantity over quality;
- emphasis upon haste;
- strict labour discipline and subordination of the trade unions to the state;
- central allocation of all materials and capital goods;
- state control of retail trade (either directly or through consumer co-operatives);
- centrally fixed prices for all consumer goods, and for produce acquired from the rural sector;
- quasi-market elements remained, in the collective farm sector (see below) and in the labour sphere.[31]

The collectivization of Soviet agriculture

The Russian peasant, working his small strip of land with a wooden plough, was the archetypal symbol of Russian backwardness. The *kulak*, or rich peasant, became the archetypal symbol of the survival of capitalism in the countryside. The collectivization offensive, launched suddenly and without warning in November 1929, sought to destroy both with one blow.[32] Within seven years, the agricultural map of the USSR had changed beyond recognition. The campaign restructured the patterns of land tenure in the countryside, creating collective farms (*kolkhozy*) and state farms (*sovkhozy*). Agriculture was mechanized. The countryside was penetrated by urban forces: party members, workers, students flooded the countryside. The party established a comprehensive degree of control over the rural sector. Viewing the map alone distorts the picture though. The use of war imagery and language – offensive, campaign, storming fortresses – accurately depicts the collectivization process. The state declared war on the peasantry. There were many, many casualties. Numerous peasants, labelled as *kulaks* were "eliminated": killed, exiled, deported. Millions starved, livestock was decimated and cannibalism was rife. The brutality of the process, the dehumanization it entailed and the suffering it engendered is given a deeply eloquent testimony by the Ukrainian peasantry welcoming the Nazi invaders of 1941 as "liberators".[33]

The collectivization drive embodied all the motifs and essential features of the Stalinist programme: class war, haste, arbitrariness, coercion, gigantomania, ideological ambitiousness, centralization, and technology as the touchstone of modernity, progress and socialism. Stalin asserted that,

> [a] radical change has taken place in the development of our agriculture from small, backward, individual farming to large-scale, advanced collective agriculture, to cultivation of the land in common, to machine and tractor stations, to artels and collective farms based on modern techniques, and finally, to giant state farms, equipped with hundreds of tractors and harvester combines. The achievements of the party consists in the fact that we have succeeded in turning the bulk of the peasantry . . . away from the old capitalist

path of development . . . to the new socialist path of development, which squeezes out the rich, the capitalists, and arms the poor and middle peasants with modern equipment, with modern implements, with tractors and agricultural machinery, thus enabling them to climb out of poverty and of bondage to the kulaks.[34]

Similar trends to those in the industrial sector can be detected, namely that while the creation of a collective farm sector was commensurate with orthodox Bolshevik theory, the outcome of this process was determined more by the imperatives of tempo, ambitiousness and class war than by the application of rationality, efficiency and realism. This is best illustrated by the fact that when the collectivization drive was launched, no-one knew what "collectivization" meant in practice.

Collectivization had always been the party's long-term objective. Large-scale, mechanized farms, organized on collectivist lines would promote a more efficient agricultural sector, increasing labour productivity and releasing labour for the industrialization drive. Output would also be increased – via extensive growth – as mechanization would allow the ploughing of "neglected and virgin land".[35] In social terms, collectivization and mechanization would shape the consciousness of the peasant, creating a socialist peasantry and destroying capitalist values and peasant individualistic norms once and for all.[36] Crucially, collectivization was to be achieved through the Leninist "voluntary" principle. Forcible collectivization was not seen as desirable or practical. At the end of the 1920s, however, collectivization was also designed with less lofty, more pragmatic, political interests in mind. An attack on the class representatives of capitalism – the *kulaks* – was necessary to discredit the Right quasi-NEPist agenda. Industrial growth required a cheap, reliable supply of grain, both for export and for urban and military requirements. Collectivization – by reducing the number of collection points, and facilitating the acquisition of grain at a price and in quantities decreed by the state – thus embodied the fulfilment of long-term Bolshevik ideals through a process driven by a combination of Stalin's personal political agenda, the enthusiasm of urban activists and the choice of means that were the quickest and most effective. Once more the means shaped and ultimately subverted the broader ideals.

The campaign was launched in an atmosphere of revolutionary maximalism, encouraging haste, extremism and class prejudice. A flavour of the ideological ambitiousness imbuing Bolshevik thinking in this period can be gleaned from Stalin's view that,

> All the arguments of "science" against the possibility and expedience of creating large grain factories each have collapsed and crumbled into dust. Practice has refuted the objections of "science", and has once again shown that "science" has a lot to learn from practice.[37]

Moreover, collectivization grew out of a conceptual and policy vacuum. What was a collective farm? What sort of land tenure should be implemented? How much should be collectivized? Which peasants would join the collective farms? None of these issues was discussed. Implementation was left to "local discretion" in the absence of clear central guidelines. The resolution of 5 January 1930 (issued in the name of the cc, but not discussed at a plenum) expressed the importance and the possibility of immediate, rapid collectivization irrespective of developments in both the countryside and the industrial sector.[38] In other words, it was to be conducted without a sufficient supply of machinery available, and irrespective of the progress made by voluntary collectivization. Implementation followed general prescriptions: purge the countryside of *kulaks*, create large-scale farms, accomplish it as quickly as possible to minimize disruption to the 1930 spring sowing. In purely quantitative terms, by 1936 90 per cent of households had been collectivized. The questions of productivity, output and the contribution of collectivization are more contested. Grain deliveries clearly increased, but the sources of this are unclear.[39]

The process itself proceeded haphazardly, brutally and rapidly after 1929. In the initial months of 1930, the emphasis was upon de-kulakization. Class war was declared upon a section of rural society,

> For the purpose of squeezing out the kulaks as a class we must break down the resistance of this class in open battle and deprive it of the productive sources of its existence and development (the free use of land, means of production, the renting of land, the right to hire labour etc.).[40]

236

Amid this chaos and coercion, local officials attempted to create gigantic *kolkhozy*, encompassing several villages, and socializing all the livestock. The peasants resisted wholesale collectivization and, in March 1930, Stalin called a halt because the chaos threatened to prevent the spring sowing. In an article, "Dizzy with success", Stalin laid the blame on local overzealousness, and called for the restoration of the voluntary principle.[41] The offensive was resumed again in the autumn of 1930 and proceeded apace for the next six years. The cost was enormous: unquantifiable human suffering, a massive famine in 1932–3 and destruction of vast quantities of livestock. Gradually over this period, the collective farm sector evolved a number of features that were eventually codified in the 1935 Model Kolkhoz Statute.

The Bolshevik preference for large farms, and for state farms over collective farms was modified in practice. From 1930 onwards, farms corresponded approximately to existing villages. Numerically *kolkhozy* predominated. *Sovkhozy* were organized as large-scale, single product structures, which paid their employees a guaranteed minimum wage.[42] The majority of *kolkhozy* were based around the *artel'* form. They were defined as "voluntary co-operatives", whose members managed the farm on a day-to-day basis. The land, horses and basic implements (e.g. ploughs) were held in common, while the livestock were still the property of individual households. After the *kolkhoz* had met the compulsory delivery quota imposed by the centre, whatever cash or produce remained was divided up between the *kolkhozniki* on the basis of a unit of value called the labour day (*trudoden'*). Labour days were calculated on the basis of the nature of the task: highly skilled tasks being rewarded more lucratively.[43] Another major concession saw the consolidation of personal livestock and a household plot within the collective farm. *Kolkhoz* markets sprang up as legitimate arenas for the sale of this personal produce. Inevitably, *kolkhozniki* spent more and more time on their personal plots. In practice, the *kolkhozy* fell short of Stalin's ideal of a fully socialized agricultural sector. The basic requirement for increased output required concessions to personal incentives. Lack of incentive to work hard was institutionalized within the *kolkhozy*. Additionally, the agricultural sector struggled to overcome the mistakes and excesses of collectivization, and the personal plot was an important tool in meeting shortfalls. The *kolkhozy* represented in Davies's words a "compromise".[44]

All these features were established in the 1935 Model Kolkhoz statute.[45] The *kolkhozy* were also part of the establishment of party control in the countryside. *Kolkhozy* chairmen were party (usually urban) appointees. Each farm had a Machine Tractor Station (MTS) which provided both machinery and political oversight (through a political department, subsequently abolished in 1934). Each political department was run by the deputy director of the MTS and contained a representative of the OGPU (secret police), who tended to do the bidding of the centre. In practice, the autonomy of the *kolkhoz* was highly limited by the interventions of the local party committee and the rural Soviet. The extensive networks of central control were designed to ensure compliance with and delivery of state quotas. This political control was reinforced by a variety of legal sanctions: execution for the theft of socialist property; criminalization of unauthorized food consumption; imprisonment for trading prior to targets being fulfilled; institution of a passport system to prevent peasant exodus from the *kolkhoz*.[46]

The collectivization process embodied the same type of shifts as in the industrial sector. The agenda of revolutionary Leftism was gradually, but not wholly, supplanted by the narrower objectives of proceeding with collectivization as quickly as possible. The achievement of 90 per cent collectivization by 1936 enabled Stalin to assert that as the *kolkhoz* was a form of socialist economic organization, a socialist economy had been built. Yet the distinction between form and content must once more be drawn. The ostensible long-term aim of the Bolsheviks had been attained. Yet the content corresponded much more closely to the specific agenda from which collectivization arose. The countryside had been purged of capitalist elements, and the farms contained no basis for capitalist-style exploitation. The voluntary principle was transgressed: peasants were cajoled and coerced into the farms. Mechanization proceeded haphazardly; few peasants knew how to work the machinery, repairs often could not be carried out, and spares were in short supply. Transport and storage problems also contributed to endemic inefficiencies. The reality of the Soviet countryside bore little resemblance to the vision of large, mechanized, technologically efficient farms that were genuinely transforming the consciousness of the peasantry in a socialist direction. This fusion of orthodox

Bolshevik forms with a Stalinist autarkic content is highlighted by the compromises and tensions running through the agricultural sector. First, socialization was restricted by the need to retain market relations and personal farming because of the appallingly low productivity within the farms. Secondly, the war waged on the peasantry required the vast extension of state power in the countryside, and the retention of the representatives of the state, as the expected transformation of peasant consciousness failed to materialize, for obvious reasons.

Society and culture of Stalinism: socialism, nationalism, inequality

In 1936 Stalin proclaimed that,

> the complete victory of the socialist system in all spheres of the national economy is now a fact . . . the exploitation of man by man has been abolished, eliminated, while the socialist ownership of the implements and means of production has been established as the unshakeable foundation of our Soviet society.[47]

A "socialist" economic system had been constructed. But what type of social relations had grown up on this economic foundation? The society that emerged in the 1930s was ridden with apparent paradoxes. Born in an atmosphere of radicalism, maximalism and proletarian class purity, it evolved into a highly conservative, traditionalist social structure. Proclaiming an era of the abolition of exploiting classes and the institution of friendly class relations between workers and peasants, the state also asserted the intensification of the class struggle as communism drew nearer. Trumpeting the victory of collectivism, the state highlighted great individual feats as evidence of the superiority of socialism over capitalism. An exploration of these paradoxes illustrates how the competing themes of the Stalinist programme – the construction of socialism and the achievement of self-sufficiency – combined to produce a perplexing amalgam of social features.

The social structure of Stalinist socialism: class struggle and inequality

The attitude of the CPSU towards social classes was conditioned by two themes. First, the thesis of the intensification of the class struggle as socialism approaches was constantly emphasized by Stalin. Continued class struggle and vigilance against internal enemies was said to be especially crucial now that the economic basis of exploitation had been removed. The defeated class enemies remained within the system, and remained as enemies because their consciousness would continue to be essentially bourgeois, irrespective of their new social position. The current danger was the difficulty in identifying the enemies in the new conditions:

> Thrown out of their groove, and scattered over the whole face of the USSR, these "have-beens" have crept into our plants and factories, into our government offices and trading organizations . . . and principally, into the collective farms and state farms. They have crept into these places and concealed their identity, donning the mask of "workers" and "peasants", and some of them have even managed to make their way into the party.[48]

These forces were said to represent a twofold danger: as agents working for the restoration of capitalism, they would undermine the Soviet system domestically, and by extension aid the global forces of imperialism. The security and independence of the Soviet state depended upon the identification and destruction of class enemies. The road to classlessness lay through intense class struggle.

Secondly, the party proclaimed that the system was now marked by a fundamental degree of social harmony and peace between classes. The abolition of private property and of exploiting classes, the creation of a socialist foundation to the economy meant that Soviet society was now composed of two friendly classes: the workers and the peasantry. They now had a fundamental identity of interests as both were deemed to be labouring classes. The continuing distinctions between them related to their differing relationship to public property: industrial workers and state farmers were classified as members of the working class because they worked with state property. Collective farmers were members of the peasantry as they worked with group property. More interestingly, the intelligentsia were now classified as a stratum of mental workers, who were serving the interests of Soviet society. They were now deemed to be an equal member of Soviet society, for two reasons. First, they were drawn overwhelmingly from the workers and peasantry. Secondly, its work was now to promote the interests of the working people, as the exploiting classes had been removed. The sum total of these changes in the class structure was that social differences, class antagonisms, contradictions were declining, and the basis for social harmony and homogeneity had been created.[49]

This proclamation of a new class structure in 1936 formalized a shift in the class identity of the Soviet state. The immediate post-revolutionary state had prioritized the interests of the proletariat. This had expressed itself in an unequal franchise and in discriminatory policies with regards to various social goods (for example, education). This approach was reinforced by the cultural revolution of 1928–31, which accentuated proletarian values and the creation of a technical intelligentsia drawn from a proletarian social background. The 1st 5YP was launched in an atmosphere of revolutionary class purity, emphasizing the motifs of the civil war.[50] However, in the aftermath of 1931, as the state focused on the tasks of promoting the successful, most effective policies to consolidate the processes of industrialization and modernization, social and cultural policies were shaped to these ends.[51] This radically modified the class-based approach to a variety of issues, including egalitarianism, the *zhenskii vopros* and educational policy.

The shift from a class motivated policy after 1931 was formalized in 1936 by the extension of the franchise to all citizens, irrespective of class. The critical issue was that of material rewards in industry. In June 1931, Stalin asserted that,

> . . . we must abolish wage equalisation and discard the old wage scales . . . we must draw up wage scales that will take into account the difference between skilled labour and unskilled labour, between heavy work and light work . . . Marx and Lenin said that the difference between skilled labour and unskilled labour would exist even under socialism, even after classes had been abolished; that only

241

under Communism would this difference disappear and that, therefore, even under socialism "wages" must be paid according to work performed and not according to needs.[52]

This is often cited as evidence of a major shift away from egalitarianism in the discourse of Soviet socialism, of the ultimate betrayal of Marxism–Leninism by Stalin. Yet the Marxist credentials of this viewpoint are impeccable. Both Engels and Marx asserted that payment in the lower phase would be according to work done, a point reinforced by Lenin. Indeed the practice of Bolshevism had reflected this, with differential wage levels, rations and privileges embedded within the structure of material rewards which emerged after 1917. Although Bolshevism did contain many who argued for a policy of strict egalitarianism, they were unable to influence either the theory or practice of Soviet socialism in a sustained way after 1917. The much-quoted example of Stalin's abolition of the partmax (the ceiling on incomes earned by party-state officials) in the mid-1930s is also viewed as further evidence of the regime's drift away from its egalitarian commitments.[53] Yet, from the civil war onwards, this principle had been honoured more in the breach than the observance.

Where Stalin appears to have shifted Soviet policy on egalitarianism was in the level of differentials between the elite and the masses, and on the nature of privilege. The favoured social groups were managers, military figures, party-state officials and key cultural figures. Managers salaries increased enormously relative to workers, primarily through bonuses. Political officers wages were no longer published, being augmented by "packets" or unauthorized payments. This monetary privilege was supplemented by unequal access to scarce food supplies during the 1930s: state stores selling food at prices far beyond the reach of the average wage earners continued to flourish.[54] The creation of this edifice of privilege was occurring at the same time as a decline in living standards for the majority of Soviet citizens. Barber has shown that at no point during the 1930s did living standards reach the levels of the late NEP period.[55]

The promotion of inegalitarianism highlights two consistent themes in Bolshevik discourse. First, material inequality would remain throughout the transition period. Secondly, although the Bolsheviks were committed to minimizing the differentials where possible, the overriding priority was to promote the wider goals of the state: the construction of a modern industrial, technologically advanced planned economy. Theoretically, Stalin reaffirmed Bolshevik orthodoxy in his report to the 17th Party Congress, outlining how equality under socialism meant equal emancipation from exploitation, equal duty to work, and equality of remuneration on the basis of work done. Equality in Marxism did not mean that "all should wear the same clothes and eat the same dishes in the same quantities".[56] Where Stalin departed from this tradition concerns the extent of inequality. This again can be explained by the emphasis upon achieving self-sufficiency in the Stalinist programme. To achieve industrialization at the necessary tempo, a structure of material incentives was required that rewarded the key groups in this process. Once more a Bolshevik principle was given a specific Stalinist content.

With regard to social equality, there was a further drift away from the radical egalitarian class-based approach of the period 1928–31. The policy of class discrimination was ended in June 1931. Stalin's speech to business executives called for the rehabilitation of the old bourgeois engineers in order to stabilize the situation in the factories.[57] Gradually, the other groups who had suffered under the cultural revolution were restored, regaining their positions and authority. The promotion of thousands and thousands of workers and working-class communists created a huge cohort of beneficiaries from the cultural revolution. Having achieved its primary aims, the policy switched away from class privilege towards a policy of consolidation of the system. This is best illustrated with reference to educational admissions policy. The proletarian bias was eschewed in favour of a selection policy that increasingly favoured ability, and ability to pay. The 1936 Constitution proclaimed that all citizens had the right to free entry to the local university. Where supply outstripped places, those with the best marks were favoured, increasingly favouring the children of white collar workers. In 1940 Stalin extended the inegalitarian thrust by charging fees for pupils in the last three years of school, and for students in universities and technical colleges.[58] The identity of the state had now shifted, away from a proletarian bias, and moving towards a more technocratic, elitist rationale, rewarding the key functional and occupational groups necessary for the administration and development of the country.

The turn away from class radicalism in education was mirrored in the attitudes towards female emancipation. Once more the radical, emancipatory agenda was supplanted by notions of emancipation through industrialization: a derivative idea whereby the construction of socialism would automatically liberate women. It was proclaimed that in the 1930s the "woman question" had been resolved.[59] The Stalinist era asserted that no special strategy for female emancipation, directed at particular issues was required. No discussion of abortion, motherhood, sexuality, child care, domestic labour took place. The work of the *zhenotdel* was halted in 1930.[60] In its stead, the state saw women as a resource, as a vital instrument for the realization of economic goals. Drawing women into the industrial workforce, as equals with their male counterparts, would demonstrate that the issue of gender equality had been solved. Between 1928 and 1940, women workers rose from 3 million to 13 million.[61] Once again the productivist, technocratic strand within Bolshevism (accentuated by the industrialization programme) triumphed over the strand that sought to prioritize the specific issues concerning women. The demographic needs of the state caused a further retreat from the radical social legislation of the post-revolutionary era. Restrictions on divorce and abortion were combined with measures to bolster the family and promote motherhood.[62] Soviet women were a collective resource for the attainment of state goals.

This outlook – that social groups were a resource to be mobilized by the state – is also excellently illustrated by the Soviet state's policy towards science in the 1930s.[63] Scientific work, and the scientific community were completely subordinated to the diktat of the party. Science was directed in a narrow, utilitarian way towards the economic and military requirements of "building socialism". Scientists were subject to an extensive system of political, ideological, financial and professional controls. Campaigns were initiated to discredit particular forms of science (especially "foreign" science), and also to isolate the Soviet scientific community from the West. Science became subject to the same "quotas" and "plans" as the rest of the economy. Purges and arrests of the scientific community punctuated the 1930s. Party figures were appointed to control scientific institutions.[64] The outcome of this was the establishment of a single party line in every branch of science. Science had become profoundly politicized. Orthodoxy reigned. As Krementsev notes, "by the end of the 1930s, a huge centralized, hierarchical, isolated, planned and politicised state science system had emerged in Russia".[65]

The normative basis of Soviet socialism: nationalism, tradition, socialist realism and heroic individualism

The shift from the policies of class war after 1931 brought a major turnabout in the normative basis of Stalinist socialism. The industrialization drive to construct socialism and achieve self-sufficiency, and the promotion of workers and peasants into the administrative elite and the intelligentsia, was reflected in the values and motifs of Stalinist cultural policy. The growth of Russian national and patriotic themes, the turn away from radical experimentation in education, law and social policy and the promotion of cultural forms in the service of socialist construction; Stalinist culture embodied the ambiguities and paradoxes of Soviet society in the 1930s.[66]

The incorporation of nationalism into the culture and worldview of Soviet socialism originated in the doctrine of "socialism in one country". In the revolutionary universe, the international socialist movement now orbited the Soviet Union. The tension between domestic considerations "build socialism!" and international considerations "overthrow western capitalism!" had shadowed Bolshevik thinking from Day One of the regime. Indeed, the collective failures of the Left in Europe by 1923 had left the party with little choice but to consolidate the revolution at home while awaiting the (inevitable) maturation of revolutionary conditions in the capitalist countries.[67] Stalin's elaboration of "socialism in one country" consolidated the primacy of the Soviet Union in the international revolutionary movement.[68] All measures necessary to defend the revolution and to promote the interests of the building of socialism in the USSR were now justified, even if this meant making a *rapprochement* with the West. From the early 1930s onwards,

> The search for alliances with the western powers, membership of the League of Nations and callous manipulation of the Comintern indicated that Stalin gave priority to the maintenance of the Soviet state above that of promoting international revolution.[69]

Although Stalin continually asserted the Soviet commitment to international revolution, the Molotov–Ribbentrop pact of August 1939 confirmed, if it needed confirming, that the interests of the Soviet state were now all that counted.

Out of the aspiration for self-sufficiency came the task of overcoming Russian backwardness, of making Russia great. This theme of national accomplishment increasingly displaced the socialist elements of Soviet socialist culture. History textbooks were rewritten reappraising Tsarist autocrats (Peter the Great, Ivan the Terrible) as progressive modernizers, irrespective of any questions of brutality or exploitation. Nationalism imparted notions of continuity and an alternative source of legitimacy for the Soviet state.[70] Alongside a revival of Russian nationalism, cultural forms became increasingly dominated by traditionalist notions: popular culture reflected elements of peasant folklorism, elite culture elements of traditional Russian "high" culture.[71] Conservative social policies predominated. In education, formal teaching methods, uniforms, compulsory pigtails and the restoration of the authority of the teacher displaced the radical prognoses of the cultural revolution.[72] Abortion and divorce were made much more difficult to obtain. Male homosexuality was recriminalized. Campaigns were launched to restore parental authority, revive ceremonial aspects to weddings and uphold strong family units as the cornerstone of socialist society.[73] These notions of tradition and conservatism grew up to promote social discipline, to sustain the new hierarchical social structure, to stabilize the system after the shock of the 1st 5YP.

Nationalism and tradition co-existed with more orthodox ideological forms. The state promoted socialist realism: cultural forms expressed in an idiom that was realistic, while incorporating what Stites calls "adventure and moral guidance"[74] and designed to promote the construction of socialism. Literature combined a number of themes designed to bolster the project of socialist construction,

> Socialist realist culture as a whole was a tortuous compromise between the art of old masters, folk culture, ideology and some elements of popular commercial art.[75]

Despite its evident eclecticism, socialist realism also espoused orthodox ideological motifs, particularly within the educational sphere. Compulsory tuition in the field of scientific communism permeated schools, colleges and universities.

The relationship between collectivism and individualism in the discourse of Stalinist socialism is an interesting one. On the one hand, the collectivist ideal was embodied in Stalin's idea of *vintiki* or cogs. Individuals were seen as components of one massive machine, all working harmoniously and in co-operation to build communism, submerging their individual identity in the collective. On the other hand, the Stalinist system consciously highlighted individuals and personal achievement as evidence of the superiority of socialism. Individuals were publicly lauded, and granted lucrative economic rewards for their outstanding contributions to Soviet life. Alexei Stakhanov's monumental productive efforts, the aviatory exploits of Chkalov, Beliakov and others were highlighted by the state, as the values they embodied were central to the functioning of the Stalinist system.[76] Individual heroism and sacrifice in the service of state goals, the struggle to master the natural environment, personal success in competition with individuals from capitalist countries fused the aims of socialist construction, national prestige and ideological competition with the West. The state promoted a particular concept of the individual – heroic, energetic, self-sacrificing – which promoted the wider socio-economic goals of the state, and created a status and incentive structure commensurate with this. Stalinist socialism sought to promote collective goals through mobilizing individuals to emulate Soviet "hero-figures" via a combination of material self-interest, personal prestige and ideologico-moral exhortation.[77] This stands in stark contrast to the Marxian idea of the realization of the individual through self-transcendence.

Complexity, plurality and eclecticism summarize the culture of Soviet socialism in the 1930s. The co-existence of different themes – nationalism, tradition, socialist realism, heroic individualism – produced a constantly shifting cultural mosaic, as the regime sought to highlight different aspects at various times.

The politics of Stalinism: party, state and society in the era of terror

Stalinism has become synonymous with terror, purges, the Cult of Personality, Show Trials, the Gulag and the growth of a monstrous police-state. Any analysis of developments in the 1930s must seek to explain the excesses, brutality, horror and irrationality of this period. Yet, it is also important to locate these "extraordinary" developments within the context of the "ordinary" politics of Stalinism: bureaucratization, disputes between centre and periphery, growth of administrative controls and expansion of the role of the party, drafting of a new Constitution, elections to the Supreme Soviet.[78] In these two areas the Stalinist programme confronted the underlying tensions in Bolshevism between a centralized apparatus of state control and the growth of popular control, between technocratic expertise and popular participation.

The "ordinary" politics of the Stalin era

Political developments in this period were conditioned by two issues. First, the enormous economic and social transformations inherent in the processes of industrialization and collectivization substantially altered the pattern of relationships between party, state and society. The enormous upheavals – population migration, rapid urbanization, deportations – created a society in flux. Controlling this process was essential if the state was to guide and direct the socio-economic transformation of the USSR.[79] Secondly, Stalin's views on the nature of the state under socialism. In 1930 Stalin argued that the power of the state would intensify with the approach of socialism.

> We are in favour of the withering away of the state, and at the same time we stand for the strengthening of the dictatorship of the proletariat, which represents the most powerful and mighty of all forms of the state which have existed up to the present day. The highest possible development of the power of the state, with the object of preparing the conditions of the withering away of the state.[80]

State and society

One of the interesting features that arise out of an analysis of the "ordinary" politics of Stalinism, is the identification of contradictory currents in the ebb and flow of the Stalinist transformation. What is not in the least surprising is the growth of centralization, bureaucratization, intellectual orthodoxy and a central role for the NKVD in the running of the system. What is more noteworthy is the persistence of the impulse for (albeit mobilized and closely directed) popular participation in state administration and a modification to the electoral arrangements of the state.

A huge party-state apparatus, organized hierarchically, which sought to bind the system together and to transmit decisions from the centre to the periphery grew up. The Soviets (particularly the rural Soviets), the MTS on *kolkhozy*, trade unions in the factories, the *Komsomol* and the judiciary were all mobilized in the attempt to regulate the new society. These organs ceased to function as democratic institutions of the state and became agencies of state mobilization. The Supreme Soviet did not meet between 1929 and 1935. The All-Union Trade Union Congress did not meet between 1932 and 1949. Of key import was the People's Commissariat of Internal Affairs (NKVD) which was created in 1934.[81] Incorporating the OGPU, the NKVD operated as a central instrument of state control as the state increasingly resorted to coercion in its dealings with society. The pivotal role of the NKVD reflects the state's desire to root out opposition and its reliance on coercion as a method of rule after 1929.

In particular, it is important to highlight that the NKVD took on many of the functions of the successor to RABKRIN (TSKK–RKI), which was the Leninist organ designed to institutionalize popular control.[82] In the late 1920s and early 1930s (certainly until 1933), Stalin used the organs of popular control and oversight as part of his campaign to attack specialists and to "unmask" saboteurs, enemy agents and "wreckers" within the economy. On the surface this appeared to be close to the Leninist vision: popular participation in mass campaigns to oversee the work of the elites. The purpose of these campaigns was closely linked to the immediate political agenda of Stalin, however, rather than the wider agenda of embedding popular control within the operation of the political system. This is easily illustrated, for when the Stalinist agenda changed, so too did the role of popular control. As Adams has related, Stalin instituted a much narrower role for TSKK–RKI. At the 17th Congress in January 1934, Stalin outlined that what the state required was, "not supervision, but [simply] checking the fulfilment of the centre's decisions".[83] Once more a Leninist ideal was given a specifically Stalinist content, as the organs of popular control became a further extension of the arm of the state. The gradual eclipse of popular control by the NKVD demonsrates the increasing centrality of coercion in the day-to-day running of the system.

The central role of the NKVD highlights two important features about state power under Stalin. First, state control penetrated every institution, agency and department, virtually politicizing every aspect of Soviet social life in the 1930s. *Kolkhozy*, factories and even party organizations were subject to the scrutiny of the NKVD. Secondly, the NKVD became a means of embedding Stalin's personal dictatorship over the party. Through the NKVD (and through his personal secretariat and the office of the chief procurator) Stalin attempted not only to watch over society, but also the party itself. The vanguard role of the party became subject to the whim of its General Secretary.[84] The central role of the NKVD in the legal system reinforced the idea of the law as an arm of the party–state dictatorship.[85]

The final arena which illustrates the growth of state power lies in the further restrictions of the autonomy of social institutions. In the field of Higher Education, the state emasculated the autonomy of the universities and managed to impose a form of intellectual uniformity and orthodoxy that laid the foundation for the growth of an exclusive, monolithic official ideology of Marxism–Leninism. Interestingly, this process arose directly out of the radicalism of the cultural revolution. Established figures in various fields were subject to scathing, public criticism by students or subordinates, either because it was of a non-Marxist nature, or because it failed to promote the immediate objectives of the state. Yet up until 1931, as Barber has shown, the regime merely narrowed the parameters of debate by defining what it was not permissible to discuss.[86] The turning-point was Stalin's intervention in a letter to the historical journal *Proletarskaya revolyutsiya*, which laid down a strict party line in an esoteric debate.[87] The imposition of intellectual orthodoxy proceeded apace over the next three years. The militant RAPP was replaced by the Soviet Writers Union. The Institute of Red Professors was disbanded.[88] This conversion of previously autonomous organizations into official arms of the state illustrates the increased "reach" of the state in this period.

Yet the impulse for popular control and popular participation did not die out completely. Stalin's advocacy of "criticism from below" during the Great Leap Forward, the nationwide discussion of the draft Constitution in 1935, the widespread populist campaign to denounce factory managers and bureaucrats, and the campaign to elect the 1937 Supreme Soviet all testify to a persistent trend towards drawing the populace into selective areas of state administration.[89] One of the paradoxes of this time was that these "populist" measures coincided with the wave of purges and arrests that swept the country after 1936. Clearly, this is far from the traditional Bolshevik conception of decentralized, popular accountable self-administration. The state sought to mobilize the people with the explicit purpose of rationalizing the efficiency of state administration and bolstering the legitimacy of the regime. The examples of the draft discussion of the Constitution and the 1937 election campaign outlined by Getty demonstrate how the state actively sought the participation and input of the population. In part, it appears to have been a propaganda/mobilization strategy. Additionally it was a measure with which the centre could criticize local officials, attempting to make the periphery more responsive to its diktats. Interestingly, Getty argues that the centre initially intended having contested, multi-candidate elections to the Supreme Soviet. Stalin, according to this view, retreated from this as local activists warned of the depth of opposition in the countryside, and the uncovering of enemies in the purges highlighted the existence of "enemies" within the system. In their stead, single candidate elections were instituted.[90]

Relations between state and society were officially described in the 1936 Stalin Constitution.[91] The description bore little resemblance to the reality of Soviet life. Yet the document, and the process of its drafting, are illustrative of the state's own perception of the changes within Soviet society, and of the image it wished to project to the West. Briefly, two issues stand out. First, the Constitution enshrined the changes commensurate with the claim that socialism had now been built. With the end of class-conflict, there would now be a direct, secret, universal franchise. Due process of law would replace class-based legality. Civil rights were proclaimed for all. Secondly, a vast range of civil rights and democratic freedoms were proclaimed: freedoms of speech, press, assembly, demonstrations, conscience; the rights to education, old age pensions, civil equality for women and national minorities, to work, to leisure. Stalin was to proclaim that, "the Constitution of the USSR is the only thoroughly democratic Constitution in the world".[92]

Yet, article 125 was prefaced with, "In conformity with the interests of the working people, and for the purpose of strengthening the socialist system . . .". The exercise of these rights and freedoms was contingent upon their reinforcing the policies of the state. Article 126 specifically outlined that the CPSU as the vanguard of the Soviet people, "is the leading core of all organisations of the working people, both governmental and non-governmental".[93] Together, these two articles enshrined the political monopoly of the CPSU, setting it above the law, and placed strict, if vague, limits on the rights of individuals. In practical terms the Constitution was meaningless. The tensions between elite and popular control, centralization and decentralization were firmly resolved in favour of the state. Little remained of Lenin's attempt to synthesize the different elements. The dictatorship of the proletariat had become a dictatorship of Stalin and the CPSU.

The Communist Party under Stalin

The evolution in the nature and role of the Communist Party after 1929 saw a continuation of the post-1917 developments. In theory, the party through its vanguard role was to play the role of "leader, guide and teacher". The party members present in all state institutions and social organizations were to provide ideological and political guidance, working to educate and enlighten and propagate the party line. The full-time party officials within the apparatus were organized hierarchically, transmitting orders from the centre, and verifying that the state institutions were implementing the policy correctly. In practice, the chaos and bureaucratization after 1929 meant that the party was to play an increasingly central role in the day-to-day operation of the system, binding it together in an attempt to ensure that the state remained able to control social and economic processes. Instead of operating via democratic centralism, the internal workings of the party continued to be marked by bureaucratism and appointmentism. Indeed, the nature and role of the CPSU under Stalin continued the trend whereby the vanguard detachment of revolutionaries evolved into an organization staffed by administrators and officials.

The exigencies of the revolution from above undermined the vanguard role both organizationally and ideologically. The organizational issue arose out of the exceptional demands placed on the party by the unleashing of collectivization and industrialization. The regional party committees began to accrue unto themselves more and more specialized functions, overseeing particular tasks (production, distribution, harvesting, labour issues and so on).[94] What was significant about this situation was that the centre held the regional party committee responsible for overseeing developments in the locality. In the atmosphere of maximalism and class war of 1928–31, the regional committees began to intervene in the day-to-day operation of factories, collective farms, Soviets, trade unions and so on, to ensure that targets were met and directives carried out. This garnering of control and responsibility, the detailed administrative interference, meant the regional committees became increasingly powerful, specialized executives in the localities. Inevitably, they neglected their formal functions of education, enlightenment, ideological leadership, agitation and propaganda. In this context the exercise of the vanguard role was virtually impossible.[95] The distinction between the party and the state became increasingly blurred, as a unified party–state apparatus was forged across the country. However, it must be noted that party control in the countryside was extremely weak in the early stages of collectivization.

The exercise of ideological and political leadership by the CPSU was severely undermined by the mass wave of recruitment into the party. The composition of the party was fundamentally altered as membership mushroomed from approximately 1.25 million members in 1928, to 3.5 million members in 1933.[96] This created its own problems. In particular there was concern about the levels of political consciousness of the new party members. Getty has detailed how the massive influx of new members affected the party:

> Many of the 1.8 million new members had no idea of the party's history or programme and were regarded as politically illiterate. Events would show that some party members did not even know the names of the leaders of the party or government, much less the details of the political platform.[97]

Two policy initiatives were designed to address these problems. The first was a *chistka* or purge of party membership in 1933, which aimed to prevent new admissions and reduce the existing numbers, so making the local organizations more effective and responsive. This was followed up by two further initiatives in 1935 and 1936 (of which more below).[98] Secondly, the party undertook a mass campaign to educate its members, to make them more politically literate. These interrelated issues – organizational and ideological – concerning the party evinced a series of responses at the 17th Congress in January–February 1934. In his report, Stalin outlined the causes of the problems bedevilling its operation,

> unhealthy moods penetrate into the party from outside [because of] the survivals of capitalism in people's minds, including the minds of certain members of our party.[99]

This was only to be expected in an era of rapid social and economic change. What was of more concern to Stalin was the inability or unwillingness of the party to respond to these "moods",

> Add to this the not very high theoretical level of the majority of members of our party, the inadequate ideological work of the party organs, and the fact that our party workers are overburdened with purely practical work, which deprives them of the opportunity of augmenting their theoretical knowledge.[100]

In terms of the organizational problems of the party, Stalin focused on the personnel. The correct general line had been implemented. The "objective conditions" in the USSR had been established for the victory of socialism. Stalin drew the following conclusion:

> It means that from now on nine-tenths of the responsibility for the failures and defects in our work rests, not on objective conditions, but on ourselves and ourselves alone . . . Bureaucracy and red-tape in the administrative apparatus; idle chatter about "leadership in general" instead of real and concrete leadership; the functional structure of our organizations and lack of individual responsibility; lack of personal responsibility in work and wage equalisation; the

absence of a systematic check upon the fulfilment of decisions; fear of self-criticism – these are the sources of our
difficulties.[101]

Stalin outlined a number of proposals to remedy both the ideological and organizational problems. The central aim was to "raise
organisational leadership to the level of political leadership".[102] In
specific terms, the measures recommended included: theoretical
and propaganda work; extensive criticism and self-criticism; purging the ranks of the party; tightening of discipline within the party;
mobilization of the masses.[103]

Stalin's approach rested upon choosing the right people. In other
words the attempt to restore the vanguard role of the party was
dependent upon the central leadership being able to change the
consciousness, outlook, values and working practices of the party
members in the localities. There were no measures addressing
directly the party's drift into an interventionist administrative organ.
At the root of this lay the conflict between the leadership's need to
sustain control and discipline, to maintain the responsiveness of the
periphery to the centre, to ensure decisions were implemented,
and the ideological imperative of developing the vanguard role of
the party. The underlying tension within the Stalinist programme –
between establishing effective measures of control and development,
and establishing structures commensurate with the underlying ideals
of Soviet socialism – was replicated once more.

The internal workings of the party itself were severely affected
by the transformation in its composition and role. It remained a
divided party. Although the "open" factionalism of the 1920s disappeared, the elite still remained divided. Disputes over the pace
and direction of economic development, the nature of planning,
collectivization, attitudes towards former oppositionists continued,
albeit in a more clandestine fashion. Divisions between centre and
periphery persisted, as the party sought to have its decisions implemented, and to extend its control over the countryside.[104] The picture
of a monolithic, centralized, disciplined vanguard of revolutionaries, obediently executing the will of Stalin is at variance with the
chaotic, divided, loosely organized, bureaucratic, administrative
structure that was the reality of the party in the 1930s. This context is
crucial in understanding the purges, terror and Cult of Personality.[105]

The "extraordinary" politics of Stalinism

The extraordinary, brutal, terrible history of the years 1936–8 has been well documented. Three issues need to be highlighted, which reflect upon the nature of party–state–society relations after 1929.[106] The first element is the emergence of Stalin, exercising enormous personal influence over the operation of the system. The creation of a Cult of Personality after December 1929 saw Stalin dominate the 1930s – both physically and politically. Poetry, art, sculpture were devoted to the semi-deification of Stalin. Literature paid homage to Stalin's genius. Political declarations were accompanied by extensive flattery and praise of the "Leader". Interpretations of this phenomenon vary from the personal (Stalin's vanity, megalomania and boundless ambition), to the political (Stalin's attempts to convert the contingent loyalty of party–state officials into unquestioning obedience), to the systemic (the extent of the divisions within the leadership, and the chaos in the system had to be concealed and glossed over. The Cult of Personality was designed to deflect attention away from this).[107] What is less contested is the growing personalization of power, and the legitimization of this phenomenon through its Russian national heritage. Stalin consciously placed himself in the tradition of ruthless, modernizing Russian autocrats: Peter I, Ivan IV.

Alongside the personalization of power, politics became increasingly dictatorial. While the party increased its day-to-day role in the running of the system, Stalin developed his own mechanisms and agencies to circumvent the obstructive party machinery. Through his own personal secretariat, through the NKVD, and through the appointment of key supporters of Stalin to central roles (Ezhov, Poskrebyshev, Vyshinsky) Stalin sought to exert his will, impose discipline, verify the work of the party–state apparatus and uncover enemies, spies, wreckers and saboteurs. Politics and policy-making were now subject to the personal interventions of Stalin.[108]

Personalization and dictatorship were accompanied by the institutionalization of coercion and terror into the system. This process came in two waves. The drive to industrialize and collectivize was couched in militaristic language which fomented the idea of "enemies" within Soviet society. The early 1930s saw terror unleashed on the peasantry, the search for "wreckers" among the specialists and technical intelligentsia, and the commencement of the cleansing of the ranks of the party. The collectivization process was accompanied by untold brutality in the state's dealings with the *kulaks*. The process of "de-kulakization" amounted to the isolation, deportation, exile and murder of peasants who were labelled *kulaks*, although the definition of *kulak* was somewhat arbitrary. Within the party, there were two attempts – in 1929 and 1933 – to cleanse the party of persons it felt to be "unsuitable".[109]

This institutionalization of coercion in the operation of the system does not adequately characterize the "extraordinary" nature of Stalinist politics in the 1930s. While purges of party membership continued throughout the 1930s, events took on a qualitatively different form between 1936 and 1938. At the end of 1934, the assassination of the first secretary of Leningrad (Sergei Kirov) witnessed the onset of a whirlwind of terror.[110] In the early stages of 1935, many were arrested in connection with Kirov's murder. After a brief hiatus, the period 1936–8 saw mass purges, arrests, and executions of people from every section of society, alongside public Show Trials of prominent Old Bolsheviks. Millions were swept into the labour camps in a period of unprecedented brutality, uncertainty, irrationality and arbitrariness.

While it is extremely difficult to explain much of this, the broad contours of the nature of the terror can be delineated. Virtually every section of Soviet society was affected, to a greater or lesser extent. Disproportionately affected by this terror were the military leaders, heads of the national republics, party intellectuals and other key figures within the elite. But it was not just members of the elite who were affected. Many ordinary individuals were caught up in this catalogue of terror. It hardly needs saying that the effects of these events were devastating, as families and lives were destroyed in a maelstrom of fear. Those arrested were either transferred into the labour camp system, which grew exponentially throughout this harrowing decade, or were summarily executed.

The two most significant institutional developments that accompanied the terror were the central role occupied by the NKVD, and the development of the Gulag system.[111] Labour camps had been a feature of the Soviet system since 1918. The origins and development of this system can be seen as being partially derived from the Bolshevik view of the transitional society. Labour was seen as an obligation. All had the duty to provide a socially useful contribution, even those who were incarcerated.[112] Additionally, forced labour was also seen as a "corrective", which would help people to amend their behaviour, to learn the "benefits" of a life subordinated to the common good, as opposed to one lived for the gratification of the self, in opposition to the state. Yet, as Bacon has demonstrated, there are limits to the extent to which the Gulag in the 1930s was a phenomenon derived directly from Bolshevik ideology.

It would appear that the growth and development of the Gulag is another example of a process that was Bolshevik in form, Stalinist in content. For while the labour camps as institutions had existed from the early days of the Bolshevik state, their rapid expansion was clearly linked to the industrialization drive, and the need to mobilize huge amounts of labour quickly and efficiently for the achievement of state goals.[113] In other words, it became an instrumental institution, designed to achieve the immediate goal of rapid industrialization and self-sufficiency. As Bacon has noted,

> . . . economic tasks dictated, of course, the location of the camps. In the midst of an industrialization campaign organised by central planners . . . it is only a small step to conclude that the economic tasks assigned to the NKVD influenced the number of inmates in the camps to a greater extent than the size of the camp population influenced the setting of plan targets.[114]

While the Gulag was a core part of the industrialization strategy, it assisted in consolidating the powers of the NKVD. Its economic empire of labour camps accorded it a central place in the day-to-day operation of the system. This also imparted a self-sustaining logic to the process of mass arrests. If the NKVD were to meet its plan targets set for the work of its camps, then this required a constant replenishing of the labour camp population, owing to the high mortality rates.[115] However, it is also clear that there is no simple relationship between the economic needs of the state and the growth of the labour camps. The sheer numbers of those executed demonstrates that increasing the forced labour population was not always uppermost in the minds of those in charge.[116] While the precise scope, extent and nature of the Gulag experience in the 1930s can be explained by the dynamics of Soviet socio-economic inter-actions, the underlying mindset of Bolshevism – that labour was a resource to be mobilized by the state in the construction of social-ism – underpinned these developments in a profound way.

Seeking a cause for these events is intensely problematic. Not only is it a subject riven with profound interpretative disputes, but at times it almost seems impossible to find any rational explanation. One thing is clear. Monocausal explanations – the evils of Stalin's personality, the inherent logic of Marxism, the plebaein nature of Russian culture – are terribly inadequate. Yet, beyond this recogni-tion of complexity, there is little agreement. A vast array of factors have to be integrated into any coherent attempts to analyze this phenomenon:

- the international context of preparations for war with Germany;[117]
- the personal political agenda of Stalin;[118]
- the target-fulfilment mentality, which reached down into the work of the NKVD;
- the demographic needs of the Gulag to supply forced labour for the state;
- the conflicts between centre and periphery within the bureaucracy;[119]
- conflicts and competition between the institutions at the centre, as each jostled for supremacy;
- the long-standing Bolshevik practice of identifying "enemies" to be rooted out;
- the exploitation of the atmosphere of denunciation for the pursuit of personal material interests (acquire a job, or get the living accomodation of the denounced) or petty vendettas;[120]
- a response to the leadership's promptings to criticize short-comings and inadequacies in the operation of the system;
- the persistence of a civil-war mentality and its application to problem-solving of a non-military nature;
- the constructivist, instrumentalist ethos of Marxism Soviet style which sought to hasten the advent of a society of perfect harmony and unity by identifying and removing dissenters/enemies.[121]

The extent of deaths and arrests is equally fiercely contested.[122] It is impossible to characterize the politics of Stalinism without integrating the entire panoply of features – personalization of power, dictatorship over the party, institutionalization of terror and police rule, labour camps, elections, constitutional campaigns – into any analysis.

Theoretical renewal under Stalin

By 1938–9 the impulse for change and transformation was petering out. With the official proclamation that socialism had been constructed in 1936, a theoretical response was required from the leadership about the transition from socialism to communism.[123] This ideological imperative for change ran counter to the political imperative of the Stalinist state which was system-maintaining. The desire for stability originated in the impulse for self-sufficiency: the increasingly hostile international arena, and the conflicts and sacrifices generated by industrialization and collectivization required measures to consolidate the position of the party and state elites. It was the latter imperative that gained the ascendancy, curbing substantive ideological and theoretical renewal for 20 years. This found expression in three ways.

First, in the revised *History of the CPSU [B]* (which set forth a highly distorted version of party history designed to accentuate Stalin's role in the making of the revolution and the construction of socialism), Stalin contributed a theoretical chapter "Dialectical and historical materialism".[124] The most significant part of this chapter was that Stalin stripped the dialectic of its transformatory implications. The orthodox Engelian interpretation of Marxist philosophy (entitled dialectical materialism) was contained in *Anti-Duhring* (emphasizing once more the central role of this text in establishing a Marxist orthodoxy among Russian Marxists). In this text, Engels outlined that there were three laws of the dialectic, which were universally applicable in all societies: the transformation of quantity into quality, the law of the unity of opposites, and the negation of the negation.[125] Within Stalin's chapter, the last law disappeared, to be replaced by two general laws about the properties of matter and nature.[126] Why did the negation of the negation disappear? The revolutionary potential within it was at odds with the desire for consolidation. If this principle was applied to Soviet society, then socialism, as the negation of capitalism would in turn be negated through the development of communism. Revolution, radical change and sharp breaks in social development were all precluded.[127]

This theme of consolidation and continuity was extended at the 18th Congress in March 1939. The materials collected and published from the Congress later that year were entitled, *The land of socialism today and tomorrow*,[128] emphasizing the extended life expected for the lower phase. Stalin's report reiterated this basic message. Although he talked of the need to outstrip the capitalist countries economically in order to lay the foundations for the future abundance of communism, it was stressed that this required further sacrifices, and "time, and no little time at that".[129] In the economic and social spheres, the tasks were now deemed to be ones of "further consolidation", "to continue to improve", "to strengthen".[130] In the last section of his speech, Stalin turned to questions of theory. Having constructed socialism, orthodoxy dictated that the state should begin to wither away, to be replaced by the self-administration of the people. Stalin rejected this view. Instead Stalin argued that the orthodox view of the state "cannot be extended to the partial and specific case of the victory of socialism in one country".[131] Hostile capitalist encirclement required a strong, coercive state with the ability to defend the USSR from attack. Internally, the function of the state was no longer the suppression of hostile classes, since they did not exist. The coercive, negative aspects of the state were now confined to "protecting socialist property from thieves and pilferers".[132] Stalin now advanced the more positive attributes – defined as "peaceful economic organisation and cultural education".[133] The state was to remain, even under communism, until the final defeat of international capitalism. The perspectives of the Stalinist leadership – consolidation and the projection of the socialist phase into the future – seemed to be confirmed by the failure of the programme commission created at the 18th Congress to draw up a new party programme to replace the obsolete 1919 party programme.[134]

Soviet socialism under Stalin 1929–41

In 1936, Stalin proclaimed that a socialist society had been built in the USSR. Was this socialist system a recognizably Bolshevik one? Scholars have tended to identify the Stalinist version of socialism with the "war communist" era, seeing in it a revival of the statist, centralizing, coercive, class war approach, contrasting markedly with the gradualist, conciliatory, market-oriented NEP period.[135] However, this view rests upon an artificially dichotomized interpretation of the two eras. A close examination of the system that emerged in the 1930s reveals a far more complex filiation between it and the theory and practice of Soviet socialism. Although Stalin did not provide a great deal of theoretical innovation after 1929, the Stalinist programme further refined and modified the dominant understanding of socialism in Bolshevik discourse, and added some completely new elements. Four trends appear to have been at work here. First, in certain areas the Stalinist programme continued and extended the Leninist synthesis. Secondly, Stalin's revolution from above conclusively resolved some of the enduring questions: the meaning of planning, the scope of state control and so on. Thirdly, the Stalinist synthesis appropriated many Bolshevik notions, but imbued them with a new content, overturning existing ideas and fundamentally altering their meaning. Finally, Stalin attempted to synthesize Soviet socialism with Russian nationalism, and the drive for self-sufficiency and autarky altered the nature of Soviet socialism in a profound way.[136]

The economics of Soviet Stalinist "socialism"

Stalin extended the underlying Bolshevik ideas about the proper shape of the economy under socialism. Stalin's programme reaffirmed the conception of socialism resting upon the values of rationalism, technocracy and productivism.[137] This manifested itself in the continual emphasis that the regime placed on "technology, expertise and the indispensability of technical and managerial skills",[138] and upon the central place of growth in the productive forces in this programme. As Walicki has noted,

> Stalin's emphasis upon the productive forces was . . . an indication that productive capacity or technological modernization should be given absolute priority and was more

important for the development of socialism than interhuman relations.[139]

The extreme statized nature of the economy after 1929 was highly reminiscent of the "war communist" period, and also of Lenin's notion that "the whole of society will have become a single factory". There was a vast accumulation of state power accompanying collectivization and industrialization. The powers vested in the central ministries and the factory managers amounted to the final subordination of the workers and their organizations – both salaried and forced labour – to the state. In specific terms, the leadership oversaw the construction of a large-scale heavy industrial sector as the basis for the growth of an industrial, modern technological society, and promoted state ownership and central planning in the years after 1928.

Despite this reiteration of the core values of Soviet socialism, Stalin infused them with a new content and meaning, which produced a markedly different outcome. The root causes of this were twofold. First, the policies of collectivization and industrialization were forged in an atmosphere of radicalism, militancy, utopianism and class war. In addition, they were linked inextricably to Stalin's personal and political struggles within the party. Economic rationality was sacrificed to the class/political impulse generated by the cultural revolution and the need to industrialize quickly. This is best illustrated with reference to collectivization. The long-term Bolshevik vision of an efficient, modern, technologically advanced, socialized agricultural economy of large-scale highly productive farms was not realized. The collective farm sector was shaped by the class imperative of de-kulakization, and by the need for a reliable supply of grain for industry and export.

Secondly, the imperatives implied in "socialism in one country" – self-sufficiency, overcoming backwardness, defensive military capability – shaped the economic processes in many ways. Most notably, economic tasks were designed for the speediest, most effective achievement of these goals. The outcome was a complex, contradictory set of structures and practices in which the long-term Bolshevik ideals were sacrificed to these more specific aims. For example, central planning was supposed to represent the triumph of rationality and the application of human reason over the spontaneity, irrationality, injustice and waste of the capitalist market. The nature of Soviet planning was far removed from this: irrational, contradictory, imprecise, inefficient. The economic sector was socialist in form, Stalinist in content.

Society and culture of Soviet Stalinist "socialism"

Similar processes were at work in the fields of culture and social policy. The radical agenda that had persisted after 1917 – to liberate and emancipate, to realize justice and egalitarianism – was finally crushed after 1931 by the conservative social policies pursued by the state. The socio-cultural sphere was still viewed instrumentally. After 1931 though, the purpose was not just the construction of socialism, but also the consolidation of the power of the state and the independence of the USSR. Policies that promoted inegalitarianism, conservative policies towards women, hierarchy and privilege replaced the radicalism of the early years. Nationalism and national defence now took priority over proletarian internationalism. The early policy of class discrimination in favour of the proletariat was dropped with the drafting of the new Constitution. Intellectual life and cultural life was dominated by the state.

The politics of Soviet Stalinist "socialism"

How do the features of Stalinist politics fit into the Soviet socialist framework? The conjunction of terror, purges, personalized power and the embedding of the rule of the NKVD within the system, with the humdrum politics of the day-to-day administration of the system, makes simple categorization impossible. The strand within Bolshevism that emphasized popular participation, democracy and local autonomy (and even its expression under Lenin in the forms of transmission belts) was further eroded in the 1930s by the state's continued emasculation of the rights and functions of social groups and public organizations. The dictatorship of the proletariat was now a number of dictatorships: of Stalin, of the party, of the state. Lenin's injunction for "less politics" had been realized. However, this was not the depoliticized, technocratic, expertise-based scientific management of society envisaged by Lenin, but the subordination of all to achieve the goals of the regime.

By 1939, the Stalinist synthesis of Soviet socialism was complete. The official state ideology proclaimed that socialism had triumphed in the USSR. From now on the task was to begin the transition to the higher phase of communism. The central question in the period after 1939 was the extent to which the theory and practice of Soviet socialism under Stalin would provide the foundation for this transition, or whether there would be further adaptations. The death of Stalin in 1953 posed this question to Stalin's successors.

Appendix: Stalinist "socialism" and the Soviet mode of production

If the question of how "Bolshevik" Stalinist socialism was is a complex one, then this is as nothing compared with the wider issue of whether it was "socialist" at all. For the purposes of this work, which traces the shifts in the Bolshevik understanding of the lower phase of communism, the issue is an interesting although slightly tangential one. While there is a degree of filiation between "Stalinism" and this understanding of the lower phase, whether this deserves the epithet of socialism is another matter. A whole spectrum of opinions exist, reflecting both the conceptual imprecision of the term socialism itself, and the ideological positions adopted by various theorists.[140] Malia has put forward an interesting argument. He maintains that by 1936, Stalin had successfully accomplished the instrumental programme of socialism: that is the negation of the central features of the capitalist mode of production. However, the outcome was not as expected for two reasons. First, the process had been an immense improvization. Secondly, the instrumental programme of socialism lacked socialism's moral programme – abundance, freedom, equality, absence of exploitation – and so it was merely the facade or structure of socialism that had emerged by 1936. Malia goes on to argue that the achievement of the moral programme was a chimera, as the measures taken to achieve the instrumental programme – which involved the overwhelming application of state power – were intrinsically inimical to the moral values of freedom and equality.[141]

Whether one subscribes to the view that the Stalinist system was a variant of state capitalism, state socialism, bureaucratic collectivism or an historically unique mode of production, the relationship between Stalinism, Bolshevism, Leninism, Marxism and socialism remains as contentious as ever.

Notes

1. J. Stalin, "A year of great change", in *Collected works*, vol. 12, p. 141.
2. The debates are summarized succinctly in C. Ward, *Stalin's Russia* (London: Edward Arnold, 1993), pp. 7–38.
3. M. Reiman, *The birth of Stalinism* (London: I. B. Tauris, 1987); C. Merridale, *Moscow politics and the rise of Stalin* (London: Macmillan, 1990); L. Viola, *The best sons of the fatherland* (Oxford: Oxford University Press, 1987).
4. J. Stalin, "The work of the joint April plenum of the CC and the CCC", in *Collected works*, vol. 11, p. 62.
5. The atmosphere of this period can be gleaned from S. Fitzpatrick, *The cultural front* (Ithaca: Cornell University Press, 1992), pp. 115–48.
6. M. Lewin, *The making of the Soviet system* (London: Methuen, 1985), p. 221; also his *Political undercurrents in Soviet economic debates* (London: Pluto Press, 1975), pp. 97–113.
7. The details of the economics of this period can be found in many texts. See for instance, A. Nove, *An economic history of the USSR* (London: Penguin, 1992), pp. 160–268. An excellent overview can be found in R. W. Davies, "Economic Aspects of Stalinism", in *The Stalin Phenomenon*, A. Nove (ed.) (London: Weidenfeld & Nicolson, 1993), pp. 39–74.
8. Lewin, *Political undercurrents*, pp. 96–117.
9. The debates on planning can be followed in depth in E. H. Carr & R. W. Davies, *Foundations of a planned economy 1926–29*, vol. 1 (London: Macmillan, 1969), chs 11, 32, 35, 36, 37.
10. Nove, *An economic history*, pp. 264–8.
11. M. Malia, *The Soviet tragedy. A history of socialism in Russia 1917–91* (New York: Free Press 1994), pp. 209–10.
12. Lewin, *Political undercurrents*, p. 105.
13. R. W. Davies, "Gorbachev's socialism in historical perspective", *New Left Review* **179**, 1990, p. 11.
14. If you feel inclined to pursue these developments in more detail, see for the early period, Carr & Davies, *Foundations of a planned economy*, chs 14 & 16; Nove, *An economic history*, pp. 213–16; D. Shearer, "Factories within factories: changes in the structure of work and management in Soviet machine-building factories 1926–34", in *Social dimensions of Soviet industrialization*, W. G. Rosenberg

& L. Siegelbaum (eds) (Bloomington: Indiana University Press, 1993), pp. 193–202.

15. Nove, *An economic history*, p. 213.
16. Lewin, *Political undercurrents*, p. 105.
17. Among the many excellent monographs see V. Andrle, *Workers in Stalin's Russia* (New York: St Martin's Press, 1988), pp. 67–111.
18. The best pieces on management/labour relations include, D. Filtzer, *Soviet workers and Stalinist industrialization* (London: Pluto Press, 1986); Andrle, *Workers in Stalin's Russia*; H. Kuromiya, *Stalin's industrial revolution: politics and workers 1928–32* (Cambridge, Cambridge University Press, 1988); Lewin, *The making of the Soviet system*, pp. 209–57; Rosenberg & Siegelbaum (eds), *Social dimensions*, chs by Davies, Kotkin and Siegelbaum; V. Andrle, *A social history of twentieth century Russia* (London: Arnold, 1994), pp. 163–93.
19. Lewin, *The making of the Soviet system*, pp. 247–56.
20. Filtzer, *Soviet workers*, pp. 116–21.
21. Ibid., pp. 35–45. Andrle, *Workers in Stalin's Russia*, ch. 4.
22. Filtzer, *Soviet workers*, ch. 9.
23. Lewin, *The making of the Soviet system*, pp. 251–6; M. Matthews, *Privilege in the Soviet Union* (London: Allen & Unwin, 1978), pp. 91–6.
24. L. Siegelbaum, *Stakhanovism and the politics of productivity in the USSR 1935–41* (Cambridge: Cambridge University Press, 1988).
25. Filtzer, *Soviet workers*, pp. 254–61.
26. Ibid., ch. 9: Andrle, *Workers in Stalin's Russia*, pp. 67–111; Davies, *The management of Soviet industry 1928–41*, in *Social dimensions*, Rosenberg & Siegelbaum (eds), pp. 109–20.
27. K. Bailes, *Technology and society under Lenin and Stalin. Origins of the Soviet technical intelligentsia 1917–41* (Princeton: Princeton University Press, 1978); S. Fitzpatrick, "Stalin and the making of a new elite", in *The cultural front*, pp. 149–82.
28. Fitzpatrick, *The cultural front*, pp. 149–65.
29. J. Stalin, "New conditions – new tasks in economic construction, in *Collected works* (Moscow: Foreign Languages Publishing House, 1955) vol. 13, pp. 53–82.
30. Bailes, *Technology and society*, chs 10–11; Fitzpatrick, *The cultural front*, pp. 165–82.
31. Lewin, *Political undercurrents*, pp. 113–14; Nove, *An economic history*, pp. 264–8; A. Nove, "Marxism and 'Really Existing' socialism", in *Studies in economics and Russia* (London: Macmillan, 1990), pp. 179–91; Davies, "Economic Aspects", pp. 56–7.
32. Collectivization has spawned a vast array of material. See S. Fitzpatrick, *Stalin's peasants* (New York: Oxford University Press, 1994); R. Conquest, *The harvest of sorrow* (London: Hutchinson,

1986); Lewin, *The making of the Soviet system*, part II; R. W. Davies, *The industrialization of Soviet Russia, I: The socialist offensive; the collectivization of Soviet agriculture 1929–30* (London: Macmillan, 1980). R. W. Davies, *The industrialization of Soviet Russia 2: the Soviet collective farm 1929–30* (London: Macmillan, 1981); M. Lewin, *Russian peasants and Soviet power* (London: Allen & Unwin, 1968); Andrle, *A social history*, pp. 143–62.

33. Conquest, *Harvest of sorrow*, argues that the horrors of collectivization were consciously engineered by the party in its struggles with the peasantry. The figures for deaths are highly contested, see the contributions in *Slavic Review* 44(3), 1985, by Wheatcroft and Rosefelde.

34. Stalin, "A year of great change", in *Collected works*, vol. 12, p. 131.

35. Stalin, "Concerning questions of agrarian policy in the USSR", in ibid., vol. 12, p. 161.

36. J. D. Bergamini, "Stalin and the Collective Farm", in *Continuity and change in Russian and Soviet thought*, E. Simmons (ed.) (Cambridge, Mass.: Harvard University Press, 1955), pp. 231–2.

37. Stalin, "A year of great change", in ibid., vol. 12, p. 135.

38. R. McNeal (ed.), *Resolutions and Decisions of the CPSU, vol. 3, 1929–1953* (Toronto: University of Toronto Press, 1974), pp. 40–3.

39. Some theorists argue that collectivization made a negative contribution to industrialization, see J. R. Millar, "Mass collectivization and the contribution of Soviet agriculture to the first five year plan", *Slavic Review* 4, 1974; H. Hunter, "Soviet agriculture with and without collectivization", *Slavic Review* 2, 1988. A counterpoint can be found in M. Ellman, "Did the agricultural surplus provide the resources for the increase in investment in the USSR during the first five year plan?", *The Economic Journal* 4, 1975.

40. Stalin, "Concerning the policy of eliminating the kulaks as a class", in *Collected works*, vol. 12, p. 189.

41. Stalin, "Dizzy with success", in ibid., vol. 12, pp. 197–205.

42. Ward, *Stalin's Russia*, pp. 50–1.

43. Davies, *The Soviet collective farm 1929–30*, pp. 68–115, 131–47.

44. Ibid., p. 175.

45. Details can be found in Nove, *An economic history*, pp. 241–5.

46. Ibid., pp. 239–52.

47. J. Stalin, "On the draft constitution of the USSR", in *Problems of Leninism* (Moscow: Foreign Languages Publishing House, 1947), p. 543.

48. J. Stalin, "The results of the first five year plan, January 7 1933", in ibid., p. 421.

49. An excellent analysis of these developments can be found in Evans, *Soviet Marxism–Leninism*, pp. 36–8.

50. S. Fitzpatrick (ed.), *Cultural revolution in Russia 1928–31* (Bloomington: Indiana University Press, 1978).

51. A good example of the shift in cultural policies and its effects upon particular groups in Soviet society can be found in J. Barber, *Soviet historians in crisis* (London: Macmillan, 1981).

52. Stalin, "New tasks – new conditions", in *Collected works*, vol. 13, p. 59.

53. Davies, "Gorbachev's socialism", p. 10.

54. Matthews, *Privilege in the Soviet Union*, pp. 91–130.

55. Cited in Ward, *Stalin's Russia*, pp. 91–2.

56. J, Stalin, "Report to the XVII Congress of the CPSU", in *Problems of Leninism*, p. 503.

57. Stalin, "New conditions – new tasks", in *Collected works*, vol. 13, pp. 71–5.

58. S. Rosen, *Education and modernisation in the USSR* (Reading, Mass.: Addison-Wesley, 1971) p. 41; Matthews, *Privilege in the Soviet Union*, pp. 114–16.

59. M. Buckley, *Women and ideology in the Soviet Union* (London: Harvester Wheatsheaf, 1989), pp. 108–38.

60. Ibid., pp. 108–20; B. Clements, "The utopianism of the zhenotdel", *Slavic Review* **51**(2), 1992, pp. 495–6.

61. Buckley, *Women and ideology*, p. 113.

62. Ibid., pp. 128–36.

63. An excellent treatment of this topic can be found in N. Krementsov, *Stalinist science* (Princeton: Princeton University Press, 1997). See also, D. Holloway, "Scientific truth and political authority in the USSR", in *Political opposition in one-party states*, L. Schapiro (ed.) (London: Macmillan, 1972), pp. 152–78; L. Graham, *Science in Russia and the Soviet Union* (Cambridge: Cambridge University Press, 1993).

64. Krementsev, *Stalinist science*, pp. 31–53; Holloway, "Scientific truth", pp. 152–60.

65. Ibid., p. 52. It is interesting to note, however, that the extent of state control was modified slightly in practice in a number of ways. First, state policy fluctuated with the oscillations in economic priorities, and was differentiated across the whole field of science. Secondly, many conflicts emerged between the different agencies engaged in overseeing science policy. Thirdly, scientists were often able to pay lip-service to party doctrine and dogma, while pursuing their own agenda simultaneously. See the conclusion to ibid.

66. R. Stites, *Russian popular culture* (Cambridge: Cambridge University Press, 1992), ch. 3. Andrle, *A social history*, pp. 203–10.

67. Details of Comintern policies and outlook can be found in, F. H. Haigh, D. S. Morris, A. R. Peters, *Soviet foreign policy, the League of Nations and Europe, 1917–39* (Aldershot: Gower, 1986); Kermit E.

McKenzie, *Comintern and World Revolution 1928–43* (New York: Columbia University Press, 1964).

68. A. Evans, *Soviet Marxism–Leninism. The decline of an ideology,* (Westport: Praeger, 1993), pp. 29–32.

69. Haigh et al., *Soviet foreign policy,* p. 125.

70. H. J. Berman, *Justice in the USSR* (Cambridge, Mass.: Harvard University Press, 1966), pp. 48–9.

71. Stites, *Russian popular culture,* pp. 64–7.

72. Rosen, *Education and modernization,* pp. 39–42; G. Hosking, *A history of the Soviet Union* (London: Fontana, 1992), p. 215.

73. Hosking, *A history,* pp. 212–15.

74. Stites, *Russian popular culture,* p. 67.

75. Ibid., p. 67.

76. Bailes, *Technology and society,* pp. 381–406; Stites, *Russian popular culture,* pp. 69–70.

77. Stites, *Russian popular culture,* pp. 65–6.

78. The debate on the politics of Stalinism is highly contested. Many "counter-communists" seek to place the terror and coercion at the centre of any analysis. "Revisionists" seek to locate it within a wider context. For the debates on the nature of Stalinism see, "New perspectives on Stalinism", *Russian Review* **45**, 1986, and **46**, 1987. Also J. Burbank, "Controversies over Stalinism: searching for a Soviet society", *Politics and Society* **19**(3), 1991. J. Arch Getty, "The politics of Stalinism", in *The Stalin phenomenon,* A. Nove (ed.) (London: Weidenfeld & Nicolson, 1993), pp. 100–37.

79. Lewin, *Making of the Soviet system,* pp. 258–86.

80. J. Stalin, "Political report of CC to XVI Congress of CPSU", in *Collected works,* vol. 12, p. 381.

81. L. Schapiro, *The communist party of the Soviet Union* (London: Methuen, 1970), pp. 403–4.

82. E. A. Rees, *State control in Soviet Russia* (London: Macmillan, 1987).

83. Cited in J. Adams, *Citizen Inspectors in the Soviet Union. The People's Control Committee* (New York: Praeger, 1977), p. 36.

84. Schapiro, *Communist party,* pp. 403–21.

85. Berman, *Justice in the USSR,* pp. 37–65; E. L. Johnson, *An introduction to the Soviet legal system* (London: Methuen, 1969), pp. 42–51.

86. J. Barber, "The establishment of intellectual orthodoxy in the USSR", *Past and Present* **83**, 1979, pp. 141–64.

87. J. Stalin, "Some questions concerning the history of Bolshevism", in *Collected works,* vol. 13, pp. 86–104. J. Barber, "Stalin's letter to the editors of proletarskaya revolyutsiya", *Soviet Studies* **28**, 1976, pp. 21–41.

88. S. Fitzpatrick, *The cultural front,* pp. 143–8.

89. G. Rittersporn, *Stalinist simplifications and Soviet complications* (Chur: Harwood Academic Publishers, 1991), pp. 64–182; J. Arch

Getty, "State and society under Stalin: Constitutions and elections in the 1930's", *Slavic Review* **50**(1), 1991, pp. 18–35.

90. Getty, "State and society", pp. 26–35.
91. S. E. Finer (ed.), *Five constitutions: Contrasts and comparisons* (Harmondsworth: Penguin, 1979), pp. 117–42.
92. J. Stalin, On the draft constitution of the USSR. Report delivered at the Extraordinary Eighth Congress of Soviets of USSR, 25 November 1936, in *Problems of Leninism*, p. 557.
93. Finer, *Five constitutions*, p. 139.
94. M. McAuley, *Soviet politics 1917–91* (Oxford: Oxford University Press, 1992), pp. 43–9; Schapiro, *Communist party*, chs 24–5.
95. McAuley, *Soviet politics*, pp. 44–5.
96. Schapiro, *Communist party*, p. 439.
97. J. Arch Getty, *Origins of the Great Purges: the Soviet communist party reconsidered* (Cambridge: Cambridge University Press, 1985), p. 21.
98. Ibid., pp. 38–92.
99. Stalin, Report on the work of the CC to the XVII Congress of the CPSU, January 26 1934, in *Problems of Leninism*, p. 498.
100. Ibid., p. 499.
101. Ibid., p. 510.
102. Ibid., p. 511.
103. Ibid., p. 511.
104. Getty, *The origins of the great purges*, pp. 10–37; Rittersporn, *Stalinist simplifications*, chs 2–4. More detailed pieces on disputes can be found in, R. W. Davies, "The management of Soviet industry", in *Social Dimensions of Soviet Industrialisation*, W. Rosenberg & L. Siegelbaum (eds) (Bloomington: Indiana University Press), pp. 105–24. R. W. Davies, "The Syrtsov–Lominadze affair", *Soviet Studies* **1**, 1981. R. W. Davies, "The socialist market: a debate in Soviet industry, 1932–33", *Slavic Review* **2**, 1984.
105. R. Tucker, "The origins of Stalin's personality cult", *American Historical Review* **84**, 1979.
106. The debate over the terror is a contentious, and bitter one. The central text on the counter-communist side is, R. Conquest, *The Great Terror: a reassessment* (London: Hutchinson 1990). The main revisionist texts are, Getty, *Origins of the Great Purges*; Rittersporn, *Stalinist simplifications*; J. Arch Getty & R. Manning (eds) *Stalinist terror* (Cambridge: Cambridge University Press, 1993).
107. Rittersporn, *Stalinist simplifications*, pp. 183–221.
108. Schapiro, *Communist party*, pp. 403–21.
109. Getty, *Origins of the Great Purges*, pp. 38–57.
110. This is a central disagreement between Getty and Conquest. See Getty, *Origins of Great Purges*, pp. 207–11; R. Conquest, *Stalin and the Kirov murder* (London: Hutchinson, 1989).

111. For a fine analysis of the development of the Gulag system, see E. Bacon, *The Gulag at war* (Houndmills: Macmillan, 1996), pp. 42–63.
112. Ibid., pp. 52–3.
113. Ibid., pp. 49–52.
114. Ibid., p. 50.
115. Ibid., p. 52.
116. Ibid., p. 52.
117. I. Deutscher, *Stalin* (London: Penguin, 1966), ch. 9.
118. Conquest, *The Great Terror*; R. Medvedev, *Let history judge* (New York: Alfred K. Knopf, 1971), pp. 289–338.
119. Getty, *Origins*, pp. 172–206.
120. A. Nove, "Stalin and Stalinism – some afterthoughts", in Nove (ed.), *The Stalin Phenomenon*, pp. 197–208.
121. L. Kolakowski, "The Marxist roots of Stalinism", in *Stalinism*, R. C. Tucker (ed.) (New York: Norton, 1977).
122. A good summary of the disputed issues can be found in Bacon, *The Gulag at war*, pp. 6–41.
123. There has been surprisingly little analysis of Stalin's theoretical contributions. A useful recent piece is A. Walicki, *Marxism and the leap to the kingdom of freedom*, pp. 426–54.
124. *History of the CPSU (Short Course)* (Moscow: Foreign Languages Publishing House, 1939), pp. 105–31.
125. Analysis of Engels' views can be found in T. Bottomore (ed.), *A dictionary of Marxist thought* (Oxford: Blackwell, 1983), pp. 120–1.
126. Stalin, "Dialectical and historical materialism", pp. 105–11.
127. Evans, *Soviet Marxism–Leninism*, pp. 52–3.
128. *The land of socialism today and tomorrow* (Moscow: Foreign Languages Publishing House, 1939).
129. Stalin, Report on the work of the CC to the XVIII Congress of the CPSU, in ibid., p. 24.
130. Ibid., pp. 32–5.
131. Ibid., p. 47.
132. Ibid., p. 50.
133. Ibid., p. 50.
134. Evans, *Soviet Marxism–Leninism*, pp. 46–7.
135. For a good overview discussion of this issue, see S. Fitzpatrick, "The legacy of the civil war", in D. Koenker et al. (eds), *Party, state and society in the Russian civil war* (Bloomington: Indiana University Press, 1989), pp. 385–98.
136. Lewin, *Making of the Soviet system*, pp. 191–208.
137. N. Harding, "Socialism, society and the organic labour state", in N. Harding (ed.), *The state in socialist society* (New York: Albany, 1984), pp. 38–45.

138. S. Smith, "Taylorism rules OK? Bolshevism, Taylorism and the technical intelligentsia in the Soviet Union 1917–41", *Radical Science Journal* **13**, 1983, p. 22.

139. Walicki, *Marxism*, p. 439.

140. H. Reichmann, "Reconsidering Stalinism", *Theory and Society* **17**, 1988, pp. 57–90; Filtzer, *Soviet workers*; Nove, "Marxism and 'Really Existing' Socialism", L. Trotsky, *The revolution betrayed* (New York: Pathfinder Press, 1973); T. Cliff, *Russia: a Marxist analysis* (London: International Socialism, 1964); M. Heller & A. Nekrich, *Utopia in power* (New York: Summit Books, 1986); T. von Laue, "Stalin in focus", *Slavic Review* **42**(3), 1983; R. Tucker (ed.), *Stalinism: Essays in historical interpretation* (New York: Norton, 1977); M. Malia, *The Soviet tragedy: a history of socialism in Russia* (New York: Free Press, 1994), pp. 211–26.

141. Malia, *The Soviet Tragedy*, pp. 224–6. I would differ from Malia's analysis in many respects, especially when he argues that "Soviet socialism was not built out of any genuine plan" (p. 223). The argument contained here is that the Bolsheviks knew generally what the structural features of socialism were, and it was Stalin's autarkic revolution which gave these features their specific content, operational practices, etc. As has been stated here before, Soviet socialist in form, Stalinist in content.

CHAPTER SEVEN

Khrushchev and Soviet socialism: burying Stalin, reviving Lenin?

How times have changed in the span of one five-year plan: in 1952 someone said that Stalin was an idiot and he was shot the very same day; recently someone announced that Khrushchev was an idiot and he got 8 years for divulging a state secret! (1957)[1]

Stalin's death evoked contradictory emotions among the Soviet people. Millions mourned. Many rejoiced. Most were merely fearful about the future. Undoubtedly, most people's lives were profoundly affected by this event. But the scale and nature of the "change" wrought by Stalin's death is more contested. In the area covered by this work – the nature of Soviet socialism – the question concerns the extent to which the regime after 1953 adapted the theory and practice of Soviet socialism. Viewing Khrushchev with the benefit of hindsight, and by comparison with his predecessor and successor, the period between 1956 and 1964 appears to be one of change, renewal, reform, of a more humane and liberal approach after the brutal horrors of Stalinism. Yet, there are significant continuities between the two eras as well. This chapter explores the relation-ship between the Khrushchevite view of socialism and the Stalinist view of socialism on the one hand, and the broader Soviet view of socialism on the other.

Contextualizing the Khrushchev era: the theory and practice of mature Stalinism 1939–53

The years from 1939 to 1953 saw few major changes to either the theory or practice of Soviet socialism. In part, this was a function of circumstance. From June 1941, the USSR was engulfed in the brutal carnage of the Second World War. The bloody, dehumanizing occupation by the Nazi army inflicted further traumas on the long-suffering Soviet citizens. Through a mixture of fierce heroism, self-sacrifice, patriotism, hard work, luck and the failings of their opponents the Soviets prevailed. The practice of the Soviet system was modified substantially in certain areas as the state sought to mobilize all constituencies in support of the war effort. This was particularly the case with regard to relations between the state and rural society. The peasants were able to benefit financially (albeit fairly modestly) from increased procurement prices (although there was little or no chance to spend their income on anything). Perhaps of greater significance was the *rapprochement* between church and state. Seeking to bind Soviet society behind the conflict, Stalin used as many forms of ideological cement as possible. The *rapprochement* with the religious authorities was born out of an attempt to synthesize state patriotism, Russian nationalism and the underlying religious sentiments of the people, particularly the rural population. Although the system was modified in certain respects, there were also tendencies that reinforced the structure and operation of the system. The rigours of running a wartime economy increased the centralized nature of economic decision-making, and maintained the heavy industry/defence priority in production. Although Stalin eventually devolved significant decision-making authority to other senior figures in the system, he remained the dominant figure, embodied as *Generalissimo*.

The Great Patriotic War (as it was to become known in official Soviet sources) had a profound impact upon the psychology of the Soviet people. The successful struggle against the Nazi invasion left the Soviet people emotionally, morally and materially devastated. A determination never to allow such an experience to be repeated underpinned Soviet foreign policy in the post-war era. In ideological terms, Stalin in particular and the party in general benefited from this struggle, as the state gained another source of legitimacy.

Building upon the nationalist sentiments and motifs propagated in the 1930s, the state portrayed the war as a national rather than a class conflict. Stalin stood four square in the tradition of great Russian leaders who had resisted foreign invasion. The war (temporarily) overturned the priority of class and national values in Soviet ideological discourse.

At the end of the war, the system was engaged in a massive reconstruction programme, seeking to make good the massive destruction of the agricultural, industrial, transport and housing infrastructure. Across this 14 year period, the system retained its essential features – central planning, bias towards heavy industry, collectivized agriculture, one-party rule, personal dictatorship, institutionalized terror, hierarchical social structure, conservative social and cultural policy – and indeed returned to many pre-war practices with regard to the church and the rural sector. The Stalinist model of socialism retained its statized, centralized essence.[2]

In international affairs there were two immensely significant developments. The advent of the cold war added a militaristic element to the competition between capitalism and socialism and prompted extensive increases in arms spending, culminating in the acquisition of nuclear capability by August 1949. The emergence of a bloc of socialist states in eastern Europe and China by 1949 had enormous implications for the Soviet understanding of socialism. While on one level it appeared to validate that the future belonged to "socialism", it was also to affect the subsequent evolution of the Soviet Union – ideologically, politically, economically and culturally – in profound and rather unexpected ways. As the first socialist state, it was necessary for the CPSU to demonstrate that it was at all times the state that was most advanced on the road to communism. This predominant position was complicated by subsequent events in which pluralism within the socialist camp – particularly between China and the USSR – became competitive rather than collaborative. Within the oscillating military context of the cold war, the Soviet state was engaged in two main rivalries after 1949: economic competition with the West, ideological competition with the East.

Ideological developments in the latter years of the Stalin era were few and far between. Stalin intervened sporadically in a restricted number of fields, most notably agronomics and linguistics.[3] The central ideological issue was the timetable of the transition to communism. The declaration that socialism had been built in 1936 raised a key question: when, and how, would the transition to communism begin? While a convincing case can be made that the involvement in world war and cold war "interrupted" the trans-formation of Soviet socialism into communism, this is only part of the story. As Evans has related, Stalin was keen to prevent discussions on this topic.[4] Stalin was motivated by a desire to play down the implications for change implicit in the notion of undertaking the transition to communism. The main document from this period is the pamphlet "The economic problems of socialism" (1952).[5] In-stead of focusing upon transformation and transition, Stalin focused upon consolidation and stability. The USSR had entered a period of preparation for the transition to communism, not the transition it-self. This entailed a commitment to the existing structures, practices and priorities for the foreseeable future. For instance, Stalin argued that collective farm property was distinct from, and inferior (in ideological terms) to state property. Transition to communism could not start until this differentiation in property relations had been overcome.[6] The implications of profound systemic change inherent in commencing the final transition underpinned Stalin's unwilling-ness to engage in public discussion.[7]

The interesting point here is that Stalin recognized that the ques-tion itself had to be addressed, and not just in a formal, rhetorical, perfunctory manner. The legitimacy of the regime continued to rest on being able to demonstrate progress towards communism. Stalin was aware of the need to validate current policies in the light of their relationship to the future society, hence his regular references to post-socialist developments. The traditional party document that set out the goals for the future was the party programme. The 1919 programme outlined the task of constructing socialism, which had been built, according to official pronouncements, by 1936. In order to substantiate Stalin's ideas about consolidation and preparation for the transition, a new party programme was required. The 18th Party Congress created a commission to prepare a new document, but nothing was ever published. The 19th Party Congress in 1952 also created another commission, but Stalin died before it could report.[8] Recent Soviet sources have shown that between 1938 and 1952, a number of drafts were circulated among the party elite.[9] This confirms the view that the party leadership were preoccupied with the question of determining the future stages of development of the Soviet state.

This had important consequences for the post-Stalin leadership. If the transition to communism was to be undertaken, this raised the prospect of profound changes. The central features of the higher phase of communism – material abundance, decentralized public self-management, withering away of money, growing equality, abolition of the distinctions between mental and manual labour, and between town and country – would transform Soviet social, economic and political structures. Yet, if commencing the transition to communism was to be postponed, the alternative – consolidating socialism – also heralded change of sorts. The imperative to catch up with and surpass the capitalist countries economically, demonstrating the superiority of socialism, remained. Yet could this be achieved on the basis of the Stalinist model of socialism? Within the new international socialist bloc, the USSR had to demonstrate its leadership in practice: as the first socialist state it had to maintain its leading role, exemplifying to the states of eastern Europe, China and elsewhere their future. The process of consolidating socialism thus also held out the prospects of change: reforming the dysfunctional elements of the Stalinist model, replacing the personal dictatorship and so on. Ideologically, there was a strong imperative for change within the practice of Soviet socialism.

There were also strong pressures inhibiting change, particularly among members of the elite who wished to consolidate the prevailing patterns of domination and subordination – politically, economically, materially – within the state. The key questions were about the scope and precise content of this change. Which elements of the Stalinist model should be retained? Which should be removed? Which should be reformed? Would Khrushchev revert back to an earlier Leninist conception of socialism? The question was complicated by the commitment of all the leaders to the core values of Soviet socialism – the leading role of the CPSU; central control and direction of all aspects of social activity; state ownership of the means of production; central planning; proletarian internationalism.[10]

But how would the post-Stalin leadership interpret the meaning of these values/features? It is at this point that the personal values, political priorities and vision of the post-Stalin leadership enter the equation. The policies of the new leadership were shaped not merely by the ideological imperatives of Soviet Marxism–Leninism, but also by the political context of Stalin's death. The CPSU had no mechanism for succession. Both the previous leaders had died in office. Who should succeed Stalin? Should it be another single leader, or a collective leadership? How should a leader (leadership) be chosen? In the context of the succession struggle, it was necessary for the leaders to differentiate themselves. By adopting particular policy stances – the priority of economic development, attitudes towards the West, social and cultural policies, pattern of political rule – they sought to distinguish themselves from their rivals. In this sense the particular shape of socialism after 1953 was forged in the crucible of the succession struggle. The combination of Khrushchev's vision, his personal policy priorities and the core features of Soviet socialism produced a distinctive synthesis, which rejected certain elements of the Stalinist model, revived aspects of the Leninist approach, while reinforcing the dominant values of Soviet socialism: statist, centralizing, technocratic, constructivist.

The politics of Khrushchevism

The politics of Stalin's death

The political legacy bequeathed by Stalin posed many difficulties for his successors. Stalin's personal dictatorship had marginalized and downgraded the party in the post-war period. No party congresses met between 1939 and 1952. The Central Committee was rarely convened. Regional and republican organs of the party exercised little authority. Stalin ruled through his personal secretariat and the Council of Ministers: the central organs of the state had a far higher status than those of the party. The pivotal role of the NKVD and its head (Lavrentii Beria) contributed to the further peripheralization of the CPSU.[11]

Of more immediate concern to the central political figures in the post-Stalin Praesidium (the new name for the Politburo) – Malenkov, Beria, Molotov, Kaganovich, Khrushchev – was the situation arising out of Stalin's death. They quickly divided up the key posts among themselves, reflecting a consensus that there should not be a single predominant figure like Stalin rather than a positive belief in the merits of collective leadership *per se*. Malenkov (nominally the most senior figure) assumed the positions of Chairman of the Council of Ministers and First Secretary of the CPSU. Under pressure he relinquished the latter post, confirming the subordinate position of the CPSU in the minds of the new leaders. Khrushchev assumed this post. Molotov assumed responsibility for foreign affairs, Kaganovich for heavy industry. Beria remained as head of the Ministry of Internal Affairs (including the NKVD).[12]

Relations between the leaders were marked by suspicion, wariness and caution. Mutual suspicion of each other's intentions combined with apprehension as to how the population would react to the death of the dictator. Malenkov, Molotov, Kaganovich and Khrushchev were united in a negative sense by their suspicion of Beria. As head of the NKVD, he appeared to be the most powerful figure, and had the potential to reimpose a regime of terror. Tentative moves were made to introduce reforms to improve the living standards of the people (including price cuts), and to reduce the arbitrary, repressive nature of the regime.[13] This tendency coincided with a growing awareness of the problems in the system of labour-camps. Riots and strikes were increasing, and the possibility of the breakdown of the entire system must have informed the thinking of the new leaders.[14]

The coincidence of these factors forced the hands of the leaders. At the July 1953 CC plenum, they moved against Beria. Having arrested him (he was later executed, in typically Stalinist fashion), they issued a statement setting out a catalogue of the problems in the system. They noted the backwardness and inefficiency of the agricultural and industrial sectors that were linked with the marginalization of the party. The domination of the party by the MVD (Ministry of Internal Affairs) was instrumental in causing these distortions. Beria, as head of the MVD was thus held accountable.[15] As Service and others have noted, the outcome of this plenum was ambiguous. A programme of generalized political and economic changes had been legitimized. The precise shape of these changes was to lead to a series of policy disputes among the leaders between 1953 and 1957.[16] The further the programme of changes progressed, the more the question of Stalin's role in creating and sustaining this system loomed ever larger. Three political developments evolved out of these initial moves in the first months of the post-Stalinist era.

First, institutionalized mass terror was ended. Beria's subordinates were also arrested. The NKVD was renamed the Committee of State Security (KGB), subordinated to the CC and was to be headed by a party appointee. The KGB lost the powers to try, sentence and execute. Their tasks were to investigate and arrest. The Ministry of Justice took over the running of the labour camps, and the other economic tasks previously associated with the MVD: canals, power-stations and so on. Gradually, during the course of 1954 and 1955, many camps were closed and amnesties granted to political prisoners who began to return to society. This created further problems, as the returnees and their relatives began to ask questions about the causes of their internment.[17]

Secondly, these developments inexorably restored the party to a central position in the system, and began to reinvigorate its internal functioning. The CC became increasingly important as a forum for decision-making and discussion of policy.[18] Thirdly, Khrushchev increased his own authority and position within the system. Malenkov was forced to resign from his position as PM in 1955, as Khrushchev prevailed in the struggle over the direction of policy, mobilizing expert opinion and coalitions of political allies behind his programme of agrarian reform.[19] Khrushchev also reinforced his own position within the party, purging 45 out of 84 secretaries, and replacing them with his own appointees, through the machinery of the secretariat.[20] Khrushchev used the very tools Stalin had adopted in the 1920s in his struggles with Trotsky, Bukharin et al. to consolidate his position.

The decisive event in consolidating Khrushchev's position was the Secret Speech condemning Stalin's crimes at the 20th Party Congress in February 1956.[21] Throughout 1955 there was a growing consensus that a searching examination of Stalin's reign had to be undertaken as the return of prisoners gathered pace. This impulse was accelerated by the publication of the Pospelov Report in 1955, which detailed the extent of the crimes and the repressions of the Stalin era.[22] The tricky issue was to decide how much to reveal without undermining the legitimacy of the system, or implicating members of the party elite or the party–state officials. The speech was delivered to a closed session of the Congress, and lasted for the best part of four hours. The Congress was stunned by the revelations about Stalin. Yet Khrushchev's position was strengthened because, even though it was a limited, compromised series of revelations that focused attention upon the personality of Stalin, he acquired moral authority from having delivered this indictment. He was also able to hint at the complicity of his rivals for power.[23]

These initial moves are illustrative of the ambiguous nature of politics under Khrushchev. These ambiguities existed on a number of levels. First, the regime had to address the dual imperative of consolidating the socialist basis of the system while embarking on the transition to communism. Secondly, the leadership were forced to confront the ambiguities and paradoxes of the Stalinist legacy. The dilemma running at the heart of the Secret Speech – conceal while revealing – was replicated in the process of transforming the Stalinist system while retaining its core features, reforming while conserving. Thirdly, Khrushchev himself was something of an ambiguous figure. He was a populist, yet increased the participation of experts and specialists in the policy-making process. He was an idealist, yet highlighted practical measures to improve the living standards of the population. He was a self-confessed Leninist, yet his thinking, mentality and approach to problem-solving were classically Stalinist. Even his character – impulsive, energetic, enthusiastic – created abrupt changes of policy and approach.

Khrushchev's interpretation of the core features of the politics of Soviet socialism arose out of this framework. The underlying issue that faced Khrushchev was how to instil dynamism into a system in which mass terror had been abandoned, without undermining the role of the party, the authority of the state or the international position of the USSR. This task underpinned his changes to the role and functioning of the party, and the relationship between state and society after 1953. The broad thrust of Khrushchev's political changes were to narrow the gap between rulers and ruled, draw the citizenry into the administration of the system while making the party–state apparatus more responsive to the policy agenda of the leadership.[24] This tension between decentralization and participation on the one hand, and elite direction and intervention on the other runs through Khrushchev's changes.

The CPSU: renewing the Leninist vanguard?

Khrushchev's innovations fell far short of addressing the party's monopoly of power. However, he did modify the way the party operated, and how it interacted with the other agencies in the system. The changes in the internal functioning, composition, structure and role of the CPSU after 1953 were developed partly to address the shortcomings in its operation under Stalin, partly to further Khrushchev's policy agenda, and partly to consolidate his own position. As many scholars have noted, the conflicts between Khrushchev and Malenkov were played out on one level as a conflict between the party apparatus (Khrushchev) and the state apparatus (Malenkov).[25] Khrushchev attempted to reinvigorate the internal life of the party, increasing the frequency of institutional meetings, granting more authority to party members vis-à-vis the full-time party officials and transforming its overall role within the system.

The recruitment practices of the Khrushchev era reflected his commitment to opening up the party to more popular involvement. Whereas Stalin had ended the policy of recruitment favouring workers and peasants, turning the CPSU into a party of the ruling cadres, Khrushchev began to reverse this. More workers and peasants were drawn into the ranks in the period 1954–61, as party membership shot up from 6.8 million in 1952 to 11.8 million in 1965.[26] While rejuvenating the composition of the party, Khrushchev also sought to change the quality of the personnel. More specialists and experts were drawn into policy-making at the centre. The new cadres were more technically minded, with more specialist knowledge to enable them to oversee the processes of industrial and agricultural production more closely and knowledgably. The other quality that Khrushchev was searching for was loyalty: an apparatus that would respond willingly to the initiatives of the centre. This led to two major overhauls of party secretaries: in 1953–6, and in 1960–1 when approximately 50 per cent were replaced.[27]

Khrushchev also oversaw a revival of the working practices of the party. The central institutions of the party met with increased frequency, especially the CC. The Party Congress – nominally its sovereign body – met in 1956, 1959 (an extraordinary Congress) and once more in 1961. Republican Congresses also met more frequently. Frequency did not improve the functioning of the Congresses though. They were still marked by sterility of debate, ritualism and uniformity, a far cry from the early years of the revolution. The revival of the CC was especially interesting. Although the Praesidium retained its position as the central decision-making forum, the CC entered the scene in two ways. First, it was expanded in size and became a means for the input of specialist advice, broadening the policy-making process. The increase in the size of the cc that this entailed – rising from 125 in 1952 to 175 full members in 1961 – rendered it more representative of a variety of opinions, although a little unwieldy as a forum for debate.[28] Secondly, it became, in Schapiro's words, an "appeal court" for conflicts in the Praesidium.[29] This was illustrated in June 1957 when Khrushchev, facing opposition to his domestic economic policies and foreign policy initiatives, was outvoted in the Praesidium (by the so-called Anti-Party group of Malenkov, Molotov, Kaganovich and Shepilov, and their associates Saburov and Pervukhin). Khrushchev argued that as he had been elected by the cc, it was they who should decide whether he should continue in his post. Having packed the cc – à la Stalin – with his supporters, Khrushchev prevailed.[30] This was an important indicator that, although Soviet leaders might continue to exercise authority in a highly personalized fashion, it was still necessary, for political survival, to pay close attention to the opinions of their colleagues and subordinates.

The revival and revitalization of the inner workings of the party were not restricted to the elite central organs. Khrushchev undertook measures to decentralize control, to take decision-making out of the hands of the full-time officials, and to allow the winds of quasi-democratization to blow through the party. It is important to locate these policies within the context of Khrushchev's overall strategy. He was not a decentralizer and democratizer *per se*. He saw these initiatives as tools for the realization of his policies. In particular, he was aware of the difficulty of making the bureaucracy responsive to the policy initiatives of the centre. Overcoming their vested interest in the preservation of the *status quo* required a mobilization of the mass party membership, alongside measures to "shake-up" the full-time paid officials.

In specific policy terms, separate departments within the apparatus of the cpsu were created in all the republics, including a bureau for the rsfsr, the first time the Russians had had their own organization. The number of full-time paid officials was reduced, as Khrushchev sought to devolve more responsibility to volunteers or part-time staff, opening avenues for the party member to participate.[31] At lower levels, Khrushchev attempted to breathe life into the meetings and discussions that took place. Constant exhortations for a more open, democratic and critical approach were made. Greater leeway for lower-level bodies to act was granted. Yet, in line with Khrushchev's general approach, criticism had to be constructive and loyal: that is, it had to reinforce the values of the leadership and promote their policies. In combination with these decentralizing moves, there were also moves initiated by the centre to revitalize the party. In October 1961 a new set of party rules were adopted by the 22nd Congress.[32] The most important change was article 25. In full it states that:

> During the elections of party organs, the principle of a systematic renewal of their membership and the succession of leadership is observed. At each successive election, the membership of the CC of the CPSU and the Praesidium is renewed by at least ¼th. Members of the Praesidium are elected, as a rule, to no more than three successive terms. Some party leaders, by virtue of their acknowledged authority or high political, organizational or other qualities, can be elected to the leading organs for an extended term . . . The membership of CC of union republic CP's, *krai* committees, and *oblast* committees is renewed by at least ⅓ at each successive election; membership of *okrug*, city and *raion* committees and of party committees of primary party organizations by ½. In the process members of these leading party organs can be elected for not more than three successive terms. Secretaries of primary party organizations can be elected at no more than two successive convocations.[33]

This compulsory rotation and renewal of party offices was designed to increase turnover, and prevent unresponsive officials from obstructing the reforms.

Khrushchev also inaugurated significant reforms of the mechanisms of popular control over the party–state machinery. The period between 1953 and 1962 saw a good deal of debate and discussion about the proper shape and functions of popular control over both party and state agencies.[34] The eventual outcome was the formation of a new Party–State Control Committee (an echo of Lenin's RABKRIN) in December 1962, with extensive powers to check on the work of party and state officials.[35] It was composed of party members, and also "representatives of TU and Komsomol organizations, of the press, and comrades of authority from among workers, kolkhozniki and intellectuals".[36] These latter two initiatives illustrate how Khrushchev attempted to combine central-directed policies with lower-level autonomy to invigorate the work of the party.

Khrushchev's interpretation of the "leading role of the party" replicated the enduring tension between the party's vanguard role – leader, guide, teacher – and its day-to-day role in the running of the system. The combined effect of Khrushchev's political changes was to place the party at the heart of the Soviet system once more. But in doing this Khrushchev extended and deepened the party's interventionist role. In other words the vanguard role was reinterpreted to reflect the party's position as the instrument of policy-making, implementation and oversight. The root cause of this lay in Khrushchev's prioritization of the practical tasks facing the CPSU of increasing production, both in terms of quality and quantity, and of promoting popular participation in the administration of the system at lower levels. This also affected the ideological arena. Khrushchev sought to increase the levels of ideological instruction within both the party and wider Soviet society, and to infuse the content with a much more practical, less abstract content. How did this evolve in practice?

In political terms, the party was to direct the work of the mass of volunteers and part-time officials who were drawn into local administration, mobilizing them to undertake key tasks. In the morass of overlapping relationships between volunteers, departments of local Soviets, party members and party officials, it was clear that the party continued to dominate.[37] The economic developments were more complex. In seeking to reduce the powers of the central ministries in Moscow, Khrushchev decentralized decision-making to lower levels in the hierarchy, while increasing the authority of the party to intervene in economic affairs. For instance, in the agricultural sphere after 1953 Khrushchev attempted to simplify the multiple lines of authority by increasing the input of the district party secretary, initially abolishing the political departments of the Machine Tractor Stations, and abolishing them altogether in 1958. This was extended in 1962 when the party was bifurcated into agricultural and industrial sections, allowing for more detailed functional specialization by party secretaries in a given locality. This amounted to the creation of two parallel structures within each party organization, whose function was to manage industrial and agricultural production.[38] As the preamble to the decree of November 1962 states:

> In our day the party is required not only to come up with the right slogan in time but also to give skilful daily concrete guidance to production, to the development of industry, agriculture and all branches of the economy.[39]

In sum, the particular interpretation of the leading role of the party which evolved under Khrushchev represents an interesting attempt to balance elite-directed expertise with (mobilized) popular participation. The interesting innovation in this respect is that the higher communist consciousness of the members of the vanguard was interpreted as not just being equipped with the scientific Marxist–Leninist worldview, but with practical, detailed knowledge and skills to enable close guidance of social, economic and political processes. This was another manifestation of technocratic Soviet socialism in action.

State and society under Khrushchev: a withering away of the state?

The relations between state and society after 1953 were profoundly altered by the abandonment of mass terror, and the downgrading of the role of the KGB in the day-to-day operation of the system. This caused the leadership to explore ways in which to renegotiate this relationship, retaining the dominant position of the party–state organs, while promoting stability and security for the population, and dynamism and support for the policies of the leaders. The key issue was the attempt to transform the patterns of authority, control and participation without undermining state control of social processes.

Coercion, legality and the rule of law

The abandonment of mass terror should not disguise the continued use of coercion and selective terror by the state. Although many camp inmates were released after 1953, elements of the Gulag system remained. The category of "political crimes" remained, although it was much more restrictive. The KGB continued its monitoring and surveillance of the population, seeking out discrepant voices. Dissent was still suppressed. The Soviet population were only exposed to those opinions or works considered to be commensurate with the ideals of the post-Stalin leadership. A concerted campaign of scientific atheism was accompanied by persecution of the church and religious believers. Medvedev & Medvedev have documented a variety of measures: closure of churches or conversion of the buildings for other purposes (garages in some cases); criminalization of religious activity in the 1961 Criminal Code and prohibition of religious instruction of minors by either parents or priests.[40] Perhaps the best example of the essentially coercive mindset pervading the system came with the extension of the death penalty in 1961. In the 1958 Criminal Code, the death penalty was restricted to the offence of treason. It was soon extended to cover a variety of economic crimes: currency speculation, black-market operations. Also in May 1961, the policy of internal exile was revived for "parasites" (an ill-defined term covering nefarious semi-legal activities).[41]

The reduction in terror was combined with a growth in "legality". In the same way that the abandonment of mass terror did not eradicate the selective use of terror, so the restoration of legality did not equate to the rule of law. The new Criminal Code in 1958 created "Socialist Legality": the legal system was placed on a more regular, predictable, systematic footing ending the arbitrariness of the Stalinist era, while the party remained essentially above the law. The new code instituted a number of key reforms:

- sentences could only be passed by the official court system;
- confessions were no longer enough for a conviction;
- penalties were reduced (maximum imprisonment from 25 years to 15, minimum from 1 year to 3 months);
- defendants were innocent until proven guilty;
- the number of cases tried in secret was reduced;
- age of criminal responsibility was raised from 14 to 16;
- measures were taken to increase the professionalism of the legal practitioners.[42]

Although these changes were subject to constant revision and inter-ference by the political authorities, they did mark a substantial change for the better for the mass of the Soviet people. The ambiguous nature of the changes – neither full-blown terror, nor rule of law – reflect the complex forces shaping the relationship between state and society in the USSR after 1953.

The growth of public self-government

Perhaps the most innovative feature of the Khrushchevite approach to societal management was the stress laid upon popular parti-cipation in the administration of localities, neighbourhoods and workplaces. At the elite level, the work of the Supreme Soviet remained formalistic and ritualized in the main. More significant change occurred lower down the hierarchy. The objective was to channel the enthusiasm and energy of the population into the work of the existing state and public organizations – TUS, local Soviets, *Komsomol* – and also to supplement their work by creating new social bodies and public organizations. A number of initiatives are worthy of mention. Comrades' courts were created by local Soviets or trade unions in order to try minor infringements of the law. The 12 members of each court would meet after work in enterprises, and impose fines or sanctions on convicted transgressors.[43] New departments comprised wholly of volunteers were assigned to local Soviets to undertake specific tasks: volunteer militias, cinemas, libraries, tree-planting, resolving housing problems, cultural pro-vision and so on. Many volunteers were assigned to existing depart-ments of Soviets and party committees. More encouragement was given to citizens to air their views, communicate with party officials and write to newspapers about problems and shortcomings. Many of these initiatives met with patchy success. The comrades' courts often became vehicles for the settlement of petty vendettas. Other volunteer departments appeared to be unable to effect any significant change in the life of localities.[44]

On one level, the purpose of this was clear: as a means of in-stilling dynamism into the system by tapping into the embers of the revolutionary enthusiasm and civic mindedness of the population. In drawing large numbers of people into the administrative functions of the state, it appeared to prefigure the eventual withering away of the state and its replacement with the public self-government of the people. Viewed from another perspective, it was part of the development of a more complex form of social control. The regime maintained its essentially mobilizational approach, channelling popular activity into regime-sponsored goals (e.g. the Virgin Lands scheme) or into politically "safe" areas, where they did not affect the party's exercise of power. Many volunteer activities were developed to make good the deficiencies of local Soviets, and so helped to improve the standards of living of the population, ameliorating any discontent. Finally, popular enthusiasm was also mobilized as part of Khrushchev's overall strategy to supervise and check on the work of the party–state bureaucracy, to make it more responsive to his initiatives. The ultimate end of all this popular participation and activity has been succinctly summarized by Walicki. He argues that the aim of this increased role for public organizations,

> was a vision with solid Marxist credentials, but [it was] a caricature. The aim was to create a voluntary conformist society free of conflicting interests . . . [He] wished to reduce the role of violence, but only on the condition that state enforced conformity would be replaced by a deeply internalised conformism capable of mobilising the masses for the active, enthusiastic and voluntary pursuit of centrally prescribed goals.[45]

Taken together, these initiatives encapsulate the ambiguous and complex nature of state–society relations under Khrushchev, in which there were measures of centralization and decentralization, populism and technocratic expertise, voluntary initiative and coercive pressure. There were echoes of the Leninist approach in much of Khrushchev's programme: the party–state control committee, mobilization of public organizations for state goals, encouraging (limited) criticism from below, as well as the tendency to favour technocratic, specialist advice and knowledge. Yet there were many features common to the whole Soviet period as McAuley identifies:

> a stress on personnel as the key resource, an emphasis on the importance of party-mindedness, and the commitment to party values by those who were running education, culture and the legal system.[46]

The politics of Khrushchevism produced a further synthesis of elite direction and popular mobilization.

Socio-cultural developments: equality, atheism and peaceful co-existence

The policy of de-Stalinization sought to remove the perceived excesses or distorted accretions of the Stalinist system. In socio-cultural terms, Stalinism had produced an hierarchical, elitist, inegalitarian social structure, with a cultural matrix dominated by conservatism, tradition, Socialist Realism and Russian nationalism. The impulse underlying these developments was to bolster the stability of the system, and to promote the immediate economic goals of the state. As the process of de-Stalinization unfolded, the need to impart dynamism and to mobilize the population necess-itated a rethink of the Stalinist approach. The question was the manner and extent to which Khrushchev would address the socio-cultural legacy he inherited. Would he reorient the system in the direction of egalitarianism and a radical, collectivist, internationalist agenda, reviving the emancipatory, radical wing of early Bolshevism? Or would he merely adapt and modify the "excesses", while retaining the orthodox Bolshevik commitment to technocracy, modernization, inequality, privilege and productivism?

Equality and Khrushchev: the promotion of less inequality

Khrushchev's approach to the questions of equality – both material and social – marks a distinct break with the Stalinist programme, without undermining or destroying the edifice of privilege that had evolved after 1917. Khrushchev's policies contained a much stronger egalitarian thrust, although measures in other areas actually rein-forced tendencies towards privilege and inequality, once more high-lighting the ambiguous, paradoxical nature of the Khrushchev era.

In terms of material equality, a number of measures were intro-duced to make the system fairer, to reduce marked inequalities and make the lives of the mass of the people less harsh and austere. Perhaps the issue of most pressing concern for the Soviet people was housing. The devastation inflicted by the Nazis, coupled with rapid urbanization had placed an unbearable burden on the housing stock. In 1955 Khrushchev undertook a massive programme of house-building, concentrated primarily in the state and co-operative sector in order to benefit those at the lower-end of the social scale. The total floor space rose from 25 million sq.m in 1955 to 62.4 million sq.m. in 1965. Additionally, the regime reduced the levels of communal apartments, opening the way for newly-weds to move into their own apartments.[47] In terms of material remuneration, the thrust was to reduce differentials. The 1956 Wages Reform sought to simplify the payment of wages.[48] A new bonus system was implemented, which reduced the high levels of bonuses that had been awarded to managers. Wage differentials were narrowed by reducing the use of piece-rates. A minimum wage was introduced. Probably the greatest beneficiaries of the policies to upgrade welfare provision were the pensioners. In 1956 a maximum pension was set (2,000 roubles per month at the All-Union level, compared with the average wage of 720 roubles).[49] Some inroads into the privileges and prerogatives of the elites had been made.

In spite of these measures to reduce differentials, the system remained an inegalitarian, privileged one. While Khrushchev attempted to improve the supply of food (and to a lesser extent consumer goods) to the population, and also abolished elements of privilege for party officials, the essential features of privilege were untouched. High salaries continued to be a secret. Restricted access to certain goods remained. Foreign currency shops were revived. Attempts to abolish the practice of "second jobs" were abandoned in the face of fierce opposition from vested interests.[50] It is in the field of educational reform that the ambiguities of the Khrushchevite approach are most evident. The thrust of his reforms were twofold. First, to increase the representation of children from worker and peasant backgrounds in the upper levels of secondary school, and in Higher Education. Secondly, to tie education more closely to the productive demands of the economy.

Khrushchev's attempts to facilitate access took a number of forms, although many measures remained on paper. The fees imposed by Stalin for study in the upper years of secondary school (essential to progress to Higher Education) were abolished, along with fees for Higher Education study. These measures were extended when Khrushchev decided to adopt a more proactive strategy. Universities and local HE institutes were to set aside a quota of places for young persons engaged in production and encourage more part-time students. Khrushchev then abolished the upper forms of secondary school in order to push all 15-year-olds directly into production for two years. Those candidates wishing to go on to HE had to undertake further study in their own time: by evening courses, correspondence courses and so on. Although some progress was made in reducing the privileged position of children from white-collar, professional backgrounds and in increasing representation from the manual strata, the achievements failed to meet Khrushchev's expectations. Some had unintended negative consequences. Preferential access to HE for candidates with prior work experience adversely affected the ability of many women to go on to HE. Many of the reforms were not implemented, or were opposed by various groups in society.[51]

Between 1956 and 1961, the state engaged in a substantial expansion of the boarding school sector.[52] This initiative combined many of the themes underpinning social policy under Khrushchev. These schools were designed to combine the inculcation of communist moral norms with practical training for work in the economy. It was felt that the boarding school option achieved a number of objectives. A longer teaching day prolonged the exposure of the children to the educational process. Moreover, the boarding school released both parents into the workforce, to contribute to the productive aims of the state. It was also a measure with an egalitarian thrust: the children targetted were those, in Kaiser's words, "deprived of normal parental care. Priority of admission is given to children of widows, unmarried mothers, and invalid parents, and to others in need of care".[53] In tandem with these more egalitarian aspirations, the educational reforms also set up more specialist, elitist academies: sciences, languages, ballet, sport, arts and others to foster excellence and specialization from an early age (usually ten or eleven). Unsurprisingly, entrance to these schools was highly competitive, and the selection process was permeated with corrupt practices, favouring the children of the elite.[54] Once more, social policy combined measures to reduce inequality with measures that increased privilege.

The question of equality for women was, in official terms, "solved". However, as Khrushchev attempted to increase the levels of political participation in the system, this entailed exploring the issue of female political participation, and the circumstances hindering this. Buckley, Lapidus and others have documented how the Khrushchev leadership became concerned with the position of women in practice, although the aim was to mobilize them as a political group to promote de-Stalinization, rather than the promotion of emancipatory measures *per se*.[55] The problem for the regime was that de-Stalinization imposed contradictory demands. Politically it meant mobilizing women, for political activity. Economically, it meant promoting more efficient productive working practices among women. Demographically, it required large families to increase the birth-rate. Abortion was relegalized to allow women to play a more central role in public life, yet it was not fully publicized because the regime realized the importance of maintaining the birth-rate.[56]

The issue of women's participation was promoted through the creation of separate organizations for women: the Women's Councils or *Zhensovety*.[57] These organizations were created at the *oblast*, *krai* and *raion* levels, and were situated within different organs: factories, farms, offices, etc. They were designed as part of the process of drawing women into active political life, educating them and promoting female productive activity. However this activity was channelled into regime-defined areas. As with the growth of other public self-organizations, their autonomy was restricted by party "direction" and "guidance". They had a number of different sections – production, culture, daily life – which promoted party policy in each of these areas. In other words they were a mobilizational resource for the party. Although, as Buckley argues, Khrushchev's innovations were important in legitimizing the idea of separate women's organizations under socialism (a move that had caused grave misgivings in the party after the revolution), the material position of women was substantially unaltered.[58] In the words of Filtzer,

> the position of women in the home or in industry altered little over the course of the 1950's and 1960's. Indeed the problems of low pay, marginalisation into manual and low-skilled jobs, harsh working conditions and the unequal sexual division of labour within the home appear as pressing today as they did 30 years ago.[59]

The normative basis of socialism under Khrushchev

What sort of values would the post-Stalin regime espouse? The Stalin regime had focused on national ideals, rather than proletarian internationalism, on personal success and individual heroism rather than collectivism, and had reached an accommodation with the church after 1941, mitigating its scientific atheism. These values were propagated as the regime sought stability and consolidation after the traumas of collectivization and industrialization. Yet it also retained a strong emphasis on productivism and constructivism. Similarly, the Khrushchev regime sought to synthesize a set of values that fostered the immediate goals of the state – repudiation of the Stalinist legacy, the promotion of economic and political change and the maintenance of social control and the authority of the CPSU – while attempting to foster cultural and educational forms appropriate to a socialist state. These overlapping aims help to explain why the Khrushchevite approach appeared to combine more "liberal", innovative forms with at times coercive and restrictive policies, as the regime sought to balance the competing claims of change and stabilization.

In the field of education, the changes to the curriculum were driven by, on the one hand, a desire to make the content more practical and vocational, creating a more qualified and skilled workforce and, on the other, by a desire to increase the ideological content, to upgrade the provision of political education at all levels of the system. The vocational content was part of a package of reforms that have become known as the "polytechnical era". Rosen has identified the core elements, as the regime attempted to combine general secondary education with industrial training. There were three aspects: (a) teaching the relationship of various theoretical subjects to their practical application in industrial processes; (b) teaching the fundamentals of production; (c) teaching vocational skills.[60]

Undergraduates were also expected to undertake a greater degree of practical training as part of their degree. Even the activities of the agitprop (Department of Agitation and Propaganda) workers, were directed at combining orthodox ideological indoctrination with more practical discussions. In the late 1950s and early 1960s, the regime undertook a concerted attempt to step up its propaganda activities, training an increased number of propagandists in its party schools and stepping up the ideological education of the populace. Evening universities of Marxism–Leninism were set up. In 1960, "People's Universities" were created, providing adult education programmes. Alongside the more formal lectures dealing with Histmat and Diamat, or the history of the CPSU, there were more informal and practical discussions on labour, technology and so on.[61] In other words, they attempted to combine ideological instruction and technical education, integrating and cementing Soviet society behind the goals of the party while promoting the economic modernization of the state.

These measures were furthered by the attack on the church and established religion undertaken by Khrushchev, emphasizing the coercive and illiberal streak running through this era. A physical campaign to close churches, persecute the clergy and prevent religious education was inaugurated in 1959, and evolved into a propaganda movement for scientific atheism, stepping up atheistic education at all levels.[62] This was not a purely destructive movement. A series of alternative secular rituals were created to replace the religious rites of birth, marriage and death. The symbols of space, technology and science were mobilized in an attempt to displace the hold of religious belief in the popular imagination, and to bolster the CPSU as the party of modernization, science and rationalism. Lenin and the October revolution were increasingly mythologized as the regime searched for a set of credible alternative icons to those provided by the church. The purpose of these twin campaigns – atheism and secularization – has been expertly summarized by Stites:

> One reason for this dual campaign was the perceived and real revival of religious activity among believers . . . Another was the obvious decline of ideology and gradual erosion of the memory of the revolution. This, together with the loosening of the repression apparatus of fear and terror led the regime to seek a new social cement . . . The anti-religious and ritual movements were, with the popularisation of space travel . . . part of a "remodernisation" movement launched by the regime to counter the effects of wartime religious emotionalism and the fantasy world Stalin had built.[63]

The assault on religion also produced an attempt to promote a secular communist moral code that emphasized collectivism, self-sacrifice and devotion to the communist cause. Although the Khrushchev era did not wholly repudiate the Stalinist focus on individuals as bearers of regime values and role models (e.g. Gagarin and the other cosmonauts), it did evince a more collectivist ethos. The principles of the moral code were published in 1961 as part of the Third Party Programme. They were:

- devotion to the communist cause; love of the socialist mother-land and of the other socialist countries;
- conscientious labour for the good of society – he who does not work, neither shall he eat;
- concern on the part of everyone for the preservation and growth of public wealth;
- a high sense of public duty; intolerance of actions harmful to the public interest;
- collectivism and comradely mutual assistance: one for all and all for one;
- humane relations and mutual respect between individuals – man is to man a friend, comrade and brother;
- honesty and truthfulness, moral purity, modesty and unpretentiousness in social and private life;
- mutual respect in the family, and concern for the upbringing of children;
- an uncompromising attitude to injustice, parasitism, dishonesty, careerism and money-grubbing;
- friendship and brotherhood among all peoples of the USSR; intolerance of national and racial hatred;
- an uncompromising attitude to the enemies of communism, peace and the freedom of nations;
- fraternal solidarity with the working people of all countries, and with all peoples.[64]

The key component stressed by Soviet scholars was the first principle: devotion to the communist cause.[65] This highlights the persistence of constructivism in Soviet discourse: the ability to consciously mould the outlook and actions of the Soviet people, and also how in all these fields (social policy, education, morality) the defining principle was the maintenance of the authority of the party.

The tension between repudiating Stalin's legacy and promoting change emerged most clearly in the literary field. With the death of Stalin, the parameters of acceptable criticism expanded, as did the number of politically acceptable topics. There were no uniform patterns during this period. Literary "thaws" would be followed by "freezes", followed by a further "thaw" and so on. The roots of these oscillations lie only partially in the ambiguities of de-Stalinization.[66] The twists and turns of state policy also reflected the divisions within the Union of Soviet Writers (USW): some individuals wished to explore new ideas, forms and conventions; many remained conservative proponents of stultifying Stalinist socialist realism. The institutional relationship between the USW and the CC Secretariat, publishing houses and editors of journals and newspapers was a constantly changing one. The publication of various pieces was the outcome of a complex series of individual negotiations between these actors, within a broad intellectual atmosphere established by the party. Lastly, literary policy was at the whim of the impulsive Khrushchev. He is reported on one occasion to have shaken the First Secretary of the USW by the lapels after literary output went beyond the limits Khrushchev wished to set for it.[67]

The trouble for the political leadership and for the heads of the politico–literary–ideological complex was attempting to keep anti-Stalinist literature within a framework that did not attack the basis of the system itself. Although the themes of socialist realism still dominated official culture, new works and writers began to challenge this orthodoxy. The flagship of the literary renaissance was *Novyi Mir* (a monthly journal) under the editorship of Alexander Tvardovsky. He published a number of works – including Solzhenitsyn's explosive *One day in the life of Ivan Denisovich* – and although he was dismissed in 1954, he was reinstated in 1958. Ehrenburg published his short novel *The Thaw*, outlining the contrasting fortunes of two writers: a defender of orthodoxy and a nonconformist. New poetry by Evtushenko and Vosnesensky explored the boundaries of the acceptable. Political satire – albeit directed at party-identified targets – mushroomed as the number of legitimate subjects for ridicule increased. One of the most interesting developments was the rapid increase in popular works of science fiction. The technological advances of the 1950s, in particular the space race, were adopted by the regime to highlight the essential superiority of socialism over capitalism, and to communicate once more the imminence of the communist era, a theme developed in the Third Party Programme.[68]

The attempt to remould the consciousness and worldview of the Soviet population in the post-1953 era across these disparate fields – education, morality, culture – gave rise to a deeper dissatisfaction with the orthodox Stalinist interpretation of Soviet Marxism–Leninism. A wide-ranging intellectual renewal began in 1955–6. It was designed to purge Soviet history, philosophy and literary policy of its Stalinist dogmas and to breathe new life into the ideological basis of party rule, legitimizing the reforms undertaken by Khrushchev at home, and consolidating the leading position of the USSR in the international socialist camp. The years between 1956 and 1961 were highly fertile ones. A new philosophy textbook – *Osnovy marksizma–leninizma* (Fundamentals of Marxism–Leninism) – was produced. A new *History of the CPSU* replaced the infamous Stalinist "Short Course". A Declaration of the Eighty-One Communist and Workers Parties in 1960 affirmed the leading position of the CPSU. In 1961, the Third Party Programme was drawn up. The theoretical innovations are analyzed more fully below.

The Soviet view of the world also shifted under Khrushchev. This was the cause of great ideological dispute both within the USSR itself (between Stalinist hardliners and de-Stalinizers) and within the socialist camp, principally between the USSR and the Chinese. Khrushchev's elaboration of the doctrines of peaceful co-existence, of a non-violent road to socialism and that war was no longer inevitable evoked a great deal of ideological dispute. Khrushchev's opponents argued that he had moved away from the fundamentals of Marxism–Leninism in the international sphere, prioritizing the interests of humanity over those of the international proletariat and denying the universality of the proletarian revolution as the motor of history.

Khrushchev's ideas were elaborated in his main report to the 20th Congress in February 1956,

> The Leninist principle of peaceful coexistence of states with different social systems has always been and remains the general line of our country's foreign policy . . . When we say that the socialist system will win in the competition

between the two systems – the capitalist and the socialist – this by no means signifies that its victory will be achieved through armed interference by the socialist countries in the internal affairs of capitalist countries. Our certainty of the victory of communism is based on the fact that the socialist mode of production possesses decisive superiority over the capitalist mode of production.[69]

Many of the themes put forward by Khrushchev revive the ideas of Bukharin from the 1920s. His argument for peaceful co-existence was based on the application of the class struggle to the realities of the nuclear era. A nuclear conflict would destroy the globe. The foreign policy of the USSR had to take account of this in framing its relations with the capitalist states. The class struggle between capitalism and socialism on a global scale had to embrace a variety of measures, but stop short of fomenting military conflicts. This revised the fundamental Leninist precept about the inevitability of war in the imperialist age. War had to be avoided. The distinctive feature of Khrushchev's conception of co-existence was that the various forms of engagement would not necessarily be conflictual, although in practice active support was given to Third World struggles. Co-existence under Khrushchev would be peaceful and competitive rather than hostile, opening the way for elements of co-operation between the two systems.[70]

Khrushchev placed economic competition between capitalism and socialism at the centre of Soviet foreign policy, reviving the views of many Soviet theorists from the 1920s. The balance of power in the world would be tilted inexorably in favour of socialism through a demonstration of the economic superiority of the latter. The non-European states would be attracted to socialism through its higher growth rates, increased economic efficiency and greater material abundance. The USSR would also actively seek to influence this process, through programmes of foreign aid to newly industrializing, post-colonial countries. Over time, the globe would become increasingly socialist, until the eventual final victory of socialism.[71]

In one sense this was an orthodox interpretation of Marxist–Leninist international relations. Socialism would eventually and inevitably replace capitalism. Conversely, Khrushchev's interpretation

301

of peaceful co-existence also brought in new ideas. The implication of projecting the class struggle as economic competition (in similar fashion to Bukharin advocating the class struggle under NEP as a form of economic competition between capitalism and socialism in the Soviet countryside) was that the idea of revolution by force of arms, or exporting revolution through an armed struggle was abandoned. The attraction of the Soviet mode of production, the variety of national cultures, economies and political systems meant that a diversity of forms of transition to socialism were now possible, including peaceful, non-violent, parliamentary transitions.[72]

Interestingly, Khrushchev's ideas also transformed Stalin's essentially nationalistic approach. Stalin's promotion of "Socialism in one country", and his advocacy of Russian nationalism identified the interests of the international proletariat with the interests of the Soviet state, and prioritized the latter. Khrushchev revived the essence of the Stalinist approach, while removing the Russian nationalist strand. The crucial factor in the concept of peaceful co-existence was to promote the performance of the domestic Soviet economy. All interests of the communist bloc had to be sacrificed for this objective. This established the USSR as the dominant part of the communist bloc, and prioritized its interests, maintaining the identity of proletarian internationalism with Soviet national interests.[73]

The evolving view of the world – part Leninist, part Stalinist, part Khrushchevite – stands as an ideal metaphor for the transitory and ambiguous nature of the Khrushchev era as a whole. Its approach to matters of social and cultural policy attempted to repudiate parts of the Stalinist legacy, to revive elements of Leninism and so create a new synthesis of the two. Although Khrushchev's achievements in this field were perhaps the most impressive of all the fields he was working in, much remained undone on his removal from power in 1964.

The economics of Khrushchevism

Economic transformation was central to Khrushchev's programme. But the nature and direction of this transformation was problematic. Many factors had to be balanced. Alleviation of Stalinist austerity required measures to increase the supply of food and consumer goods. The cold war required investment in defence and heavy industries, and in military technology. Economic competition with the West compelled the leadership to demonstrate the superiority of the Soviet economy. Announcing the imminent transition to communism could only be validated in practice through greater efficiency, technological advance and material abundance. The choice of economic policy was also determined by the politics of the leadership struggle. Each of the candidates adopted a set of policy priorities (agriculture, heavy industry, consumer goods), and entered coalitions to acquire power and outmanoeuvre opponents. Khrushchev's general approach was to prioritize the agricultural sector, while providing a greater degree of balance between light and heavy industry, without abandoning the traditional commitment to the latter. What was unclear after 1953 was the extent to which the economic reforms would fundamentally transform the economic basis of Stalinist socialism, or would merely tinker with its internal functioning or shift its priorities without changing its essential features.

Khrushchev and Soviet agriculture

Khrushchev tied himself to the improvement of the Soviet agricultural sector in the leadership struggle after 1953. In opposition to Malenkov, who favoured increasing the supplies of consumer goods (fridges, televisions, cars, etc.), Khrushchev emphasized the importance of increasing food supplies to improve the day-to-day lives of the Soviet people. The problems he faced were enormous. Chronic underinvestment, the lack of a viable incentive structure, poor infrastructure (transport, storage, etc.), technological backwardness and excessive bureaucratic control had produced an agricultural sector with endemic low productivity. Khrushchev's reforms of Soviet agriculture were ambitious, grandiose plans that ultimately failed to meet the expectations he aroused. The details of the reforms and their successes and failures have been well documented elsewhere.[74] Within the analytical framework of this work, Khrushchev's changes retained the essential structure of Soviet agriculture created by Stalin, although significant changes were introduced in certain areas.

The structure of Soviet agriculture

The basic organizational unit of Soviet agriculture remained the *kolkhoz* or collective farm. The rationalization and merger of the *kolkhozy*, which had begun in 1950, was accelerated under Khrushchev. Simultaneously, there were also moves to convert *kolkhozy* into *sovkhozy* or state farms (ideologically the latter structure was preferred by the state, as state property was considered to be superior to group property). By 1958 there were 69 100 (larger) *kolkhozy* (compared with 125 000 in 1950).[75] The wider organizational picture underwent significant change. Initially moves were made to shift the locus of decision-making further down the hierarchy and to increase the autonomy of the farms in their production decisions. A decree of March 1955 sought to enable the *kolkhoz* to have a greater say in its internal production affairs. The Agricultural Ministry in Moscow lost much of its power to oversee the sector as a whole.[76]

The most important developments were the changes in the functions of the MTS from 1953 until their abolition in 1958. They lost their political supervisory role, and became more closely linked to the productive process. More qualified agronomic personnel were assigned to the MTS, and the MTS director was supposed to work with the *kolkhoz* farm chairman in meeting the delivery obligations of *kolkhoz*. Having upgraded the authority of the party to supervise the work in the countryside, it was decided in 1958 that there was no longer a role for the MTS, which was subsequently abolished. The farm machinery was sold to the *kolkhozy*.[77] The decentralizing thrust was not applied consistently. In 1962, recentralizing measures – embodied in the creation of Territorial Production Agencies – were introduced. Further reorganizations (recentralizing ones) were planned just before Khrushchev was removed.[78] In sum, the structure of the system remained centralized, subject to bureaucratic and political interventions and incapable of generating genuine autonomy for the farms.

The operation of Soviet agriculture: plant more, plough more, pay more

The attempts to increase agricultural output followed a twin track approach. Measures were adopted to address the internal operation of the system: attempting to increase productivity through altering the system of incentives, increasing the use of mechanization, agricultural techniques, fertilizer and so on. As with other aspects of Khrushchev's rule, it was one step forwards, two steps backwards. In the immediate aftermath of Stalin's death, procurement quotas were reduced, and the prices paid by the state increased. Taxes on farmers were reduced. Restrictions on private plots were lessened, so that by 1958 peasant private plots had no compulsory delivery obligations. The regime began to develop concerns about the growth of incomes from private plots, and so restrictions were reimposed. This stop-start, haphazard approach to the agricultural sector failed to generate a coherent system of incentives, as the reforms stopped well short of marketization and the introduction of profit and loss economic measures. Other reforms – in particular the abolition of the MTS that impoverished many farms and left them unable to employ or repair their farm machinery – undercut the thrust of these changes.

The state also undertook a series of campaigns to increase output through extensive ploughing, planting, and rearing of livestock. The most famous of these campaigns was the Virgin Lands scheme.[79] This was a mass mobilization campaign to plough up a huge area of SE European Russia (North Kazakhstan and western Siberia) which began in 1954. The new quantity of land cultivated equated, according to Nove, to an area the size of Canada![80] Initially the results were encouraging. The results could not be sustained, however. Soil erosion, inattention to local conditions, climatic unsuitability, and waning popular enthusiasm all contributed to a declining yield. In the short-term it was successful. In the long-term it was irrelevant, as it failed to address the structural operational causes of Soviet agricultural failure. Another campaign – to extend the planting of maize – was less successful, for similar reasons.[81] Other campaigns to increase the use of fertilizer and the levels of mechanization also met with patchy success.

Khrushchev set out ambitious targets for agriculture. The 7 Year Plan for agriculture, adopted in 1958, should have increased output by 70 per cent by 1965. In 1963, the harvest was so bad that grain had to be imported from the West. Although the 1964 harvest was much better, the damage to Khrushchev's personal and political authority had been done. These failures were a substantial part of Khrushchev's removal from office in October 1964. The reasons for the failures are many-sided, and too complex to do justice to here.[82]

What is noteworthy is that while these measures did bring some improvements in agricultural output, in the peasants standard of living, and in raising the political profile of Soviet agriculture, they merely extended the Stalinist, extensive approach to economic development. Rather than moving towards a more efficient, balanced, high productivity rural economy, these campaigns replicated the inefficiencies endemic within the system. Efforts to increase the technological efficiency of the sector were submerged within Khrushchev's campaigning, mobilizing, populist, interventionist, hectoring, Stalinist style.

Khrushchev and Soviet industry

In spite of the raised profile of the Soviet agricultural sector, industrial development remained the lodestar of the Soviet economy. Expansion of the industrial economy was central to the process of de-Stalinization, and to the domestic and international standing of the USSR. The immediate years after 1953 were a period of rapid economic growth. Many of the indices of the 5th 5YP (1950–55) were exceeded, fuelling the optimism and utopianism that was embodied in the Third Party Programme and the proclamation that the transition to communism could begin. However, there was a significant economic slowdown after 1960, which contributed in no small measure to his downfall. Industrial developments under Khrushchev followed a familiar pattern, mixing an essentially Stalinist approach with a partial return to a neo-Leninist type strategy, accomplished via a series of organizational changes.

Economic strategy between 1953 and 1957 was shaped by an interaction of political and economic issues. A new (6th) 5YP was required. The plan was discussed extensively during 1955 and was adopted at the 20th Party Congress in February 1956. It set out a traditionally Stalinist set of priorities. Emphasis was laid on growth rates, heavy industry (especially metallurgy and energy) and on the creation of large-scale projects:

> The primary tasks . . . are to be the continued development of heavy and light metallurgy, of the oil, coal and chemical industries, accelerated rates of construction of power-generating stations, and ensuring the rapid growth of machine-building.[83]

306

At the same time, the shift towards a more consumer-oriented set of priorities was highlighted. The means for the achievement of higher growth was another synthesis of typically Stalinist strategies with post-Stalinist means. The 6th 5YP set out to exploit rapaciously and extensively the natural resources and raw materials of the eastern regions of the country, as a means of creating the energy producing base of the system. This was an extension of the Stalinist extensive growth strategy. At the same time, the plan called for moderniza-tion, technical progress, specialization and the growth of labour productivity, that is intensive growth. Khrushchev highlighted the importance of learning from the technological developments in the West, and of reducing the levels of bureaucracy in the economy.[84]

Within a year the 6th 5YP had been abandoned. The official explanation stated that the plan was flawed, as the levels of invest-ment set out were infeasible. Whether this explanation was accur-ate is difficult to judge. The political wranglings behind this decision are more easily detectable. The abandonment of this plan saw a move by Khrushchev's opponents to restrict his economic auth-ority. The appointment of Pervukhin as an economic overseer was mooted. Khrushchev hit back with moves to decentralize economic authority to the regions, thus disbanding the central economic ministries, the power-base of his opponents.[85] When Khrushchev prevailed in the struggle with the so-called "anti-Party" group, his plans for decentralization – the 1957 *sovnarkhozy* reforms – were implemented (of which more below). In the light of this structural change, and of Khrushchev's ascendancy, a new plan was prepared for the 7-year period between 1959–65.[86] Embodying the optimistic and buoyant atmosphere of economic success and technological achievement (Sputnik's successful launch), this new plan was subject to subsequent upward revisions. To what extent did Khrushchev's economic strategy mark a departure from the Stalinist model in practice?

The structure and operation of the economy: sovnarkhozy *and central planning under Khrushchev*

The *sovnarkhoz* reforms were the first of a bewildering series of changes to the structure and functioning of the centrally planned economy between 1957 and 1963. Measures to decentralize were followed by recentralizing ones. These were chaotic times for officials, managers and workers alike, as Khrushchev increasingly frantically searched for a way to make the economy responsive. The reform failed. The *sovnarkhozy* were abandoned within a year of Khrushchev's fall, and the central ministries restored. How were they supposed to work?

The political context of this reform has already been set out. The economic arguments in favour of decentralizing the economy were set out during the February 1957 cc plenum. It was argued that the increasingly specialized nature of economic decision-making required new organizational and management structures,

> As industry develops, one is confronted with a question of increasing urgency: should one continue to proceed in the sphere of organisational forms for the management of industry along the line of a further splintering of technical, economic and administrative management by creating at the centre a constant succession of new specialised branch ministries and departments, or should one, rather, seek more flexible forms for managing the economy, forms that are better suited to the features peculiar to the given stage of development?[87]

The *sovnarkhoz* reforms were a new form of management, appropriate to the new stage of development of the Soviet economy, building on and replacing the branch system of administration that had consolidated under Stalin. A decentralized form of economic administration would be more flexible, more responsive and better suited to local conditions. It was hoped that it would solve many of the problems embedded in the centralized system: departmentalism, lack of co-ordination, inflexibility, waste, inefficiency, lack of quality.

Khrushchev's reform abolished the majority of the central industrial ministries. In their place 105 regional economic councils (the *sovnarkhozy*, harking back to an earlier Bolshevik economic form of management during the civil war) were created. At the same time, the powers and functions of GOSPLAN were extended. Its task was to co-ordinate the individual plans of each *sovnarkhoz*, and to provide central direction of key economic indicators: prices, supplies, wages. The *sovnarkhozy* were under the jurisdiction of the republican Council of Ministers. Small-scale local industry remained under the control of the local authorities. Initially, all the enterprises in the region covered by each *sovnarkhoz* were subject to its direction (save the armament, chemical and electricity branches which retained their central ministry).[88] As the system evolved, the structure of each *sovnarkhoz* changed. By 1962, each *sovnarkhoz* had developed its own branch form of administration, as well as general departments (dealing with labour, wages, personnel, etc.). The *firma* – a conglomeration of a number of enterprises into one body – was also developed. The general contours of the 5YP were developed at the centre by GOSPLAN. McAuley describes the relationship between each enterprise and the *sovnarkhoz* in the planning process,

> In July or August the director would set up a commission of leading personnel, party and union representatives to work on a project plan for the following year. This would be based upon the current indices and the general directives of the 5YP. The project was then sent to the *sovnarkhoz* to be studied and altered in the light of any further directives from above, and was returned to the enterprise for further suggestions. It then went back to the *sovnarkhoz* for any final alterations and for ratification before being presented to the enterprise by the end of December.[89]

The *sovnarkhoz* reforms were themselves reformed a number of times after 1957. In 1960, co-ordinating agencies were created for republics with multiple *sovnarkhozy*. In 1961, the USSR was divided into 17 economic regions, each controlling six *sovnarkhozy*. In 1962, a number of (advisory) state committees were created. Gosplan was reorganized twice, and a Supreme Economic Council (VSNKh) created to co-ordinate the co-ordinating agencies. In 1963, the number of *sovnarkhozy* was reduced to 47. These changes were inexorably moving in the direction of re-centralization. Khrushchev was removed before any other changes could be introduced![90]

Did this decentralization change the nature of the Soviet planning process? The thrust of the Khrushchevite reforms – to create a more productive, technological economy, increasingly oriented

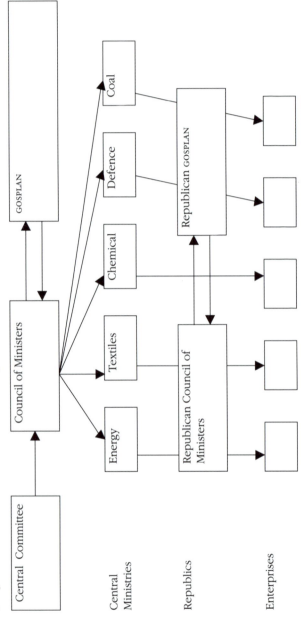

Figure 7.1 Organizational changes to the Soviet economy under Khrushchev 1957–63. The structure prior to 1957 (simplified version): the centralized "branch" system.

Under the branch system, directives were sent down from the central party/state institutions – via GOSPLAN – to the lower-levels with instructions as to how much to produce, for whom and so on. The problem for the policy-makers was that the vertical organization of the system, divided up into the branches of each industry, bred what was known as *vedomstvennost* or departmental mindedness. Each branch was more concerned with its own interests than with the efficient functioning of the economy as a whole.

Figure 7.2 Organizational changes to the Soviet economy under Khrushchev 1957–63. The *sovnarkhoz* reforms of 1957: decentralized regional economic councils.

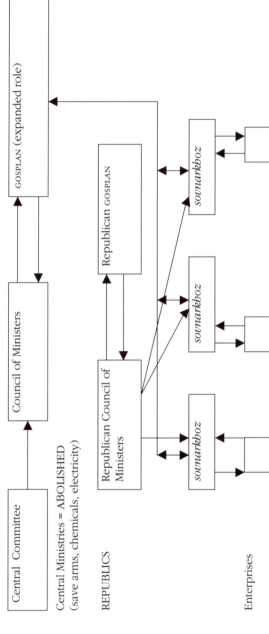

Under the 1957 *sovnarkhoz* reforms, Khrushchev decentralized decision-making in the economy. Partly to devolve decision-making closer to the point of production, and partly to destroy the power of the central ministries which were the power-base of his opponents. GOSPLAN had its role expanded, its task being to co-ordinate the plans of each *sovnarkhoz*. Each *sovnarkhoz* was responsible for all the enterprises in its region. The larger republics had multiple *sovnarkhoz*. Unfortunately, *vedomstvennost* was replaced by *mestnichestvo* or localism. Each *sovnarkhoz* was more interested in promoting the interests of its region rather than taking a national approach. 105 *sovnarkhozy* were created.

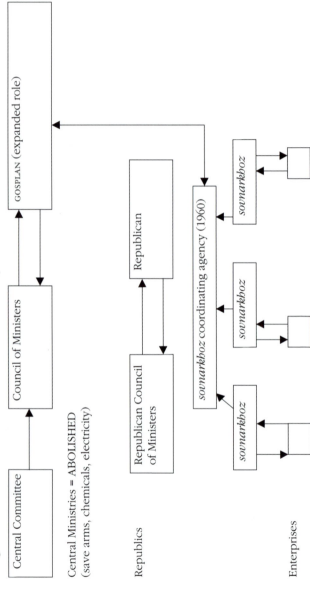

Figure 7.3 Organizational changes to the Soviet economy under Khrushchev 1957–63. The further reorganizations of Nikita Khrushchev: recentralization creeps back.

Central Committee

Council of Ministers

GOSPLAN (expanded role)

Central Ministries = ABOLISHED
(save arms, chemicals, electricity)

Republican

Republics

Republican Council of Ministers

sovnarkhoz coordinating agency (1960)

sovnarkhoz

sovnarkhoz

sovnarkhoz

Enterprises

Under the 1960 reorganization, Khrushchev attempted to address the issue of *mestnichestvo* by creating a number of co-ordinating agencies in republics with multiple *sovnarkhozy*. In this way it was hoped to bring a greater degree of rationality into the decision-making at republican levels, thus ending the problems of duplication, waste, inefficiency and irrationality.

312

Figure 7.4 Organizational changes to the Soviet economy under Khrushchev 1957–63. Once more on the reorganizations of Khrushchev: a new regional structure.

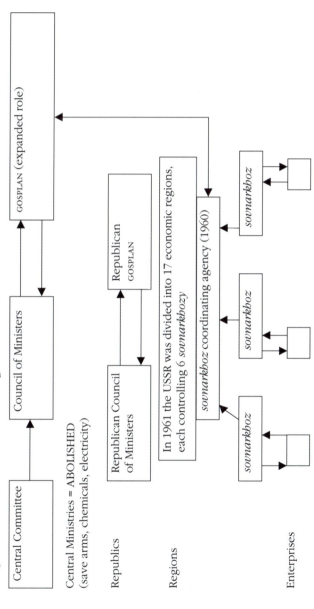

The inability to co-ordinate the Soviet economy continued, so in 1961, Khrushchev introduced further measures to try and streamline the operation of the *sovnarkbozy*. An economic regional structure was imposed on top of the republican structure. Each region controlled six *sovnarkbozy*.

Figure 7.5 Organizational changes to the Soviet economy under Khrushchev 1957–63. Reorganization mania: 1962 and all that.

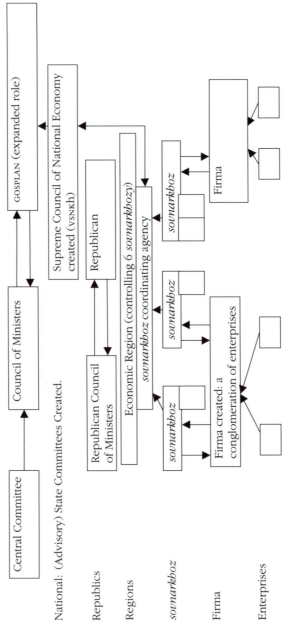

In 1962 things got really complicated. New institutions at the centre emerged, to co-ordinate the co-ordinating bodies, and provide advice for the policy-making bodies. At the *sovnarkhoz* level, each *sovnarkhoz* developed its own branch system of administration. Thus by 1962, Khrushchev's reorganizations had managed to achieve departmental mindedness and localism. Further concentration at lower levels occurred with the incorporation of enterprises into firma.

The final change in 1963 was to reduce the number of *sovnarkhozy* to 47.

towards consumers – compelled the planners to attempt measures to shift production away from purely physical indicators, and to focus instead upon quality, cost-reduction, profitability, greater product mix and so on. Managers were given a degree of greater autonomy, and various measures of carrot and stick were implemented to make enterprises conform to the latest central initiative.[91] The problem was that these initiatives did not replace the issuing of commands based on physical output. They co-existed with them. The retention of the setting of physical targets, disaggregated for republics, regions and enterprises was not altered. Prices were still set centrally, with no regard for consumer demand. Plan fulfilment remained the overriding priority for enterprise managers.

The reforms to the structure and operation of the command economy failed. At the heart of their failure lies the fact that they were essentially an organizational solution to a systemic problem within the centrally planned economy, and were generated partly by elite political manoeuvrings. This was no genuine decentralization of decision-making. All the problems of the centralized system were reproduced at local levels, with the added problems of localism, making central co-ordination wellnigh impossible. Each *sovnarkhoz* naturally looked after the interests of that region before the wider interests of the economy as a whole. The essence of the Stalinist approach to central planning remained. The new added-in components merely complicated the planning system further, creating further dysfunctionalities. The system of priority planning for rapid development of a few key sectors had (just about) functioned in the 1930s. Trying to adapt this to a modern, complex, technological economy, based on consumer demand and driven by high labour productivity, proved impossible. Policies embodying measures of economic rationality could not be combined with the Stalinist command–administer system. It was one or the other.

Management and labour under Khrushchev: reviving the trade unions?

The Stalinist system was based upon the harsh exploitation of the workers, and the total subordination of the collective organizations of the workers to the interests of the state. A series of severe labour decrees were promulgated, which instituted a regime of strict discipline to prevent labour turnover, absenteeism and the like. With the abandonment of mass terror in 1953, the coercive labour edifice had also to be dismantled. With what would it be replaced? How would the regime seek to motivate and stimulate the workers to work harder? What role would the trade unions play in the system? Would they remain, as Lenin devised, "transmission belts"? Or, would there be a return to an agenda of worker participation in factory management? This was a crucial issue for the leadership, as an increase in labour productivity was central to the economics of de-Stalinization.

The repeal of Stalinist labour legislation began in 1956. The punitive decrees of 1940 and 1941 were removed, allowing workers to leave jobs and find another without fear of the consequences. Absenteeism was to be dealt with locally by the relevant managerial authorities. Important improvements to workers conditions were also made. Wage rates were raised. A minimum wage was introduced. Working hours were shortened. Improvements covered other fields as well: maternity rights, holidays, pensions to name but a few.[92] The following year the state set about putting a more positive framework in place. The Model Internal Labour Regulations of January 1957 gave the workers a greater degree of job security, by creating a graduated series of reprimands and disciplinary measures before dismissal. Appeals against dismissal were also made easier.[93] The overall effect fell far short of the principles of the 1922 Labour Code. These initiatives to create more "liberal" labour legislation inexorably led to a review of the role and structure of the trade unions.

A cc plenum of 16/17 December 1957 addressed the issue of the work of the trade unions. Within a framework of increased participation and authority for the trade unions within the workplace, the decree reiterated the traditional Bolshevik rationale of the role of a trade union in a socialist society,

> The trade unions are called upon to intensify their work of enlisting the working people in the management of production, to increase still further the creative initiative and activism of the working masses in the building of communism in our country, and to rally them still more strongly behind the communist party. The central task of the trade

unions is to mobilise the masses for the struggle for a further powerful upswing in all branches of the economy.[94]

Reforms to the operation of the trade unions covered a number of areas. Its overall structure was altered to be more closely configured to the institutional architecture of the *sovnarkhozy*. Within each region a new committee – the *oblsovsprof* – was formed, corresponding to the *sovnarkhozy*. The central organs were retained, and continued to work with the government in formulating policy on labour relations. At regional levels, the *oblsovsprof* were responsible for implementing decisions passed down from above, while overseeing the work of the *sovnarkhoz* concerning safety and other issues.[95]

The cc decree was critical of the failures of union committees to defend the rights and positions of workers. Within the factory itself, the trade unions were granted greater powers and opportunities to participate. The union committee had a greater say in settling labour disputes. No worker could be fired without the agreement of the union committee. The unions were to have greater powers to enforce collective agreements between management and workers. Greater consultation over bonuses, wages and other matters was instituted.[96] Perhaps the major innovation was the creation of a permanent production meeting within the factory. These were elected bodies of representatives of the trade union, management, engineering and technical personnel, office workers, party and *Komsomol* workers. Their remit was to improve the work of the factory in meeting its plan, and also in reducing costs, increasing efficiency and so on. A secondary objective was to draw the workers more meaningfully into the production process itself.[97] The central aim of the trade union legislation was, in Filtzer's words,

> to foster the belief among workers that, with greater democratization, they would become active participants in the management of their own enterprises, and indeed of society at large . . . to give workers a feeling that the regime was "for them", that after the years of alienation from the political process workers now had an ally in the regime, and together they would build socialism within everybody's lifetime.[98]

But these changes fell a long way short of economic democracy. This was no revival of workers' control. The basic Bolshevik framework that developed after 1918 was retained. The factory was run on the basis of one-man management, combined with participation from below. The central task of the unions was to assist in the fulfilment of the plan target. They were still transmission belts, with a key role to play in educating the workers and disseminating party propaganda. They were still directed by the party. They were still agents of mobilization in party campaigns. They still continued to be a means of checking on the work of factory managers for the elites. Labour relations became more coercive again after 1961. The workers remained subordinate to "their" state.

Ideological and theoretical renewal under Khrushchev

De-Stalinization in practice was matched by similar processes in the field of theory. The stultifying intellectual atmosphere of late Stalinism had to be challenged as part of the process of change. The dogmatic orthodoxy of the Stalinist interpretation of Marxism–Leninism encased Soviet intellectual life in a rigid framework, which prevented discussion of new ideas and alternative policy proposals. As Khrushchev drew increasing numbers of consultants and experts into the policy-making process, the vacuity and inappropriateness of Stalinist ideological formulae became apparent. A wide-ranging process of ideological renewal was initiated, as they sought to move away from the simplistic dogmas of the *Short Course*. Six new projects were inaugurated between 1958 and 1961: (a) a new book of Marxist theory, *Fundamentals of Marxism–Leninism*; (b) a new philosophy textbook, *Fundamentals of Marxist Philosophy*; (c) a new History of the CPSU; (d) a new Party Programme (the third one); (e) a new three volume anthology of Soviet literature; (f) a statement derived from the 1960 Conference of 81 Communist and Workers Parties, outlining the principles governing relationships within the socialist bloc.

The outcome of this ideological renewal reflected the ongoing struggle between reformers and defenders of orthodoxy within the politico-ideological hierarchy. A number of creative "collectives" were set up to work on these projects. The complexion of these works reflected the political values of the leaders of these collectives. The textbook on Marxist theory, *Fundamentals of Marxism–Leninism*, was a (relatively) innovative work, headed by the old Bolshevik, Otto Kuusinen. By contrast, the *History of the CPSU* was drawn up under the guidance of B. N. Ponomarev, and although it removed the worst distortions of the *Short Course*, very few "blank spots" were filled in. Within many of these works, there can be detected an upsurge in utopianism and optimism about the future, inspired and fomented by Khrushchev's bold pronouncements and plans.[99] An interesting consequence of this intellectual renewal was the emergence of a number of institutes that quickly earned reputations as centres of innovative and creative thought, particularly in economics and international relations. These institutes – and their scholars – were to play a central role in the intellectual renewal after 1985.[100]

The central ideological document of the Khrushchev era was the Third Party Programme, which was adopted by the party at the 22nd Congress of the CPSU in October 1961. The party programme was the key ideological statement of the CPSU. It was not just a doctrinal statement though. It had to set out the leading role of the USSR in the socialist bloc, while detailing the requirements of building socialism/communism at home. It was an indicator of the correlation of forces within the party, and an expression of the dominant values of the leadership.[101] The details of the drafting process are a little unclear. Khrushchev announced the formation of a drafting commission at the 20th Congress in 1956. Substantive work did not begin until 1958, which was then postponed in the light of the convening of the extraordinary 21st Congress in 1959, at which Khrushchev set out a series of ambitious economic goals for the USSR.[102] The key issue was Khrushchev's identification of a new stage of historical development for the Soviet state,

> the XXI Congress of the CPSU is guided by the USSR's entry into a new era of historical development. Socialism in our country has achieved a complete and final victory . . . Under the party's guidance the Soviet people have achieved such victories of socialism in all areas of economic and socio-political life that the creation of the material and technical basis of communist society and the

planned transition to communism have become practically realisable tasks.[103]

An extensive series of discussions and negotiations ensued between 1959 and its adoption in October 1961. The final content was by no means uncontested. Many defenders of the Stalinist line – in particular Molotov – wished to focus on the completion of the construction of socialism, before turning to the transition to communism. Khrushchev's general line prevailed however.[104]

The final line of the Party Programme states (in capitals!): "THE PARTY SOLEMNLY PROCLAIMS: THE PRESENT GENERATION OF SOVIET PEOPLE SHALL LIVE UNDER COMMUNISM!"[105] The timetable was as follows. Between 1961–70, the USSR, in the process of creating the material–technical basis of communism, would outstrip the USA in production per head of population. Between 1971–80, the material and technical basis of communism will be created, and so, "a communist society in the main will be built in the USSR. The construction of communist society will be fully completed in the subsequent period".[106] Why did Soviet ideology take this markedly more optimistic, utopian turn at this point?

The impressive economic growth rates of the mid-1950s created an atmosphere of optimism, fuelled by the technological achievements of the Soviet space industry. The growth of the international socialist bloc and the anti-imperialist revolutions in the Third World had ended hostile capitalist encirclement according to Khrushchev, opening the way for a reduction in the coercive powers of the state. Further improvements in economic performance, particularly in the area of labour productivity, were thought to be imminent, given the psychological lift provided by the end of mass terror and the apparent victory in the economic competition with the West.[107] The content of the party programme was also determined by a number of political factors. It would be misleading to see it arising purely out of a shift in the economic and technological nature of the system. Domestically, Khrushchev attempted to assert his authority over the Stalinists/conservatives in the Central Committee. Asserting the imminent transition to communism implied change and transformation, rather than consolidation and stability. For instance, the growth of public self-government would preclude a return to a terroristic coercive state. The revival of utopianism can be seen as a function of the end of mass, random terror, as the party sought to inspire and enthuse, rather than terrorize and coerce the people.

The party programme was not just for domestic consumption though. The content was also driven by the dynamics of the tensions within the socialist bloc, and in particular the rift between the cpsu and the Chinese Communist Party (ccp).[108] The ccp – highly critical of the condemnation of Stalin and the doctrine of peaceful co-existence – were seeking to challenge the hegemony of the ussr within the socialist bloc. The Soviets were increasingly aware of the ccp's desire to begin a "Great Leap Forward" to communism. The proclamation that the ussr was embarking on the transition to communism was a bold attempt to cement its position as the leader of the socialist bloc. But there was more than just ideological conflicts involved in this dispute. Duevel has argued that the Chinese position was that the more advanced socialist countries should be prioritizing the development of the less advanced states, rather than promoting their own development. In other words, the ussr should be funding and aiding Chinese economic development rather than their own.[109] On this reading the party programme was designed to maintain the ussr's priority position within the socialist bloc. The interests of all other socialist states were to be subordinated to those of the ussr, rather than vice versa.

Socialism and communism in the Third Party Programme

How "orthodox" was the view of socialist and communist society as set out in the programme? Khrushchev specified the nature of the transition from socialism to communism in more depth than Soviet ideologists heretofore. In his view socialism as a transitional society had two phases: construction of socialism, and creating the material–technical basis of communism. Communism itself would have two stages: basic and completed communism. But what was the relationship between the two? It is clear that Khrushchev saw communism growing out of socialism organically. They shared many similar features, but also there were key, qualitative distinctions in certain areas. According to Evans,

> Khrushchev spoke of three main tasks to be accomplished during the full-scale construction of communism. The main

economic task would be to build the material and technical base of communism. The principal social task would
be the elimination of distinctions between social classes,
resulting in the creation of a classless, communist society.
In politics, society would prepare itself for the "complete implementation of the principle of communist self-
government".[110]

In the light of embarking upon the transition to communism, the
Third Party Programme began to spell out the meaning and content
of many of the features of the future society as set out in Soviet
Marxism–Leninism. Although this mainly dealt with features of communism, there were also interesting adaptations to the theory of the
state and party under socialism.

Within the programme, a fundamental shift in the nature of the
state was announced,

> Having brought about the complete and final victory of
> socialism – the first phase of communism – and the transi-
> tion of society to the full-scale construction of communism,
> the dictatorship of the proletariat has fulfilled its historic
> mission and has ceased to be indispensable in the USSR
> from the point of view of the tasks of internal develop-
> ment. The state has become a state of the entire people, an
> organ expressing the interests and the will of the people as
> a whole.[111]

This was a major theoretical development, as Marxism had almost
always identified the state as an instrument of class rule. Now the
All-People's State represented all Soviet citizens (although a leading
role for the proletariat was still reserved, without saying what this
meant in practice). This idea was a repudiation of the Stalinist idea
of the strengthening of the state with the approach of socialism
because of the intensification of the class struggle. How could the
elaboration of a new state form be reconciled with the traditional
belief in the "withering away" of the state under communism?
Khrushchev's thesis was that the construction of communism
would mean the withering away of particular functions of the state
(coercion, repression) and by extension of the organs responsible

for these functions (police, army, courts). Other functions of the state (cultural, economic and so on) would remain, and in this sense the state under socialism would also be developed and extended.[112] The performance of many of these tasks by the state would be carried out by transfer to public organizations, and by drawing more people into the operation of state bodies themselves, particularly the Soviets. The process of "withering away" was a complex one in Khrushchev's theory. While certain features of the state would begin to diminish immediately, other non-coercive features would disappear on the basis of the internal transformation of the state apparatus itself. The state would remain in place in the era of basic communism. Its final disappearance was postponed until the advent of finished communism, when the final economic preconditions of communism had been met, and when socialism had consolidated its victory finally in the international arena, precluding the need for organs of national defence.[113]

While the state was changing its nature and beginning to wither away (in part), the party programme outlined that,

> The period of the full-scale construction of communism is characterised by a further enhancement of the role and importance of the communist party as the leading and guiding force of Soviet society.[114]

The basis for the enhanced role for the party rested in guiding Soviet society towards communism. The withering away of the state agencies placed a greater premium on the conscious guidance by the vanguard: public self-government and popular participation had to be channelled by the party if communism was to be reached. While the state would start to wither away as communism approached, the party would become increasingly central to the running of the system.

The programme affirmed the central features of communism: material abundance, increasing social homogenization, distribution according to need. In the preamble to part two, communism was defined as,

> a classless social system with one form of public ownership of the means of production and full social equality of

323

all members of society; under it, the all-round development of people will be accompanied by the growth of the
productive forces through continuous progress in science
and technology; all sources of public wealth will gush forth
abundantly, and the great principle "From each according to his ability, to each according to his needs" will be
implemented.[115]

What was the specific meaning of these ideas given within the programme? Material abundance was viewed as the provision of high-
quality consumer goods, an abundance of choice of foodstuffs, an
apartment for every family. In terms of equality and distribution
according to need, it was emphasized that full social equality and
the disappearance of money would only emerge under finished
communism. In the meantime, material inequality would remain,
although the differentials would be reduced. This would be done
in two ways. First, the wages of the lower paid would be rapidly
increased. Secondly, the state would increasingly provide a number
of public services free of charge to the population: education, health,
pensions, public transport, public catering to name but a few. It
was envisaged that by 1980 about 50 per cent of the real income of
the Soviet people would be provided by the state, and the proportion of personal requirements met from wages would gradually
shrink. In this way the state would approach distribution according
to need, although distribution according to labour would continue.[116]
Finally, social relations under communism would become increasingly homogenous. Distinctions between town and country, mental
and manual labour would be gradually overcome. In the main this
was derived from two developments. First, the changes in the nature of ownership relations. The group property of the *kolkhozy*
would be gradually transformed into state property. Secondly, the
advances in agricultural technology would increase the productivity of the agricultural sphere, while upgrading the educational
and skill levels of rural workers.[117]

Khrushchev's conception of communism, while clearly orthodox in its identification of its central features, also departed from
orthodoxy in some ways. The continued existence of the state,
commodity–money relations, distribution according to labour and the
growth in the role of the party in the stage of "basic" communism

emphasizes that Khrushchev was keen to hedge in the transformation inherent in the transition to communism. The continued role for central authorities, and the postponement of the final qualitative changes to Soviet society reflected Khrushchev's desire to preserve elements of the present even while transforming the system. Another illustration of the tension between change and continuity running throughout the Khrushchev years.

Khrushchev and Soviet socialism

Khrushchev has been variously described as a Stalinist, a liberal communist, a neo-Leninist, a hare-brained schemer, an opportunist.[118] The existence of such diverging interpretations reflects the transitional and paradoxical nature of the Khrushchev era, as well as the quirks of Khrushchev's character. But where does Khrushchev stand in the history of Soviet socialism? Did he maintain the essentials of the Stalinist approach, or did he, as he claimed, mark a return to Leninism?

It is clear from the ideological works of the Khrushchev era, that the underlying values and principles of the Khrushchev era reflected the dominant values of Soviet socialism: scientific, rationalist, productivist, constructivist, technocratic. His view of communism confirmed the hegemony of the modernist interpretation of Marx, in which the realm of freedom was to be enjoyed outside of labour, in which humanity would dominate nature, in which human fulfilment resided in leisure and material plenty. The most astonishing expression of the technocratic, scientific, optimistic outlook of the CPSU under Khrushchev comes at the end of the textbook, *Fundamentals of Marxism–Leninism*. Here the authors set out the vistas of human development that would open up in a communist society. Developments in science would enable humanity to solve all problems, and to perfect themselves physically and spiritually. For instance, it was suggested that scientific developments would enable a communist society to – prolong man's life to 150–200 years, to conquer old-age and fatigue, to learn to restore life in case of untimely accidental death; place at the service of man all the forces of nature; render completely harmless natural calamities; learn to control the weather.[119]

It then went on to conclude that, "there is no limit, nor can there be any, to the inquiring human mind".[120] The Khrushchev era reaffirmed the Bolshevik commitment to science and technology, planning and social engineering as the means by which the future society would be constructed. The agenda of radical egalitarianism, decentralized direct democracy and popular self-government remained submerged. The main change after 1953 was that Khrushchev shifted and modified the specific meaning or content of many of the core features of Soviet socialism Stalin-style: the leading role of the party, central planning, proletarian internationalism and so on.

The economics of Soviet socialism

In the economic sphere, the continuities with the Stalinist synthesis were most marked. The economy continued to be thoroughly statized. The essential features of the Stalinist command economy – predominance of state ownership, central planning through the issuance of commands based on physical targets, centralized supply system, hierarchical organization, priority to heavy industry and defence, fetishization of economic growth – remained virtually unchanged. The 7YP of 1959–65 outlined further investment in metallurgy, energy and defence industries. The innovations introduced by Khrushchev – higher priority for agriculture, more balanced approach to the production of consumer goods, decentralization of decision-making to the regional level – were shifts of emphasis or organizational changes. The basic structure, functioning and principles of the economy were further consolidated under Khrushchev.

The politics of Soviet socialism

In political terms, Khrushchev represented a return to a neo-Leninist type strategy, although he continued with many of the political practices established by Stalin. In particular, the abandonment of institutionalized mass terror, the enhancement of the role of the CPSU and the revival of popular participation in the actvities of local government and within factories point back to Lenin's strategy of channelling popular activism towards state-directed goals with the party providing ideological guidance. The development of socialist legality was also crucial in removing the more arbitrary and coer-cive aspects of the state. Khrushchev's continued selective use of terror, his increasing concentration of power in his own hands, and his use of the secretariat to consolidate his own position while undermining those of his opponents, are all deeply reminiscent of Stalin's political manoeuvrings (although many would argue that these traits first emerged under Lenin).

Political developments after 1953 were concerned with trying to impart dynamism and legitimacy into a system stripped of mass terror and personal dictatorship. Khrushchev was no democratizer *per se*. Popular participation and criticism from below was an in-strument of the leadership for the achievement of its wider systemic goals. It remained a regime of mass mobilization. There was never going to be a retreat from the leading role of the cpsu, or the domination of state over society. The continued Bolshevik prefer-ence for technocratic solutions to social problems and societal man-agement is evidenced by the increasing input from specialists in the policy-making process. Khrushchev aimed to synthesize party-led popular participation and technocratic decision-making.

Socio-cultural aspects of Soviet socialism

It was in the field of social and cultural developments that Khrushchev was able to make the most decisive break with the Stalinist synthesis. There are two reasons for this. First, there were fewer ideological obstacles to be overcome. Secondly, the resist-ance of the vested interests within the system was minimal in this area (with the notable exception of his educational reforms). With far greater scope, and far less resistance, Khrushchev was able to stamp his personal authority on this area.

In terms of social policy, the system became more egalitarian and more welfarist in orientation, while retaining its collectivist thrust. The living standards of the population gradually rose. This contrasted markedly with the inegalitarian, hierarchical, stratified, conservative nature of Stalinist social policy, which had as its goal the consolidation of the state, and the preservation of the privileges of the ruling stratum. Yet, this was not a move towards a radically egalitarian system. Soviet society remained dominated by privilege. Khrushchev's approach mitigated the extent of this privilege. In cultural/worldview terms, there was a conspicuous retreat from the overtly Russian nationalist approach of Stalin. Yet Khrushchev continued the fundamental Bolshevik principle of subordinating the interests of the international socialist movement to the interests of the Soviet state. The instrumental approach to cultural policy – subordinating everything to the goals of the state – remained at the heart of the Khrushchevite era.

Notes

1. D. Sturman, "Six leaders in search of character", *Survey* **28**(3), 1984, p. 209.
2. Details on this period can be found in G. Hosking, *A history of the Soviet Union* (London: Fontana, 1992), pp. 261–325; A. Nove, *An economic history of the USSR* (London: Penguin, 1992), pp. 269–323; T. Dunmore, *The Stalinist command economy: the Soviet state apparatus and economic policy 1945–53* (London: Macmillan, 1980).
3. For philosophical developments, see R. T. De George, *Patterns of Soviet Thought* (Ann Arbor: University of Michigan Press, 1966), pp. 179–201. See also E. Simmons (ed.), *Continuity and change in Russian and Soviet thought* (Cambridge Mass.: Harvard University Press, 1955), esp. the chapters by Erlich, Gurian, Dobzhansky, Marcuse, Barghoorn. An excellent piece on Lysenko is, N. Krementsov, *Stalinist science* (Princeton: Princeton University Press, 1997).
4. A. Evans, *Soviet Marxism–Leninism: the decline of an ideology* (Westport: Praeger, 1993), pp. 48–52.
5. J. Stalin, *Economic problems of socialism* (Moscow: Foreign Languages Publishing House, 1952). For a commentary/discussion see, De George, *Patterns of Soviet thought*, ch. 10. Also, A. Walicki, *Marxism and the leap to the kingdom of freedom* (Stanford: Stanford University Press, 1995), pp. 448–52.
6. Walicki, *Marxism and the leap*, p. 449.
7. Evans, *Soviet Marxism–Leninism*, pp. 52–4.
8. Ibid., pp. 46–7, 51–2.
9. L. A. Openkin, "I. V. Stalin: poslednii prognoz budushchego", *Voprosy istorii KPSS* **7**, 1991 (cited in ibid., p. 55, fn 8); N. Barsukov, "Kommunisticheskiye illyuzii khrushcheva", in *Dialog* **5**, 1991, pp. 75–83.
10. M. Suslov in *Pravda*, 7 November 1956.
11. L. Schapiro, *The communist party of the Soviet Union* (London: Methuen, 1970), pp. 555–8.

12. R. Medvedev & Z. Medvedev, *Khrushchev: the years in power* (Oxford: Oxford University Press, 1977), pp. 46–55; M. McAuley, *Politics and the Soviet Union* (Harmondsworth: Penguin, 1977), pp. 173–5.
13. M. McAuley, *Soviet politics 1917–91* (Oxford: Oxford University Press, 1992), p. 62.
14. Hosking, *A history*, pp. 326–33.
15. R. Service, "The road to the XX Party Congress: an analysis of the events surrounding the CC plenum of July 1953", in *Soviet Studies* **33**(2), 1981, pp. 232–45.
16. Ibid., pp. 240–5; Medvedev & Medvedev, *Khrushchev*, pp. 24–65.
17. Medvedev & Medvedev, *Khrushchev*, pp. 39–42; J. Keep, *Last of the Empires* (Oxford: Oxford University Press, 1995), pp. 76–81; McAuley, *Politics and the Soviet Union*, pp. 168–73.
18. McAuley, *Politics and the Soviet Union*, pp. 168–79.
19. Medvedev & Medvedev, *Khrushchev*, pp. 24–55.
20. Keep, *Last of the Empires*, pp. 68–9.
21. The text of the speech can be found in N. Khrushchev, *Khrushchev Remembers* (London: Little Brown, 1971).
22. Hosking, *A history*, p. 334.
23. R. Sakwa, *Soviet politics* (London: Routledge, 1989), pp. 66–70.
24. Ibid., pp. 75–6; M. McCauley (ed.), *Khrushchev and Khrushchevism* (London: Macmillan, 1987), pp. 9–29.
25. For example, Sakwa, *Soviet politics*, pp. 64–5.
26. Keep, *Last of the Empires*, p. 66. For a detailed breakdown, see T. H. Rigby, *Communist party membership in the USSR 1917–67* (Princeton: Princeton University Press, 1968).
27. Ibid., pp. 66–72.
28. Ibid., pp. 69–71.
29. Schapiro, *Communist party*, p. 591.
30. R. W. Pethybridge, *A key to Soviet politics: the crisis of the anti-party group* (New York: Praeger, 1962).
31. Schapiro, *Communist party*, pp. 594–5; Hosking, *A history*, pp. 349–50.
32. The rules can be found in G. Hodnett, *Resolutions and decisions of the CPSU*, vol. 4 (Toronto: University of Toronto Press, 1974), pp. 264–81.
33. Ibid., pp. 270–1.
34. J. Adams, *Citizen inspectors in the Soviet Union* (New York: Praeger, 1977), ch. 3.
35. Ibid., pp. 298–303.
36. Ibid., p. 300.
37. Keep, *Last of the Empires*, pp. 69–76.
38. Hodnett, *Resolutions and decisions*, pp. 292–8.
39. Ibid., p. 292.

40. Medvedev & Medvedev, *Khrushchev*, pp. 150–1.
41. Hosking, *A history*, pp. 350–3.
42. Keep, *Last of the Empires*, pp. 81–3.
43. Ibid., pp. 74–83. Details on how they worked in practice can be found in M. McAuley, *Labour disputes in Soviet Russia 1957–65* (Oxford: Clarendon Press, 1969), pp. 191–3.
44. Keep, *Last of the Empires*, pp. 74–6; Hosking, *A history*, pp. 351–2.
45. Walicki, *Marxism and the leap*, p. 515.
46. McAuley, *Soviet politics*, p. 69.
47. Keep, *Last of the Empires*, pp. 96–9; Hosking, *A history*, pp. 353–4.
48. D. Filtzer, "The Soviet wage reform of 1956–62", *Soviet Studies* **41**, 1989, pp. 88–110.
49. M. Matthews, *Privilege in the Soviet Union* (London: Allen & Unwin, 1978), p. 104.
50. Ibid., pp. 94–6, 108, 128–9.
51. Ibid., pp. 114–17.
52. M. Kaser, "Soviet boarding schools", *Soviet Studies* **20**(1), 1968/69, pp. 94–105.
53. Kaiser, "Soviet boarding schools", p. 96.
54. Hosking, *A history*, pp. 355–6.
55. M. Buckley, *Women and ideology in the Soviet Union* (London: Harvester Wheatsheaf, 1989), pp. 139–60; G. Lapidus, *Women in Soviet society* (Berkeley: University of California Press, 1978), pp. 120–2, 241–6.
56. Buckley, *Women and ideology*, pp. 156–69.
57. Buckley, *Women and ideology*, pp. 140–55.
58. Ibid., p. 159.
59. D. Filtzer, *Soviet workers and de-Stalinisation* (Cambridge: Cambridge University Press, 1992), p. 180.
60. S. Rosen, *Education and modernization in the USSR* (Reading, Mass.: Addison-Wesley, 1971), p. 43.
61. Ibid., pp. 44–6.
62. J. Dunstan, "Atheistic education in the USSR", in G. Avis (ed.) *The making of the Soviet citizen* (London: Croom Helm, 1987), pp. 50–79.
63. R. Stites, *Russian popular culture* (Cambridge: Cambridge University Press, 1992), p. 145.
64. Hodnett (ed.), *Resolutions and decisions*, p. 279.
65. J. Scanlan, *Marxism in the USSR* (Ithaca: Cornell University Press, 1985), pp. 264–5.
66. Keep, *Last of the Empires*, pp. 120–31.
67. J. Garrard & C. Garrard, *Inside the Soviet Writers' Union* (New York: I. B. Tauris, 1990), p. 78.
68. Stites, *Russian popular culture*, p. 145.
69. Cited in R. V. Daniels, *A documentary history of communism, vol. 2: Communism and the world* (London: I. B. Tauris, 1985), p. 224–5.

70. R. C. Tucker, *The Soviet political mind* (London: Pall Mall Press, 1963), pp. 210–23.
71. Ibid., pp. 218–22.
72. Ibid., pp. 192–7; Evans, *Soviet Marxism–Leninism*, pp. 71–4.
73. Tucker, *Soviet political mind*, pp. 219–20.
74. M. McCauley, *Khrushchev and the development of Soviet agriculture: the Virgin Lands programme* (London: Macmillan, 1976); Medvedev & Medvedev, *Khrushchev*, pp. 56–65, 94–128.
75. Nove, *An economic history*, p. 338.
76. Keep, *Last of the Empires*, pp. 104–5.
77. Ibid., pp. 105–7.
78. Nove, *An economic history*, pp. 364–70.
79. McCauley, *The development of Soviet agriculture*; Nove, *An economic history*, pp. 332–4.
80. Nove, *An economic history*, p. 333.
81. Medvedev & Medvedev, *Khrushchev*, pp. 123–8.
82. Ibid., pp. 81–128; Nove, *An economic history*, pp. 364–70.
83. Hodnett (ed.), *Resolutions and decisions*, p. 46.
84. A. Nove, "Industry under Khrushchev", in *Studies in economics and Russia* (London: Macmillan, 1990), pp. 106–7.
85. Ibid., pp. 106–8.
86. Hodnett (ed.), *Resolutions and decisions*, pp. 124–32.
87. Ibid., pp. 83–4.
88. Nove, *An economic history*, pp. 344–6.
89. McAuley, *Labour disputes*, p. 61.
90. Nove, *An economic history*, pp. 361–4. See also R. F. Miller, "Khrushchev and the Soviet Economy: management by reorganisation", in *Khrushchev and the communist world*, R. F. Miller & F. Feher (eds) (London: Croom Helm, 1984), pp. 108–38.
91. Ibid., pp. 356–60.
92. Filtzer, *Soviet workers*, pp. 36–8.
93. Ibid., pp. 38–41.
94. Hodnett (ed.), *Resolutions and decisions*, p. 103.
95. McAuley, *Labour disputes*, pp. 66–7.
96. Ibid., pp. 67–73.
97. Ibid., pp. 66–7.
98. Filtzer, *Soviet workers*, pp. 42–3.
99. Walicki, *Marxism and the leap*, p. 517.
100. See M. Sandle, "Russian think-tanks 1956–1996", in *Think-tanks in comparative perspective*, A. Denham & D. Stone (eds) (Manchester: Manchester University Press, 1998).
101. M. Sandle, "The final word: the draft party programme of July/August 1991", *Europe/Asia Studies* **48**(7), 1996, pp. 1131–3.
102. Barsukov, "Kommunisticheskiye illyuzii", pp. 76–8.
103. Hodnett (ed.), *Resolutions and decisions*, p. 129.

104. The debates on the content of the programme can be found in *The Road to Communism* (Moscow: Progress, 1961). For a western evaluation see R. Schlesinger, "The CPSU programme: historical and international aspects", *Soviet Studies* **13**, 1961/62, pp. 303–20.

105. The text of the programme can be found in Hodnett (ed.), *Resolutions and decisions*, pp. 167–264. Quote is on pp. 263–4.

106. Ibid., p. 211.

107. Evans, *Soviet Marxism–Leninism*, pp. 57–60.

108. For details on the Soviet–Chinese rift, see R. F. Miller & F. Feher (eds), *Khrushchev and the communist world*, chs 5 & 6; D. Zagoria, "Russia and China: two roads to communism", in *The future of communist society*, W. Laqueur & L. Labedz (eds), (New York: Praeger, 1962), pp. 137–45; C. Duevel, "The CPSU programme: Guide for world communism", in *The USSR and the future*, L. Schapiro (ed.) (Munich: Institute for the study of the USSR, 1962), pp. 232–52.

109. Duevel, *The CPSU programme: guide for world communism*, pp. 242–5.

110. Evans, *Soviet Marxism–Leninism*, pp. 61–2.

111. Hodnett (ed.), *Resolutions and decisions*, p. 234.

112. Ibid., pp. 234–42; Evans, *Soviet Marxism–Leninism*, pp. 93–8. See also, R. Hill, "State and ideology", in *Khrushchev and Khrushchevism*, M. McCauley (ed.) (London: Macmillan, 1987); R. E. Kanet, "The rise and fall of the 'All-People's State': recent changes in the Soviet theory of the state", *Soviet Studies* **20**(1), 1968, pp. 81–93; G. Brinkley, "Khrushchev remembered: on the theory of Soviet statehood", *Soviet Studies* **24**(3), 1972/73, pp. 387–401.

113. Evans, *Soviet Marxism–Leninism*, pp. 96–9.

114. Hodnett (ed.), *Resolutions and decisions*, p. 259.

115. Ibid., pp. 208–9.

116. Evans, *Soviet Marxism–Leninism*, pp. 69–71.

117. Ibid., pp. 77–82.

118. Good appraisals of Khrushchev can be found in Sakwa, *Soviet politics*, pp. 79–82; Medvedev & Medvedev, *Khrushchev*, pp. 171–9; M. McCauley, "Khrushchev as leader", in *Khrushchev and Khrushchevism*, M. McCauley (ed.), pp. 9–30; F. Feher, "The social character of Khrushchevism: a transition or a new phase?", in *Khrushchev and the communist world*, Miller & Feher (eds), pp. 12–38; J. Azrael, "Khrushchev Remembered", *Soviet Union* **2**(1), 1975, pp. 94–101; G. Breslauer, "Khrushchev reconsidered", *Problems of Communism* **25**, pp. 18–33, 1976.

119. O. Kuusinen (ed.), *Fundamentals of Marxism–Leninism* (London: Lawrence & Wishart, 1961), p. 876.

120. Ibid., p. 876.

CHAPTER EIGHT

Brezhnev and developed socialism: technocratic socialism in power

After the American landing on the moon, Brezhnev orders Soviet cosmonauts to land on the sun in the shortest possible space of time. "But the temperatures there are so great it isn't possible to get near it!" complain the scientists. "Then make the landing at night," orders Brezhnev.

Introduction

The fall of Khrushchev in 1964 was the first time a Soviet leader had been removed from power. His successors were Leonid Brezhnev and Alexei Kosygin, as the Central Committee decided (once more) to return to a more collectivist approach to leadership. They inherited a complex legacy, which was to shape the nature of Soviet socialism from 1964 until Gorbachev's accession to power in March 1985. At an immediate level, they were forced to confront the ambiguous legacy bequeathed by Khrushchev of organizational chaos, economic and agricultural problems, political dissatisfaction among the party–state bureaucracy and rising discontent among the masses, witnessed by the riots at Novocherkassk in 1962. The new leadership were also faced with Khrushchev's prediction about the advent of communism: only 16 years to go. At a deeper level, they were still confronted with the legacy of Stalinism. The command economy had to be made more efficient and productive, the political system had to be enervated without reverting back to mass terror and without undermining the leading role of the CPSU. Further advances in the economic race with the West had to be combined with the consolidation of the CPSU in the world socialist system.

The circumstances surrounding the fall of Khrushchev were critical in shaping the post-Khrushchev era. At a Central Committee plenum in October 1964 it was stated that,

> Khrushchev allowed serious mistakes in his work, made thoughtless and hasty decisions, and played organisational leapfrog . . . [he] concentrated all the power in the country in his own hands and began to abuse it . . . Khrushchev surrounded himself with advisors from among his relatives . . . He was lavish and indiscriminate in his promises. At the sessions of the Praesidium, Khrushchev shouted, swore, insulted members . . . and used dirty language . . . It is harder to struggle with a living cult than a dead one. If Stalin destroyed people physically, Khrushchev destroyed them morally.[1]

Although Khrushchev's fall was precipitated by policy failures on virtually every front, the underlying cause was the political alienation of Khrushchev from the key groups within the system: the party–state bureaucracy and the military. The 1964 palace coup has been termed a "bureaucratic counter-revolution".[2] Khrushchev had no support within the party or the state by 1964. His constant reorganizations, reshuffles, and populist campaigns had undermined the security of tenure of the *apparatchiki*. The removal of mass terror should have enabled the *nomenklatura* to have enjoyed the privileges of their elite position. Khrushchev's campaigning reorganizations prevented this. The lower and middle echelons of the party were agitating for his removal.

This is of fundamental importance in understanding the subsequent evolution of Soviet socialism after 1964. The new leadership were brought to power on the wave of a deep-seated desire of the elite for political stability and security of tenure. This became embodied in the slogan of the Brezhnev era: trust-in-cadres. This was an implicit social contract between the political elite and the party–state officials. The elite promised stability. The officials promised to co-operate with the policy proposals for change sent down from above. But this posed a problem for the leadership. If the policies of mass terror and party-directed populism were ruled out, by what means could the dynamism required to initiate change be imparted? How could the command economy be reformed, if the system was directed towards self-sustenance and stability? The answer to these questions lay in the adoption by the elite of an essentially technocratic approach to policy-making, emphasizing the hegemony of elite-based, depoliticized, expertise-based approaches to the management of society. Before they could embark upon this approach, it was necessary to address the legacy of Khrushchevism.

The de-Khrushchevization of Soviet society 1964–71

Removing Khrushchev's unpopular policies proceeded with almost indecent haste after 1964. The bifurcation of the party into industrial and agricultural sections was abolished and regional party committees were reunited. The compulsory rotation of posts and limited tenure was abandoned. In the economic sphere, the Ministry of Agriculture re-emerged, the *sovnarkhozy* were abolished in September 1965, GOSPLAN had its full planning authority restored and the agricultural TPAS disappeared. The central industrial ministries were restored. Organizational stability dominated after 1965. The RSFSR bureau of the CPSU was removed in 1966. In social policy, the vocational and egalitarian thrust of the education reforms were abandoned.[3]

The broad thrust of the Khrushchevite policy agenda was maintained to a high degree after 1964, however. The priority accorded to agriculture was continued, albeit without the Khrushchevite "excesses". Prices for produce were raised, restrictions on private plots were reduced, and overall levels of investment increased substantially. In industrial terms, the eighth 5YP (1965–70) set out ambitious targets, which continued the trend of establishing a higher priority for consumer goods. The search for ways to improve the efficiency and functioning of the command economy continued. Debates among scholars over the ways and means of economic reform, over the causes of inefficiency and economic slowdown, had evolved from the late 1950s. Perhaps the most well known contribution in this debate came in 1962 when Liberman published his article, "Plan, Profit, Premium" in *Pravda* on 9 September. He argued that bonuses to managers should be linked to the generation of profit, and that in general the managers should be granted more autonomy.[4]

This impulse for change was reflected in the 1965 reforms to industrial planning, which became known as the Kosygin Reform (named after the Prime Minister).[5] This was the decree that abolished the *sovnarkhozy* and restored the central ministries, while simultaneously granting greater autonomy and discretion for factory managers. It would be wrong to see this as a measure of radical decentralization. In abolishing the regional and republican powers of economic administration, it restored certain powers to the centre, while devolving other powers to the enterprise level. A number of specific changes were introduced into the production process at the enterprise level, including reducing the number of central indicators to be met by the managers, greater emphasis upon profit and less upon quantity, more scope for horizontal links between enterprises and greater use of mathematical techniques. The attempt to combine these initiatives with the restoration of the authority and powers of the central ministries proved unworkable. The central authorities continued to intervene, to issue commands. Shortages undermined the drive for profit and the price mechanism remained divorced from demand. The compromised, half-hearted nature of this reform partially accounts for its failure. By the early 1970s it had fizzled out, and the traditional forms of central planning had reasserted themselves.[6]

The practice of dealing with Khrushchev's policy initiatives was well underway by 1966. The question of Khrushchev's theoretical and ideological legacy was more tricky. There was a conspicuous retreat from the promises of the Third Party Programme, as the accumulating problems within the economy called into question the attainment of communism by 1980. Yet there was a reluctance formally to abandon the timetable in the programme. The response of the leadership was the gradual elaboration of a new concept: Developed Socialism.[7] The theorist responsible for its full development was Fedor Burlatskii (who was also responsible for the idea of the All-People's State), although there had been a number of references to "developed" or "mature" socialism from scholars throughout the 1960s.[8] Between 1967 and 1971 (when it was fully elaborated at the 24th Congress of the CPSU) an increasing number of references were made to this concept. By the time of the Congress, no more references were made to the idea of the "full-scale construction of communism".[9]

The concept of Developed Socialism came both to shape and embody the nature of Soviet socialism under Brezhnev. Although its values and priorities reflect those of the traditional model of Soviet socialism, Developed Socialism arose out of a very specific political and theoretical context. Faced with the problem of Khrushchev's grandiose claims about the proximity of communism, the Soviet leadership were in something of a dilemma. If the USSR was no longer engaged in the construction of communism, on what basis could it claim to be the dominant state in the socialist bloc? All the countries were "socialist". Developed Socialism became a means of differentiating the USSR from the other socialist countries, while asserting its leading role: it was the first state to undertake the construction of a "developed socialist" society. It also had a domestic application. The leadership had to reassure the bureaucracy that change would be measured and gradual. By removing the utopian, transformatory implications of Khrushchev's full-scale construction of communism, Developed Socialism became a celebration of the system's maturity, focusing on the perfection of the existing system. But Developed Socialism had also to outline the way in which developments and changes would take place. In this sense it needed to be a modernizing doctrine that sought to create intensive, balanced, efficient growth within the existing institutional framework.

At first it represented a further and fuller delineation of the nature of the post-revolutionary development of Soviet society towards communism. In time, however, it was to become a full-blown doctrine that touched upon almost all aspects of Soviet society. From 1971 onwards a large number of articles appeared in many journals (for example, *Kommunist* and *Voprosy Istorii KPSS*) dealing with the form and content of Developed Socialism, and indeed the period 1971–81 has been characterized by one Soviet theorist as the era of Developed Socialism.[10]

Evans has noted the distinctive view of the periodization of socialism after the revolution contained within Developed Socialism. There were now four stages between capitalism and communism:

337

1) a transitional stage of building socialism (1917–36);
2) a socialist society "in the main", which was constructing a developed socialist society (1936 onwards);
3) developed socialism attained in the 1960s;
4) communism (at an unspecified time in the future).[11]

For Brezhnev and others, socialism ceased to be a brief transitional period between capitalism and communism. It was a long historical phase, marked by its own laws of social development, not all of which had been revealed by the unfolding of the historical process. This argument maintained that the difference in the degree of the development of socialism had become so great as to require a qualitative distinction. Fedoseev noted that:

> Developed Socialist society is not considered by us as something midway between socialism and communism . . . It is a socialist society attaining a developed condition, characterised by the all-round disclosure of the advantages of socialism.[12]

This was a fundamental revision of the orthodox view of the transition from capitalism to communism. Communism was now postponed until the distant future. Socialism was now a prolonged historical phase in its own right, markedly distinct from communism. In Brezhnev's words, Developed Socialism was, "that stage of maturity of the new society, when the restructuring of the totality of social relations on the collectivist principles internally inherent to socialism is being completed."[13]

The emphasis now lay in "perfecting" socialist society, in focusing upon the present tasks within the socialist phase. The transition to communism was now postponed until the potential within socialism itself had been exhausted.

Developed Socialism provided the ideological and conceptual framework for the evolution of Soviet socialism after 1971. Although Soviet socialism evolved into a technocratic, elitist, expertise-based, incrementalist and gradualist approach to societal management and social progress during the 1970s, this was not the inexorable outworking of the application of the principles of Developed Socialism. When Burlatskii first discussed the concept in depth, he emphasized its reformist potential. The greater scope for rational planning and rapid increases in productivity inherent in the Scientific and Technological Revolution (str) imparted a sense of optimism to ideological pronouncements of the late 1960s and early 1970s, although falling short of Khrushchevian expectations. The original conception of Developed Socialism also continued the emphasis upon popular participation in political processes. But this was different from the mobilizing, campaigning participation of Khrushchev. The higher educational levels of the population would enable the people to participate in a more informed, rational manner. This participation would enhance the scientific nature of decision-making, as there would be an improved flow of information from lower levels of the system. Alongside an optimistic, reformist, participatory strand, Developed Socialism also contained the fullest expression of the technocratic, rationalistic, scientific ethos within Soviet socialism. This latter strand was embodied in two concepts that dominated the thinking of Soviet theorists in the 1970s: the str and the Scientific Management of society.

Julian Cooper stresses that "one cannot speak of a generally accepted Soviet theory of the str and its consequences".[14] However, there was a degree of consensus on many basic questions.[15] Almost all theorists viewed the transformations in science and technology as revolutionary, forming an integral part of the general revolutionary transition from capitalism to communism. Science was being increasingly transformed into a direct productive force and the str gave rise to profound social consequences. These consequences stemmed from the changed place of the worker in the production process, but they produced different results according to the social system in which they occurred. According to Soviet theorists, only under socialism, with its societal-wide planning and management, its stress on the development of individuals and the use of science and technique for the interests of society as a whole, could these processes be mastered and utilized progressively. Under capitalism the existing contradictions were merely intensified by the str.[16] According to Hoffmann & Laird, Soviet theorists stressed that "only a unified society led by the cpsu and under 'public control' can make full use of the str and its consequences".[17]

The most obvious impact of the str lay in the regime's approach to policy-formulation and decision-making. The planning, administration and guidance of society now became the crucial sphere for the translation of scientific-technical changes (and the consequent socio-economic development) into actual policies that would attempt to realize the widely accepted political goals of modernization and stability. One of the unintended consequences of the way in which the STR was conceptualized in the USSR was its constriction of creativity and initiative. The feeling of optimism that the STR communicated about the ability of the regime to solve problems, mediate conflicts and further the progress of Soviet society towards communism, endowed the leadership with a belief in their ability to plan optimally and to "manage" society. This became a "legitimization" of the close conscious control of social processes, which left little room for initiative and creativity, and may have been a contributory factor in the emergence of passivity and stagnation in Soviet society. The STR posed a twofold problem for the leadership. First, how could the new scientific and productive potential that was becoming available be harnessed in order to foster the further development of socialism? Secondly, how could this process be mastered and consciously controlled in order to avoid some of the deleterious consequences suffered by capitalist society (pollution, growing unemployment and inequality owing to increased rewards for capital)?[18] The response of Soviet theorists to the challenges posed by the STR was the elaboration of the idea of the Scientific Management of society.

"Scientific Management" became the dominant theme of administrative theory and practice under Brezhnev. Indeed it has been described by Western scholars as the *sine qua non* of Developed Socialism.[19] The traditional view of the administrative sphere under socialism was that the state would wither away and would be replaced by the self-management of the people. Developed Socialism, while emphasizing the growth in the level of popular involvement in the tasks of administering society, now put greater emphasis on Scientific Management as the means of realizing a "scientific" transition to communism. Perhaps the main Soviet proponent of Scientific Management was Viktor Afanas'yev, who defined it as:

> The systematically exercised, conscious and purposeful influence by man on the social system as a whole or on its separate aspects . . . on the basis of the knowledge and

use of the objective laws of socialism and its progressive trends, in order to ensure its effective functioning and development.[20]

It is easy to see why Scientific Management was perceived as the crucial integrating element of Developed Socialism. Its dual emphases expressed the existence of a methodology or of technologies for the optimization of socio-economic planning and guidance on the one hand, and the need to preserve and enhance the role of the party and state elites to control and master the management process and its skills on the other.[21] It became the embodiment of both the "means" and "ends" of Brezhnevite socialism. Its aim was to provide a means of pursuing the (often conflictual) goals of modernization and stability. It sought to achieve this by combining the close control of social and economic processes with the introduction of the latest scientific and technical changes. In Soviet terms it was the point at which the "subjective factor" (i.e. the conscious action of individuals in history) met the objective laws of social development or *zakonomernosti* in order to realize socialism's progress towards communism.[22]

Taken together, it is evident that the combined impact of the STR and of Scientific Management was to affirm that Developed Socialism lay squarely within the traditional discourse of Soviet socialism. Developed Socialism embodied the rationalism, optimism, and constructivism that had underscored Marxist and Bolshevik philosophy. The achievements of the STR meant that the technology existed (or soon would exist) to enable the leadership to guide and control social processes. This would be achieved through Scientific Management. This belief in turn reinforced the optimism that a society could be "built" that was conflict-free and had removed the basis of exploitation and oppression. What is significant to note is that Developed Socialism did not emerge fully-formed, and did not remain static. It evolved as the leadership applied their principles to the reality of the USSR in the 1970s. As the decade progressed, the technocratic, incremental emphasis gradually displaced the reformist, participatory strand. While reinforcing the underlying philosophy of Soviet socialism, how did Developed Socialism interpret the features of the traditional model of Soviet socialism?

341

Developed Socialism and the practice of Soviet socialism

The economics of Developed Socialism

The economic aspects of Brezhnevite socialism were based on minimal change. The essential features of the Soviet economy – state ownership and direction, central planning, hierarchical organization, emphasis upon growth, plan fulfillied – remained. Brezhnev's approach, although punctuated by attempts to reform and improve the functioning of the economy, also continued the policy priorities of the Khrushchev era. Agriculture remained at the centre of the policy agenda, and industrial growth was to be a balance between the production of producer goods, and the needs of consumers. The essential distinction between the two eras was in the means chosen to pursue these ends. Khrushchev chose mobilization, energy, reorganization, speed, confrontation. Brezhnev chose consensus, gradualism, incrementalism, technocracy.

The 8th, 9th and 10th 5 year plans outlined ambitious but not extreme rates of growth, including the aim of increasing the production of consumer goods more rapidly than capital goods (although it was unrealized in practice).[23] The increase in the volume of consumer goods was highlighted by the leadership for a number of reasons. Primarily, it reinforced the higher level of development reached by the Soviet economy. The earlier priority on heavy industry was appropriate for the embryonic stages of building socialism. Now, a more balanced approach was required. Additionally, in political terms it legitimized the regime at home. Increasing the standard of living would reduce the dissatisfaction of the Soviet people. This appeared to overturn the traditional Soviet emphasis upon the growth of the productive forces of the economy as the motor of economic progress, repeating the arguments put forward by Malenkov in the 1950s.[24] In reality, Brezhnev was attempting to develop both sectors in tandem, rather than sequentially. This created problems for the leadership, as the military and defence sectors required investment in heavy industry, which subverted this aspiration over the long term.

The leadership attempted to transform the type of growth, shifting towards intensive growth (based upon a more efficient utilization of existing resources, the application of new technology and so on), and towards output measured in qualitative terms, rather than purely quantitative. The problem was that this strategy of intensive, qualitative growth was undermined by the seeming imperviousness of the command economy to reform. The planning process continued to be dominated by the central ministries and by a target-fulfilled mentality. The acquisition of new technology from the West during the period of *détente* in the 1970s was a central component of the reform strategy of the leadership.

Agriculture under Developed Socialism

A number of initiatives were tried in the agricultural sphere. Organizationally, the practice of merging *kolkhozy* with *sovkhozy* continued. Moves were also mooted to create agro-industrial complexes, combinations of *kolkhozy*, *sovkhozy*, retail outlets and processing plants. Investment was increased substantially, as were the prices paid by the state for agricultural produce. More encouragement was given to peasant private plots.[25] One of the more interesting developments was the revival of the link or brigade system. Groups of workers would draw up a contract with the management for certain tasks, and be paid on results. The results were positive: increased output, decreased costs. In practice it was subverted by the opposition of the obstructive bureaucracy.[26] The final initiative under Brezhnev came in 1982, with the announcement of the Food Programme. In practice it was little more than a repetition of former policies: reorganization and increased subsidies. By the end of the Brezhnev era, agriculture was in crisis. Meat and grain had to be imported. Subsidies had rocketed. Although production had increased, productivity had not. Rural life was grim, and rural outmigration by the young was gathering pace. Agricultural failure remained a permanent headache for the party.[27]

Industry under Developed Socialism

The changes to the functioning of the Soviet industrial economy between 1971 and 1982 were minimal. The aspiration to make the planning process more precise and scientific found its most coherent expression in the elaboration of SOFE (System of the Optimal Functioning of the Economy).[28] Echoing the earlier Taylorist tendencies of the Bolshevik state, a group of economists and mathematicians believed it was possible to increase labour productivity and efficiency through a scientifically validated plan, using computer technology to draw up accurate plans and estimates of inputs. It failed. Not only did it prove impossible to generate the necessary hardware, but most managers, foremen and workers ignored the computer projections, preferring instead to rely on traditional methods to fulfil their plan target and the military were extremely reluctant about sharing their technological expertise.[29]

The only other industrial innovations of note came in 1973 and 1979. In the first reform, a number of enterprises were merged into production-associations, thus physically reducing the number of units involved in the planning process.[30] At the end of the decade, a number of changes were introduced, which attempted to make the planning system more responsive to criteria of quality, more cost-sensitive, more attuned to technological innovation. This merely had the impact of increasing the number of indicators for managers. The command economy remained intact. There was no real decentralization, no use of market levers, no radical worker democratization within the factories. The structure, organization and functioning of the centrally planned economy continued essentially as it had since the 1930s.

The politics of Developed Socialism

The CPSU and Developed Socialism

Soviet socialism had rested upon party hegemony in political life. By the 1970s the nature of the party had changed from the original ideal of an elite vanguard of revolutionaries, armed with Marxism–Leninism, providing ideological and political leadership. Of the adult population, 11 per cent were now members of the party. In sociological terms, the composition of the party was far more diverse. Members tended to be educated, and drawn from the professional and technical strata of society. It housed a great diversity of opinions: Stalinists, reformers, Russian nationalists, technocrats, careerists, Leninists, minority nationalists. There were generational divides (particularly between the Stalin and post-Stalin generations).[31] Much did not change though. Centralism and appointmentism prevailed over democracy. It remained a privileged, hierarchical body. Its monopoly on power was unchallenged. Developed Socialism outlined a threefold transformation of the party. The leading role was to grow; the style of work was to be modernized and placed on a more scientific footing; and the party was to be internally transformed into a party of All-The-People.[32]

The changes to the party were spurred by a number of factors. To cope with the multiplicity of socio-economic and scientific and technical changes it was necessary that the party begin to use more modern, scientific techniques in leading society. In addition, Soviet society was becoming an increasingly complex and diverse organism to manage. This was evident with the increased use of specialists in policy-formulation, the increase in the number of actors participating in the political process, and the proliferation of vested interests seeking to obstruct, retard or accelerate change. Finally, the "1964 compromise" (in which officials were given assurances of stability and job security in return for compliance with the reformist goals of the leadership) meant that the ability of the party elite to bring about thorough, substantial change was fundamentally compromised by the commitment to stability.[33]

The growth in the leading role of the party was seen in Soviet literature as having both objective and subjective elements, reflecting the "traditional" concept of the party's role, and the specific changes to that role posed by the present stage of development. The former were classified as political, organizational and ideological functions, which represented policy-making, supervision of the administrative sphere, the inculcation of the values and norms commensurate with the level of development attained by Soviet society, and the elaboration of new theoretical concepts to give direction and legitimacy to the changes. The growth of this aspect of the party's role was usually explained as a logical response to the unfolding of the laws of social development. It stemmed from the nature of the tasks involved in the building of socialism and communism.[34]

The "subjective factor", i.e. the conscious action of individuals and bodies upon the historical process, became far more significant under Developed Socialism. In managing an increasingly complex socio-political and economic entity the party's role became radically transformed. For instance, a more complex socio-political organism required more co-ordination and integration. Overcoming vested interests, resistance to change, a competitive bureaucratic milieu, and eliciting contributions from more actors and participants (to help formulate policy and implement decisions) forced the party to adopt a more interventionist stance.[35] The conditions of Developed Socialism thus imposed on the party a multifaceted dilemma. First, to maintain its traditional role while assuming a more activist, interventionist stance: what Hoffmann & Laird have described as being that of "co-ordinator, integrator, regulator, mobilizer and energizer."[36] Secondly, to modernize both society and itself, while maintaining its commitment to stability.

The modernization of the style and content of the party's work complicated this dilemma. The process of attempting to manage a Developed Socialist society "scientifically" as a means of controlling and guiding the changes imposed by the STR, rendered both the existing management skills and practices obsolete. In terms of style, this meant the adoption by party officials of leadership and integrative roles, as opposed to command and petty oversight. In terms of content, this required the adoption of new scientific techniques of management, and on a broader scale required the retraining and rejuvenation of the party officials.

> We need people who combine a high level of political consciousness with a sound professional training, people who can knowledgably tackle the problems of economic and cultural development, and are well-versed in modern methods of management.[37]

Developed Socialism modified and adapted certain elements of the party's leading role, without really shifting its emphases or introducing any radical innovations. In fact, the new Constitution of 1977 enshrined the nature of the party's leading role in article 6,

> The leading and guiding force of Soviet society and the nucleus of its political system, of all state organisations and public organisations, is the CPSU. The CPSU exists for the people and serves the people. The Communist Party, armed with Marxism–Leninism, determines the general perspectives of the development of society and the course of the home and foreign policy, directs the great constructive

work of the Soviet people, and imparts a planned, systematic and theoretically substantiated character to their
struggle for the victory of communism.[38]

The tension between ideological guidance and day-to-day intervention was resolved to some extent by articulating that methods of
Scientific Management were an intrinsic part of the role of the party.
In practice, very little changed. The party officials continued to
administer, and proved impervious to exhortations to change their
ways of working. Having abandoned mass terror, and Khrushchev's
constant reorganizations as a means of shaking up and controlling
the party apparatus, the policy of trust-in-cadres proved incapable
of changing the party's mode of operation. Consequently, the CPSU
became increasingly prone to stasis, corruption and immobilism. Its
raison d'être became a defence of its own positions, privileges and
status. After 1977–78, the governing style of the elite – *après moi
le déluge* – infected the whole party. A more stark contrast with
Lenin's vision of a dedicated vanguard of revolutionaries is hard to
imagine.

State, society and the individual

Although Brezhnev initially reiterated the Khrushchevite stress on
the All-People's State, this soon disappeared from Soviet discourse.
After 1971, the state under Brezhnev attempted to strike a balance
between the prerogatives of the state and the rights of the individual, and between popular participation and elite, technocratic
management of social processes. Although the Brezhnev era is
often seen as being little more than a neo-Stalinist renaissance, a
close analysis reveals that while the system did become more repressive and illiberal in certain areas, it also continued many of the
post-Stalinist practices initiated by Khrushchev.

A distinctive feature of decision-making in this period was the
use of specialists. As policy-making became more complex, so the
leadership increasingly consulted with specialist groups: agricultural, judicial, educational, foreign policy.[39] In addition, the whole
decision-making process was far more deliberative, rational and
consensual. The Khrushchevite mobilizational approach was replaced by a far more orderly and stable process under Brezhnev. Its

central elements were a coalition of the major institutions within the system – cc, Secretariat, kgb, military – with more specialist groupings representing specific policy areas. Two items of note here. First, the political elite still directed and controlled this process. No real autonomy for specialists was created. However, on occasions it was possible for a coalition of groups to effect political change, rather than merely having input into the policy process. The most well known case is that of Lake Baikal. A collection of scientific figures, environmentalists and journalists argued for measures to protect the lake – the largest freshwater one in the world – from pollution by a factory making tyres for the Soviet air force.[40] They prevailed, emphasizing the scope for action which did occasionally occur. Secondly, this was an extension of a process inaugurated by Khrushchev, rather than a wholly new development. Western specialists remain deeply divided over the way to categorize and conceptualize these developments: institutional pluralism, bureaucratic pluralism, corporatism, imperfect monism, within-system pluralism, totalitarianism without terror. All have been applied to this period.[41] However the system is conceptualized, it is clear that policy-making was more routinized, with greater participation from a variety of groups at elite level.

At the same time, greater efforts were made to increase popular participation. The state continued its attempts to draw the population into the administration of local affairs, to encourage communication between elite and masses, and to consult the population during the elaboration of key policies. Letter-writing – to newspapers, journals, party organizations and Soviet bodies – was encouraged by the elite in order to obtain information on the attitudes and priorities of the leadership.[42] Perhaps the greatest effort at popular consultation was the mass nationwide discussion undertaken before the adoption of the 1977 Constitution (mirroring the discussion undertaken by Stalin in 1935–6). Approximately 140 million people took part and 400,000 amendments were sent in, of which 150 were adopted (all are official figures).[43] There were other examples. As ever, the topics and parameters of the discussion were centrally determined. The regime continued to be a mobilizational one: the Soviet calendar was punctuated by a widespread array of collective assemblies to celebrate the achievements and traditions of the state: the October Revolution, the Great Patriotic War, May

Day and so on. The Brezhnev era added a number of new rituals to the Soviet political calendar.[44] The nature of this mobilization had changed though. The mobilizational campaigns of the 1930s and 1950s had amalgamated central goals with popular enthusiasm. By the 1970s the well of popular enthusiasm had run dry. A campaign to build the Siberian railway dismally failed to enthuse the population.[45]

The increasing focus upon scientific management, stability and gradual, incremental change diffused any lingering ideological ardour. Cynicism and apathy grew apace. Although the system remained a participative one, the nature of this participation had changed, becoming far more complex and differentiated. The original Leninist vision of combining elite guidance with popular control had evolved out of all recognition. "Elite guidance" meant extensive state control over society. "Popular control" had become an individualized form of participation in various elite directed processes: election campaigns, letter writing, collective assemblies, nationwide discussions. The best example of this combination of elite guidance with popular participation lies in the arena of popular control. The reforms to the Party–State Control Committee introduced in 1968 reflect the new attitude to public participation under Brezhnev. The new leadership were intensely critical of the populist approach of Khrushchev. Under the new arrangements, there was to be a strict delineation of the functions of citizen inspectors. The latter were to investigate problems in the day-to-day working of the local area, leaving the party to apply the sanctions against transgressors. In addition, the party sought citizen inspectors who were also members of the party. This converted the citizen inspectors into an informal or auxiliary organ of the party.[46]

By the mid-1970s, the practice of popular participation and oversight – a constant theme of Bolshevik ideology – was still alive and well in the functioning of the Soviet state. The nature and extent of this oversight had changed radically, however. The inspector was now involved in checking that state and party directives were being carried out, and in feeding back information into the policy process. But the party exercised close tutelage over these activities, and was also heavily involved in the selection of the inspectors. In sum, the role of the citizen inspectors under Brezhnev demonstrated the technocratic, de-politicized nature of mass political activity in the Soviet Union in the 1970s. Popular participation was to be an adjunct of the party-led, expertise dominated, scientifc management of Soviet society.[47]

The relationship between the powers of the state, and the rights of the individual under Brezhnev was also complex. On one level, the system appeared to become more repressive and coercive, moving back towards a form of neo-Stalinism. The KGB enhanced its position within the elite. Repression and harassment of dissidents – individuals willing to express unorthodox or heretical views – increased substantially, commencing in 1966 with the trial of Sinyavsky and Daniel.[48] The continued existence of labour camps, the increased use of "psychiatry" to "treat" dissidents, and the subordination of the judiciary to the party all reflect the repressive and arbitrary nature of the Brezhnev regime. At the same time, the more stable and orderly approach to socialist legality was maintained. There was no likelihood of a return to the Stalinist arbitrary mass terror. Indeed, there was something of a weakening of the hostile anti-religious campaigns of the Khrushchev era, although harassment of believers still continued.

The dissident phenomenon is an interesting example of the first shoots of a semi-organized, unofficial, clandestine opposition movement. It grew out of the Sinyavsky and Daniel trial, and was concerned primarily with the human rights abuses committed by the state against Soviet citizens. The aim of the movement was to highlight the disparity between the ostensible rights and freedoms enshrined in the Soviet constitution, and the reality of life in the USSR. The movement rested on *samizdat'* (self-publishing): copies of reports detailing human rights abuses were circulated throughout a clandestine network, and also given to Western journalists. Individuals would receive one copy, and then make six further copies. The recipients would then follow the same procedure and so on. Although the original concern encompassed civil and human rights – freedom of speech, conscience, assembly, religion, greater openness – this soon spread to environmental, cultural and national issues. This pluralism came to encompass the political complexion of many of the dissidents. Voices could be heard extolling Russian nationalist ideals, neo-Leninism, Western liberalism and other themes. Interestingly, dissident concerns were at the centre of the reforms introduced by Gorbachev after 1985.

The general contours of the relationship between the state and the individual were enshrined in the 1977 Constitution. Adopted on the 60th anniversary of the 1917 revolution, it was hailed as a major achievement of the regime by Brezhnev. Although it detailed a barrage of rights enjoyed by the Soviet citizenry – work, leisure, health care, welfare, housing, education, freedom of speech, press, assembly, conscience, personal inviolability – these were all undermined in two ways. First, the constitutionally guaranteed leading role of the CPSU enshrined its monopoly on power. Secondly, individual rights and freedoms were constrained by two basic provisos:

article 59 stated that: "citizens' exercise of their rights and freedoms is inseparable from the performance of their duties and obligations".[49]

article 39 stated that: "enjoyment by citizens of their rights and freedoms must not be to the detriment of the interests of society or the state, or infringe the rights of other citizens".[50]

The basic premise was that the interests of the collective were prior to, and greater than, those of the individual. Moreover, the rights of the individual were state-based, and were then delegated to the individual from the state. There were no natural rights for Soviet citizens, and no autonomous sphere for individuals outside of the reach of the state. The state was the great benefactor, delegating rights and freedoms. Developed Socialism, in this respect, lies firmly in the Soviet tradition of state-based, anti-individualistic socialism.

Society and culture of Developed Socialism

Privilege and equality

The Brezhnevite approach to the questions of material and social inequality was somewhat paradoxical. Although there was general continuity with the Khrushchev era in terms of policy priorities, in certain areas there was a revival of Stalinist practices. This is most clearly illustrated with reference to the question of privilege and material equality. The Brezhnev era saw a renewed emphasis upon rewarding the elites, increasing incentives for those at the summit of the hierarchy. The egalitarian thrust of Khrushchev's educational policies were in the main abandoned. The vocational elements were removed, and special grants for gifted children increased. The changes benefited the children of the elites (although there were other measures to help the children of the masses also).[51] Privileges for the *nomenklatura* – more housing, foreign currency shops, access to shortage goods, holiday homes – were extended. Rewards for decorated individuals – Heroes of Socialist Labour, war veterans – were extended, and new state honours and titles were created.[52] The relaxation of political controls and oversight of the bureaucracy created more settled and orderly life for most officials. Arising out of this was the mushrooming of nepotism, patronage networks and corruption.[53]

On the other hand, the extent of privilege did not return to Stalinist levels, and in some areas significant measures were taken to address continued underprivilege. Subsidies of key items – rents, food, heating, transport – grew inexorably. Wages for workers also rose during the 1970s. The regime's prioritization of consumer goods (although the results in both quantitative and qualitative terms were disappointing) and food supplies raised the living standards of the mass of workers and peasants. Diets were more balanced. Ownership of cars, televisions and fridges rose substantially. These improvements must be tempered by an awareness of the poor quality and unreliability of many of these items, the frequent unavailability of spare parts, and the time spent queueing.[54] The biggest "winners" under Brezhnev were the agricultural workers. The levels of material remuneration for state and collective farmers were increased over and above those of industrial workers, and professional groups. Some of the more glaring inequalities in the lives of collective farmers were also removed. The internal passport system was gradually phased out after 1974. The electrification of rural areas was virtually completed by 1973. Collective farm workers now qualified for state pensions.[55]

How were these developments conceptualized within Developed Socialism? Stalin dramatically increased the privileges and benefits of the elite while suppressing the living standards of the workers and peasants. Khrushchev narrowed the differentials while retaining the edifice of privilege. Brezhnev's approach was to increase the living standards of those at the bottom without undermining the privileges of those at the top. In other words, Developed Socialism envisaged the erosion of inequality arising out of a general rise in the living standards of the population, not by redistributing from the privileged to the underprivileged. As Evans notes,

> The improvement in the material wellbeing of groups with lower-incomes was to be paid for out of the increments in the total of social benefits created by economic growth so that it would be possible to enhance the standard of living of the less affluent groups without reducing the rewards to more privileged strata.[56]

The issue of female emancipation returned, rather surprisingly, to the socio-political agenda. Rather surprisingly because it had been "solved" under Stalin. It returned to the agenda primarily for socio-economic reasons. The declining growth and birth rates in the 1970s compelled the leadership to explore the roots and connections of these twin processes. This revived discussions of the problems and issues facing women at home and at work. These issues were legitimized by the concept of Developed Socialism. The task was now to perfect social relations under socialism in order to lay the foundations for the emergence of a classless, egalitarian, socially homogenous society under communism. All obstacles and hindrances to the achievement of these objectives had to be researched and discussed, and this obviously included obstacles to women's emancipation.[57]

These developments in material rewards and social equality were linked by their subordination to the socio-political and economic goals of Developed Socialism. Maintaining privilege while seeking to eradicate underprivilege reflected the elite's commitment to maintaining the position of the bureaucratic hierarchy while simultaneously improving the standard of living of the masses. In this way, political stability and ideological legitimacy could be maintained. Similarly, the greater focus upon women's issues did not mean a revival of the early Bolshevik emancipatory strand embodied by Kollontai and others. It was generated by the narrow, immediate needs of the state to raise levels of production and increase the birth rate. Once more social policy was subordinated to the productivist requirements of the Soviet state.

The normative basis of Developed Socialism: *détente*, militarism, Russian nationalism and nostalgia

The formative components of the worldview of the CPSU underwent some significant revisions after 1964. In international terms, the CPSU under Brezhnev continued its policy of peaceful, competitive co-existence with the West. A new era had emerged though. Before the Second World War, socialism had been unable to prevent war breaking out. The aftermath of the war reconfigured the relationship between socialism and capitalism, opening up the emergence of peaceful co-existence. By the 1970s the growth in military and nuclear technology, and in particular the reality of MAD (Mutually Assured Destruction) resulting from nuclear proliferation meant that a new situation had emerged: *détente*. Capitalism could no longer expect to defeat the socialist system by military means. The prospects for peace, and for a more co-operative emphasis in co-existence, were greatly improved. Yet Soviet theorists (as well as their counterparts in the USA) still viewed *détente* as part of the ongoing process by which socialism would overcome capitalism. According to Shenfield,

> Detente enables the socialist countries to reduce their military burden, and . . . to develop democracy more easily and overcome "deformations" caused by international tension. Anti-communism becomes a less effective ideological weapon against working-class struggle in the capitalist countries. Detente in general eases imperialist pressure on the revolutionary movement, reducing the danger of "export of counter-revolution".[58]

Once again *détente* was partially derived from the domestic economic needs of the USSR. Reducing the military burden enabled a shift of resources to consumer goods. The more relaxed international atmosphere facilitated the import of Western technology, allowing the state to modernize the economy without enormous investment. The acquisition of Most Favoured Nation status for the USSR from the US government meant substantive economic benefits, which were to filter through to the Soviet economy in the mid-1970s. The highpoint for the Brezhnev regime in its international prestige and status came in 1975 at Helsinki with the signing of the OCSE accords.[59]

In the domestic sphere, the Brezhnev regime introduced a number of new components to the value-system of Soviet socialism. In essence, these innovations were designed to consolidate the position of the CPSU at home, to bolster its legitimacy and to sustain the more consensual, conservative approach to societal management. This meant a move away from the more confrontational and radical approaches of Khrushchev. The anti-religious, atheistic campaign was toned down, and the vocational slant to education was also abandoned, being replaced with a more orthodox academic curriculum. Gradually the contours of the Brezhnevite worldview emerged. It was one which sought to synthesize its emphasis on science and technology with nostalgia, conservatism, militarism and the trappings of superpowerdom.

A distinctive feature of the Brezhnevite value system was a revival of the Stalinist approach. First, towards the middle of the 1970s a new personality cult began to grow up around Brezhnev, in which criticisms of Stalin subsided, and the achievements of Brezhnev were excessively praised. Brezhnev appropriated the title that had been bestowed upon Stalin: *vozhd'*. He became General Secretary and Chair of the Praesidium of the Supreme Soviet. The practice of naming streets, towns, etc. after leaders was revived. He awarded himself numerous prizes: the Lenin Peace Prize, the Lenin Prize for Literature. This was no Stalinist cult though. Brezhnev was ridiculed for his intellectual mediocrity in popular satire of the time. The second revival of Stalinist themes saw the re-emergence of Russian nationalism within the official discourse of the state. In the late 1960s, a significant number of intellectuals began to espouse Russian nationalist values. In part this was a response to the flowering of minority nationalism within the other republics. In part it was also an attempt to fill the spiritual void left by the decline in religious faith, and the retreat from the utopianism inherent in Khrushchev's imminent transition to communism. The toning down of Khrushchev's anti-religious campaign has its roots in this Russian nationalist revival: the closure of churches was said to be doing irreparable damage to Russian cultural treasures.[60] But in other respects the state was unable to revive the Stalinist approach, particularly in mobilizing the population for state goals. The attempts to enthuse the population for the task of constructing BAM (the Baikal–Amur Mainline railway) singly failed to excite the revolutionary ardour of the Soviet people, unlike many of the industrial projects of the 1930s.

The revival of Russian nationalism was used by the regime as a form of ideological cement. The focus on the past – especially the Second World War – served to consolidate the regime, and to give it an alternative source of legitimacy as the economy began to slow down towards the end of the 1970s. The attempt to graft Russian nationalist themes onto traditional Marxist–Leninist categories was highly reminiscent of the latter years of the Stalin regime. Cultural policy reflected this conservative bent. Gradually, a constrictive orthodoxy was imposed on literature, arts and history writing. The parameters of official culture were broad. Themes of technological advances were combined with a revival of traditional Russian folk values, embodied in a revival of rural prose that glorified the "lost" rural past. The popularity of the rural prose school – comprising the authors Rasputin, Belov and others – is no surprise to Stites: "The prospect of the disappearance of the peasant way of life . . . induces many to gaze fondly upon the countryside as the last refuge of real Russian values: honesty, simplicity, harmony, stability, family warmth."[61]

The other predominant theme of cultural policy was the extensive use of militaristic symbols, and the closer integration of military-patriotic themes into the everyday life of the Soviet citizen. There was a constant flow of novels concerning the Great Patriotic War. It also emerged in the most unlikely places. In the field of circus entertainment,

> About 80 students were accepted annually from some 3000 applicants to the [circus] academy where they learned all the genres of the trade and the rudiments of Marxist ideology which they were expected to incorporate into their acts. In practice this meant a regular dose of patriotism, war songs and even documentary footage of German atrocities.[62]

Militaristic themes pervaded every aspect of Soviet life. The Soviet ritual calendar had many days devoted to the Soviet armed forces. Ostensibly ideological parades – May Day for instance – became vehicles for displays of military might. Military training was integrated fully into the lives of educational establishments. Overlaying this turn towards militarism was the sense of pride in the superpower status of the USSR. This was manifested in the enormous amount of time and attention devoted to the propagation of the achievements of the Soviet state, especially those activities that reinforced the notions of the superiority of socialism over capitalism. Great political capital was made out of the space race, and the superiority of Soviet technology over that of the West. Similarily the sporting achievements of the Soviet bloc countries appeared to demonstrate in practice the superiority of the Soviet way of life over the capitalist way of life. The economy may have been slowing down, but socialism was still able to outperform capitalism.

The Brezhnev regime remained committed to the core values of Soviet socialism: collectivism, egalitarianism, internationalism. The particular content and interpretation of these components was distinctive to the Brezhnev era. From the early 1970s Soviet scholars had been discussing the idea of a specific "socialist way of life", an idea that was officially adopted by the leadership at the 25th Party Congress in 1976.[63] Its emergence against a backdrop of economic slowdown and agricultural reverses is not without significance. The leadership asserted that the superiority of socialism over capitalism could not be measured solely using the criteria of economic productivity, levels of consumption and so on. The USSR had a number of advantages: its way of life was qualitatively superior to that of the capitalist countries. What were the essential features of this way of life? There was little agreement among Soviet scholars. Brezhnev briefly mentioned some attributes at the 25th Party Congress: collectivism, comradeship, unity and friendship of nations and moral health.[64] However, the specific meanings of these values proved somewhat elusive. In fact it is probably accurate to suggest that these values were defined negatively: the "socialist way of life" was often reduced to little more than a negation of capitalism's features: individualism, selfishness, immorality. The elimination of negative phenomena in Soviet society would leave a "socialist way of life" *in situ.*

The significance of the "socialist way of life" lies in the elite's modification of the productivist ethos of Soviet socialism. The onset of economic problems undermined the Soviet claims that socialism was superior to capitalism and would inevitably supersede it. The leadership had to find a way to tone down the consumerist expectations of the Soviet population while buttressing the superiority of the socialist system. Soviet ideological pronouncements noted that a narrow focus on increasing the material standard of living tended to create acquisitive and proprietorial attitudes, which were inappropriate in a Developed Socialist society. Consequently, it was necessary to reaffirm collectivist, fraternal values within socialist society. The notion of a "socialist way of life", with its implications of little more than moral superiority for socialism, is illustrative of the growing pessimism of the Brezhnev leadership, and of the continued dominance of the impulse to conserve and consolidate the existing system. The underlying constructivist ethos – of shaping the values and outlook of Soviet citizens – remained. But the ends had shifted from the creation of a communist society, to the buttressing of the position of the Soviet state.

Developed Socialism and the Soviet model

Developed Socialism sought to adjust and adapt the essential traits of the Soviet system to the demands of modernization. Its emphases were upon stability, gradual, evolutionary change and the need to "perfect" the existing institutions. Its chosen methods were incrementalist and technocratic. Organizationally it stressed centralism, hierarchy and the close, conscious management of social processes. In terms of its underlying philosophy, Developed Socialism lay firmly within the traditional model of Soviet socialism. The themes of rationalism and constructivism were embodied in the belief in "social engineering" which underscored Developed Socialism. It was possible consciously to plan the "construction" of a socialist society. Moreover, the plan to divert two Siberian rivers in order to irrigate vast areas of land illustrated the lingering tenacity of the Bolshevik belief in the ability of humanity to overcome any obstacle in its attempts to construct the new society. The realization of a complete "socialist way of life", with its own morality and culture, and of a "New Soviet Personality" could be engineered on the initiative of the party. Personalities could be moulded through education, propaganda and training. Although, the communist utopia was indefinitely postponed, Developed Socialism embodied the technocratic, scientific, norms of orthodox Soviet socialism.

What specific meaning and content did Developed Socialism ascribe to the core features of the Soviet model of socialism? In economic terms, the essential features of the command economy were restored and consolidated: central planning, state ownership, managerial authority within the factory. The attempts to bring about changes were mere adaptations of the existing structures (the Production-Association reform of 1973), and modifications to its *modus operandi* (increasing use of computers/mathematical techniques). The critical issue was that these innovations did not replace the process of target-fulfilled by quota, but co-existed with them. In terms of economic priorities, the era of Developed Socialism maintained the more balanced post-Stalinist approach, investing heavily in agriculture and consumer goods. The traditional emphasis upon heavy industry did not disappear. It metamorphosed into a growing impetus to apply the advances in science and technology to the productive process, in order to increase the efficiency and productivity of the economy, laying the basis for further economic advances and the modernization of the armed forces.

In the political sphere, the approach adopted by Brezhnev synthesized a variety of themes. The party retained its central role as the agency of social transformation and management, continuing the Khrushchevite revival of the party. However, the precise exercise of this leading role differed fundamentally from Khrushchev's. Instead of adopting the role of campaigner, mobilizer, energizer in tandem with the mass activism of the population, the party adopted a technocratic, depoliticized approach. Political leadership and decision-making was about finding the most rational, efficient means to manage society, not about the growth of public self-government. This was distinct from the Stalinist approach. Although repression increased, and the KGB played a greater role in the running of the system, there was no return to mass terror, and the CPSU was the central political organ. This was distinct from the Leninist synthesis, as the popular mobilizational strand was absent from the politics of Developed Socialism. The persistence of central authority – the party and the state – long into the future, emphasized the continuing hegemony of statism and centralism in Bolshevik discourse.

In socio-cultural terms, the traditional Bolshevik commitment to collectivism, egalitarianism, productivism and proletarian internationalism continued to be mitigated by the ongoing need of the state to legitimate itself in the eyes of its own population and of the world socialist system, and to maintain itself in power. Peaceful co-existence, privilege, consumerism and the "socialist way of life" were combined with militarism, nationalism, traditional Russian folk culture and technocracy to create an eclectic hotch-potch of values underpinning Developed Socialism.

Postscript: Developed Socialism after Brezhnev

The Brezhnev era delivered a period of relative economic prosperity, political stability and a reduction in international tension. However, many social, economic and political problems had accumulated in Soviet society by the time of Brezhnev's death in 1982. Growth rates were slowing appreciably. According to a range of economic indicators, the USSR was slipping down the league table. Corruption was rife. The leadership were ageing, and personnel turnover was slowing down. Massive environmental problems were accumulating. The workforce was increasingly cynical, apathetic and alienated. Alcoholism, drug addiction and other symptoms of social and moral decay became apparent. Ostrich-like, the regime were unwilling or unable to confront these problems. As Stites asserts, "instead of answers and solutions, it offered smug slogans about progress".[65]

The succession of Andropov in 1982 gave elite backing to a (limited) theoretical rejuvenation, although this process had already been set in train by the time of Brezhnev's death. This can be seen in the debate on contradictions that occurred among Soviet social scientists from 1981 to 1984.[66] This debate was primarily a response to the 1980–81 Solidarity crisis in Poland. This provided a great challenge for Marxist–Leninist theorists who had to come to terms with how to conceive of such crises in a supposedly crisis-free socialist society, which was progressing towards communism. This debate played an important role in undermining Developed Socialism, as it called into question the ability of the existing dominant concepts to explain the nature of Soviet society in the early 1980s. The growing plethora of problems was increasingly at variance with the view, propounded by Developed Socialism, of a crisis-free and progressive advance towards communism. This debate on contradictions was the first major step in the theoretical de-Brezhnevization of Soviet society.

The accession of Andropov brought about a shift in the orientation of the regime, which now was faced with the reality of dealing with the stagnation of the latter Brezhnev years. Indeed it was Andropov who set in motion the process of de-Brezhnevizing Soviet society, a process that eventually led to *perestroika*. Some of the more general features of Andropov's brief tenure as General Secretary have been fairly well documented.[67] Economically and socially, Andropov was viewed by some Western analysts as a "'progressive': flexible, undogmatic, conscious of the need for reform in many economic and social areas and committed to *détente*".[68] While many of his initial policy pronouncements were concerned with the area of increasing discipline (as a way of promoting greater economic efficiency from within the system: i.e. stricter curbs on alcoholism, absenteeism, etc.), he was also seen as a figure who favoured more fundamental changes (in terms of agricultural and economic reform) to deal with the problem of falling growth rates and consistently poor harvests.[69]

Andropov's views of the socio-political structure greatly contributed to the process of undermining the worldview of Brezhnevite socialism, which tended to view socialism as a gradual crisis-free linear progression towards communism. He tended to view Soviet society more critically (or was more prepared to express his views) and on the whole was more realistic and frank about its shortcomings, and consequently about the urgency of change. This more realistic and critical approach gave rise to a number of interesting themes, many of which conflicted with the dominant themes of Developed Socialism. First, it allowed for the possibility of clashes, tensions and crises. Secondly, there were clearly problems within the Soviet system that could not be rationalized as "vestiges" of capitalism, but which were attributable to shortcomings within the socialist system itself. Thirdly, the process of the growing social homogeneity of the Soviet population clearly had a long distance to traverse, in the light of the divergent interests and tensions that existed, or could arise. On a general level Andropov clearly contributed to the undermining of Developed Socialism, by questioning (implicitly) the linear crisis-free view of socialist social development.

These emphases are reinforced when Andropov's specific views of Developed Socialism are analyzed. In contrast to Brezhnev who, by the 24th Congress, tended to view the attainment of a Developed Socialist society as something of a *fait accompli*, or as an accomplished theoretical fact, Andropov, while accepting that a Developed Socialist society had been reached, was moving away from this position. He brought into question the level of progress attained by Soviet society, as well as the extent of the theoretical comprehension of social processes in Soviet society.[70] According to Andropov, the Soviet Union had reached only the beginning of "the long historical phase" of mature socialism. The task now was to "perfect" Developed Socialism: this necessarily meant revealing some of the problems and difficulties ("subjective" and "objective") that had to be overcome in the process of "perfection". In this way, Andropov was able to move away from Brezhnev's emphasis on the consolidation of what had been achieved (implicit in his representation of Developed Socialism as an accomplished fact) and to emphasize in turn the need for changes and major improvements, both to forestall conflicts and to progress towards communism.[71]

Andropov also questioned the ability of the existing theoretical concepts, embodied in Developed Socialism, to comprehend the nature of Soviet society in the 1980s. In a speech to the party veterans, he asserted that, "frankly speaking, we have not yet properly studied the society in which we live and work and have not fully disclosed its inherent laws".[72] In an attempt to rectify this situation and to overcome the widespread theoretical sterility and dogmatism in Soviet theory at this time, Andropov advocated the "creative use of ideology". If Soviet theory was to be relevant to the problems confronting society, it could not rest upon outdated and inadequate formulae, but had to be developed rigorously in line with practical developments. It was clear from Andropov's own analysis of Soviet society that theoretical developments were necessary to take account of the new problems and conditions. As the dominant ideological and theoretical concept of a mature socialist society, Developed Socialism was clearly inadequate (or was being inadequately interpreted by Soviet scholars) and would have to be included in any theoretical rejuvenation that occurred.[73] Andropov's untimely death meant that these themes were unable to be thoroughly pursued. However, he clearly played a vital role in initiating the de-Brezhnevization of Soviet society and in undermining Developed Socialism.

It is probably fair to characterize Chernenko's period in office as a hybrid: neither a return to Brezhnev's policies and values, nor a direct continuation of what Andropov had started. What seems to have occurred is that the trends inaugurated by Andropov slowed appreciably under Chernenko, without undergoing a significant change in direction. For example, continuity was maintained through the campaign targeted against corruption. Conversely, the decentralization of industrial decision-making was implemented in a watered-down fashion.[74] Teague also emphasizes that Chernenko fell back on Marxist–Leninist slogans as a substitute for Andropov's labour discipline campaign: seeking greater effort and efficiency through increased exhortations and propaganda campaigns (commemorating the 50th anniversary of Stakhanovism).[75] Similarily, Chernenko shared many of Andropov's perceptions of Developed Socialism. Chernenko started from the assertion that Marxism–Leninism requires "creative development" and must oppose all forms of "dogmatism and ossification". In particular, in stressing the need for ideological flexibility, Chernenko seems to have been undermining the ideological legacy of Suslov (the chief ideologist of the Brezhnev years) by urging a reassessment of "seemingly indisputed theses".[76] This led Chernenko to reach many conclusions similar to those reached by Andropov. The USSR had entered the stage of Developed Socialism, although they were only at the beginning of this prolonged period. The attainment of Developed Socialism, while being an implicit recognition of the mature and developed nature of the Soviet system, should not, according to Chernenko, be interpreted either as signifying its total perfection, or lead to the idealizing of what has been achieved. In this way Chernenko was able to advocate realistic and sober assessments of Soviet society and of the need to "perfect" and "improve" all aspects of Soviet society.[77]

The continuities with Brezhnev, both for Andropov and Chernenko, are far more evident than the changes though. The principles and underlying philosophy of the traditional model of Soviet socialism remained virtually untouched by Andropov and

Chernenko's innovations. The arrival of Gorbachev as General Secretary brought a radical critique of Brezhnevite socialism, and ultimately a complete transformation of the principles and philosophy of the Soviet model of socialism.

Notes

1. R. V. Daniels, *A documentary history of communism* (London: I. B. Tauris, 1985), p. 354.
2. Details on Khrushchev's overthrow can be found in W. Hahn, "Khrushchev's ouster", *Problems of Communism* **40**, 1991; R. Medvedev & Z. Medvedev, *Khrushchev: the years in power* (Oxford: Oxford University Press, 1977), pp. 168–89.
3. R. Sakwa, *Soviet politics* (London: Routledge, 1989), pp. 84–6; A. Nove, *An economic history of the USSR* (London: Penguin, 1992), pp. 371–6.
4. M. Lewin, *Political undercurrents in Soviet economic debates* (London: Pluto Press, 1975), pp. 135–6.
5. Ibid., pp. 183–5; Nove, *An economic history*, pp. 374–6.
6. J. Keep, *Last of the Empires* (Oxford: Oxford University Press, 1995), pp. 233–7.
7. It was first mentioned by Brezhnev in 1967. See, "Pyat 'desyat let' velikh pobed sotsialisma", in *Leninskim kursom*, vol. 12 (Moscow: Progress, 1970). For Western analyses, see A. Evans, *Soviet Marxism–Leninism: the decline of an ideology* (Westport: Praeger, 1993), pp. 105–39; D. Kelley (ed.), *Soviet politics in the Brezhnev era* (New York: Praeger, 1986); D. Kelley, "Developed Socialism: a political formula for the Brezhnev era", in *Developed Socialism in the Soviet bloc*, J. Seroka & S. Simon (eds) (Boulder: Westview Press, 1982).
8. F. Burlatsky in *Pravda*, 21 December 1966, p. 2.
9. The Khrushchevite programme was ignored in official discourse until the discussions surrounding the new Constitution in 1976/7, when there was a mini-revival of utopianism in Soviet discourse.
10. R. Kosolapov, *Developed Socialism: theory and practice* (Moscow: Politizdat, 1982), p. 62. See also, A. Butenko, "O razvitom sotsialisticheskom obshchestve", *Kommunist* **6**, 1972, pp. 48–58; F. Burlatsky, "Politicheskaya sistema razvitogo sotsializma", *Kommunist* **12**, 1979, pp. 62–73.
11. Evans, *Soviet Marxism–Leninism*, pp. 108–9.
12. P. N. Fedoseev, "Postroenie razvitogo sotsialisticheskogo obshchestve v SSSR – torzhestvo idei leninisma", *Kommunist* **2**, 1974, p. 18.
13. L. I. Brezhnev, *Report to the 24th CPSU Congress 1971* (Moscow: Progress, 1971), p. 24.

14. J. Cooper, "The STR in Soviet theory", in *Technology and communist culture*, F. J. Fleron (ed.) (New York: Praeger, 1977), p. 167.
15. Ibid., pp. 167–75.
16. E. P. Hoffmann & R. F. Laird, *Technocratic socialism: the USSR in the advanced industrial era* (Durham: Duke University Press, 1985), pp. 12–16.
17. Ibid., p. 16.
18. Ibid., pp. 8–18.
19. Ibid., p. 60. Other works on scientific management include, V. Afanas'ev, "Nekotorie aspekti nauchnogo upravlenie obshchestvom v SSSR", in *Sotsialniye i politicheskiye problemy razvitogo sotsializm* (Prague: Mir i sotsialisma, 1978). Afanas'ev, *Nauchnoe upravlenie obshchestvom* (Moscow: Progress, 1971). Afanas'ev, *Nauchno-tekhnicheskaya revolutsiya, upravlenie, obrazovanie* (Moscow: Progress, 1975).
20. V. Afans'ev, *Soviet democracy in the period of Developed Socialism* (Moscow: Progress, 1979), p. 131.
21. D. R. Kelley, *The politics of Developed Socialism* (Westport, Greenwood Press, 1986), pp. 110–15.
22. Ibid., pp. 139–43.
23. Nove, *An economic history*, pp. 376–7.
24. A. Nove, *Stalinism and after* (Boston: Unwin Hyman, 1989), p. 166.
25. Keep, *Last of the Empires*, pp. 244–9.
26. Ibid., pp. 249–51.
27. Ibid., pp. 251–2.
28. Ibid., pp. 237–8.
29. Ibid., p. 238.
30. A. Nove, *The Soviet economic system* (Boston: Allen Unwin, 1986), pp. 69–74.
31. M. McAuley, *Soviet politics 1917–91* (Oxford: Oxford University Press, 1992), p. 86.
32. E. Chekharin, *The Soviet political system under Developed Socialism* (Moscow: Novosti, 1976), pp. 251–67; Kosolapov, *Developed Socialism*, pp. 162–71.
33. Kelley, "Developed Socialism: a political formula", pp. 10–18.
34. Kosolapov, *Developed Socialism*, chs 2, 7; V. Kas'yanenko, *KPSS: organizator stroitelstva razvitogo sotsializma* (Moscow: Politizdat, 1974), ch. 5.
35. P. Cocks, "Retooling the directed society: administrative modernisation and Developed Socialism", in *Political developments in Eastern Europe*, J. Triska & P. Cocks (eds) (New York: Praeger, 1977), pp. 65–70.
36. Hoffmann & Laird, *Technocratic socialism*, p. 41.
37. Brezhnev, *Report*, p. 36.
38. S. E. Finer (ed.), *Five constitutions* (Harmondsworth: Penguin, 1979), pp. 149–50.

39. J. Hough & M. Fainsod, *How the Soviet Union is governed* (Cambridge, Mass.: Harvard University Press, 1979), pp. 422–3.
40. Keep, *Last of the Empires*, p. 260.
41. V. Bunce, "The political economy of the Brezhnev era", *British Journal of Political Science* **13**, 1983, pp. 129–58; G. Breslauer, "On the adaptability of welfare-state authoritarianism", in *The Soviet polity in the modern era*, E. Hoffmann & R. Laird (eds) (New York: Aldine, 1984); J. Hough, "The Soviet Union: petrification or pluralism?", in *Problems of Communism* **21**(2), 1972, pp. 25–45.
42. Hough & Fainsod, *How the Soviet Union is governed*, pp. 298–9.
43. Ibid., p. 200; R. Sharlet, "The new Soviet constitution", in *Problems of Communism* **26**, 1977, pp. 1–24.
44. C. Lane, *The rites of rulers* (Cambridge: Cambidge University Press 1981), appendix B: The Soviet ritual calendar.
45. M. McAuley, *Soviet politics*, p. 85.
46. Adams, *Citizen inspectors*, pp. 94–174.
47. Ibid., pp. 151–63.
48. Hosking, *A history of the Soviet Union*, pp. 413–15.
49. Finer, *Five constitutions*, p. 163.
50. Ibid., p. 158.
51. M. Matthews, *Privilege in the Soviet Union* (London: Allen & Unwin, 1978), pp. 91–114.
52. Ibid., pp. 119–26.
53. J. P. Willerton, *Patronage and politics in the USSR* (Cambridge: Cambridge University Press, 1992).
54. Keep, *Last of the Empires*, pp. 228–31.
55. Ibid., pp. 252–5.
56. Evans, *Soviet Marxism–Leninism*, pp. 134–5.
57. M. Buckley, *Women and ideology in the Soviet Union* (New York: Harvester Wheatsheaf, 1989), pp. 161–90.
58. S. Shenfield, *The nuclear predicament. Explorations in Soviet ideology* (London: Routledge, 1987), p. 25.
59. Sakwa, *Soviet politics*, p. 280.
60. Keep, *Last of the Empires*, pp. 284–300.
61. R. Stites, *Russian popular culture* (Cambridge: Cambridge University Press, 1992), p. 150.
62. Ibid., p. 164.
63. Evans, *Soviet Marxism–Leninism*, pp. 141–50.
64. L. Brezhnev, *Report to the 25th Congress 1976* (Moscow: Progress, 1976), p. 57.
65. Stites, *Russian popular culture*, p. 149.
66. An excellent summary of this debate can be found in E. Kux, "Contradictions in Soviet socialism", in *Problems of Communism* **33**, 1984, pp. 1–27.

67. A. Brown, "Andropov: discipline and reform", in *Problems of Communism*, Jan/Feb 1983, pp. 18–31; I. Zemtsov, "Andropov", *Crossroads* **3**, 1983.
68. Brown, "Andropov", p. 25.
69. Ibid., pp. 24–6.
70. Y. Andropov, "Ucheniye Karla marksa i nekotoriye aspekty stroitel'stva sotsializma v SSSR", in *Kommunist* **3**, 1983, pp. 9–23.
71. Andropov, in *Pravda*, 16 June 1983, pp. 1–2.
72. Andropov, in *Pravda*, 16 August 1983, p. 1.
73. Andropov, "Ucheniye", p. 19.
74. E. Teague, "Chernenko's first year", in *Radio Liberty Research Bulletin*, 46/85, 2 February 1985, p. 2.
75. Ibid., p. 3.
76. K. Chernenko, cited in M. Zlotnik, "Chernenko's platform", in *Problems of Communism* **31**, 1982, pp. 70–74.
77. K. Chernenko, "Urgent questions of the party's ideological and mass-political work", in *Current Digest of the Soviet Press* **35**(24), 1984, pp. 1–3.

PART FOUR

The demise of scientific socialism

CHAPTER NINE

Gorbachev and Soviet socialism: The rise and fall of Humane Democratic Socialism

Old Soviet Adage:

There's no unemployment, yet nobody works.
Nobody works, yet the plan still gets fulfilled.
The plan gets fulfilled, yet there's still nothing in the shops.
There's nothing in the shops, yet every fridge is full.
Every fridge is full, yet everyone still complains.
Everyone complains, yet the same people keep getting
elected.

Introduction

The death of Chernenko in 1985 brought Mikhail Gorbachev to power. His period in office witnessed a series of profound changes, which transformed the global political, economic and ideological landscape. Within the Soviet context, the reform process of *perestroika* or restructuring, led to a process of radical change that culminated in the collapse of the communist system and the end of the Soviet Union. Somewhat hidden amid this swirling vortex of change was a fundamental reconceptualization of the traditional Soviet model of socialism. Originating in a critical reappraisal of Developed Socialism within a new version of the Third Party Programme, this new concept of Soviet socialism – Humane

Democratic Socialism – emerged in 1989/90, and was substantiated within official Soviet discourse in the Draft Party Programme of July/August 1991. The combined impact of these "revisions" was to abandon the core features of the orthodox Soviet model, and to bring about a fundamental shift in the worldview of the CPSU. The orthodox commitment to scientific socialism was replaced with an ethical, humanistic approach. Gorbachev social-democratized Bolshevism.

The structure of this chapter traces the origins and development of this new concept of socialism. It is not organized chronologically, as the dismantling of the old form of socialism occurred concurrent with the elaboration of the new. Instead, the following analysis sets out the variety of factors – theoretical, political, economic, social and international – that shaped Humane Democratic Socialism, before setting out the essential features of the centrepiece of Gorbachev's ideological renewal.

Why a new concept of socialism?

The first signs of a debate concerning a new model of socialism emerged in October 1988. Ideology chief Vadim Medvedev wrote an article in *Pravda*, which was derived from a speech at an international social science conference on the contemporary meaning of socialism.[1] Within a year, there had been something of an intellectual flowering, which culminated in Gorbachev's "*Sotsialisticheskaya ideya i revolutsionnaya perestroika*" (The socialist idea and revolutionary perestroika) in November 1989, which set out his view of the essential values and structures of a future Soviet socialist society. This in turn laid the groundwork for the CPSU's platform for the 28th Congress "Towards Humane, Democratic Socialism".[2] Why did this debate occur?

The search for a new model of socialism was the logical outcome of two interlinked processes. The first was the practical process of restructuring Soviet society. The reforms proved to be far more radical and comprehensive than the leadership initially envisaged. As the extent of the problems was revealed, the need for a radical transformation became apparent. This in turn meant a re-evaluation of the foundations of the Soviet theoretical edifice: the nature of socialism.

The problem was that the dominant conception of socialism ante *perestroika* was a participant factor in the crisis within Soviet society. The vast catalogue of problems that had accumulated by the early 1980s – falling economic growth rates, growing technological lag from the West, a plethora of negative social phenomena, growing social passivity and inertia, highly bureaucratized and formalistic political processes – required a radical solution. However, Developed Socialism as a doctrine was unable to supply this. It sought to adjust and adapt the essential traits of the Soviet system to the demands of modernization, emphasizing stability and gradual evolutionary change. As Gorbachev's solution entailed an increasingly radical programme, involving the attempt to unleash a (managed) process of popular initiative and creativity, Developed Socialism became increasingly disfunctional in this respect.[3] Developed Socialism was also unable to confront some of the contemporary problems common to all social systems: the implementation of the Scientific and Technological Revolution, environmental survival and, also, how to conceive of the role of the individual in society. The process of renewal, and the simultaneous growth of global problems were gradually revealing the theoretically bankrupt and historically exhausted nature of Soviet Brezhnevite/neo-Stalinist socialism. By mid-1988, it was clear that the next step would be to start the process of reconceptualization.

The uncertainty engendered by the changes also had an impact. Questions were asked in journals, newspapers and among ordinary citizens. Where are we going? What will our society look like if these changes succeed? Are we not renouncing socialism? The new concept of socialism emerged partly in response to these questions. To give *perestroika* legitimacy, direction and content, it became necessary to provide a sound theoretical basis for the changes and to affirm in the eyes of the population that the reforms were more than just a collection of *ad hoc* policies. The leadership had a definite aim, and a strategy for pursuing it.

The important thing to note about this debate was that it was not just an abstract discussion about the meaning of socialism at the end of the twentieth century. It was also a political project, tied inextricably to the processes of political and economic renewal, and this had major implications for the reconceptualization of Soviet socialism.[4] The content of a "renewed" Soviet socialism was shaped as much by "political" factors, by the necessity of bringing about a successful transition to an efficient economic system, as by the reanimation or reinterpretation of socialist values and principles. This proved to be a source of considerable "tension" within Soviet socialism, as the values considered to be an integral part of the socialist project struggled for hegemony with the demands of creating an efficient socio-economic system. The outworking of this tension between instrumentalism and idealism was to play an important part in shaping the final form and content of Soviet socialism. There was also another tension at play. While attempting to combine successful reform with doctrinal purity, *perestroika* had also to maintain the CPSU in power. This imposed on the new view of socialism that emerged the need to promote change while defending some of the "old" principles and values of Soviet socialism, as they provided a rationalization of the party's role.

Soviet socialism in transition: from Developed Socialism to Humane Democratic Socialism (via Developing Socialism)

The central concepts and values of renewed Soviet socialism grew out of the theoretical and practical developments after 1985. The framework was initially conditioned by the normal process of leadership succession in the USSR: an attack on the legacy of the predecessor.

The decline and fall of Developed Socialism

The immediate measures to de-Brezhnevize Soviet society struck mainly at the most obvious aspects of corruption and degeneration among the personnel. Attacks on the privileges of the party and state elites were increased, and there was a steady flow of personal criticism of Brezhnev, his leadership style, his capabilities and his achievements. *Pravda* categorized his rule as one of "flattery, obsequiousness, sycophancy and fawning".[5] There were clear political reasons for these measures, as Gorbachev sought a scapegoat for problems and a means of bolstering his own authority. But the analysis swiftly moved away from the shortcomings of the system, and from Brezhnev himself, towards an attempt to discover the reasons why there was a pre-crisis situation in the Soviet system by the early 1980s. The initial response was to abandon Developed Socialism and elaborate the concept of stagnation (*zastoi'*).[6]

As de-Brezhnevization proceeded, Developed Socialism was emptied of its content, abandoned and replaced (initially) by the concept of *uskorenie* (the "acceleration of socio-economic development"). A key stage in this process was the publication of a revised version of the Third Party Programme in 1986. The 26th CPSU Congress in 1981 had called for a revised programme to be drawn up. The resulting document paid scant attention to the concept of Developed Socialism. A close reading of the text reveals that the concept of *uskorenie* now occupied a central place in Soviet discourse:

> The Third Programme of the CPSU in its present updated edition is a programme for the planned and all-round perfection of socialism, for Soviet society's further advance to communism through the country's accelerated socio-economic development.[7]

Marginalization of Developed Socialism was followed swiftly by criticism and abandonment. In his speech to the 27th CPSU Congress, Gorbachev outlined,

> It is proper to recall that the thesis on Developed Socialism has gained currency in our country as a reaction to the simplistic ideas about the ways and period of time for carrying out the tasks of communist construction. Subsequently however, the accents in the interpretation of Developed Socialism were gradually shifted. Things were not infrequently reduced to just registering successes. It became a peculiar vindication of sluggishness in solving outstanding problems. Today . . . this approach has become unacceptable.[8]

On this reading, although Developed Socialism was an appropriate corrective to Khrushchev's timetable for the direct transition to communism, the problems lay in subsequent interpretations of it. It became an inherently conservative doctrine that fostered complacency and operated by extolling the positive aspects of Soviet society. The resulting theoretical sterility and ideological dogmatism glossed over any problems that existed, and so hindered their resolution. Finally, Developed Socialism produced among the population a mentality of stagnation and apathy that snuffed out creativity and stifled the emergence of dynamism. The need for radical change and to impart creativity and initiative meant removing the concept that seemed to be entirely opposed to these priorities.[9] After the 27th Congress references to Developed Socialism gradually disappeared.

A qualitative turning-point in the treatment of the Brezhnev era occurred at the January plenum of the Central Committee in 1987.[10] As *perestroika* widened its scope, so the basic structures and worldview of Brezhnevite socialism increasingly came under attack. The immediate consequence of this was the emergence of the concept of *zastoi* as a characterization of the Brezhnev years. This concept was at first applied to the late 1970s and early 1980s. However it was quickly extended to cover the whole of the Brezhnev era. This marked a shift towards an analysis that sought to comprehend the "objective", root causes of the problems of the Soviet system which emerged under Brezhnev. It raised some uncomfortable questions for the new leadership. Was stagnation purely a Brezhnevite or post-Stalinist phenomenon, or was it something inherent within the Soviet model? In this way, the process of de-Brezhnevization inexorably evolved into a re-evaluation of Stalin and Stalinism.

At the 1987 January plenum, Gorbachev catalogued in detail the various ills of the latter Brezhnev period (as well as for the first time identifying the situation in the USSR as a "crisis"). The crux of his approach was to relate the crisis of the late 1970s and early 1980s to a much wider context: the theoretical and practical legacy of the 1930s and 1940s, and the inability or unwillingness of subsequent leaders to address these issues.[11] This speech laid the foundations for a series of debates and articles addressing the origins and nature of the "braking mechanism" (the configuration of factors causing the slowdown in economic growth, and the rise of the related negative socio-political phenomena). Soviet scholars began to debate and discuss the nature of the Stalinist system and its evolution under Brezhnev.

One of the keynote contributions was from Gavriil Popov, who coined the phrase the "Administrative System". This was characterized as a mechanism of government and economic management based upon administrative methods, which was excessively centralized, hierarchical and bureaucratic.[12] This idea provided a starting-point for a radical critique of the form and content of Brezhnevite socialism. Many of the themes that Popov's analysis highlighted (the nature of the socialist management apparatus, overcentralization, hierarchy, the stifling of creativity, the growth of passivity and inertia) were developed further by Soviet scholars in their analysis of the braking mechanism. Towards the end of 1987 and at the beginning of 1988 a series of articles and discussions appeared, concerned with various aspects of the Brezhnev years. The fullest discussion of the braking mechanism was contained in the pages of *Voprosi Istorii KPSS* at the beginning of 1988.[13] This was the documentation of a discussion that had been sponsored by the Central Committee of the CPSU, held at the Institute of Marxism–Leninism.[14] The main conclusion from this debate was that any analysis of the braking mechanism had to take account of the existence, to a greater or lesser extent, of a link between the Stalinist system and the system which crystallized under Brezhnev. It became clear to many academics and reformers that to eliminate the problems that accumulated under Brezhnev required measures which addressed the basic elements of the system, laid under Stalin, not just the innovations introduced by Brezhnev.

The critique of the operation of the traditional model embraced the following themes: (a) a rejection of "barracks" or "regimental" socialism which was authoritarian and hierarchical; (b) a rejection of the dehumanizing, bureaucratic, statist form of socialism in which people perceived themselves to be mere "cogs" (*vintiki*) in a huge machine; (c) a repudiation of a form of socialism which lacked a clear moral underpinning, had no spiritual content, and no respect for the dignity or cultural requirements of a person; (d) a rejection of socialism in which one group or body exercised an ideational monopoly and in which there was no genuine pluralism of opinions or openness with regard to the dissemination and availability of information.

Criticism was especially directed against the role of the state and the amount of centralization in the system. State ownership was equated with "no-one's" ownership, contributing to the growth of alienation. The commitment to collectivism and egalitarianism had become little more than crude levelling, creating grey uniformity and drab conformity. This critique was extended to the basic philosophical themes of Soviet socialism. The criticism of the neglect of the individual, and of their moral and spiritual needs reflected the general dissatisfaction with the productivist one-dimensional view of individuals being shaped primarily by their material conditions of existence. On the other hand some core elements of the traditional model remained untouched: the leading role of the party, a belief in the superiority of central planning over the market, and a general philosophy marked by rationalism and constructivism.

The theory and practice of perestroika

The content of the new concept of socialism also arose out of the reform process itself. In elaborating a series of measures to overcome the crisis facing the USSR, the CPSU embarked on a journey that led to some fundamental revisions of the core features of the traditional model. These measures had a significant impact in shaping the renewal of Soviet socialism. The catalogue of problems to which *perestroika* was directed have been well documented elsewhere, and scarcely need repeating here.[15] The problem for the leadership was that the answer to the economic stagnation was not just economic growth, but economic growth of a new kind: based around efficiency, productivity, greater product quality and the increased application of new technology. In the Soviet context though this meant more than just the modernization of an outdated and inefficient productive process: the problem was also rooted in the cultural and institutional legacy of Stalinism.[16] The gradual radicalization of *perestroika* revealed that many of the core features of the traditional model of Soviet socialism were a constituent part of the problem.

The search for remedies for the ills of the Soviet economy began along similar lines to those employed by Andropov: campaigns to extract greater productivity from the workforce (anti-corruption, anti-alcohol, quality control) with measures to streamline the bureaucracy. The deepening of the reforms led to organizational changes, similar to those outlined in the 1965 Kosygin reforms: greater autonomy for managers and more scope for worker participation were included in the 1987 Law on the State Enterprise.

It seemed a possibility at one point that a form of worker self-management might have emerged.[17] This decree also included measures to allow loss-making firms to be declared bankrupt. The deepening economic problems in 1988 and 1989 led to more far-reaching reassessments of the core features of Soviet socialism. Alternatives to state ownership began to be proposed and discussed. Co-operatives were allowed to operate. Individuals were allowed to provide services. The taboos on hired labour were gradually removed. The market (either in combination with, or instead of, central planning) began to be viewed in a more positive light.

Perestroika was distinguished from previous attempts at reform by its attempts to combine political and economic changes. Gorbachev sought to integrate popular participation and to revive Soviet democracy in order to facilitate the changes in the economy. The rapid progress of political reform demonstrates the dynamic nature of the internal momentum generated by the democratization process. In January 1987, a "watershed" plenum for political reform occurred. Its proposals, which at the time seemed fairly radical, included: electoral reforms (possibility of secret ballots for party secretary posts); contested (multi-candidature) elections to the Soviets; greater popular involvement at all stages of the election campaign; elections in factories for managers; and a greater role for legislative organs over their executive counterparts.[18] At the 19th Party Conference in June 1988 it was deemed necessary to deepen the political reforms. The role of the Soviets was to be upgraded, allowing them greater autonomy of action by separating them from the influence of the party. In turn, the CPSU was to have its internal processes democratized and its wider role in society reduced to broad ideological and political tasks (as opposed to day-to-day involvement in local social and economic affairs).[19]

By the spring of 1990, events had overtaken Gorbachev's original vision of a democratized socialist pluralism within a one-party state. The CPSU began to be seen as part of the problem, not the solution. In March 1990, the constitutional guarantee of the leading role of the party, article 6, was abandoned. The political system appeared to have a distinctly "westernized" look: an embryonic parliamentary system, with the separation of powers, checks and balances, the rule of law, an executive Presidency, political pluralism. A multi-party system was emerging, fitfully by 1991.[20] The reform process did not just criticize the negative aspects of Soviet socialism. It also began to develop alternative policies and new structures, and these fed into the debates on the shape of the new concept of socialism.

Perestroika was a time of radical conceptual innovation, as well as of political, economic and social change. The emergence of new concepts and ideas to tackle the vast catalogue of problems had a profound impact upon the form and content of Soviet socialism Gorbachev-style. The emergence in April 1985 of the strategy of "The acceleration of socio-economic development" marked the first appearance of new theoretical concepts designed to confront the problems of Soviet society.[21] The overall objective was the transition of Soviet society to a qualitatively new condition. *Uskorenie*, as a concept, was concerned above all with raising the rate of economic growth. However, it was to be a new quality of growth: efficient, productive and intensive, and also a wider package of measures dealing with the political and social aspects of economic reform. *Uskorenie*, as a result, brought forth a number of concepts.

The most well known idea is that of *perestroika* or restructuring.[22] Although initially quite limited in scope, it evolved and developed into a fundamental concept touching all aspects of Soviet society (in sometimes unexpected ways). Indeed, Gorbachev began to talk of *perestroika* as a "revolution", "I would equate the word *perestroika* with the word 'revolution' . . . the reforms mapped out . . . are a genuine revolution in the entire system of relations in society."[23] *Perestroika* also sheltered three important concepts that played a key role in reshaping the philosophical and normative basis of Soviet socialism: the "human factor"; *glasnost'* (openness); and *demokratizatsiya* (democratization). The "human factor" contained elements that were clearly instrumental to the reforms, and themes which fed into the debates on renewing Soviet socialism. As a part of the reform process, the "human factor" was a vital component, helping to stimulate policies that allowed the workers to feel as if they were in charge of their workplace, and so gave them a greater moral and material interest in the outcome of their work. Trying to encourage popular participation, personal independence, hard work and individual initiative was viewed by the leadership as a way of overcoming the mentality of dependency and formalism, by allowing the population simultaneously to alter the institutional framework of society, and their own values and attitudes.

Conceptually speaking, though, the general ethos underpinning the adoption of the "human factor" was quite revealing. The Soviet population was now deemed to have a diversity of interests that had to be taken into account in the formation of policy.[24] This had major implications for a system that was based around the rule by an elite who claimed to know and be pursuing the "true" interests of the Soviet population, and was a significant shift in Soviet thinking. The recognition of diversity was a necessary precondition for the legitimation and acceptance of a pluralistic political and economic milieu. More generally, the turn towards the human being as an individual, as an active subject in the historical process, can be seen as the start of the reaction against the dehumanizing, alienating aspects of neo-Stalinist state socialism.

Glasnost' played a pivotal role in the reform process. The merits of a frank, honest, critical appraisal of the past and the present became apparent. The reassessment of Soviet history, and especially of Stalin and Stalinism, of NEP and war communism, was an important self-cognitive tool in the attempt to understand their own society better.[25] Of particular interest was the positive appraisals of two previous eras – NEP and the Khrushchev leadership – which were both seen as progressive times that were reactions against the excessive state power and centralization of war communism and Stalinism, respectively. Moreover, the respective reforms under NEP and Khrushchev – broadly liberalizing and participatory – also occurred within a framework of one-party rule, giving historical legitimacy to Gorbachev's project. *Glasnost'* also contributed to the attempt to destroy both the old system, with its peculiar institutional immobilism and mentality of dependency and apathy, and the opposition to the newly emerging system. A fundamental precondition for the emergence of democratic participation and popular initiative and creativity was to create an atmosphere in society whereby the citizen felt that party and state officials were accountable and responsible to them, and where grievances could be aired and redress obtained. By encouraging greater accountability and openness in the work of public bodies, corrupt and/or incompetent officials came to realize that they could no longer remain immune from criticism, and the citizenry acquired greater confidence to speak out. In other words, *glasnost'* was an integral part of the strategy of galvinizing support "from below" for the reforms, and for overcoming opposition.[26]

The promotion of *glasnost'* had a wider conceptual significance though. The willingness on the part of the leadership to tolerate the public expression of ideas, a diversity of views, a clash of opinions and to promote dialogue had profound implications for Soviet society. Toleration of pluralism, and a broader scope for debate signified a move towards a genuinely public sphere of civic awareness and action. For Gorbachev, this was an essential precondition for the resurrection of public morality, and formed the basis for a healthy democracy.[27] The sprouting of a public sphere, of "socialist" pluralism, of dialogue and tolerance imparted two new elements into Soviet thinking. Policy formation had to be marked by realism and the acceptance of diversity. The party had to, in his words, "learn to overcome the inveterate discrepancy between reality and the proclaimed policy".[28] It also led to a "weakening of the demand for belief in the infallibility of the party or the interpreters of the ideology".[29] The scope for debate and disagreement was inherently widened, and the party's claim to know the "true" interests of society, which was the central plank in rationalizing the leading role of the cpsu, was significantly eroded. *Glasnost'* marked another important shift in Soviet thinking.

Demokratizatsiya was seen as the key to the success and irreversibility of *perestroika*. For the leadership, the strategy of democratization was a vital expedient. If support was to be galvanized, and opposition overcome, then people would have to support the changes through active participation. As well as being a strategy designed to encourage participation from below, it can also be seen, arguably, as part of a new "social contract" in which political reforms aimed to offset the problems in the economic sphere by allowing people to articulate their interests, and express their grievances, giving them an authentic stake in the success of the changes.[30] In Gorbachev's words, structures needed to be created whereby the people would "feel that they are their own masters and creators. A house can only be put in order by a person who feels that s/he owns this house".[31]

Conceptually, democratization highlighted the needs and interests of individuals, and also the need to treat society as a complex amalgam of individuals, groups and strata, with diverse and at times conflicting interests, and not as an homogenous entity. This meant the creation of structures and processes that promoted the peaceful and consensual settlement of conflicts, that protected the rights of individuals, that allowed genuine participation and real choice, and that permitted genuine democratic control from below and so prevented abuses of power. In other words, democratization was seen as a shift towards a more democratic and humanistic rationalization of social processes, which emphasized choice, participation and diversity.

The shift in Soviet thinking on foreign affairs was perhaps more profound than that on domestic affairs. Gorbachev's reform project hinged on the creation of a more peaceful, co-operative international atmosphere that would enable a shift of resources to the domestic economy, and facilitate the acquisition of Western technology and credits. The theoretical renewal in foreign affairs became known as New Political Thinking (NPT hereafter). Smirnov, in an extended discussion, defined NPT in the following way:

> NPT is not a dogma or set of rules, but is an on-going dialogue with the international community and a joint search for global truth and justice. It does not claim a knowledge of absolute truth. Its realism is based on a recognition of the diversity of interests and goals of the world's different societies and of the international community as a whole.[32]

Its basic thesis was that the modern world required a new atmosphere of co-operation and toleration. The defining principle of NPT was that the world should be viewed as an interdependent and integral whole. While there would still be antagonisms, interdependence, owing to the rapid growth of scientific and technical progress, had reached the stage whereby humanity had only one common fate: either "perish under the weight of contradictions, or find a path for their solution".[33] Interdependence had two distinct but interrelated strands. The first was the recognition of the functional integration of the world economy and of global communications. The second was the growing concern with global problems, especially universal security for mankind in the nuclear era and the possibility of ecological catastrophe. Both threatened humanity and so required international co-operation.[34]

The other main principle of the NPT was the primacy of common human values over national or class interests and values.[35] This was closely linked to the issues raised by the threat of global catastrophe. In the face of the possibility of the extermination of both humanity and the Earth itself "a concern for the survival of the human race, that is to say a concern for the individual as an absolute value, for ensuring their basic rights, the right to life is given top priority".[36] Human values must take priority over class ones in an age of the possible total annihilation of the species, thus placing an objective limit on the utility of class-based approaches to the world.

One of the most interesting themes of NPT was its response to the problems posed by trying to conceive of the role of the individual in the modern world. These problems included not only the means of guaranteeing the protection of universal human values and rights – social justice, human rights, equality before the law – but were also concerned with the changing role of the individual in society and at work as a result of the impact of the STR. This referred mainly to areas such as leisure time, working practices and so on.[37] This new approach to the role of the individual was the start of a fairly basic shift in Soviet thinking. The passive, constrictive role for the individual in Brezhnevite neo-Stalinist socialism had to yield to an outlook that placed a premium upon the individual as an active agent in the historical process. The problems of implementing the STR had a major impact in this area. Under Brezhnev the attempt was made to "manage" these processes, to guide their implementation consciously. There was a general failure to see that the STR required a policy which focused on the creative input of the individual, both in society as a whole and also at work, in order to stand any chance of succeeding. The new technological innovations resulting from the STR required workers with higher educational and skill levels. These developments, for Cooper, raised the issue "of greater democracy in economic life and for improved opportunities for creativity and self-expression".[38] The new humanistic emphasis on the individual in Soviet thinking was more than just a part of the leadership's mobilizing strategy for successful economic reforms. It was part of a much wider reappraisal, which went to the very core of the philosophical basis of the new Soviet conception of socialism.

Summarizing the joint impact of the changes in Soviet domestic and foreign policy thinking provides some very interesting insights. The break in domestic thinking with neo-Stalinist concepts was accompanied by a break with the neo-Stalinism of Soviet foreign policy thinking. Soviet society was viewed as a complex, diverse, conflictual organism in which social differentiation, political pluralism and a "clash of opinions" were inevitable features. Soviet thinking now began to stress the need for realistic appraisals, stripped of ideology and dogma, and the importance of placing the individual at the centre of the new society. In international terms there was a shift from "proletarian internationalism to progressive humanism".[39] This was a move away from a narrow, class-based confrontational stance, towards a posture emphasizing common human values, co-operation and consensus, but also included a shift in the means of resolving problems in which politics and dialogue acquired primacy over military-based solutions. "Progressive humanism" emphasized realism, humanism, diversity, and toleration.

Perestroika *and Developing Socialism*

Between the rejection of Developed Socialism and the emergence of Humane Democratic Socialism in late 1989/early 1990, the concept of "Developing Socialism" arose. This was an interesting moment in the evolution of Soviet socialism, as the leadership sought a way of disassociating themselves from parts of the traditional model, without abandoning those elements that rationalized the continued domination of the CPSU and its ideas. This hybrid of "old" and "new" reflected the basic dilemma of trying to implement change while at the same time limiting it. The concept of *uskorenie* provides a good example of this co-existence of old approaches with new goals. The economic approach of *uskorenie* was meant to produce a new type of growth: intensive, efficient, productive, technological. Yet the economic plans of the CPSU remained tied to a fetishization of economic growth *per se*. The leadership were attempting to transform the structural basis of the system, while also increasing growth. "Old" thinking died hard.

The concept of Developing Socialism was introduced and developed by Gorbachev and Alexander Yakovlev,[40] although it was Georgii Smirnov, the Director of the Institute of Marxism–Leninism in the late 1980s, who played the most prominent role in the conceptualization of Developing Socialism.[41] It was never defined precisely or substantively, but comprised a number of themes. Developing Socialism's recognition of contradictions, conflicts and a diversity of interests within Soviet society was a notable departure from the traditional model. Developed Socialism had little or no recognition of diversity. Another innovation was the commitment to pluralism, tolerance and a consequent rejection of intellectual uniformity. Developing Socialism acknowledged that no one group or person had a monopoly on the truth. This in turn meant a commitment to learn from the positive and negative aspects of others. This was in stark contrast to Developed Socialism which saw the party line as always embodying the "correct" view of the world and the true interests of Soviet society. Other ideas and opinions had no legitimacy, and the experiences of others were a testament to the inherent correctness of the cpsu's policies. Attitudes to the role of the individual also shifted markedly. The stress on differing and diverse interests in Developing Socialism was an attempt to redress the balance between individual, collective and the general interests of Soviet citizens. Society should be guided by a more individualistic and humanistic ethos, one which accepted people as they were and attempted to produce policies that expressed these interests. The approach to the individual should be holistic, encompassing the individual's life in its totality, including moral, cultural and spiritual aspects, which had been areas of wanton neglect. Perhaps the most significant development was the downgrading of the class interests of individuals and the upgrading of personal, group, regional and even common human interests as the basis of its worldview. Developing Socialism emphasized a more humanistic, democratic bent. Under Developed Socialism, the collective interest was deified. Individuals, groups, regions all existed to construct the material–technical base of communism, which was the end to which all resources – human and natural – were to be subordinated. Moral, ethical and spiritual concerns were consequently played down as they were secondary to the overriding goal: the construction of a Developed Socialist society, guided and directed by the Soviet state.

Developing Socialism was forged out of the ambiguities of *perestroika*. While it revised many of the traditional elements of the Soviet model, it also upheld many of the core features. Developing

Socialism reflected the underlying tension running through *perestroika*, attempting to combine continuity and change. In the period between 1987–88 the Gorbachev leadership was looking for a way to renew Soviet socialism while retaining its core features: the leading role of the party, central planning, state ownership and control. This entailed combining new initiatives with these traditional commitments. Hence:

Traditional Model	**Developing Socialism**
Public ownership	Mainly public ownership (with private elements)
Central planning	Plan/Market
Leading Role of Party [LRP]	LRP/socialist pluralism

This table encapsulates the transitional nature of Developing Socialism, standing between the scientific approach of Developed Socialism and the ethical approach of Humane Democratic Socialism. This transitory, Janus-like nature was manifest in the underlying values of Developing Socialism.

An uneasy co-existence of two conflicting philosophical outlooks within *perestroika* became evident. The constructivist outlook that underpinned Developed Socialism and which expressed the basis of Soviet Marxism–Leninism since 1917 existed, in diluted and modified form, at the heart of *perestroika*. The language of *perestroika* betrayed the tenacity of this philosophical position. Society had to be "restructured", "renovated", and "reorganized". The new state of Soviet society was still implicitly seen as something that could be "built" "from above", albeit with vastly upgraded participation and input "from below". *Perestroika* was still basically a constructivist doctrine, although *perestroika* also contained the seeds of the new philosophy. This implied a turn to the individual, to their needs and interests, to enable them to control their own lives and environment meaningfully. This by extension implied the recognition that society and social processes were not something that could be managed, individual personalities could not be created or moulded.

Perestroika sought to give expression to discourses of both constructivism and humanism and this tension was reproduced within

Developing Socialism. This ambiguity – science or humanism – was evidence of a major problem. Developing Socialism had its roots in the philosophical outlook of the former concept of Soviet socialism, and this compromised its attempt to give expression to the new ideas and values. A comparison of the philosophical values of the traditional model and of Developing Socialism might look like this:

Traditional Model	**Developing Socialism**
Collectivism	Modified collectivism
Social harmony	Social diversity
Productivism	Holistic view of person
Optimism/progressivism	Realism
Constructivism	Constructivism
Rationalism	Rationalism & moralism
Proletarian internationalism	Progressive humanism

The long-term significance of Developing Socialism is that it marked a staging-post in the erosion of traditional Soviet socialist concepts and consequently created the possibility for a new model of socialism based on ethical, humanistic, democratic principles to emerge. This concept marked the beginning of the shift away from Soviet socialism as a "scientific" doctrine. Why did this shift occur, and what did it imply, if anything?

The legacy of the Stalinist past had created an endemic antipathy and disillusionment towards "scientific" socialism. This legacy and the emergence of genuine political pluralism after March 1990 meant that Soviet socialism had to couch its appeal in terms of being the most morally acceptable doctrine – partly to distance itself from the disillusionment with scientific socialism, and partly to present itself in a favourable light in order to vie with other doctrines. In the same way that the CPSU was now faced with competition from other groups and movements, so socialism had to face competition from other ideas, which forced it to adapt to the new circumstances. Finally, the whole idea of "scientific" socialism, with its emphases on certitude, optimism and truth seemed inappropriate in a situation marked by growing uncertainty, realism and conflicts.

The implications of this shift were twofold. On one level, it removed the last vestige of a belief in the ability of an enlightened elite (in this case a vanguard party) to guide society and reconstruct it along rational lines. The adjective "scientific" as applied to the traditional model had expressed the inherent correctness of party policy, the party's knowledge of the general laws of social development and its ability to construct a socialist society on the basis of this knowledge. This was now no longer the case. More importantly, it relativized the socialist idea, and so opened the way for genuine political and ideological pluralism. Once it had been accepted that there was not one single truth, and that no group could claim to be the one "legitimate source of political initiative",[42] then it became evident that socialism as a doctrine was no longer "correct", but just one option that had to struggle for hegemony. Socialism was no longer an automatic stage on the way to communism, but became one optional set of social arrangements among many alternatives.

A new concept of socialism emerged from a complex sociopolitical, economic and doctrinal context. The new vision of socialism had to contribute to the transformation of the system, while maintaining those in power who sponsored it. It had to respond to the imperatives of domestic reform, and to the global pressures for change. It had to repudiate the perceived distortions of the traditional model (renouncing the legacy of statism, social engineering and scientific socialism) while rescuing the idea of socialism from the widespread disillusionment associated with it. As Sakwa put it, Soviet socialist theorists had to find a Third Way between moving away from the crisis of "Actually Existing Socialism" and lapsing into something approaching radical liberalism.[43] The demise of Developing Socialism created the preconditions for the emergence of the new concept of Soviet socialism expounded by Gorbachev: Humane Democratic Socialism.

Humane Democratic Socialism: an emperor with no clothes?

The search for a renewed concept of Soviet socialism was taken up by the Soviet scholarly community after October 1988. Within a number of key theoretical journals – *Kommunist* (the theoretical journal of the Central Committee), *Voprosy filosofii*, *Sovetskoe gosudarstvo i pravo* – many discussions ensued on the problems and issues raised by the need to revise the Soviet model of socialism. Prominent contibutions from Boris Kurashvili, Anatoli Butenko, Fedor Burlatsky, Len Karpinsky, Georgii Smirnov, Georgii Shakhnazarov, Oleg Bogomolov and others were central to the reshaping of the party's view of socialism. The first sign of an official codification of these debates came on 26 November 1989 when Gorbachev published his statement of faith "The socialist idea and revolutionary *perestroika*" (although there had been intimations of "humane" socialism in the preceding two years). At the February 1990 plenum, the platform "Towards Humane Democratic Socialism" was adopted. This formed the basis for the draft programmatic documents of the 28th Congress of the CPSU, which was convened in July 1990. At the Congress, a commission was formed to redraft the party programme on the basis of this new platform. The composition of the draft programme was a rather tortuous, highly politicized process that was finally completed when the draft was published in *Pravda* on 8 August 1991.[44] The coup intervened before the programme could be ratified or implemented. Humane Democratic Socialism died at birth.

It is possible, on the basis of the documents published, to evaluate the nature of Humane Democratic Socialism (HDS hereafter), and so to compare it with the orthodox model. The vision of socialism, and its component parts, was not a static one. There was a significant degree of theoretical evolution between November 1989 and 1991.

Humane Democratic Socialism: the socialist vision

> The socialism we want to build through *perestroika* is a society with an efficient economy, a high scientific, technological and cultural level and humanitarian social structures, a society that has democratized all aspects of social life and created the necessary conditions to encourage people's creative endeavour and activity.[45]

Gorbachev's overall vision, stressing humanism, democracy, morality and the individual as its guiding principles, proved to be an eclectic mixture based on a synthesis of general world experience, national peculiarities, a re-reading of Marx and Lenin, and the theory and practice of European Social-Democracy. No longer was Soviet socialism to be defined as: "if it's not capitalism, then it must be socialism". The worldview of HDS seemed to be defined more along ethical, individualistic lines as it sought to react against what went before, while simultaneously responding to the demands of integration into global civil society. In practical policy terms though, it seemed to offer little more than a rehashing of European Social-Democracy or welfare capitalism, opting for a radical injection of West European economic forms alongside an active social policy.

One of the most significant revisions in the nature of socialism was the emphasis upon its contingent, continually evolving nature. The traditional view had seen it as a transitional society with a set of key features that had to be consciously constructed as part of the process of reaching communism. Now socialism was no longer viewed as a set of features defined in advance. It was a "creative endeavour" that could not define *a priori*. The precise nature of HDS would unfold during the course of its emergence. In the search for legitimating reference points for this approach, the Gorbachev leadership focused on two: the Lenin of NEP (liberalized mixed economy eschewing the statist authoritarianism of war communism, generally pragmatic approach to societal management), and the humanistic early writings of Marx. The implications of this were momentous. The purpose of the party was no longer to construct an abstract series of structures which constituted the transition phase.

The cornerstone of Gorbachev's vision was that of freedom (*svoboda*). This freedom was perceived as the expression of true human individuality through association with other individuals: that is, a return to Marx's view that in overcoming self-alienation and alienation from others, an individual becomes truly and fully human only in his/her solidarity and community with others. In reality, Gorbachev was to espouse a form of freedom closer to traditional liberal political philosophy, than "early" Marx's views.[46] For Gorbachev, the individual had to become the alpha and omega, the measure of all things. This rediscovery of individual liberation in Soviet socialist discourse was primarily a reaction, as Gorbachev himself admitted:

> In the name of wrongly understood collectivism, human individuality was ignored, the development of the personality

was hampered, the reasonable confines of freedom were drastically narrowed under the pretext of the priority of the collective over the individual.[47]

The result had been to emasculate the humanitarian essence of the socialist ideal, and it is this that Gorbachev wished to restore. This was first expressed in the idea that common human values took precedence over class values, and it was precisely the repudiation of the class-based, "hatred" approach to the world that HDS opposed.[48] According to Amelina, Lenin's functional approach to morality destroyed the ethical basis of socialism, and gave socialism a utilitarian content that drained its humanistic essence. This in turn made possible the striving of the "Administrative System" to erase the sphere of personal interests, by identifying the traditional social norms (charity, compassion, etc.) as "bourgeois deviations" or "vestiges".[49] The "return" to humanism, or more properly, to "socialism with a human face", had a number of aspects.

Freedom did not mean merely freedom from economic exploitation, but also from the suppression and appropriation of the will of the individual: culturally, spiritually, religiously, racially, etc. No longer was a person to be treated as a one-dimensional economic being. The opposition to all forms of exploitation was extended into a concern for all facets of an individual's personality: creating the preconditions for the economic independence of a person was meaningless if they were spiritually or culturally emasculated, and unable to realize their true potential. Emphasis was now given to the qualitative and spiritual aspects of an individual's existence, and the aim was to allow the emergence of an integral human being: owner and worker, producer and consumer, citizen.[50] This was a clear shift away from the productivism of the traditional model. The emphasis upon individuals, their interests, ideals and needs, required a strong democratic imperative. This was reflected not only in the need to promote and encourage pluralism, diversity and individual creativity, but also in the striving to create structures that guaranteed equality before the law, and that upheld the basic rights and dignity of the individual.

This vision of HDS clearly represented an attempt to break with the past, while creating a society that could respond to the social, political and economic challenges of rapid technological advances and integration into the world community: changing work patterns and techniques, growing division of labour, an increased need for specialization and so on. At the 28th Party Congress in July 1990, a society of Humane Democratic Socialism, embodying the ideals outlined above, was described as having three main components: (a) the state, which is subordinate to society, guarantees the protection of the rights, freedoms, honour and dignity of the people; (b) the individual is the aim of social development; (c) the transformation of the working people into the masters of production.[51]

How were these interpreted in the specific arenas of economics, politics and socio-cultural policy?

The economics of Humane Democratic Socialism

Economic transformation ran at the heart of *perestroika*. Unlike previous reformist initiatives under Khrushchev and Brezhnev, the economics of *perestroika* embraced the structures and principles underlying the operation of the Stalinist command economy. The radical momentum generated by the increasingly desperate search for solutions to the USSR's economic malaise overtook the core features of the Soviet economy: central planning and state ownership. Both were deemed to be constituent components of the causes of economic failure. But with what would they be replaced?

The overall vision was one that combined both efficiency and high labour productivity, with humanism and social justice. In other words socialism was now defined as a set of principles to be realized, not institutional features to be constructed. Creating a socialist society based on these principles meant utilizing whatever economic mechanisms would most efficiently produce these values. In general terms Humane Democratic Socialism sought to integrate the progressive productive forces and advanced technologies of the world economic system into the Soviet Union, and, in addition, to implement distribution according to work done. This, in turn, required the use of incentives and differentiation of incomes, to stimulate productivity and greater efficiency. In terms of humanism and social justice, a socialist economy should:

> enable the individual to be master again with full rights, to return the individual to the means of production, to the

land, to overcome alienation, to stimulate interest and strengthen the work motivation of each individual.[52]

Defining socialism according to a set of values removed the ideological taboos associated with the market, private ownership, hired labour. The 28th Party Congress in July 1990 attempted to realize these principles, by steering a path between the "old" and the West.[53] Both the old model of strict administrative allocation and the "Western" path of immediate denationalization of the means of production and unfettered marketization of the economy were rejected, as:

> Each of them contradicts the main values of socialism and world practice, leads to the limitation of the inalienable rights of an individual, and is not able to create a highly effective system of management.[54]

The optimal economic arrangement for realizing these principles was said by Gorbachev to be the "mixed economy".[55] Two key features stand out: the regulated market economy and the introduction of a variety of forms of ownership.

From central planning to the regulated market economy

> Moving towards the market, we are not moving away from socialism, but to a fuller realization of society's possibilities.[56]

The move away from the system of central planning began in earnest with the 1987 Law on State Enterprises. Measures were adopted that decentralized decision-making and reduced the powers of the central ministries. The number of central ministries was reduced. Enterprises were given more autonomy in deciding what to produce, and the republics also acquired more autonomy. This decree not only shifted the locus of decision-making, but also altered the nature of the planning process. Much more power was given to the enterprise to decide on what to produce. This was embodied in the principle of *khozraschet* or profit and loss accounting. At the same time, GOSPLAN and the central ministries were to reduce the number of plan indicators that the enterpise had to fulfil. State orders were to be the main link between the enterprise and the ministry. Having fulfilled their state order, the enterprise was free to seek out its own contracts. The Law hoped to create horizontal links among enterprises and to make them more responsive to consumer demand. *Khozraschet* created the scope for the use of market levers while retaining elements of the planned approach to economic management. The enterprises were also supposed to balance their books, in order to make them more productive and cost-sensitive.[57]

The reform was a compromise, and inexorably it failed. Enterprises were unwilling to seek out contracts. Ministries were unwilling to allow the enterprises to exercise their autonomy. As with the 1957 *sovnarkhozy* reforms, and the 1965 Kosygin reforms, the central ministries reasserted their powers. Gorbachev chose in 1990 to move much more quickly towards a fuller implementation of marketization within the Soviet economy, which led to a far-reaching reassessment of the market and the use of commodity–money relations under socialism. Soviet theorists and politicians began to make more neutral statements about the market in 1987. Between 1989 and 1991, the central issue was the attempt to find the optimum balance between planning and market elements, and to define the nature of planning under Humane Democratic Socialism.

The market held a number of attractions for Gorbachev, but it was not to be unfettered. State regulation, through the indirect levers of financial policy and the direct intervention of social policy, was to remain a key part of an Humane Democratic Socialist society. The market was now not merely ideologically and philosophically acceptable for socialists, according to Gorbachev, but was also a necessary component of both a successful reform and a healthy socialist society. Ideologically speaking, the market was neutral. It was no longer a feature uniquely associated with capitalism: it had been produced by human civilization and could be appropriated by any particular social system.[58]

The most interesting development was the recognition of the *socialist* attributes that the market could bring to the Soviet system. On the one hand this was an obvious attribute of the market: providing the dynamism and efficiency for an economy that could be integrated into the world economy, and meet the socialist aspiration to raise the people's standard of living, through the creation of a productive, innovative, entrepreneurial society. On the other hand, the market was also said to meet the requirements of socialist humanism and social justice, in three ways. First, the market provided a bulwark to the political democratization of Soviet society by creating the framework for the economic freedoms of the individual, "the market democratises economic relations, and socialism is inconceivable without democracy".[59] Only within a market framework could there co-exist a variety of forms of ownership and economic management that expressed the "private interests of the people".[60] This stimulated the growth of economic freedoms and provided the basis for independent business activity. At the same time, the market supplied the preconditions for a genuine socialization of the Soviet economy:

> ... the creation of free associations of producers, joint-stock companies, production and consumer co-operatives, associations of leaseholders and entrepreneurs ... is the high road to a genuine socialisation of production on the principles of free will and economic expediency.[61]

At one and the same time, the market supposedly allowed the individual to pursue their private interests, while creating a truly collectivist society.

Secondly, the market implemented another basic principle of socialism: distribution according to work done. By providing an equilibrium between demand and supply, and so putting an end to the problem (seemingly endemic to a Soviet-style economy) of shortages, the market ensured that people could turn their wages into goods, and so reward highly productive labour. This also prevented the flourishing of groups and individuals who thrived on the profits gleaned from exploiting the shortages.[62]

Thirdly, the market promoted a more effective system of social security and social protection. Unleashing market forces in the Soviet economy would in the long-run increase the national wealth through the impetus this gives to labour productivity. This would then allow the raising of the ceilings of the guaranteed minimum levels of wages, pensions, allowances, and the increased provision of health care, education, housing, pensions, etc. Through an active state social policy, the less well-off members of society could benefit from the all-round increase in economic efficiency and productivity.[63]

What sort of regulation did Gorbachev envisage? The role for the state in the economy was highly circumscribed, in comparison with what went before. This was especially evident with regard to the scope and tasks of the plan in a regulated market economy. The planning system was to operate through indirect levers: taxes, interest on credit, pricing, state orders, customs duties, legislation, etc. The purpose of this planning was to undertake what the market could not do: implement long-term major scientific and technical advances, develop the infrastructure and protect the environment. State regulation did not merely encompass the economic processes, but also the economic and social consequences of a regulated market. Gorbachev repeatedly emphasized the need for an active, extensive social policy in order to uphold the principle of social justice and defend the position of the needy. It appeared that the economy was geared to the creation of a system that stimulated individual initiative, innovation and productivity, while protecting the less well-off against adversity.

From state ownership to a mixed economy: patterns of ownership and control

The issue of property ownership forced its way onto the policy agenda after 1986. In order to overcome the alienation of the Soviet working people from the means of production and to increase their interest in the outcome of their labour, encouragement was to be given to diverse forms of ownership. Initially, this took the form of lifting the restrictions on individual forms of labour, and on the creation of co-operatives. As the reform process proceeded, the emphasis shifted towards a destatization of ownership forms. The starting-point was to remove the monopoly of state ownership of the means of production. Interestingly, however, there was a convergence in the type of ownership relations to replace traditional state ownership. In the socialist vision ownership relations had to fulfil two criteria: they had to overcome the alienation of the individual from the means of production, and must make them the master of the means of production. The reformist imperative in the economy was to restore dynamism, efficiency and productivity. As a result, HDS combined these two themes to propose a diversity of ownership forms:

> We associate solving the vital issue of the socialist revolu-
> tion with the attainment of a plurality of forms of ownership:
> how to overcome the alienation of man from the means
> of production, from ownership – we thereby combine
> socialism with the private interests of the people.[64]

HDS, in advocating a variety of forms of ownership (municipal,
state, co-operative, joint-stock, private), sought to overcome both
the alienation from capitalist property relations (where ownership
is predominantly privately owned) and the alienation from full state
ownership (where no-one owns the means of production). In this
way true economic freedom was to be realized, as the individual
was able to determine how to undertake their "independent business activity". The only thing that was not allowed was the traditional formula of "excluding the exploitation of man by man".[65]

The transition from "formal" to "real" socialization was described
by Gorbachev as a move to a mixed economy, including private
ownership. However, private ownership was to play a highly constrained role, and he maintained in July 1990 that no-one would be
compelled to join private enterprises against their will.[66] In other
words, hired labour was alright now, as long as you consented to it!
Policy initiatives in the areas of land reform and privatization of
state-owned enterprises taken by the RSFSR and other republics in
1991 seemed to suggest that the provisos concerning a limited role
for private ownership, and the inadmissability of the exploitation
of man by man had been swept away in the rush to embrace
full-blooded market relations. The overall impression is that HDS
was distinguished from other socio-economic formations more by
degree than by principle: there was to be a plurality of forms of
ownership, of which private was a small part, and in which socialized forms (associations of lease-holders, co-operatives, state)
predominated. In the same way, hired labour (and therefore
exploitation) was now permissible, as long as it was voluntarily
entered into.

The other path eschewed by the adoption of market relations
and diverse forms of property ownership was the increase in worker
participation in the management of enterprises. Under the 1987
Law on the State Enterprise, a Work Collective was created that
had significant input into the operation of the enterprise. This

was gradually discarded, as the moves towards a market system gathered pace. The rejection of bureaucratic, statist centralized management of the economy had not resulted in a reanimation of a modernized form of workers' participation in the economy, or of a radical economic democratization.

The politics of Humane Democratic Socialism

The initial vision underpinning the politics of *perestroika* was very similar to that which animated Khrushchev: political leadership exercised by a revived communist party, alongside greater popular participation in the organs of local government, greater freedom of discussion, and more room for political activity from autonomous social groups. Political pluralism under *perestroika* was to be a pluralism of opinions, within socialist parameters. The party was to be revived by sweeping out the old, the corrupt and the incompetent, democratizing its internal life and withdrawing from day-to-day supervision of the economy into a broader ideological and political leadership role. This attempt to maintain one-party rule within a pluralist, democratized system was destroyed during 1989 and 1990 as Soviet society rose up and undermined the authority of the party. The emergence of a pluralistic, competitive socio-political milieu, of an embryonic civil society, of new institutional arrangements, compelled the leadership to incorporate these new developments into the political values of HDS.

The CPSU under HDS: from vanguard to parliamentary party

Under Developing Socialism, the leading role was renewed, involving a greater degree of political and ideological guidance, alongside a commitment to tolerate "socialist" pluralism of opinions and groups. However, even as Gorbachev, Medvedev et al. were defending this renewed leading role it was being undermined on three fronts. First, the revolution "from below" during 1989 gradually undermined the authority and political credibility of the party. The elections to the 1989 Congress of People's Deputies (which removed many high-ranking party officials), the growth of nationalist movements, the collapse of communism in eastern Europe and the miner's strike all presented a massive challenge to the CPSU.

Secondly, internally, the party was in turmoil. Different groupings emerged with competing visions of the way forward. Radical democrats (Democratic Platform), orthodox Marxist–Leninists, moderates and radical socialists (Marxist Platform) all coalesced, destroying the monolithic façade of party life. Thirdly, the rationale of the leading role of the party, as we have seen, was undermined by the conceptual innovations introduced by *perestroika*: conflicts, diversity, pluralism.[67]

The challenges to the leading role were recognized by Gorbachev in his keynote article of November 1989, which seems to be one of the first signs of the shift in the rationalization of the party's leading role. Gorbachev admitted that in the future the leading role might be abandoned: "At the present complex stage, the interests of the consolidation of society . . . point to the need for keeping a one-party system."[68] Retaining this leading role, alongside a pluralistic political system, had become a question of expediency, not doctrinal purity. Maintaining the integrity of the system, defending socialist ideals and a successful reform of the system became the *raison d'être* of the party's leading role, not its claim to ideological truth.[69] The seminal moment came at the February 1990 plenum of the CPSU, when Gorbachev finally recognized that it was no longer feasible to retain a constitutional guarantee of the party's leading role in a pluralistic society.[70] Article 6 was abandoned, and this represents a key moment in the shift from the traditional model of scientific socialism, to the new model of ethical, humanistic socialism. Although it was clear that Gorbachev still hoped and believed that the party would continue to play the leading role in society (although in an informal sense), the recognition that the political system was now *de facto* pluralistic was an immense shift in the politics of Soviet socialism.

Under HDS, the defining principle of the political system was: "the free competition of socio-political organisations within a constitutional framework". The role of the party in a HDS society was fourfold: theoretical (evaluating society and elaborating a strategy to promote socialism), ideological (defending the philosophy and morality of the CPSU), political (conducting campaigns, elections, etc.), organizational (implementing its guidelines and decisions). But the important difference was the constitutional and competitive framework within which the party now had to operate. This shift was recognized and confirmed by the draft party programme of August 1991.[71] The cpsu now had to accept that it had to fight for power, that it might well be in opposition and that it would need to co-operate with other political movements. In short, the cpsu now had to transform itself into a parliamentary party.

This shift from vanguard to parliamentary body had further implications. The perception of the social base of support of the party was modified. The working class had always had a privileged position in the representative discourse of the party (even in the era of the party of the whole people). That privileged position now disappeared: "[the party] can count on the realization of its pro-grammatic aims only by consistently expressing and upholding the interests of all working people." The party was now to draw its support from the whole of Soviet society: no social group was to enjoy a privileged position. Membership of the party was also thrown open, being available to all (including religious believers). Rule by the vanguard – a core component of Soviet socialism – had been abandoned.

Individual rights and state power under HDS

Party documents from this period recognize the massive changes in the political landscape. Many of the features of Western liberal democracy – multi-party pluralism, rule of law, constitutional order, separation of powers – were acknowledged. Gorbachev's report to the 28th Congress described HDS as the replacement of the Stalinist model of socialism with "a citizen's society of free people".[72] The focus upon the individual as the measure of all things placed the issue of civil rights and freedoms, and the means of securing them, firmly in the forefront of the party's policy. This caused not only a profound renegotiation of the powers and functions of the state, but also deeply altered the whole nature of the political and legal system in order to institutionalize and defend these rights.

The basic parameters of this "citizens" society involved the in-corporation of the international norms on human rights into the theory and practice of the ussr, extending the Europeanizing theme of *perestroika*. These included the basic rights (life, liberty and property), and freedoms (to choose one's place of residence, to emigrate, to confidentiality, of expression, press, information and conscience).[73] These norms were clearly seen as a priority, as they were described as the "central, strategic" task of the party.[74] This emphasis on the rights of the individual entailed a redefinition of the relationship between the individual, society and the state. The balance shifted away from the state and towards the individual and civil society.

Under the 1977 Constitution individual rights and liberties were highly prescribed. The basic ethos was that the rights of the individual were state-based, and were then delegated to the individual from the state. In the words of Lukasheva, the task now was to move away from the idea of the "state as the benefactor endowing a person with rights".[75] The individual now delegated a certain amount of authority to the state, which was constituted on the basis of the rights of individuals, and which had, in turn, to safeguard them. For Migranyan, the individual had inalienable rights, and dwelled in an autonomous sphere upon which neither state nor society should encroach.[76] This shift emerged partly from the attempt to overcome the arbitrary nature of the Administrative System, which failed to provide legal safeguards for an individual, and which gradually eroded the basic human attributes of decency, conscientiousness and respect for others. It was also part of the attempt to restore a morality based on the common human values of respect for the dignity, privacy and autonomy of others. How did the party envisage realizing these rights?

In the section "Towards genuine people's power", the party advocated three main tasks: the formation of a civil society, in which the state must exist for the sake of the person; the strengthening of the law-governed state to ensure the equality of all before the law, and the independence of the courts; and a thorough democratization of the entire political system, which involved the free competition of all socio-political organizations, and the separation of legislative, executive and judicial powers.[77] Faced with criticism that HDS was nothing more than the assimilation of the norms and values of Western liberal-democracy, Gorbachev argued that the humanization and democratization of Soviet society was no mere capitulation to liberal values, but was carried out "within the framework of the socialist choice".[78] Whatever the precise nature of state power under HDS, there was now a recognition of the priority of the interests and rights of the individual.

The socio-cultural sphere under HDS

Reviving the Soviet economy via the introduction of market mechanisms and diverse forms of ownership entailed reconceptualizing the approach to material rewards, social differentiation and social justice. The need to stimulate productivity, hard work, technological innovation and economic competition forced a rethink of the CPSU's traditional commitment to, and understanding of, collectivism and egalitarianism.

There was now a recognition that to create a productive and efficient society required a complete reassessment of the way in which the individual was treated and conceived of. In many ways this echoed the critique of stagnant collectivist societies which had been prevalent in liberal political philosophy.[79] According to this view, a social system stagnates when it is deprived of its basic motive force for development: the creative self-determination of individuals, their interests, and their own sense of moral responsibility for their actions. If governments fail to respect the autonomy of individuals, treating them instead as means to an abstractly imposed end, then that society will stagnate and eventually collapse: "Human beings think and work creatively only when they are free, independent and motivated by self-interest."[80] Only in this way, according to Tsipko, could socialism become more efficient than capitalism, and thereby supply the material wants and needs of its citizens.

The shift in the Soviet conception of human nature has been described as the move from a form of abstract collectivism towards "possessive individualism".[81] Migranyan argued that Soviet theorists, "in the heat of the struggle against bourgeois individualism . . . threw out the baby with the bathwater".[82] In attempting to negate selfishness, Soviet theorists underestimated the attributes of *laissez-faire* individualism, which promoted the impressive development experienced by capitalism in the nineteenth century (the notion of self-sufficiency as an expression of an individual's reliance on their own hard work), and which, through the emergence of a healthy civil society, ensured individuals of protection against an intrusive state.[83] Remedying this situation required a fundamental rethink of the Soviet view of human nature. The basic postulate was to take individuals as they were, not as the leaders or the ideologists or the theories thought they should be. Policies, structures and institutions had to be tailored and shaped with this aim in mind. This implied two further things. People were complex organisms, with a vast array of motivations and aspirations, needs and desires springing from their widespread social affiliations, cultural traditions and beliefs, and also their biological impulses. This forced a recognition of the primacy of personal interests over class affiliations and so, in turn, of values such as acquisitiveness and materialism.[84] Encouragement had to be given to individual enterprise and initiative, to the desire for private and co-operative forms of ownership in the economy. This attempt to foster a political and socio-economic milieu that would stimulate elements of "possessive individualism" was a radical shift. Previously, all manifestations of individual acquisitiveness and personal proprietorial instincts were seen as evidence of the continued existence of bourgeois attitudes, which were entirely incompatible with the values of the New Person and so had to be eradicated.

Now, individualism was seen as the "inevitable mainspring of progress and that 'I' is the universal controlling and motive force".[85] Individual were now deemed to be the best judge of their own best interests, and encouragement should be given to the fostering of the values of hard work, self-improvement and enterprise. However it would be misleading to see this process as the unbridled march towards a society of purely selfish individuals, lacking any kind of collectivist ethos. Possessive Individualism it may have been; unmitigated it was not. For alongside the recognition of the priority and primacy of the individual and their interests was the wider application of this principle, which in many ways was a return to Marx's dictum that "the free development of each is the condition for the free development of all". In Soviet theory, the pursuit of individual wellbeing was now seen as the condition of a common wellbeing, as a means of satisfying the wider social interest.

The fundamental issue here was how precisely to overcome this dichotomy between an ethos of personal acquisition and gain, with the goal of promoting a spirit and an ethos of fraternity, co-operation and altruism, values fundamental to the socialist vision. This dichotomy ran at the heart of Gorbachev's project, and by extension runs at the heart of socialism proper. Gorbachev tried to reconcile his view of people fully realizing their individuality through their communal links and through human solidarity, with the need to encourage entrepreneurialism and personal gain. Adherents to the socialist cause, faced with this injection of a substantial dose of liberal political philosophy into the socialist patient, were faced with a number of tasks, if the pursuit of personal and private interests was to reap public benefit.

Initially this required a reassessment of the concept of equality, or of the commitment to an egalitarian, collectivist society. Within the historical traditions of socialism, "equality" has been a highly "contested" concept. In its most "pure" form it expresses the idea of the community as being the highest form of individualism, in which self-denial and altruism are the key to self-realization.[86] The problem facing Gorbachev and other theorists of HDS, was how to reconcile their commitment to egalitarianism with the need to in-crease the efficiency and productivity of the economy. On the one hand, material differentiation was to be encouraged to promote individual freedom and creativity to get the economy moving again. On the other hand, they were committed to a society of social justice and human solidarity. The concept of "equality" was caught within the vortex of the reformist imperative (introducing elements of liberal political philosophy into the system) and the socialist vision (which remained loyal to collectivism and social justice).

Echoing the Stalinist moves of the early 1930s, Soviet theorists attacked the *uravnilovka*, or equalization, which they argued had dominated Soviet social policy after Stalin:

> . . . the modern idea of equality does not imply a mech-anical and deadening levelling of society. Equality is about giving each individual the chance to reveal to the full his/ her potential . . . In order to breathe the air of freedom, it is necessary to crack the shell of equality.[87]

The idea of equality within the discourse of HDS attempted to synthesize these two imperatives. Discussions ensued on the mechanism for implementing material rewards for the population. Greater stress was laid upon the use of material incentives to reward work, as scholars discussed the viability of maintaining the exten-sive subsidized services provision available to the population. This caused a threefold reassessment of the traditional Soviet approach to equality. First, equality was now redefined as something close to equality of opportunity or life-chances. Secondly, a much more sustained critique of the edifice of privilege entered the public domain after 1987–8. As the party moved into a competitive socio-political situation, the partial removal of restrictions on information flows led to the airing of criticisms of the benefits and perks available to the *nomenklatura*. As the party attempted to implement a system of distribution that rewarded performance, hard work and industry, the justification for unearned rewards was increasingly untenable. Finally, tying rewards to performance would inevitably increase the levels of material differentiation. Gorbachev repeatedly emphasized the need for an active social policy to protect the vulnerable strata of society. In the statement adopted by the 28th Congress, seven provisions outlined the nature of these social guarantees:

1) create an integral social security system for low income and large families, ensuring that the combined level of pay, pensions and allowances is not below the subsistence level;
2) ensure a guaranteed level of housing, education, medical services and other benefits, while developing paid services and a housing market;
3) implement a major health care programme;
4) improve the position of women, and child-care and maternity provision;
5) improve the position for children's care;
6) ensure equal opportunities for young people;
7) improve the lot of invalids, servicemen and veterans.[88]

In addition, a series of measures were outlined to cushion the population against the almost inevitably adverse consequences of a switch to a regulated market economy: indexing incomes, and creating a mechanism to cope with structural changes in employment and to retrain those made redundant.[89] The meaning of social justice in HDS was elaborated rather vaguely in the 1991 draft party programme,

Due reward for labour and talent is an indispensable condition of progress in industry, science and culture. Competition, enterprise and initiative on the part of those who create material goods and spiritual assets should be combined organically with social guarantees to citizens, and special concern by society for socially vulnerable strata.[90]

In the area of social equality, especially gender relations, there was little change in the official policy of promoting greater opportunities for women to work and to participate in public life,

> We are in favour of strengthening economic and social guarantees and improving the working conditions of women, daily life and the family. The CPSU supports the efforts of the state and independent women's organizations directed towards rendering aid to families of modest means, the real equalization of opportunities for women and men in all spheres of life . . . and expanding opportunities for women to engage in self-education, art and sports.[91]

The biggest advance during these years was not a shift in official policy, but the greater degree of discussion of women's issues facilitated by *glasnost'*. The approach adopted by Gorbachev continued the line that the "woman question" had not been solved, reflecting the more pessimistic, realistic tone of HDS.

The shifts in the understanding of collectivism and egalitarianism are illustrative of a much more profound shift in the worldview of Soviet socialism. The abandonment of proletarian internationalism, and the adoption of what may be termed "progressive humanism" forced a fundamental rethink of the approach to international affairs. HDS recognized a profound reassessment of the priority accorded to class interests and to common human values. Common human values were now deemed to be prior to, and higher than, the narrow class interests of any social class. Realizing the class interests of the proletariat was best achieved by struggling for the interests of humanity as a whole. In the draft party programme, the CPSU was now to be guided,

> by the principles of humanism and panhuman values. The all-round development of man and his harmonious interaction with nature are the main guidelines for progress in the modern world.[92]

This caused a reappraisal of attitudes towards capitalism and the West. Perhaps the main reappraisal was the rejection of the view of the world as being divided into two hostile "camps" – capitalism and socialism – which were diametrically and irreconcilably opposed to each other. Gorbachev stated that while a class-based analysis of the causes of the nuclear threat and other global problems was still relevant, the appearance of weapons of universal destruction placed, "an objective limit [on] class confrontation in the international arena".[93] The priority of universal human values imposed the need to accept economic and ideological competition, but to keep this within a peaceful, co-operative framework. The co-operative aspects of co-existence now took clear precedence over the competitive ones.

Three interrelated factors came to encapsulate the Soviet approach to international affairs under Gorbachev. The first was the recognition of diversity, or the so-called "Sinatra Doctrine".[94] In other words, as Gennadi Gerasimov outlined, each state could do it "their way". Differences between states – cultural, political, national – were inevitable, beneficial and to be respected by all. The relative merits of different systems had to be judged by their ability to protect the basic rights and freedoms of the individual. As all peoples have the right to choose independently the socio-economic and political system of their preference, and this right to choose cannot be violated by decision-makers from elsewhere (although with the usual proviso that freedom must always be exercised in tandem with responsibility), international affairs must be conducted democratically. Problems that arise between states must be resolved politically – through negotiation and compromise – and not militarily. Gorbachev stressed the importance of dialogue between nations.

The great dichotomy of "capitalism" and "socialism" which dominated Soviet political thinking and practice was comprehensively rejected by Georgii Shakhnazarov, a leading Soviet theorist and close adviser to Gorbachev. According to Shakhnazarov, the cold war was the result of geopolitical and military factors: it was clearly an exaggeration to state that economic differences were greater between Czechoslovakia and Austria or the two Germanies, than between, for instance France and Japan, or Poland and North Korea. "Within system" differences often outweighed "between system" ones. Drawing distinctions between countries could not be done simply according to an arbitrary definition of their economic structure, and so the division of the world into two "camps" could not be sustained.[95]

The reassessment of "two-campism" led to further re-evaluations that went to the very heart of the understanding of capitalism and socialism in Soviet discourse. The rejection of the Stalinist thesis about the inimicable hostility of capitalism and socialism meant a move away from the view that everything that was Soviet was socialist and thus inherently "Good"; while everything in the West was capitalist and thus "Bad". The two systems were no longer seen in stark, diametric opposition. The picture painted by Soviet theorists was far more complex, diverse and multifaceted.[96] A number of broad themes emerged.

First, there were structures and processes common to capitalism and socialism. In the course of human civilization, forms and structures emerged that were neutral and independent of system, and could therefore exist equally legitimately under both socialism and capitalism.[97] Boris Kurashvili, an outspoken proponent of reform, maintained that a "frontier zone" existed between the capitalist and socialist countries. This "zone" contained some of the general properties of human civilization (for Kurashvili, these were commodity production and political democracy) which had to be appropriated by socialism if it was to derive maximum benefit from them.[98] Shakhnazarov took this one stage further. He did not just suggest that some capitalist social relations could be used under socialism. In an interesting interpretation of Marx's view that socialism comes into being bearing the "birth-marks" of capitalism, he refuted the widespread interpretation of this remark, which suggests that remnants of capitalism would continue to exist for sometime after the socialist revolution. Instead he put forward the view that these "birth-marks" were certain fundamental features of the socialist system that were inherent in capitalism. In other words socialism acquired them "genetically" from its predecessor. In this view, socialism inherited two of the basic elements of social life characteristic of all socio-economic systems: market production and statehood in politics.[99]

The rejection of the "irreconcilable hostility" thesis was reinforced by the growing awareness of the fundamental changes within the capitalist countries of the West. This acknowledgement of the changes in capitalism, going one step further than the recognition of common human structures, in turn contributed to a reassessment of both socialism and Western Social Democracy.[100] Capitalism had evolved beyond recognition from its classic nineteenth century form. Through the planning of scientific and technical progress, the expansion of the social sphere and a general turn towards differing forms of socialization, Western society was said to have undergone major social changes, during which it acquired new social features. Among the most significant cited were the high rewards for skilled labour, the growth of a comprehensive system of welfare provision, and the increased access available to both information and the political system for citizens. This turn towards a greater use of planning and of differentiated forms of socialization fundamentally altered the nature of capitalism, a change that, for some Soviet theorists, remained virtually unscathed by the assaults on public intervention from Reaganomics and Thatcherism in the West. Not only did capitalism take into account the interests of the economically dominant class, but it now had to ensure that the basic needs of society were met. In other words, through a process of self-adaptation, capitalism acquired many structures and processes that socialists had usually appropriated as their own. This was attested to in practice by the examples of Sweden or Austria.[101]

There were not two completely different, although internally uniform, systems. The world was now said to contain societal "amalgams", in which elements of different systems existed in differing proportions.[102] Interestingly, Shakhnazarov argued that the countries of western Europe all appeared to be "capitalist" in production and "socialist" in distribution, rejecting the view that the two systems were hermetically sealed and diametrically different. This entailed a further twofold reassessment. First, the relative advantages of capitalism and socialism were weighed and balanced. Higher productivity was seen as the overwhelmingly favourable feature of capitalist societies. Socialism, conversely, demonstrated the advantages of socialization and of the need for rational planning. Secondly, the whole experience of European Social Democracy was reappraised. Both Gorbachev and Medvedev called for a reinterpretation of the social-democratic experience.[103]

The significance of this reassessment of the relationship of capitalism and socialism is that it destroyed once and for all the proclamations concerning the inherent, historical and moral supremacy of socialism over capitalism. Socialism was no longer the inevitable future for all capitalist countries. Most of the defenders of socialism (except perhaps for the guardians of orthodoxy) were forced to concede that socialism had advantages in some areas (greater rationality, better welfare protection and a greater emphasis on social justice), and capitalism had proved more effective in others (economic efficiency and material satisfaction).[104] The unbroken progress of history, through capitalism, to socialism and ultimately to communism could no longer be sustained in the light of this evidence. This notion destroyed one of the central pillars of the ideological legitimacy of the cpsu. Moreover, the position of the ussr as the trailblazer and head of the international revolutionary movement was fatally weakened by these developments.

Underpinning the approach to the international sphere within hds was the yearning to rejoin the mainstream of European civilization, to integrate the ussr into the cultural, economic and social developments of the rest of the world. Gorbachev ended the traditional Bolshevik ambiguity with regard to attitudes towards the West. Gorbachev was a Europeanizer and Westernizer, and these values were embodied in hds.

In domestic affairs, hds also oversaw a massive shift in the normative basis of Soviet socialism. At the heart of hds ran a commitment to pluralism, moralism, spirituality and humanism which displaced both Marxism–Leninism and its core components of scientific atheism and class prejudice. This had implications in a number of different fields. In the sphere of education the first signs of change came in the field of history, which was the first area spotlighted by *glasnost'*. Dissatisfaction began to be expressed publicly about the state of Soviet history textbooks. In the spring of 1988, it was decreed that the history examinations had been abolished owing to the ongoing debates about Soviet history and the unsatisfactory nature of the textbook.[105] By September 1988 a new textbook had been prepared, although it met with immediate criticisms and was itself replaced by a book prepared by the State Committee for Public Education, which came out in 1989. Once more it became outdated, and a competition was announced for the completion of another textbook in December 1990.[106]

From 1988–9 onwards changes began to become apparent in other fields as well. In October 1989 decree 685 was issued, which dealt with "The restructuring of the teaching of social sciences in Higher Education Institutions". This created an overnight transformation in the content of the university curriculum, removing the compulsory study of Marxist–Leninist concepts and creating the preconditions for the emergence of a pluralistic educational system.[107] Significantly, this transformation occurred prior to the abandonment of article 6. What did this decree say? Social science core courses had previously been: CPSU history; Marxist–Leninist philosophy; scientific communism; political economy. These were now to become: socio-political history of the twentieth century; philosophy; problems in the theory of contemporary socialism; political economy.[108]

This marked a shift away from the privileged position of Marxism–Leninism in the curriculum, as students were now to examine a wide variety of theories and worldviews, and to place Marxism–Leninism within a much wider historical and conceptual framework. Aside from the changing content, two important organizational changes also emerged. Individual institutions were to have a degree of independence in the organization of their teaching. The State Committee would set general programmatic courses, but 20 per cent of the curriculum could be set by the universities themselves, including the right to introduce their own specialized courses, or to publish their own treatises. This move away from an exclusive concentration on Marxism–Leninism was confirmed in February 1990 when examinations in Marxism–Leninism were abandoned to be replaced by ones in socialist theory.[109]

Another interesting example of the pervasiveness of the retreat from Marxism–Leninism prior to 1990 was the debates and discussions surrounding the new philosophy textbook. In its previous guises it was entitled: *Foundations of Marxism–Leninism* or *Introduction to dialectical and historical materialism*. This became *Introduction to philosophy*, and with the change in title came a marked shift in content. Under the editorial supervision of Ivan Frolov (appointed by Gorbachev as editor of *Pravda* in 1989), the new textbook reflected the interests and themes that Frolov had been exploring for some time: individuals and their mode of existence, rather than materialistic dialectics.[110] Students of philosophy in the

Soviet Union now had a text that dealt with both Marxist and non-Marxist philosophy, and with the general history of philosophy. According to Buccholz:

> ... the absence in the new textbook of a chapter on the so-called "basic question of philosophy" ... is tantamount to removing the cornerstone of the entire structure of dialectical and historical materialism. [In] renaming these subjects ... a crucial part of Marxism–Leninism has been dismantled.[111]

With regard to the CPSU's commitment to scientific atheism, the first example of a slight shift came in 1988. Elaborate celebrations were staged to commemorate the millennium of Christianity being introduced into Russia. This apparently caused tension between the Council for Religious Affairs (CRA) (a state body which, being reformist in tone, began to concern itself with defending believers interests) and the propaganda and atheistic departments of the party.[112] In March of 1988, Kharchev, the former head of the CRA, spoke of the need to look anew at religion. In an interesting quote cited by Melnick, Kharchev stated:

> Questions arise as to what is more advantageous to the Party – a believer in God, one who does not believe in anything, or one who believes in both God and communism.[113]

Of the three, Kharchev preferred the latter. These articles of Kharchev prefigured the emergence of "new thinking" in the field of scientific atheism. The discussion proceeded along two separate, although related, axes: the attitudes of the party towards religion and believers, and the attitudes towards scientific atheism. The starting-point for the reassessment of the latter was an article by Viktor Garadzha entitled "*Pereomyslenie*" (rethinking) in *Nauka i religiya*, of January 1989.[114] Calling for a re-evaluation of the entire system of atheistic education and propaganda, his article initiated a debate concerning the efficacy of atheistic methods and aims. The new values appeared to be toleration and dialogue. The "old" crude approaches were to be eschewed in favour of respect for the feelings of believers and the need to engage in constructive dialogue.

413

Atheism was to be pursued by winning the arguments, not crushing buildings or menacing individuals, and not through crude propaganda.[115] However, this point should not be overstated, as the guardians of atheistic orthodoxy still maintained their firm and unequivocal opposition. But it is clear that some of the principles of NPT filtered through to the sphere of atheistic education, a point that was attested to by the growth of religious instruction in schools.

The shifting emphasis in atheistic methods and goals was mirrored by the accommodation undertaken by the party in its attitudes towards religion as an alternative worldview. The law on "Freedom of conscience and religious organizations"[116] adopted in October 1990 was highly significant. The main provisions can be divided into three sections: individual and group; church and state; and international. The overall purpose was to guarantee freedom of conscience, expression and worship, and equality of rights and interests of citizens. Now, however, each citizen "enjoys the right to express and spread convictions" about their religion. The sections dealing with church/state and group/state were especially illuminating in the light of previous state policy. Article 5 established the separation of church and state and the equality of all denominations before the law. State interference in religious activities was proscribed, and state funding of atheistic propaganda was forbidden, testifying not only to the separation of church and state, but also to that of party and state. According to Article 12, religious organizations now also had access to the mass media and the right to create means of mass information. Educationally, they could set up religious schools and training seminaries (article 6), and could own property and engage in economic activities (articles 17 and 18). The international dimension was significant for slightly different reasons. Article 31 stated that:

> If an international treaty to which the USSR is a signatory has established rules other than those contained in the legislation on freedom of conscience and religious organisations, the rules of the international treaty shall apply.[117]

The priority given to the international treaties (the 1981 UN Declaration on the Elimination of all Forms of Intolerance and Discrimination Based on Religion or Belief, and the Document of the CSCE in

Vienna from 1989, especially) is yet another example of the incorporation of European norms of morality and human rights into Soviet theory and practice.[118] These themes were also reflected in the latest draft of the CPSU programme. Freedom of conscience, spiritual freedom, respect for all believers was stressed. No mention was made of atheism at all.

HDS also overturned the traditional Bolshevik approach to questions of morality. Previously Marxism–Leninism subordinated the moral freedom of the individual to the needs of the state. *Perestroika* caused a complete reassessment of Marxist–Leninist moral philosophy. The renewed emphasis on justice, compassion, freedom, charity and spiritual values reflected the priority of universal human values, and the return to a Judaeo – Christian based moral code, in turn reflected the wider absorption of Russia into European civilization. Morality no longer had a class basis, and was no longer prescribed by obligations or ends. This shift in moral philosophy reinforces the themes explored above. *Perestroika* forced Soviet Marxism–Leninism to recognize the importance of moral and spiritual questions, and the paucity of an approach to the world that concentrated almost wholly upon material issues, and on an economistic, productivist view of the individual. Finally, it also signified the new status of individuals, who were now no longer necessarily bound by their social obligations in the exercise of their moral freedom.

The cultural policy of the state under *perestroika* underwent a similar transformation. Initially, the CPSU maintained its instrumentalist constructivist approach. Under *glasnost'*, it sought to develop cultural forms, and to promote particular cultural phenomena that fostered the conception of reform favoured by the leadership. The rapid progress of *glasnost'* produced a dazzling array of spontaneously produced cultural trends, which the CPSU was unable to control and was forced to recognize. As Stites outlines,

> Popular culture at the peak of *glasnost'* reflected above all the . . . splintering and pluralism of values in Soviet society: new and old, urban and rural, cosmopolitan and chauvinistic, religious and anti-religious, rational and mystical . . . But it also indicated spontaneity, freedom, competition, individualism – a market place of ideas and feelings.[119]

The recognition and legitimation of cultural spontaneity marked the demise of the constructivist approach to social and cultural management. There was to be no more social engineering.

The culmination of the transformation of the value-system of Soviet socialism was reflected in the reduced status and importance of Marx, Engels and Lenin in Soviet discourse. The Founding Fathers had previously occupied a sacrosanct position, immune from criticism. The progress of *glasnost'* produced a flood of criticisms that created the conditions for the CPSU to begin to draw upon other socialist thinkers and intellectual traditions in the formulation of its new worldview. The draft party programme proclaimed that,

> The CPSU is built on the devotion of its members to certain ideological values. For us the chief of these is the idea of Humane Democratic Socialism. While restoring and developing the initial humanist principles of the teaching of Marx, Engels and Lenin we include in our ideological arsenal all the wealth of our own and world socialist and democratic thought.[120]

The worldview of the CPSU was a diverse, eclectic, pluralistic one, far removed from the scientific, constructivist, Marxist–Leninist basis of the orthodox model of Soviet socialism.

The draft party programme of August 1991: the social-democratization of Bolshevism

The whole gamut of theoretical and ideological changes in the period after 1985 were embodied in the draft party programme of August 1991, which Gorbachev managed to hijack and turn into a personal statement of faith by by-passing the official drafting commission.[121] This recognized the massive ideological reappraisal at the heart of HDS: the abandonment of teleological historical materialism, and with it the demise of a belief in the future communist society, stateless, classless, harmonious and free from exploitation. Communism ceased to be the ostensible goal towards which the Soviet system was moving. As Gooding has shown, not only were references to Khrushchev's proclamation of the imminent advent of communism heavily criticized, but references to communism itself steadily declined, to the point where it could be said to have been abandoned.[122] Although this was clearly a continuation of the entire post-revolutionary practice (Khrushchev excepted) of postponing the transition to communism, it marks a qualitative break. No longer was there even a formal commitment to communism as the social system which would follow a "restructured" Soviet society. The first draft of the 1991 party programme contained no references at all to communism. The reworked version of August 1991 outlined communism to be nothing more than a "social ideal". This *de facto* abandonment of the teleological element inherent in Soviet historical materialism was clearly tied to the emergence of an ethical concept of socialism. Implicit within HDS was the realization that the evolutionary progressivist optimism of the traditional model of Soviet socialism was misplaced. The possibility of crises, conflicts and revolutions under socialism, the admission that socialism had a lot to learn from capitalism, led inexorably to the conclusion that the historical process was no longer a scientific project governed by observable and knowable laws.

This abandonment or "withering away" of communism also caused a profound reassessment of socialism as a transitional society between capitalism and communism. Previously, it was seen as something that was doomed to pass away (sooner or later), as a transition period, and so was merely a means to a higher goal. Now though:

> Socialism is no longer a stage in the transition to communism, but becomes an end in itself, an absolute rather than a conditional goal, and one whose prospects of being realised can only be damaged by the perpetuation of communist values.[123]

The debates that were spawned by the theoretical renewal inherent in *perestroika* (imperatives of the NPT, empirical historical studies and the acceptance of the existence of neutral structures and processes), and the implications of the retreat from scientific socialism, combined to cause a reassessment of capitalism, socialism and communism in Soviet theory. The abandonment of Marxist historicism, of socialism as a society that transcends capitalism, of the vanguard role of the party, of the class-based view of the world, were all recognized in the draft party programme. *De facto* the CPSU had abandoned its commitment to, and belief in, orthodox Marxism–Leninism. The belief-system of the CPSU was essentially similar to those of West European social democratic parties. The Bolshevik programme – to transform the world – was finally laid to rest.

Humane Democratic Socialism in historical perspective

The core values contained within HDS were those of humanism, democracy and freedom, symbolizing the triumph of ethical socialism over its scientific predecessor. Not only did *perestroika* undermine the core institutional features of the orthodox model in practice – the leading role of the party, central planning, state ownership – but it also destroyed the understanding of the underlying principles of Soviet socialism: rationalism, productivism, constructivism, collectivism. While Khrushchev and Brezhnev had modified the Stalinist interpretation to a greater or lesser extent, their overall approach remained within the parameters of the orthodox interpretation of Soviet socialism which came to predominate after 1917. HDS represents a complete break with the principles and values of the Soviet model of socialism, without returning to the radical, decentralizing, emancipatory, workerist agenda that had existed within early Bolshevism, but which had been gradually displaced by a more technocratic, statist conception. HDS ended the historic split within the international socialist movement in 1914.[124]

The core ideas re-evaluated by HDS concerned the state, the market, class and property.[125] Orthodox Soviet socialism had viewed the state as the primary agent for change, class as the basic divide in politics, the market as a mechanism instituting inequality and irrationality, and private property as a source of exploitation and alienation. HDS turned these ideas on their head. Gorbachev stressed that the participation of society, and the groups and individuals within it, was vital to the creation of a self-sustaining process of change and renewal. State power and ownership merely created a different form of alienation. Overcoming this meant a radical shift of power and control to society and to individual citizens. As mentioned above, the rejection of the primacy of class values was transformed into embracing universalist humanitarianism: the interests of humanity were now prior to those of the proletariat. Similarily, both the market and private property were no longer viewed exclusively as the source of patterns of domination and subordination. Instead it could, given the right socio-economic milieu, become a means of bolstering the freedom and autonomy of groups and individuals, granting them a source of independence from the state and so creating greater opportunities for political and economic equality.

The problem in trying to assess this concept is that these values and ideas were the result of a whole variety of intellectual influences, as well as reformist imperatives. This eclecticism embraced Lenin, Marx, Eurocommunism, Social Democracy and others. It is clear that this widespread reliance on a variety of sources reflected the need to evolve a concept or doctrine that could embody the vortex of contradictory pressures which Gorbachev found himself in. The relation of Gorbachev to Lenin is an interesting one. Gorbachev, like all the General Secretaries before him, asserted the need to return to Lenin. However, it was the nature of this "return" that is worthy of note. The most consistent theme was the invocation of Lenin as both revolutionary and arch-pragmatist, linking the two leaders through their style of leadership and their approach to politics. Gorbachev eschewed many of the traditional elements of Leninism, enthusiastically embraced others and modified yet other aspects. The most obvious theme was that *perestroika* represented the rediscovery of the threads of NEP as a method of building socialism, especially the liberalizing measures in the economy. The analogy with NEP was not wholly accurate though, given the disparity between Lenin's political centralization (restrictions on other parties and curtailing inner-party democracy) and Gorbachev's democratization and "socialist" pluralism. Perhaps the crucial similarity was the historical choice: NEP represented the rejection of war communism, *perestroika* the rejection of Stalinism.[126]

Much of Lenin and Leninism was discarded. The emphasis on class, the international solidarity of the proletariat juxtaposed to the forces of Imperialism, the restrictions on alternative political groupings. However, a strong core of the political aspects of Leninism were retained by Gorbachev. The Leading Role of the Party was defended by Gorbachev right up until its abandonment in March

1990, even within the changing political conditions brought about by democratization. (Indeed, Gorbachev still retained his faith in the party after the August coup.) This latter development also led, in Sakwa's words, to the revival of "a participatory form of democracy based on the Soviets".[127] This return to what Sakwa has termed "commune democracy" involved the attempt to create a form of democracy which entailed mass participation, within the confines of a one-party system. Participatory, commune democracy rejected the parliamentarism, separation of powers and checks and balances of liberal democracy as a sham, masking the domination of the ruled by their rulers. Socialist, commune democracy emphasized instead the active participation of the masses. It was clear that this vision underpinned Gorbachev's policy initiatives in this area in 1987–8, as he sought the activization of the Soviets and a renewal of the leading role of the party. The Soviets were to act as functioning representative and administrative bodies, drawing in the people, while the party was to renounce its day-to-day involvement in managing social and economic affairs. Instead, the party was to take on ideological and political "guidance", and act as a forum for the articulation and aggregation of the interests of the "informals".

Although, in political terms, this can be seen as an attempt to create a modified form of Leninist commune democracy, the evolution of Gorbachev's thought in tandem with the dynamics of the reform process meant that it was not a static conception. Gradually, Gorbachev began to introduce elements of liberal democracy (separation of powers, two-tier parliamentary system, Executive Presidency) into the political system. At root, this turn away from modified Leninism arose from the realization that the Leading Role of the Party was unsustainable and a hindrance to the progress of the reforms. Party and state had to be separated. The demise of party-led *perestroika*, and the emergence of what Sakwa has termed "Presidential *perestroika*" meant the end of "modified" Leninism as a component part of Gorbachev's ideological platform, although it played a key role in its emergence.[128]

Just as Lenin of NEP became a source of ideas, inspiration and legitimacy, so too did the "early" Marx. Many of the themes of Marx's writings prior to 1848 – such as alienation and individual creativity – had emphasized basic humanitarian values. In his struggle with the effects of the Administrative System upon the consciousness and psychology of the Soviet population, these themes resonated within Gorbachev. It was also evident that Gorbachev viewed individual freedom in humanistic Marxist terms. The phrase, the free development of each as the condition for the free development of all, encapsulated his vision of socialism:[129] a society of human solidarity and fraternity, in which the individual realizes him/herself through transcending their own narrow desires and interests. The priority or order is the significant thing though: human solidarity comes through the emancipation of the individual, not the other way around. Human autonomy, open-ended history and an assertion of the significance and importance of the individual in socialism, all these themes reflected a shift in the philosophical priorities of Soviet socialism, and a return to the "early" Marx.

The internal dynamics of *perestroika*, involving a growing radicalization of the economic and political spheres, gradually transformed Gorbachev's thinking. The initial combination of neo-Leninism (involving commune democracy in the political sphere, and moves towards more decentralized, self-managing structures in the economy) and humanistic Marxism, was transformed into a combination of social democracy and radical liberalism. Economically, the "mixed" economy became the centrepiece. A balance was to be struck between plan and market, public and private (and other forms of) ownership. Social policy emphasized the importance of welfare, health care, improved pensions, etc. Politically, the structures and institutions of liberal democracy became acceptable, involving the attempt to create a representative constitutional democracy, and a functioning civil society protected by the rule of law. In philosophical terms, the new ethos was an amalgam of "watered down" collectivism and possessive individualism. Gorbachev's ideological platform evolved to the point where the wholesale borrowing of "Western" concepts and values had displaced whole sections of the former "orthodoxy".

Evaluating HDS is not easy. It is vital to take account of the context (rapidly accelerating pace of change), and of the evolutionary process which the ideas of Gorbachev and his advisers underwent. It seems clear that the initial phase of *perestroika* (c. 1987–90) was an attempt at a social democratization of Leninism: more market, more private initiative, greater political autonomy for non-party groups, but all within a socialist, one-party system. Subsequent developments witnessed the abandonment of the framework of neo-Leninism. The attempt to synthesize the elements of neo-Leninism (a one-party system and revitalized Soviets) with some elements of Western liberal democracy collapsed. Ideas, values and concepts that were alien to Soviet Marxism–Leninism were injected into it. Instead of revitalizing the patient, the medicine hastened its demise. The result was the rapid evolution of a concept of socialism that at times appeared to be little more than a form of welfare capitalism or perhaps a relative of European Social Democracy. The problem was that in reacting against statist socialism, and asserting the importance of individual autonomy and freedom, HDS found it increasingly difficult to prevent itself collapsing from social democracy into welfare capitalism and radical liberalism.[130]

The 1991 draft party programme stands as a testament to the momentous changes the USSR and the CPSU underwent in the period after March 1985. Before the CPSU had the opportunity to implement HDS, the system was embroiled in the August coup. Scientific socialism was dead. Ethical socialism was swept away in the tumult surrounding the demise of communism.

Notes

1. V. Medvedev, "Sovremennaya kontseptsia sotsializma", in *Pravda*, 5 October 1988, p. 4. The basic issues and problems raised at the conference are summarized in "Protivorechie sovremennogo sotsializma", *Obshchestvennie Nauki* **1**, 1990, p. 15–28.
2. M. S. Gorbachev, "Sotsialisticheskaya ideya i revolutsionnaya perestroika", *Pravda*, 26 November 1989, pp. 1–3; K gumannomy, demokraticheskomy, sotsialisticheskomy obshchestvy", *Pravda*, 7 February 1990, p. 1–3.
3. F. Burlatsky, "Kakoi sotsializm narodu nuzhen?", *Literaturnaya gazeta*, 20 April 1988, p. 2.
4. J. Farr, "Understanding political change conceptually", in *Political innovation and conceptual change*, T. Ball et al. (eds) (Cambridge: Cambridge University Press, 1989).
5. *Pravda*, 10 November 1985, p. 1.
6. See the collection, *Brezhnev: the period of stagnation* (Moscow: Novosti, 1989). F. Burlatsky, A hero of times past, *Guardian*, 17 December 1988, p. 19.

7. Cited in S. White, *Soviet communism: programme and rules* (London: Routledge, 1989), p. 42.
8. M. Gorbachev, *Report to the 27th CPSU Congress* (Moscow: Novosti Press, 1986), p. 114.
9. Ibid., p. 114–16.
10. M. Gorbachev, *On perestroika and the party's personnel policy*, 27 January 1987 (Tass transcript, 1987). The plenum was postponed three times before finally meeting.
11. Gorbachev, *On perestroika*, pp. 10–18.
12. The term was first coined in Popov's review of Aleksander Bek's novel, *The new appointment*, published in *Nauka i zhizn'*, April 1987, pp. 54–65. For a Western assessment see, V. Andrle, "Beyond the Administrative System", *Detente* **12**, 1988, pp. 17–21.
13. "O sushchnosti mekhanizma tormozhenie", *Voprosy istorii KPSS* **1**, 1988, pp. 128–34. "Nekotorie problemy razvitiya obshchestve v 70 gody. Deistvie mekhanizma tormozhenie", in *Voprosy istorii KPSS* **2**, 1988, pp. 110–33.
14. See especially the wide-ranging discussion, "Problemy razrabotki kontseptsii sovremennogo sotsializma", *Voprosy filosofii* **12**, 1988, pp. 31–71.
15. For a good short summary of the problems facing the Soviet leaders see, R. Parker, "Assessing perestroika", *World Policy Journal* **6**(2), 1989, pp. 264–96.
16. R. Amann, "Searching for an appropriate concept of Soviet politics: the politics of hesitant modernisation", *British Journal of Political Science* **16**(4), 1986, pp. 477–82.
17. R. W. Davies, "Gorbachev's socialism in historical perspective", *New Left Review* **179**, 1990, pp. 15–18, 22–5.
18. Gorbachev, *On perestroika*, pts 1 and 2.
19. *XIX vsesoyuznaya konferentsiya kommunisticheskoi parti sovetskogo soyuza: stenograficheskii otchet'* (Moscow: Politizdat, 1988).
20. On the political reforms see S. White, *After Gorbachev* (Cambridge: Cambridge University Press, 1992).
21. This concept received its first full theoretical elaboration in A. Aganbegyan, "Strategiya uskorenie sotsial'no-ekonomicheskogo razvitiya", *Problemy mira i sotsializma* **9**, 1985, pp. 13–19.
22. M. Gorbachev, *Perestroika: new thinking for our country and the world* (London: Fontana, 1987), pp. 34–7.
23. M. Gorbachev, "Perestroika neotlozhna: ona kasaetsya veskh i vo vsem", *Pravda*, 2 August 1986, p. 2.
24. T. Zaslavskaya, O stratgeii sotsialnogo upravlenie perestroiki, in *Inogo ne dano* (Moscow: Progress, 1988), pp. 9–50.
25. B. Kurashvili, "Modeli sotsializma", *Sovetskoe gosudarstvo i pravo* **8**, 1989, pp. 99–110.

26. H. Smith, *The new Russians* (London: Vintage, 1990), pp. 79–173.
27. Gorbachev, *Perestroika: new thinking*, p. 76. See also Gorbachev's memoirs, *Zhizn' i reformy* [2 vols] (Moscow: Novosti, 1995), pp. 314–33.
28. Ibid., p. 76.
29. R. Sakwa, *Soviet politics* (London: Routledge, 1989), p. 212.
30. P. Hauslohner, "Gorbachev's social contract", *Soviet Economy* **3**(1), 1987, pp. 54–89; Gorbachev, *Zhizn' i reformy*, pp. 423–67.
31. Gorbachev, *On perestroika*, p. 39.
32. W. Smirnov, "New political thinking: Problems and prospects", *Social sciences* **19**, 1988, p. 216.
33. G. Shakhnazarov, "Political leadership in the nuclear era", *Social Sciences* **19**, 1988, p. 53.
34. S. Shenfield, *The nuclear predicament* (London: Routledge, 1987), pp. 61–2; Gorbachev, *Zhizn'*, vol. 2 part 3.
35. V. Petrovsky, "All-embracing universal security", *Social Sciences* **19**(3), 1988, pp. 39–40.
36. Ibid., p. 40.
37. P. Fedoseev, "Man in the modern world", *Social Sciences* **19**(2), 1988, pp. 8–17; I. Frolov, "Global problems: man and his outlook", in ibid., pp. 29–43.
38. J. Cooper, "The Soviet economy in transition", in *The Soviet revolution*, J. Bloomfield (ed.) (London: Lawrence & Wishart, 1989), p. 122.
39. J. Bloomfield, in ibid., p. 246.
40. The first mention by Gorbachev was in his speech at the January 1987 plenum. It was most fully elaborated by him in his speech, "October and *perestroika*: the revolution continues" (especially part 2 "Developing Socialism and *perestroika*") in *Pravda*, 3 November 1987, pp. 1–2. The fullest account of Yakovlev's views came in his keynote article in *Vestnik* **6**, 17 April 1987, "Dostizhenie kachestvenno novogo sostayaniya sovetskogo obshchestva i obshchestvennie nauki". This was followed in 1987 and 1988 by a number of important articles and discussions. See for example: "O protivorechiyakh razvivayushchegosya sotsializma", *Politicheskoe obrazovanie* **2**, 1988, pp. 25–8; and a round-table in ibid., **12**, 1988, pp. 33–48.
41. The key article is G. Smirnov's, "Tvorchestvo teorii razvivayush-chegosya sotsializma", *Kommunist* **12**, 1987, pp. 19–32. See also his "Revolutsionnaya sut' obnovleniya", *Pravda*, 13 March 1987, pp. 2–3; and "Teoreticheskoe osmislenie protsessov obnovleniya sotsializma", *Obshchestvennie nauki* **6**, 1988, pp. 5–19; K voprosu o leninskoi kontseptsii sotsializma, *Politicheskoe obrazovanie* **1**, 1989, pp. 12–21.
42. L. Kolakowski, *Main currents of Marxism* (Oxford: OUP, 1978) vol. 2, p. 391.

43. R. Sakwa, *Gorbachev and his reforms 1985–90* (London: Phillip Allan, 1990), p. 103.
44. M. Sandle, "The final word: the draft party programme of July/ August 1991", *Europe–Asia Studies* **48**(7), 1996, pp. 1131–50.
45. M. Gorbachev, "Sotsialisticheskaya ideya", *Pravda*, 26 November 1989, p. 2.
46. Walicki, *Marxism and the leap to the kingdom of freedom*, p. 539.
47. Ibid., p. 2.
48. Gorbachev, *Perestroika: new thinking*, pp. 135–60; E. Amelina, "Socialist ideal: class hatred or humanism?", *Social Sciences* **1**, 1990, pp. 44–55.
49. Amelina, "Socialist ideal", p. 54–5.
50. "Towards Humane Democratic Socialism: the CPSU Programme of the 28th Congress", in *BBC Summary of World Broadcasts*, [SWB] SU/0821, C2/1–8, 20/7/90. The first version of the draft party programme was translated in *BBC SWB* 26 July 1991, SU/1134 C1/1–7. The revised version was translated in *BBC SWB*, 9 August 1991, SU/ 1146 C1/1–7.
51. "Towards Humane Democratic", p. 2.
52. M. Gorbachev, "Address to Belorussian Academy of Sciences", in *BBC SWB* SU/1009 C1/1–14, p. 4.
53. "CPSU resolution on economic policy and market relations", in *BBC SWB* SU/0820 C1/17–18, 19 July 1990.
54. Ibid., p. 17.
55. M. Gorbachev, "On the transition to the market economy", in *BBC SWB* SU/0873 C1/1–4, 19 September 1990, pp. 2–3. For Gorbachev's reflections on economic reform, see, *Zhizn' i reformy* **1**, ch. 11.
56. M. Gorbachev, "Report to the 28th CPSU Congress", in *BBC SWB* SU/0807 C1/1–18, 4 July 1990, p. 1.
57. W. Joyce, "The law of the state enterprise", in *Gorbachev and Gorbachevism*, W. Joyce et al. (eds) (London: Cass, 1989), pp. 71–82.
58. G. Shakhnazarov, "De-ideologisation of inter-state relationships", *Social Sciences* **1**, 1990, pp. 38–56.
59. Gorbachev, "On the transition", p. 2.
60. Ibid., p. 1.
61. Ibid., p. 2.
62. Ibid., p. 2.
63. Ibid., p. 2.
64. Gorbachev, "On the transition", p. 1. For a Western assessment, see P. Hanson, "Ownership issues in *perestroika*", in *Socialism, perestroika and the dilemmas of economic reform*, J. Tedstrom (ed.) (Boulder: Westview Press, 1990), pp. 65–96.
65. "Platform for the 28th CPSU Congress", in *BBC SWB* SU/0688 C1/1–11, 14/2/90, p. 4.

66. Gorbachev, "Report to the 28th CPSU Congress", p. 5.
67. G. Gill, *The collapse of a single party system* (Cambridge: Cambridge University Press, 1994).
68. Gorbachev, "Sotsialisticheskaya ideya", p. 1.
69. Ibid., p. 2. See also Gorbachev's memoirs, *Zhizn' i reformy*, vol. 1, ch. 17.
70. The proceedings of this plenum can be found in *Pravda*, 6 February 1990, pp. 1–2.
71. Revised draft party programme, pp. 5–7.
72. Gorbachev, "Report to 28th Congress", p. 1.
73. 28th Congress programme, p. 3. Sakwa, *Gorbachev*, p. 397.
74. 28th Congress programme, p. 3.
75. Lukasheva was a participant in the discussion in "Individual, society, state", *Soviet Sociology*, Sept/Oct 1990, pp. 37–60.
76. A. Migranyan, "Vzaimootnosheniya individa, obshchestva i gosudarstva v politicheskoi teorii marksizma i problemy demokratizatsiya sotsialisticheskogo obshchestva", *Voprosy filosofii* **8**, 1987, pp. 75–91.
77. 28th Congress programme, p. 3.
78. Ibid., p. 2.
79. See, for example, D. Manning, *Liberalism* (London: Dent, 1976).
80. A. Tsipko, cited in E. Teague, "Soviet theoreticians debate the human factor", in *Radio Liberty Research Bulletin*, 385/89, 6/8/89, pp. 10–12.
81. J. Scanlan, "Ideology and reform", in *Gorbachev's reforms: Japanese and US assessments*, P. Juviler & H. Kimura (eds) (New York: Aldine de Gruyter, 1988), pp. 49–62.
82. Migranyan, "Vzaimootnosheniya", p. 86.
83. Ibid., p. 88.
84. Scanlan, "Ideology and reform", p. 60–1.
85. J. Gooding, "Gorbachev and democracy", *Soviet Studies* **42**(2), 1990, p. 200.
86. R. N. Berki, *Socialism* (London: Dent, 1976), p. 25.
87. V. Kuvaldin, "Equality v. freedom", *Moscow News* **11**, 1990, p. 7.
88. 28th Congress programme, p. 3.
89. Ibid., p. 4.
90. *Pravda*, 8 August 1991, p. 3.
91. Ibid., p. 3.
92. Ibid., p. 3.
93. Gorbachev, *Perestroika: new thinking*, p. 146.
94. A phrase coined by Gennadi Gerasimov, the foreign policy spokesperson of the foreign ministry.
95. G. Shakhnazarov, "V poiskakh utrachennoi idei", *Kommunist* **4** and **5**, 1991, pp. 18–31, and 16–30, respectively. For a Western assessment,

see M. Sandle, "Georgii Shakhnazarov and the Soviet critique of historical materialism", *Studies in East European Thought* **49**, 1997, pp. 109–33.

96. E. Batalov, "Prospects of socialism and utopian consciousness", *Social Sciences* **20**(3), 1989, pp. 84–6.

97. Shakhnazarov, "De-ideologisation", pp. 38–56; E. Primakov, "Capitalism in the interrelated world", *Social Sciences* **19**(4), 1988, pp. 48–61.

98. Kurashvili, "Modeli", pp. 109–10.

99. Shakhnazarov, "De-ideologisation", p. 45.

100. Ibid., p. 52–4. For a Western assessment, see H. Timmermann, "The CPSU's reassessment of international social-democracy", *Journal of Communist Studies* **5**(2), 1989, pp. 173–84.

101. Timmermann, "The CPSU's", pp. 176–82; C. Aitmatov, in *Izvestiya*, 4 June 1989, p. 2.

102. Shakhnazarov, "De-ideologisation", pp. 47–8.

103. Timmermann, "CPSU's reassessment", pp. 175–6.

104. A. Sabov, Shvedskaya spichka, in *Literaturnaya Gazeta*, no. 15, 11/4/90, p. 14. A. Shakol'skii, Sotsialisticheskii korolstve shvedska, *Argumenty i fakty* **17**, 1990, p. 4.

105. The resolution was published in *Uchitel'skaya Gazeta* 21/5/88.

106. R. W. Davies, "*Soviet history in the Gorbachev revolution*" (Houndmills: Macmillan, 1989); T. Ito (ed.), *Facing up to the past. Soviet historiography under perestroika* (Sapporo: Hokkaido University 1989); V. Tolz, New history textbooks for secondary schools, *Radio Liberty Research Bulletin*, 396/89, 22/8/89, pp. 5–7.

107. A. Buccholz, "The ongoing deconstruction of Soviet Marxism–Leninism", *Studies in Soviet Thought* **40**, 1990, pp. 231–40.

108. Ibid., pp. 231–3.

109. Cited in *Izvestiya*, 4 February 1990, p. 2.

110. Buccholz, "The ongoing deconstruction", pp. 232–5.

111. Ibid., p. 234.

112. A. James Melnick, "Scientific atheism in the era of *perestroika*", *Studies in Soviet Thought* **40**, 1990, pp. 223–9.

113. Ibid., p. 224.

114. V. Garadzha, "Pereomyslenie", *Nauka i religiya*, January 1989, pp. 2–5.

115. Melnick, "Scientific atheism", p. 224.

116. *Pravda*, 9 October 1990. For a commentary see S. J. Roth, "The new Soviet law on religion", *Soviet Jewish Affairs* **20**(2–3), 1990, pp. 23–7.

117. *Pravda*, 9 October 1990.

118. Sakwa, *Gorbachev*, p. 397.

119. R. Stites, *Russian popular culture* (Cambridge: Cambridge University Press, 1992), p. 203.

120. Revised draft party programme, p. 4.
121. Excellent context for this whole period can be found in Gorbachev, *Zhizn' i reformy*, vol. 2, part 5.
122. Gooding, "Gorbachev and democracy", pp. 198–202.
123. Gooding, "Gorbachev and democracy", p. 202.
124. A. Evans, *Soviet Marxism–Leninism* (Westport: Praeger, 1993), p. 200.
125. Sakwa, *Gorbachev*, pp. 114–16.
126. C. Smart, "Gorbachev's Lenin: the myth in service to *perestroika*", *Studies in Comparative Communism* **23**(1), 1990, pp. 5–22.
127. Sakwa, *Gorbachev*, p. 112. See also his, "Commune democracy and Gorbachev's reforms", *Political Studies* **37**(2), 1989, pp. 224–43.
128. Sakwa, *Gorbachev*, pp. 162, 169–99.
129. C. J. Arthur (ed.) *Marx and Engels: the German Ideology* (London: Lawrence & Wishart 1970), pp. 182–6.
130. Sakwa, *Gorbachev*, p. 383.

Conclusion: history and Soviet socialism

Q: What is the definition of socialism?
A: The longest road from feudalism to capitalism.

A number of obituaries for the Soviet Union, and for Soviet social-ism are beginning to emerge as the dust from 1989–91 settles. His-torians, political scientists and other commentators have reflected on the critical significance of these events, marking either the end of modernity, the end of "The short twentieth century", the demise of the political project derived from the Enlightenment, or even the end of History.[1] Two issues conclude this analysis of the origins, evolution and demise of the Soviet model of socialism. The first is, what does this analysis tell us about the historical development of Soviet socialism, and of the importance of ideas in shaping the history of socialism in the Soviet Union? Secondly, what does the future hold for "socialism" as a political doctrine?

Soviet socialism in historical perspective

The adoption of an historical perspective on the unfolding of Soviet socialism throws up some extremely interesting insights. Extrapo-lating from the above analysis, the key factors in shaping the Soviet model of socialism were as follows. First, the understanding of the transition phase they inherited from Marx, Engels and Kautsky, mediated through the experience of the German war economy during the First World War. As Feher has noted,

> Marxism–Leninism was an even more arbitrary selection from the menu of Marxian philosophy, and resulted in the philosophy's curtailment and fragmentation . . . Marxism–Leninism threw overboard the entire humanistic legacy of Marx's philosophy.[2]

The Bolshevik preference for certain socio-economic and political forms – non-market, centralist, statist, planned, technocratic – was reinforced by the circumstances of economic, cultural and technological backwardness, chaos, war and international hostility after 1917, which led to the erosion of the democratic, decentralizing, radical, emancipatory strand of Bolshevism. The other defining moment came with the revolution from above and the development of "socialism in one country". The need for "haste", the accent on Bolshevik tempos and the project to "overcome backwardness" now co-existed in Bolshevik discourse with the project of constructing socialism. This had two effects. First, the precise meaning of concepts such as "planning" were finally resolved (and were to maintain virtually unchanged until 1990). Secondly, as Hobsbawm has noted, "Bolshevism turned itself into an ideology for rapid economic development for countries in which the conditions of capitalist development don't exist".[3] The Bolshevik emphasis upon the growth of the productive forces in order to lay the foundations for material abundance was displaced by the commitment to growth at any cost as quickly as possible. The rationalist, productivist heart of Leninist Bolshevism was replaced by the autarkic, crudely productivist heart of Stalinist Bolshevism.

Soviet socialism displayed a great deal of heterogeneity over this period, along a number of axes. The first of these relates to the rhythms of the process of building socialism: radical, energetic phases of activity (war communism, revolution from above, Khrushchevism, *perestroika*) which would give way to more gradualistic, measured phases of development (NEP, the Brezhnev era). This rhythm is overlain by a further contrast between methods of building socialism that were centralist and statist (war communism, Stalinism,

Brezhnevism), and those that favoured a greater degree of decentralization and liberalization (NEP, Khrushchevism, *perestroika*). The method of building socialism under Bolshevism displayed a remarkable degree of diversity and heterogeneity.

A third issue is the relationship between theory and practice in the successive phases in the building of socialism. In the eras of "war communism", NEP, Khrushchev and *perestroika*, theory was modified and refined in the light of the changing practice of the CPSU, albeit within the parameters of the general understanding of socialism in Bolshevik discourse. The two exceptions to this were the Stalinist era (in which "socialism in one country" preceded the economic and social transformations of the 1930s), and the Brezhnev era (where Developed Socialism was elaborated concomitant with the abandonment of Khrushchevite practices). It is no surprise that these two eras are seen as the most dogmatic, conservative, intellectually stultifying times of Soviet history, as the elaboration of theory helped to encase the structures and practice of Soviet socialism within a narrow constricting framework that vastly reduced the optional paths of social development open to the party leadership.

Bearing this diversity in mind, one of the striking features of the theory and practice of Soviet socialism was the degree of continuity and stability exhibited between 1917 and 1985. The worldview of Bolshevik Marxism–Leninism – constructivist, rationalist, productivist, technocratic – continued to underpin the process of building socialism in the USSR after 1917 (and indeed remained during the early stages of *perestroika*). The CPSU also maintained a striking commitment to the core features of "socialism" as a transition phase, as derived from their readings of Marx, Engels and Kautsky and from the practice of the German war economy: central planning, state ownership, central direction of social processes, leading role of the communist party, proletarian internationalism. The stability or rigidity of the core features of the ruling ideology has long been remarked upon by Western commentators.[4] Although the precise meaning of many of these features was subject to periodical reinterpretation in the light of political imperatives (especially the leading role of the party, and the commitment to proletarian internationalism), the party maintained that socialism was a transitional society defined according to a set of structural features to be consciously constructed.

431

How important have these ideas been in the course of development of Soviet history? Malia has recently argued that,

> Thus, the essence of the communist system and the unity of the Soviet experience are defined by a single and supreme task – the "building of socialism". And it is because Western social science has by and large refused to take this ideological aim seriously that Sovietology has failed so woefully to understand its subject.[5]

The views set out here concur with this statement. The understanding of "socialism" as a transitional society profoundly shaped the practice of Soviet socialism. However, it is important to qualify this by locating each particular interpretation of the transition phase generated by Lenin, Stalin, Khrushchev, Brezhnev and Gorbachev within the specific Soviet/international context out of which it arose. There was something of a dialectical relationship between the understanding of socialism and Soviet reality which forged successive syntheses of Soviet socialism after 1917. Only through the adoption of an historical perspective, which affords the possibility of tracing the degrees of continuity and change, is it possible to perceive the central role of the ideas, beliefs and presuppositions of the CPSU in determining the course of Soviet history, and at the same time to perceive the areas in which real life refused to yield to Bolshevik diktat, causing a refining of their theory in the light of this new practice. Soviet history requires a knowledge of the ideas, values and beliefs that animated its leaders, as they significantly determined the course of events from 1917–91.

One final point. What of socialism as a political doctrine after the "failure" of the Soviet "experiment"? The reasons for this failure are manifold, and deeply disputed. Economic failure, ethnic protest, political stasis, international pressure have all been identified as central factors in the collapse of the Soviet system. But what of the doctrinal roots of this process? To what extent was the failure of Soviet socialism the inexorable outworking of tendencies inherent within either socialism or Marxism?

The Marxist roots of Soviet socialism have been widely discussed by a number of theorists, both East and West.[6] Kolakowski argues that Marx's aspiration for universal human emancipation was rooted in a desire to achieve a perfectly unified human community. As civil society is a forum for the expression of private, and conflicting interests, it is necessary to dissolve civil society in the political society of public life (that is the state).[7] He goes on to state that,

> far from promising the fusion of civil with political society, the Marxian perspective of unified man is more likely to engender, if put into practice, a cancerous growth of quasi-omnipotent bureaucracy . . . and the dream of perfect unity may come true only in the form of a caricature: as an artificial unity imposed by coercion from above.[8]

Aleksander Tsipko also searched out the Marxist roots of Stalinism during the late 1980s. He blamed the flawed concept of human nature in Marx, arguing that this led the Bolsheviks to attempt to mould individuals and to engineer a particular form of personality among its citizens, which became the rationale for the intrusion of the state into all areas of the lives of Soviet citizens.[9]

Blackburn has responded to the question of Marxism's responsibility. He argues that while it is one-sided and distorted to argue that Marxism was directly responsible for Soviet socialism, Marxists and other socialists cannot argue that there is no link between the two. He argues,

> So with Marxism the gaps, errors and inadequacies in what Marx had to say about, for example, the rule of law, or the rights of the individual, or the need for checks and balances in political structures, or the abolition of commodity-money relations, do not constitute the essence of Marxism, as some would like to claim; but they may have some responsibility, direct or otherwise, for the practices of what used to be called "actually existing socialism".[10]

The many critiques of the practice of Soviet socialism from a variety of Marxist perspectives testify, according to Blackburn, to the enduring validity of Marxism as a doctrine, and to its ability to develop critical perspectives on all forms of oppression and exploitation.

Malia and Kolakowski extend their critique of Marxism to socialism as a whole. Malia argues that there are two components to socialism: a moral one and an instrumental one. The former refers to "democratic equality", the latter to the abolition of private property. To achieve this goal, the market must also be overcome, and this requires the massive imposition of state power. Transplanted to Russia, the absence of the necessary socio-economic prerequisites for the building of socialism required the intervention of a political body (in this case the Leninist vanguard) to carry this out, accumulating state power in the hands of a few individuals. In other words, Malia argues that the entire Soviet experience was a direct result of socialism itself, of the contradictory impulses running at the heart of the doctrine itself.[11] He states that, "the Soviet experiment turned totalitarian not despite its being socialist but because it was socialist".[12]

Many theorists, by way of contrast, have sought to rescue socialism as an ideal and a political movement in the wake of the collapse of the Soviet Union. There are two aspects to this project, a doctrinal one and an historical one. In historical perspective, the situation faced by contemporary socialists centres on their ability to explain the failure of the Soviet system as a particular, specific set of circumstances peculiar to the ussr between 1917–91. Hobsbawm argues that the Soviet experiment was not designed "as a global alternative to capitalism".[13] On these grounds it is not permissible to universalize the experience of "actually existing socialism". It must be analyzed within its particular historical context. In doctrinal terms, the particular mix of socialist values that emerged after 1917 (synthesizing rationalism and egalitarianism in Berki's terms)[14] has no bearing on the other variants of socialism within the world. The collapse of Soviet socialism represents the demise of the Enlightenment-based strand of socialist theory, which expressed the emancipatory power of knowledge and human reason. Its like will not be seen again, and not many people have mourned its passing. The viability and validity of varieties of socialism that outline moral or ethical imperatives, and which express a fundamental yearning for a fairer, not a more rational society, remains intact. But has socialism become little more than a purely moral standpoint?[15]

The enduring issue to be addressed is the lack of practical examples of societies that are functioning according to broadly socialist principles. The crisis within the countries of European social-democracy (particularly Sweden and Austria) in the 1980s seemed to confirm the conservative criticisms of socialism. But as attention has switched to the continued defects and flaws within capitalism among contemporary social theorists, so there has begun a renewal of socialist thought and doctrine. Most socialists now accept that the attempt to abolish or overcome market relations was a deeply flawed project. On the other hand, the bankruptcy of the New Right faith in unfettered market forces has been demonstrated by the results of "shock therapy" in eastern Europe and elsewhere.[16] The pressing problems of the world – global poverty, environmental degradation – have thrown the spotlight onto the flaws and defects of contemporary capitalism. The key processes for socialists, according to Blackburn, were

> to explore ways in which economic processes can draw on the skills and initiative of millons of independent agents, and yet remain responsive to democratically agreed social priorities . . . and to socialise the market.[17]

Socialism will continue the attempts to synthesize liberty, equality and justice. Its appeal will remain, as Hobsbawm argues, because "socialists are there to remind the world that people, and not production come first".[18] Such an epitaph could be fittingly inscribed on the tombstone of Soviet socialism.

Notes

1. Among the many works that have recently appeared, see the following: E. Hobsbawm, *Age of extremes. The short twentieth century* (London: Michael Joseph 1994); M. Malia, *The Soviet tragedy: a history of socialism in Russia* (New York: Free Press, 1994); R. Skidelsky, *The world after communism* (London: Macmillan, 1995); F. Fukuyama, *The end of history and the last man* (New York: Free Press, 1992); W. Laqueur, *The dream that failed* (Oxford: Oxford University Press, 1994); R. V. Daniels, *The end of the communist revolution* (London: Routledge, 1993); Z. Brzezinski, *The grand failure: the birth and death of communism in the twentieth century* (London: Macdonald, 1990); J. P. Arnasson, *The future that failed. Origins and destinies of the Soviet model* (London: Routledge, 1993); R. Blackburn (ed.), *After the fall. The failure of communism and the future of socialism* (London: Verso, 1991).

2. F. Feher, "Marxism as politics: an obituary", *Problems of Communism* **41,** 1992, p. 15.
3. Hobsbawm, "Out of the ashes", in Blackburn, *After the fall*, p. 318.
4. This point is forcibly and persuasively argued by J. Cooper, "Construction . . . reconstruction . . . deconstruction", in *Perestroika: the historical perspective*, C. Ward & C. Merridale (eds) (London: Edward Arnold, 1991), pp. 161–7.
5. M. Malia, "From under the rubble, what?", *Problems of Communism*, **41**, 1992, p. 103.
6. See the contributions by Kolakowski and Markovic in R. Tucker (ed.), *Stalinism: Essays in historical interpretation* (New York: Norton, 1977). See also M. Malia, *The Soviet tragedy. A history of socialism in Russia* (New York: Free Press, 1994); R. Miliband, *Socialism for a sceptical age* (Cambridge: Polity Press, 1994); D. Joravsky, "Communism in historical perspective", *American Historical Review* **99**, June 1994, pp. 837–57.
7. L. Kolakowski, "The myth of human self-identity", in *The socialist idea*, L. Kolakowski & S. Hampshire (eds) (London: Weidenfeld & Nicolson, 1974).
8. Ibid., p. 31.
9. A. Tsipko, "Istoki stalinizma", in *Nauka i zhizn'*, nos. 11 & 12 1988, 1 & 2 1989.
10. Blackburn, "*Fin de siècle*: socialism after the crash", in *After the fall*, p. 178.
11. Malia, "From under the rubble", pp. 103–5.
12. Malia, *The Soviet tragedy*, p. 498.
13. Hobsbawm, *Age of extremes*, p. 497.
14. R. N. Berki, *Socialism* (London: Dent, 1976).
15. J. Habermas, "What does socialism mean today?", in *After the fall*, pp. 25–46.
16. Hobsbawm, *Age of extremes*, pp. 497–9.
17. Blackburn, "Introduction", in *After the fall*, pp. x–xi.
18. Hobsbawm, *Out of the ashes*, p. 324.

Chronology of party conferences and congresses

1st Congress of RSDLP	March 1898
2nd Congress	July–August 1903
3rd Congress	April–May 1905
1st Conference	December 1905
4th (Unification) Congress	April–May 1906
2nd Conference	November 1906
5th Congress	May–June 1907
3rd Conference	August 1907
4th Conference	November 1907
5th Conference	January 1909
6th Conference	January 1912
7th Conference	April 1917
6th Congress	August 1917
7th Congress	March 1918
8th Congress	March 1919
8th Conference	December 1919
9th Congress	March–April 1920
9th Conference	September 1920
10th Congress	March 1921
10th Conference	May 1921
11th Conference	December 1921
11th Congress	March–April 1922
12th Conference	August 1922
12th Congress	April 1923
13th Conference	January 1924
13th Congress	May 1924

14th Conference	April 1925
14th Congress	December 1925
15th Congress	December 1927
16th Conference	April 1929
16th Congress	June–July 1930
17th Conference	January–February 1932
17th Congress	January–February 1934
18th Congress	March 1939
18th Conference	February 1941
19th Congress	October 1952
20th Congress	February 1956
21st Congress	January–February 1959
22nd Congress	October 1961
23rd Congress	March–April 1966
24th Congress	April 1971
25th Congress	February–March 1976
26th Congress	February–March 1981
27th Congress	February 1986
19th Conference	June–July 1988
28th Congress	July 1990

Chronology of main ideological texts of Soviet socialism

1902	What is to be done? (Lenin)
1903	Adoption of Party Programme
1916	Imperialism: the highest stage of capitalism (Lenin)
1917	State and revolution (Lenin)
	Can the Bolsheviks retain state power? (Lenin)
1918	The immediate tasks of the Soviet Government (Lenin)
	The Proletarian Revolution and the renegade Kautsky (Lenin)
1919	Second Party Programme Adopted
	ABC of Communism (Bukharin & Preobrazhensky)
1920	Terrorism and communism (Trotsky)
	The economics of the transition period (Bukharin)
1921	Tax-in-kind (Lenin)
	Fourth Anniversary of the October Revolution.
	The New Economic Policy and the tasks of the Political Education Departments.
	Report on the New Economic Policy.
	The importance of gold now and after the complete victory of Socialism. (All Lenin).
1922	Testament (Lenin)
1923	On co-operation (Lenin)
	How we should reorganize *Rabkrin* (Lenin)
	Better fewer but better (Lenin)
1924	Foundations of Leninism (Stalin)
	October Revolution and the tactics of Russian Communists (Stalin)

1925	Concerning the New Economic Policy and our tasks (Bukharin)
	The road to socialism and the Worker-Peasant Alliance (Bukharin)
1926	On the problems of Leninism (Stalin)
1928	Notes of an economist (Bukharin)
1929	A year of great change (Stalin)
1931	The tasks of business executives (Stalin)
1939	*A History of the CPSU* (B): *Short Course.*
1952	Economic problems of Socialism (Stalin)
1958–60	Fundamentals of Marxism–Leninism
	Fundamentals of Marxist philosophy
	History of CPSU
	Anthology of Soviet literature
	Conference Statement of 81 Communist and Workers' Parties
1961	Third Party Programme
1967	Elaboration of concept of Developed Socialism
1986	Third Party Programme (Revised Edition)
1989	Socialist idea and revolutionary *perestroika* (Gorbachev)
1991	Draft Party Programme Adopted.

Glossary of key terms/acronyms

apparatchiki	member of the apparatus
artel'	Organizational form of collective farm, mixing collective and private practices
ARCS	All-Russian Congress of Soviets
CC	Central Committee of Communist Party
CHEKA	Extraordinary Commission for Suppression of Counter-revolutionary Sabotage and Speculation
CPSU	Communist Party of the Soviet Union
chistka	purge or cleansing
glasnost'	openness
glavki	Management organs of Soviet industry, arranged vertically into branches. Became a force for centralization in economic structure.
GOELRO	State Electrification Commission
GOSPLAN	State Planning Commission
GPU	State political administration
Gulag	Chief Administration of Camps
HDS	Humane Democratic Socialism
KGB	Committee of State Security
khozraschet	profit and loss accounting
kolkhoz	collective farm
kombedy	Committees of Poor Peasants
kommuna	Organizational form of collective farm, in which everything is socialized
Komsomol	Communist Youth League
kulaks	"rich" peasantry

441

MTS	Machine Tractor Stations
Narkomprod	Commissariat of Food Procurement
Narkompros	Commissariat of Enlightenment
NEP	New Economic Policy
NKGK	People's Commissariat of State Control
NKVD	Commissariat of Internal Affairs
NOT	Scientific Organization of Labour
NPT	New Political Thinking
OGPU	secret police
perestroika	restructuring
prodnalog	tax-in-kind
Prolet'kult	Proletarian Culture Movement
RABKRIN	Commissariat of Workers' and Peasants' Inspection
razverstka	Requisitioning of grain from the peasantry
RSDLP	Russian Social Democratic Labour Party
RSFSR	Russian Socialist Federation of Socialist Republics
smychka	economic alliance
sovkhoz	state farm
sovnarkhoz	Regional Economic Council
Sovnarkom	Council of People's Commissars
SR	Socialist Revolutionaries
STO	Council of Labour and Defence
STR	Scientific and Technological Revolution
TOZ	Organizational form of Collective Farm, loosely organized on collectivist principles
uchraspred	Account and Distribution section
uskorenie	acceleration of socio-economic development
USSR	Union of Soviet Socialist Republics
VSNKh/ *Vesenkha*	Supreme Council of the National Economy
VTSIK	Supreme Council of the National Economy
Zhenotdel	The Women's Department of the CC Secretariat
zhenskii vopros	Woman question
Zhensovety	Women's Council

Select bibliography

Adams, J. *Citizen inspectors in the Soviet Union* (New York, 1977).

Akhapkin, Y. (ed.). *First decrees of Soviet power* (London, 1970).

Amman, R. Searching for an appropriate concept of Soviet politics: The politics of hesitant modernization. *British Journal of Political Science* **16**, pp. 475–94, 1986.

Andrle, V. *Workers in Stalin's Russia* (New York, 1988).

Andrle, V. *A social history of twentieth century Russia* (London, 1994).

Anon. *Inogo ne dano* (Moscow, 1988).

Anon. *The land of socialism today and tomorrow* (Moscow, 1939).

Anon. *The road to communism* (Moscow, 1961).

Arnasson, J. P. *The future that failed. Origins and destinies of the Soviet model* (London, 1993).

Arthur, C. J. (ed.). *Marx and Engels: the German Ideology* (London, 1970).

Atkinson, D. *The end of the Russian land commune 1905–1930* (Stanford, 1983).

Atkinson, D., A. Dallin, G. Lapidus (eds). *Women in Russia* (Hassocks, 1978).

Avis, G. (ed.). *The making of the Soviet citizen* (London, 1987).

Azrael, J. Khrushchev remembered. *Soviet Union* **2**, pp. 94–101, 1975.

Bacon, E. *The Gulag at war* (London, 1996).

Bailes, K. Alexei Gastev and the Soviet controversy over Taylorism. *Soviet Studies* **29**, pp. 373–94, 1977.

Bailes, K. *Technology and society under Lenin and Stalin. Origins of the Soviet technical intelligentsia 1917–41* (Princeton, 1978).

Ball, A. Lenin and the question of private trade in Soviet Russia. *Slavic Review* **43**, pp. 399–412, 1984.

Barber, J. Stalin's letter to the editors of proletarskaya revolyutsiya. *Soviet Studies* **28**, pp. 21–41, 1976.

Barber, J. The establishment of intellectual orthodoxy in the USSR. *Past and Present* **83**, pp. 141–64, 1979.

Barber, J. *Soviet historians in crisis* (London, 1981).

Batalov, E. *Prospects of socialism and utopian consciousness. Social Sciences* **20**, pp. 85–96, 1989.

Bauman, Z. *Socialism: the active utopia* (London, 1976).

Beilharz, P. *Labour's utopias* (London, 1992).

Bender, F. The ambiguities of Marx's concepts of "Proletarian Dictatorship" and "Transition to Communism". *History of Political Thought* **2**, pp. 525–55, 1981.

Benvenuti, F. *The Bolsheviks and the Red Army 1918–22* (Cambridge, 1988).

Bergman, J. The idea of individual liberation in Bolshevik visions of the New Soviet Man. *European History Quarterly* **27**, pp. 57–92, 1997.

Berki, R. N. *Socialism* (London, 1975).

Berman, H. J. *Justice in the USSR* (Cambridge, Mass., 1966).

Bideleux, R. *Communism and development* (London, 1985).

Blackburn, R. (ed.). *After the fall. The failure of communism and the future of socialism* (London, 1991).

Blank, S. Soviet institutional development during NEP: a prelude to Stalinism? *Russian History/Histoire Russe* **9**, pp. 325–46, 1982.

Bloomfield, J. (ed.). *The Soviet revolution* (London, 1989).

Boettke, P. J. The Soviet experiment with pure communism. *Critical Review* **2**(4), pp. 149–82, 1988.

Boettke, P. J. *The political economy of socialism: the formative years 1918–28* (Boston, 1990).

Bottomore, T., et al. (eds). *A dictionary of Marxist thought* (Oxford, 1983).

Bova, R. On perestroika: the role of workplace participation. *Problems of Communism* **36**, pp. 76–86, 1987.

Brinkley, G. Khrushchev remembered: on the theory of Soviet statehood. *Soviet Studies* **24**, pp. 387–401, 1972–3.

Brinton, M. *The Bolsheviks and workers' control* (London, 1970).

Brovkin, V. *The Mensheviks after October: socialist opposition and the rise of the Bolshevik dictatorship* (London, 1987).

Brown, A. Andropov: discipline and reform. *Problems of Communism* **32**, pp. 18–31, 1983.

Brown, A. *The Gorbachev factor* (Oxford, 1996).

Brown, A. (ed.). *New thinking in Soviet politics* (Oxford, 1992).

Brus, W. Utopianism and realism in the evolution of the Soviet economic system. *Soviet Studies* **40**, pp. 434–43, 1988.

Brus, W. & M. Laski. *From Marx to the market. Socialism in search of an economic system* (Oxford, 1989).

Brzezinski, Z. *The grand failure. The birth and death of communism in the twentieth century* (London, 1990).

Buccholz, A. The ongoing deconstruction of Soviet Marxism–Leninism. *Studies in Soviet Thought* **40**, pp. 231–40, 1990.

Buckley, M. *Women and ideology in the Soviet Union* (London, 1989).

Burbank, J. Controversies over Stalinism: searching for a Soviet society. *Politics and Society* **19**, pp. 325–40, 1991.

Burbank, J. Lenin and the law in revolutionary Russia. *Slavic Review* **54**, pp. 23–44, 1995.

Burke, J. P., L. Crocker, L. Legters (eds). *Marxism and the good society* (Cambridge, 1981).

Burlatsky, F. *Khrushchev and the first Russian spring* (London, 1991).

Carr. E. H. *Socialism in one country*, [2 vols] (London, 1965).

Carr, E. H. *The Bolshevik revolution*, [3 vols] (London, 1966).

Carr, E. H. Introduction. In *ABC of Communism*, N. Bukharin & E. Preobrazhensky (eds) (Harmondsworth, 1969), pp. 13–51.

Carr, E. H. & R. W. Davies. *Foundations of a planned economy 1926–29*, [3 vols] (London, 1969).

Carver, T. *Engels* (Oxford, 1981).

Channon, J. The Bolsheviks and the peasantry: the land question during the first eight months of Soviet rule. *Slavonic and East European Review* **66**, pp. 593–624, 1988.

Chase, W. Voluntarism, mobilization and coercion: Subbotniki 1919–21. *Soviet Studies* **41**, pp. 111–28, 1989.

Churchward, L. *The Soviet intelligentsia* (London, 1973).

Clements, B. The utopianism of the zhenotdel'. *Slavic Review* **51**, pp. 483–96, 1992.

Cohen, S. Bukharin, Lenin and the theoretical foundations of Bolshevism. *Soviet Studies* **21**, pp. 436–57, 1969/70.

Cohen, S. *Bukharin and the Bolshevik revolution* (Oxford, 1980).

Cohen, S. *Rethinking the Soviet experience* (Oxford, 1985).

Cohen, S., A. Rabinowitch, R. Sharlet (eds). *The Soviet Union since Stalin* (London, 1980).

Cohen, S. & K. vanden Heuvel. *Voices of glasnost'* (New York, 1989).

Conquest, R. *The politics of ideas in the USSR* (New York, 1967).

Conquest, R. *The harvest of sorrow* (London, 1986).

Conquest, R. *Stalin and the Kirov murder* (London, 1989).

Conquest, R. *The Great Terror. A reassessment* (London, 1990).

Conquest, R. *Stalin: breaker of nations* (London, 1993).

Cooper, J. Construction . . . reconstruction . . . deconstruction. In *Perestroika: the historical perspective*, C. Ward & C. Merridale (eds) (London, 1991), pp. 161–67.

Crick, B. *Socialism* (Milton Keynes, 1987).

Daniels, R. V. *The conscience of the revolution: communist opposition in Soviet Russia* (Cambridge, Mass., 1960).

Daniels, R. V. *A documentary history of communism*, [2 vols] (London, 1985).

Daniels, R. V. The "Left Opposition" as an alternative to Stalinism. *Slavic Review* **50**, pp. 277–85, 1991.

Daniels, R. V. *The end of the communist revolution* (London, 1993).

Davies, R. W. *The industrialization of Soviet Russia I. The socialist offensive: the collectivization of Soviet agriculture 1929–30* (London, 1980).

Davies, R. W. *The industrialization of Soviet Russia II. The Soviet collective farm 1929–30* (London, 1981).

Davies, R. W. The Syrtsov–Lominadze affair. *Soviet Studies* **33**, pp. 29–50, 1981.

Davies, R. W. The socialist market: a debate in Soviet industry, 1932–33. *Slavic Revew* **2**, pp. 201–23, 1984.

Davies, R. W. *Soviet history in the Gorbachev revolution* (Houndmills, 1989).

Davies, R. W. (ed.). *From Tsarism to the New Economic Policy* (Houndmills, 1990).

Davies, R. W. Gorbachev's socialism in historical perspective. *New Left Review* **179**, pp. 5–27, 1990.

Davies, R. W., M. Harrison, S. Wheatcroft (eds). *The economic transformation of the Soviet Union 1913–45* (Cambridge, 1994).

Day, R. B. *Leon Trotsky and the politics of economic isolation* (Cambridge, 1973).

Day, R. B. (ed.). *Nikolai Bukharin: Selected writings on the state and the transition to socialism* (New York, 1982).

De George, R. T. *Patterns of Soviet thought* (Ann Arbor, 1966).

Deutscher, I. *Trotsky: the prophet unarmed* (Oxford, 1959).

Deutscher, I. *Stalin* (London, 1966).

Dobb, M. *Soviet economic development* (London, 1966).

Dobrin, S. Lenin on equality and the Webbs on Lenin. *Soviet Studies* **8**, pp. 337–57, 1957.

Dunmore, T. *The Stalinist command economy: the Soviet state apparatus and economic policy 1945–53* (London, 1980).

Eissenstat, B. (ed.). *Lenin and Leninism* (Lexington, 1971).

Engels, F. *Anti-Duhring* (Peking, 1976).

Erlich, A. *The Soviet industrialization debate* (Cambridge, Mass., 1960).

Evans, A. B. Developed Socialism in Soviet ideology. *Soviet Studies* **29**, pp. 409–28, 1977.

Evans, A. B. The decline of Developed Socialism? Some trends in recent Soviet ideology. *Soviet Studies* **38**, pp. 1–23, 1986.

Evans, A. B. The Polish crisis in the 1980s and adaptation in Soviet ideology. *Journal of Communist Studies* **2**, pp. 263–85, 1986.

Evans, A. B. The new program of the CPSU: Changes in Soviet ideology. *Soviet Union* **14**, pp. 1–18, 1987.

Evans, A. B. Rereading Lenin's *State and Revolution. Slavic Review* **46**, pp. 1–19, 1987.

Evans, A. B. Rethinking Soviet socialism. In *Developments in Soviet politics*, S. White, A. Pravda, Z. Gitelman (eds) (London, 1992), pp. 28–47.

Evans, A. B. *Soviet Marxism–Leninism. The decline of an ideology.* (Westport, 1993).

Farber, S. *Before Stalinism* (Cambridge, 1990).

Figes. O. *Peasant Russia, civil war* (Oxford, 1990).

Figes. O. *A people's tragedy. The Russian revolution 1891–1924* (London, 1996).

Filtzer, D. Preobrazhensky and the problem of the Soviet transition. *Critique* **9**, pp. 63–84, 1978.

Filtzer, D. *Soviet workers and Stalinist industrialization* (London, 1986).

Filtzer, D. The Soviet wage reform of 1956–62. *Soviet Studies* **41**, pp. 88–110, 1989.

Filtzer, D. *Soviet workers and de-Stalinisation* (Cambridge, 1992).

Fitzpatrick, S. *The Russian Revolution 1917–39* (Oxford, 1994).

Fitzpatrick, S. *The Commissariat of Enlightenment: Soviet organization of education and the arts under Lunacharsky* (Cambridge, 1970).

Fitzpatrick, S. The "soft line" on culture and its enemies: Soviet cultural policy, 1922–27. *Slavic Review* **33**, pp. 267–87, 1974.

Fitzpatrick, S. *Russia in the era of NEP* (Bloomington, 1985).

Fitzpatrick, S. The Bolsheviks' dilemma: class, culture and politics in early Soviet years. *Slavic Review* **47**, pp. 599–613, 1988.

Fitzpatrick, S. New perspectives on the civil war. In *Party, state and society in the Russian Civil War*, D. Koenker, et al. (eds) (Bloomington, 1989), pp. 3–23.

Fitzpatrick, S. *The cultural front: power and culture in revolutionary Russia* (Ithaca, 1992).

Fitzpatrick, S. *Stalin's peasants* (New York, 1994).

Fitzpatrick, S. (ed.). *Cultural revolution in Russia* (Bloomington, 1978).

Fleron, F. J. (ed.). *Technology and communist culture* (New York, 1977).

Fukuyama, F. *The end of history and the last man* (New York, 1992).

Garrard, J. & C. Garrard. *Inside the Soviet writers' union* (New York, 1990).

Gerner, K. & S. Hedlund. *Ideology and rationality in the Soviet model* (London, 1989).

Getty, J. Arch. *Origins of the Great Purges: the Soviet communist party reconsidered* (Cambridge, 1985).

Getty, J. Arch. State and society under Stalin: Constitutions and elections in the 1930s. *Slavic Review* **50**, pp. 18–35, 1991.

Getty, J. Arch. & R. Manning (eds). *Stalinist terror* (Cambridge, 1993).

Gilison, J. *The Soviet image of utopia* (Baltimore, 1975).

447

Gill, G. *The collapse of a single-party system* (Cambridge, 1994).

Gleason, A., P. Kenez, R. Stites (eds). *Bolshevik culture* (Bloomington, 1985).

Gooding, J. Gorbachev and Democracy. *Soviet Studies* **42**, pp. 195–231, 1990.

Gooding, J. Perestroika as revolution from within: an interpretation. *The Russian Review* **51**, pp. 36–57, 1992.

Gooding, J. Lenin in Soviet politics, 1985–91. *Soviet Studies* **44**, pp. 403–22, 1992.

Gorbachev, M. *Perestroika: new thinking for our country and the world* (London, 1987).

Gorbachev, M. Sotsialisticheskaya ideya i revolyutsionnaya perestroika. *Pravda*, 26 November 1989, pp. 1–3.

Gorbachev, M. *Zhizn' i reformy*, [2 vols] (Moscow, 1995).

Graham, L. *Science in Russia and the Soviet Union* (Cambridge, 1993).

Gregor, R. (ed.). *Resolutions and decisions of the CPSU: vol. 2 1917–29* (Toronto, 1974).

Guroff, G. Lenin and Russian economic thought: the problem of central planning. In *Lenin and Leninism*, B. Eissenstat (ed.) (Lexington, 1971), pp. 183–215.

Hagen, M. von. The NEP, perestroika and the problem of alternatives. In *Socialism, perestroika and the dilemmas of Soviet economic reform*, J. Tedstrom (ed.) (Boulder, 1990), pp. 40–64.

Hagen, M. von. Civil-military relations and the evolution of the Soviet socialist state. *Slavic Review* **50**, pp. 268–76, 1991.

Hahn, W. Khrushchev's ouster. *Problems of Communism* **40**, pp. 109–15, 1991.

Haigh, F. H., D. S. Morris, A. R. Peters. *Soviet foreign policy, the League of Nations and Europe 1917–39* (Aldershot, 1986).

Haimson, L. *The Russian Marxists and the origins of Bolshevism* (Cambridge, Mass., 1955).

Hanson, S. *Time and revolution. Marxism and the design of Soviet institutions* (Chapel Hill, 1997).

Harding, N. *Lenin's Political Thought*, [2 vols] (London, 1983).

Harding, N. Socialism, society and the organic labour state. In *The state in socialist society*, N. Harding (ed.) (New York, 1984), pp. 1–50.

Harding, N. *Leninism* (Houndmills, 1996).

Hauslohner, P. Gorbachev's social contract. *Soviet Economy* **3**, pp. 54–89, 1987.

Heller, M. & A. Nekrich. *Utopia in power* (New York, 1986).

History of the CPSU (Short Course) (Moscow, 1939).

Hobsbawm, E. *Age of Extremes. The short twentieth century* (London, 1994).

Hodnett, G. *Resolutions and decisions of the CPSU*, [vol. 4] (Toronto, 1974).

Hoffmann, E. P. & R. Laird. Soviet views of the "scientific-technological revolution". *World Politics* **30**, pp. 615–44, 1978.

Hoffmann, E. P. & R. Laird. *Technocratic Socialism: the USSR in the advanced industrial era* (Durham, 1985).

Hough, J. The Soviet Union: Petrification or pluralism? *Problems of Communism* **21**, pp. 25–45, 1972.

Hough, J. *Russia and the West. Gorbachev and the politics of reform* (New York, 1990).

Hough, J. & M. Fainsod. *How the Soviet Union is governed* (Cambridge Mass., 1979).

Hosking, G. *A history of the Soviet Union* (London, 1992).

Howard, M. C. & J. E. King. A history of Marxian economics, [2 vols] (Houndmills, 1989).

Hunt, R. N. Carew. *The theory and practice of communism* (Baltimore, 1963).

Ito, T. (ed.). *Facing up to the past. Soviet historiography under perestroika* (Sapporo, 1989).

Johnson, E. L. *An introduction to the Soviet legal system* (London, 1969).

Joravsky, D. Communism in historical perspective. *American Historical Review* **99**, pp. 837–57, 1994.

Joyce, W., H. Ticktin, S. White (eds). *Gorbachev and Gorbachevism* (London, 1989).

Kanet, R. E. The rise and fall of the All-People's state: recent changes in the Soviet theory of the state. *Soviet Studies* **20**, pp. 81–93, 1968.

Kaser, M. Soviet boarding schools. *Soviet Studies* **20**, pp. 94–105, 1968/69.

Keep, J. *Last of the Empires* (Oxford, 1995).

Kelley, D. R. Developed Socialism: a political formula for the Brezhnev era. In *Developed Socialism in the Soviet bloc*, J. Seroka & S. Simon (eds) (Boulder, 1982), pp. 3–18.

Kelley, D. R. *The politics of Developed Socialism* (Westport, 1986).

Kelley, D. R. (ed.). *Soviet politics in the Brezhnev era* (New York, 1986).

Khrushchev, N. *Khrushchev remembers* (London, 1971).

Kimmerling, E. Civil rights and social policy in Soviet Russia, 1918–36. *The Russian Review* **41**, pp. 24–46, 1982.

Koenker, D., W. Rosenberg, R. Suny (eds). *Party, state and society in the Russian Civil War* (Bloomington, 1989).

Kolakowski, L. The myth of human self-identity. In *The socialist idea*, L. Kolakowski & S. Hampshire (eds) (London, 1974).

Kolakowski, L. *Main Currents of Marxism* (Oxford, 1978).

Kolakowski, L. & S. Hampshire (eds). *The socialist idea* (London, 1974).

Krementsov, N. *Stalinist science* (Princeton, 1997).

Kurashvili, B. Modeli sotsializma. *Sovetskoe gosudarstvo i pravo* **8**, pp. 99–110, 1989.

Kuromiya, H. *Stalin's industrial revolution: politics and workers 1928–32* (Cambridge, 1988).

Kuusinen, O. (ed.). *Fundamentals of Marxism–Leninism* (London, 1961).

Kux, E. Contradictions in Soviet socialism. *Problems of Communism* **33**, pp. 1–27, 1984.

Labedz, L. (ed.). *Revisionism* (London, 1962).

Lampert, N. *The technical intelligentsia and the Soviet state* (London, 1979).

Lapidus, G. *Women in Soviet society* (Berkeley, 1978).

Laquer, W. & L. Labedz (eds). *The future of communist society* (New York, 1962).

Laue, T von. Stalin in focus. *Slavic Review* **42**, pp. 373–89, 1983.

Leggett, G. *The Cheka: Lenin's political police* (Oxford, 1981).

Lenin, V. I. *What is to be done?* (Moscow, 1902).

Lenin, V. I. *State and revolution* (Petrograd, 1918).

Lenin, V. I. *Collected works*, [45 vols] (Moscow, 1960–70).

Lenin, V. I. *Selected works*, [3 vols] (Moscow, 1967).

Leonhard, W. *Three faces of Marxism* (New York, 1974).

Lewin, M. The immediate background to Soviet collectivisation. *Soviet Studies* **17**, pp. 162–97, 1965/66.

Lewin, M. *Russian peasants and Soviet power* (London, 1968).

Lewin, M. *Political undercurrents in Soviet economic debates* (London, 1975).

Lewin, M. *The making of the Soviet system* (London, 1985).

Lichtheim, G. *Marxism: an historical and critical study* (London, 1961).

Lichtheim, G. *A short history of socialism* (London, 1983).

Liebman, M. *Leninism under Lenin* (London, 1975).

Lih, L. Bolshevik *razverstka* and war communism. *Slavic Review* **45**, pp. 673–88, 1986.

Lih, L. Political testament of Lenin and Bukharin and the meaning of NEP. *Slavic Review* **50**, pp. 241–52, 1991.

Lih, L. The mystery of the ABC. *Slavic Review* **56**, pp. 50–72, 1997.

Lih, L., O. Naumov, O. Khlevniuk (eds). *Stalin's letters to Molotov* (New Haven, 1995).

Lincoln, B. *Red victory* (New York, 1990).

McAuley, M. *Labour disputes in Soviet Russia 1957–65* (Oxford, 1969).

McAuley, M. *Politics and the Soviet Union* (Harmondsworth, 1979).

McAuley, M. *Soviet politics 1917–91* (Oxford, 1992).

McCauley, M. *Khrushchev and the development of Soviet agriculture: the Virgin Lands programme* (London, 1976).

McCauley, M. (ed.). *Khrushchev and Khrushchevism* (London, 1987).

McLellan, D. *Karl Marx: his life and thought* (London, 1974).

McLellan, D. (ed.). *Karl Marx: selected writings* (Oxford, 1977).

McLellan, D. *Marxism after Marx* (London, 1979).

McLelland, J. Utopianism versus revolutionary heroism in Bolshevik policy: the proletarian culture debate. *Slavic Review* **40**, pp. 403–25, 1980.

McNeal, R. H. *Resolutions and Decisions of the CPSU.* Vol. 3 1929–53 (Toronto, 1974).

McNeal, R. H. *Stalin. Man and ruler* (Houndmills, 1988).

Malia, M. *Alexander Herzen and the birth of Russian socialism* (New York, 1961).

Malia, M. From under the rubble, what? *Problems of Communism* **41**, pp. 89–106, 1992.

Malia, M. *The Soviet tragedy: a history of socialism in Russia* (New York, 1994).

Malle, S. *The economic organization of War Communism* (Cambridge, 1985).

Marx, K & F. Engels. *Selected works* (London, 1968). Esp: *Socialism: utopian and scientific; Manifesto of the communist party; Critique of the Gotha Programme; The civil war in France; Letter to A. Bebel.*

Marcuse, H. *Soviet Marxism* (New York, 1961).

Matthews, M. *Soviet social structure* (London, 1972).

Matthews, M. *Privilege in the Soviet Union* (London, 1978).

Mayer, R. The dictatorship of the proletariat from Plekhanov to Lenin. *Studies in East European Thought* **45**, pp. 255–80, 1993.

Medvedev, R. *Let history judge* (New York, 1971).

Medvedev, R. & Z. Medvedev. *Khrushchev: The years in power* (Oxford, 1977).

Melnick, A. James. Scientific atheism in the era of perestroika. *Studies in Soviet Thought* **40**, pp. 223–9, 1990.

Merridale, C. *Moscow politics and the rise of Stalin* (London, 1990).

Meyer, A. G. *Leninism* (Cambridge, Mass., 1957).

Meyer, A. G. The war scare of 1927. *Soviet Union/Union Sovietique* **1**, pp. 1–25, 1978.

Miliband, R. *Socialism for a sceptical age* (Cambridge, 1994).

Miller, R. F. & F. Feher (eds). *Khrushchev and the communist world* (London, 1984).

Narkiewicz, O. Stalin, War Communism and collectivization. *Soviet Studies* **18**, pp. 20–37, 1966/67.

Nove, A. Lenin and the New Economic Policy. In *Lenin and Leninism*, B. Eissenstat (ed.) (Lexington, 1971), pp. 155–71.

Nove, A. New light on Trotsky's economic views. *Slavic Review* **41**, pp. 84–97, 1981.

Nove, A. *The Soviet economic system* (Boston, 1986).

Nove, A. *Stalinism and after* (Boston, 1989).

Nove, A. *Studies in economics and Russia* (Houndmills, 1990).

Nove, A. Marxism and "really existing" socialism. In *Studies in economics and Russia* (London, 1990), pp. 179–91.

Nove, A. *An economic history of the USSR* (Harmondsworth, 1992).

Nove, A. (ed.). *The Stalin phenomenon* (London, 1993).

Ollman, B. Marx's vision of communism. *Critique* **8**, pp. 4–41, 1977.

Parker, R. Assessing perestroika. *World Policy Journal* **6**, pp. 264–96, 1989.

Patenaude, B. Peasants into Russians. The utopian essence of war communism. *The Russian Review* **54**, pp. 552–70, 1995.

Pethybridge, R. *A key to Soviet politics: the crisis of the anti-party group* (New York, 1962).

Pipes, R. *The Russian Revolution 1899–1919* (London, 1990).

Pipes, R. *Russia under the Bolshevik regime* (London, 1994).

Plamenatz, J. *German Marxism and Russian Communism* (London, 1954).

Radkey, O. *The sickle under the hammer: the Russian Socialist-Revolutionaries in the early months of Soviet rule* (Columbia, 1963).

Radzinsky, E. *Stalin* (London, 1996).

Read, C. *Culture and power in revolutionary Russia* (London, 1990).

Read, C. *From Tsar to Soviets. The Russian people and their revolution 1917–21* (London, 1996).

Rees, E. A. *State control in Soviet Russia: the rise and fall of the Workers' and Peasants' Inspectorate* (London, 1987).

Reichmann, H. Reconsidering Stalinism. *Theory and Society* **17**, pp. 57–90, 1988.

Reiman, M. *The birth of Stalinism* (London, 1987).

Remington, T. *Building socialism in Bolshevik Russia* (Pittsburgh, 1984).

Remington, T. A socialist pluralism of opinions: Glasnost' and policy-making under Gorbachev. *The Russian Review* **48**, pp. 271–304, 1989.

Rigby, T. H. *Communist Party membership in the USSR 1917–67* (Princeton, 1968).

Rittersporn, G. *Stalinist simplifications and Soviet complications* (Chur, 1991).

Robinson, N. Gorbachev and the place of the party in Soviet reform. *Soviet Studies* **44**, pp. 423–43, 1992.

Rosen, S. *Education and modernization in the USSR* (Reading, Mass., 1971).

Rosenberg, W. Russian labour and Bolshevik power: social dimensions of protest in Petrograd after October. In *The workers' revolution in Russia in 1917: the view from below*, D. Kaiser (ed.) (Cambridge, 1987), pp. 98–131.

Rosenberg, W. & L. Siegelbaum (eds). *Social dimensions of Soviet industrialization* (Bloomington, 1993).

Sakwa, R. Commune Democracy and Gorbachev's reforms. *Political Studies* **37**, pp. 224–43, 1989.

Sakwa, R. *Soviet politics* (London, 1989).

Sakwa, R. *Gorbachev and his reforms 1985–90* (London, 1990).

Sandle, M. The final word: the draft party programme of July/August 1991. *Europe–Asia Studies* **48**, pp. 1131–50, 1996.

Sandle, M. Georgii Shakhnazarov and the Soviet critique of historical materialism. *Studies in East European Thought* **49**, pp. 109–33, 1997.

Scanlan, J. *Marxism in the USSR* (Ithaca, 1985).

Scanlan, J. Ideology and reform. In *Gorbachev's reforms: Japanese and US assessments*, P. Juviler & H. Kimura (eds) (New York, 1988), pp. 49–62.

Schapiro, L. *The Communist Party of the Soviet Union* (London, 1970).

Schapiro, L. *Origins of the communist autocracy: political opposition in the Soviet state* (London, 1977).

Schapiro, L. (ed.). *The USSR and the future* (Munich, 1962).

Scheibert, P. Lenin, Bogdanov and the concept of proletarian culture. In *Lenin and Leninism*, B. Eissenstat (ed.) (Lexington, 1971), pp. 43–57.

Schlesinger, R. *The spirit of post-war Russia* (London, 1947).

Seroka, J. & S. Simon (eds). *Developed Socialism in the Soviet bloc* (Boulder, 1982).

Service, R. *The Bolshevik party in revolution 1917–23*, [3 vols] (London, 1979).

Service, R. The road to the XX Party Congress: an analysis of the events surrounding the CC plenum of July 1953. *Soviet Studies* **33**, pp. 232–45, 1981.

Service, R. *Lenin: a political life*, [3 vols] (London, 1985, 1991, 1994).

Service, R. *A history of twentieth century Russia* (London, 1997).

Sharlet, R. The new Soviet constitution. *Problems of Communism* **26**, pp. 1–24, 1977.

Shenfield, S. *The nuclear predicament. Explorations in Soviet ideology* (London, 1987).

Siegelbaum, L. *Stakhanovism and the politics of productivity in the USSR 1935–41* (Cambridge, 1988).

Siegelbaum, L. *Soviet state and society between revolutions 1918–29* (Cambridge, 1992).

Simmons, E. V. (ed.). *Continuity and change in Russian and Soviet thought* (Cambridge, Mass., 1955).

Sirianni, C. *Workers' control and socialist democracy* (London, 1982).

Skidelsky, R. *The world after communism* (London, 1995).

Smart, C. Gorbachev's Lenin: the myth in service to perestroika. *Studies in Comparative Communism* **23**, pp. 5–22, 1990.

Smith, S. Taylorism rules OK? *Radical Science Journal* **13**, pp. 5–27, 1983.

Sochor, Z. Soviet Taylorism Revisited. *Soviet Studies* **33**, pp. 246–64, 1981.

Stalin, J. V. *Problems of Leninism* (Moscow, 1947).

Stalin, J. V. *Economic problems of socialism* (Moscow, 1952).

Stalin, J. V. *Collected works*, [13 vols] (Moscow, 1955).

Swain, G. *The origins of the Russian Civil War* (London, 1996).

Stites, R. *Revolutionary dreams. Utopian dreams and experimental life in the Russian revolution* (Oxford, 1989).

Stites, R. *Russian popular culture: entertainment and society since 1900* (Cambridge, 1992).

Szamuely, L. *First models of socialist economic systems* (Budapest, 1974).

Tedstrom, J. (ed.). *Socialism, perestroika and the dilemmas of economic reform* (Boulder, 1990).

Thompson, T. L. *Ideology and policy: the political uses of doctrine in the Soviet Union* (Boulder, 1989).

Timmerman, H. The CPSU's reassessment of international social-democracy: Dimensions and trends. *Journal of Communist Studies* **5**, pp. 173–84, 1989.

Traub, R. Lenin and Taylor: the fate of "scientific management" in the (early) Soviet Union. *Telos* **37**, pp. 82–92, 1978.

Trotsky, L. *The revolution betrayed* (New York, 1973).

Trotsky, L. *Terrorism and communism* (London, 1975).

Tsipko, A. Istoki stalinizma. *Nauka i zhizn'* **11** & **12**, 1988, **1** & **2** 1989.

Tucker, R. C. *The Soviet political mind* (London, 1963).

Tucker, R. C. The origins of Stalin's personality cult. *American Historical Review* **84**, pp. 347–66, 1979.

Tucker, R. C. (ed.). *Stalinism: essays in historical interpretation* (New York, 1977).

Urban, G. R. *Stalinism* (Aldershot, 1982).

Valkeneier, E. K. New Soviet thinking about the Third World. *World Policy Journal* **4**, pp. 651–74, 1987.

Viola, L. *The best sons of the fatherland* (Oxford, 1987).

Volkogonov, D. *Stalin. Triumph and tragedy* (London, 1991).

Walicki, A. *A history of Russian thought from the enlightenment to Marxism* (Oxford, 1980).

Walicki, A. *Marxism and the leap to the kingdom of freedom* (Stanford, 1995).

Waller, M. *The end of the communist power monopoly* (Manchester, 1993).

Ward, C. *Stalin's Russia* (London, 1993).

Ward, C. & C. Merridale (eds). *Perestroika: the historical perspective* (London, 1991).

Wetter, G. *Dialectical materialism* (New York, 1958).

White, S. & A. Pravda (eds). *Ideology and Soviet politics* (London, 1988).

White, S. *Soviet Communism: Programme and rules* (London, 1989).

White, S. Democratization in the USSR. *Soviet Studies* **42**, pp. 3–24, 1990.

White, S. Rethinking the CPSU. *Soviet Studies* **43**, pp. 405–28, 1991.

White, S. *After Gorbachev* (Cambridge, 1992).

Whitefield, S. *Industrial power and the Soviet state* (Oxford, 1993).

Wildman, A. *The end of the Russian imperial army*, [2 vols] (Princeton, 1980, 1987).

Willerton, J. P. *Patronage and politics in the USSR* (Cambridge, 1992).

Williams, R. C. *The other Bolsheviks. Lenin and his critics 1904–14* (Bloomington, 1986).

Woodby, S. *Gorbachev and the decline of ideology in Soviet foreign policy* (Boulder, 1989).

Woodby, S. & A. B. Evans (eds). *Restructuring Soviet ideology: Gorbachev's new thinking* (Boulder, 1990).

Wright, A. *Socialisms* (Oxford, 1986).

Yanowitch, M. *Controversies in Soviet social thought: democratization, social justice, and the erosion of official ideology* (Armonk, 1991).

Zlotnik, M. Chernenko's platform. *Problems of Communism* **31**, pp. 70–74, 1982.

Index

ABC of Communism, The 130, 132, 133
Administrative System 376–7, 392, 402, 421
agriculture 69–71, 109–11, 303–6, 343
All-People's state 322, 336, 347
Andropov, Y. 360–63, 378
anti-party group 285, 307
artel' 111
associations 229–30

Beria, L. 280
Bogdanov, A. 33, 106, 124
Bolshevik
    Party 1–2, 16, 33, 79–81, 115–16
    ideology 34, 44–6, 69, 72, 86–8, 96, 131, 139, 349, 430–32
Bolshevism 4, 77, 83–5, 87–8, 98, 107, 125, 163, 165, 169, 172, 173, 182, 200, 203–4, 217–18, 231, 242, 244, 259, 292, 372, 416, 430–32
Brest-Litovsk Treaty 61, 68, 85, 96, 129

Brezhnev, L.
    cultural policy 354–8
    economics 342–4
    ideology 337–42
    politics 347–51
    social policy 351–3
Bukharin, N. 34, 85, 86, 105, 108, 123, 124, 131, 133, 134–5, 200–6, 301, 302
Burlatskii, F. 336, 338, 390

Central Committee 76, 115, 117, 152, 166, 228, 282, 284–5, 308, 316, 334, 348, 376, 377
centralization 15, 20, 38, 47, 62, 68, 79, 81, 87, 96, 99, 114–15, 121, 191–2, 229
CHEKA 70, 76–7, 81, 112–14, 122, 168
Chernenko, K. 363–4, 371
China 277, 279
Chinese communist party 321
chistka 167, 254
civil war 95, 101, 109–10
cold war 277, 303

collectivization 110–11, 203, 213, 234–9, 263
communism, *see* Marx.
Communist Party of the Soviet Union (CPSU) 4, 240, 252–6, 279, 283–8, 321, 334–5, 344–7, 351, 359, 374, 379, 385, 386, 388, 399–401, 407, 412–13, 415, 416, 418, 422, 431
comrades courts 290
Congress of People's Deputies 399
Conquest, R. 1
Constituent Assembly 72–3
constitutions
    1981 78–9, 103
    1936 243, 251–2
    1977 346, 348, 351, 402
constructivism 16, 23, 46, 85, 126, 142, 341, 358, 387, 415
co-operatives 185–6, 201, 379
Council of Labour and Defence (STO) 98, 100, 109
Council of Ministers 280
criminal code
    1958 289
    1961 289
cult of personality 247, 255–6, 355
cultural policy 123–6, 142, 169, 175–6, 245–7, 356–8

Davies, R. W. 189, 229, 237
Democratic Centralists 118, 120, 143, 162
democratization 62, 380, 382–3, 402, 419
détente 343, 354, 361
Developed Socialism 336–42, 345–6, 352–4, 358–63, 373–6, 386, 431
Developing Socialism 385–9, 399

dictatorship of the proletariat 15, 18–20, 25, 35–43, 71–2, 77, 78, 105, 113–14, 121, 129, 134–5, 137, 141–2, 216, 252, 264
dissent 350

eastern Europe 277, 279
education 85, 142, 173–4, 243, 250, 293–4, 296–7, 411–13
egalitarianism 11–12, 45–6, 82–3, 122–3, 170–73, 242–5, 292–6, 352–3, 403–7
Engels 12–13, 15, 19–20, 25–8, 30, 45, 71, 108, 260, 416, 432
expressivist 12
Ezhov 256

firma 309
Fitzpatrick, S. 2, 173–4
foreign concessions 158–9

Gastev, A. 107
Getty, J. Arch 251, 253
glavki 64, 98–100, 229
glasnost' 380–82, 407, 411, 415–16
GOELRO 107, 109
Gorbachev 152, 350, 364
    Bolshevism 416–22
    Brezhnev era 374–8
    economics 393–9
    freedom 391–2
    Leninism 419
    political reform 379–80, 399–402
    social policy 403–11
    theoretical renewal 380–85
GOSPLAN 108, 109, 227–8, 308–9, 335, 394
Great Patriotic War 276–7, 356
Gulag 247, 257–9, 289

human factor 380–81
Humane Democratic Socialism 372, 389–416, 418–22

ideology 1, 2, 127, 265, 276
industrialization 200, 205–8,
    212–13, 226–7, 230–33, 258,
    263

Kaganovich, L. 280–81, 285
Kamenev, L. 113
KGB 282, 289, 348, 350, 359
khozraschet 158, 159, 229, 394–5
Khrushchev, N.
  communism 321–5
  de-Stalinisation 292, 318
  equality 292
  fall 333–5
  ideology 318–21
  Leninism 291, 302, 325–6
  literature 299
  peaceful co-existence 301–2
  politics 280–88
  religious policy 297
  sovnarkhozy 307–15
Kirov, S. 257
kolkhozy 229, 234, 237–8, 249,
    250, 304, 324
Kollontai, A. 124, 353
kombedy 71, 109–10
kommuna 111
Komsomol 125, 138, 140, 249, 287,
    290, 317
Kosygin, A. 336, 378, 395
Kritsman, L. 65, 66, 127
Kronstadt 151, 152, 162
Krzhizhanovskii, S. 107, 188
kulaks 70–71, 156, 201, 203, 214,
    234–6, 257
Kuusinen, O. 319

labour camps 103, 231, 257–9, 281
labour code
  1918 103
  1922 159, 316
labour policy 67–70, 102–5, 136,
    159–61, 230–33, 315–18
Land Code 156

Larin 62, 88, 108
law 168–9, 250, 288–90
Left communists 86, 102, 118
Lenin
  and Bolshevik leaders 62, 85, 86
  Can the Bolsheviks retain state
    power? 34
  culture 124–5
  factions 117–18, 162–4
  Kautsky 34, 45, 86, 132
  militarization of labour 104–5
  party 32–3, 39–41, 140–42
  prodnalog 152–7
  specialists 38–9, 45, 122
  State and revolution 33–45, 137,
    190
  war communism 128, 131–2,
    138–9, 176–85
  workers control 34, 43–4, 59
Leninism 2, 210, 419–22
Lih, L. 95–6, 110, 128, 132, 184,
    201

Machine Tractor Station 238, 249,
    287, 304
Malenkov, G. 280–82, 284, 285,
    303, 342
Malia, M. 1, 2, 10, 96, 433–4
Marx
  communism 13–16, 20–25, 28
  *Critique of the Gotha
    Programme* 13, 15, 18, 20
  socialism 15–20
  Russian Road 29
Marxism 2, 127, 220, 243, 259, 322,
    421, 432–3
  Russian, 30–33
Marxism–Leninism 1, 2, 220, 242,
    280, 288, 297, 300, 322, 344,
    363, 412–13, 411, 415, 418,
    422
Medvedev, V. 372, 399, 410
militarization of labour 102–5, 107,
    136

Military Opposition 118, 120, 143
Molotov, V. 280–81, 285, 320
Molotov–Ribbentrop Pact 246
moral code 298

Narkomprod 98
Narkompros 125, 174
nationalization 59–61, 96–9, 129, 157
NEP 56, 128, 143, 151–3, 176–93, 200–1, 205–6, 229, 302, 381, 391, 419, 420, 430–31
New Political Thinking 383–5
NKVD 112–13, 168, 230–31, 233, 249–50, 256, 258, 281, 282
nomenklatura 334, 352, 406
Nove, A. 127, 189, 305

oblsovsprof 317
OGPU 238, 249
orgburo 116, 166

Paris Commune 18–20, 35
Party Congresses
    8th 103, 107, 116, 120
    9th 102, 105
    10th 105, 151–4, 160, 162–4, 166, 167, 177
    11th 161, 167
    17th 243, 249, 254
    18th 261, 278
    19th 278
    20th 282, 300, 306, 319
    21st 284, 319
    22nd 284, 286, 319
    24th 337, 362
    25th 357
    26th 375
    27th 375–6
    28th 390, 393, 394, 401, 406
Party Programme
    1903 33, 132
    1919 130, 132, 139, 261, 278
    1961 298, 300, 306, 319–25, 336

1986 371, 375
1991 372, 390, 406, 407, 416–18, 422
perestroika 152, 361, 371, 373–4, 376, 378–89, 393, 399–401, 415, 417, 419–21, 430–31
Pipes, R. 1, 2
planning 47, 99–100, 108–9, 187–9, 201–2, 204, 205, 207, 227–9, 394–7
Plekhanov, G. 25, 30, 45
Politburo 116, 152, 165, 280
populism, 29–32
Pospelov report 282
Praesidium 280, 284
Preobrazhensky, E. 129, 200, 207
prodnalog 152–3, 156, 161, 177, 182
productivism 24, 27, 46, 82, 84, 87, 104, 122, 126, 132, 133, 244, 262, 357–8, 415, 430
Prolet'kult 124–5
propaganda 126, 296–7, 363

rationalism 10–12, 23, 27, 46, 67, 106, 132, 187, 262, 341, 358, 430
razverstka 110
Red Army 113–14, 122, 138, 164, 172
revolutionary decrees 58–9

science policy 244–5
Scientific and Technological Revolution 339–40, 346, 373, 384
Scientific Institute of Labour (NOT) 107, 188
scientific management 340–41, 347, 349
secretariat 116, 166, 348
self-sufficiency 211–15, 219
Shakhnazarov, G. 390, 408, 410
Shakhty trial 232

show trials 164, 257
Sinatra doctrine 408
smychka 154, 177, 202–4, 205
socialism in one country 203, 206,
    208–11, 228, 245, 263, 302,
    431
socialist way of life 357–8
socialist realism 246
Solidarity 360
Solzhenitsyn, A. 299
sovkhozy 111, 234, 237, 304
sovnarkhozy 98–100, 307–15, 317,
    335, 336, 395
Sovnarkom 61, 64, 74, 76, 77, 81,
    98, 104, 109, 114, 117, 158,
    228
Stakhanovism 231, 247, 363
Stalin 166, 200, 203, 206, 207
    collectivization 234–36
    The economic problems of
        socialism 278
    equality 242–3
    ideals 211
    linguistics 277
    party 255
    theory 260–61
    Trotsky 208–11
Stalinism 151, 247–8, 265–6,
    276–80, 292, 333, 378, 381,
    419, 430, 433
Stalinist model 208, 226, 233,
    262–5, 401
state capitalism 59, 61, 69, 86, 155,
    176–85
state control
    NKGK 120
    RABKRIN 120–21, 165, 249, 286
    TSKK-RKI 249
    Party-State Control Committee
        286, 291, 349
subbotniki 103
Suslov, M. 363
Sverdlov 81, 116

Taylorism 69, 101, 106–8, 187, 343
technocracy 67, 82, 87, 88, 96, 101,
    106–7, 119, 121, 126, 132, 187,
    244, 262, 342
terror
    Red 112–13, 168
    Stalinist 218, 256–60
TOZ 111
trade unions 59, 67–9, 101–2,
    104–6, 119, 125, 138, 139–40,
    159–60, 165, 249, 287, 290,
    316–18
Trotsky 102, 104–5, 108, 113, 123,
    124, 131–2, 134–6, 138,
    140–41, 152, 200, 205–11
trust-in-cadres 334–5
trustification 97–8, 158
Tvardovsky, A. 299

Union of Soviet Writers 299
uskorenie 375, 380, 385

Vesenkha/VSNKh 64–5, 68, 97, 100,
    101–2, 109, 160, 227–8, 309
virgin lands 291, 305

war communism 57, 95–6, 126–43,
    262, 381, 391, 430–31
women's emancipation 82–3,
    122–3, 142, 170–72, 244,
    294–5, 353, 407
workers' control 58, 61, 62–7, 84,
    101–4, 107, 119, 159
Workers' Opposition 118, 120, 143,
    162, 166

Yakovlev, A. 385

zastoi 375–6
Zhenotdel 122–3, 125, 169, 170–71,
    244
Zhensovety 295
Zinoviev, G. 209